ECONOMIC HISTORY

KEYNESIANISM VS. MONETARISM

FINANCE, MONEY AND BANKING

KEYNESIANISM VS. MONETARISM

And other essays in financial history

CHARLES P. KINDLEBERGER

Routledge
Taylor & Francis Group

LONDON AND NEW YORK

First published in 1985

Reprinted in 2006 by
Routledge
2 Park Square, Milton Park, Abingdon, Oxon, OX14 4RN

Transferred to Digital Printing 2007

Routledge is an imprint of Taylor & Francis Group

British Library Cataloguing in Publication Data
A CIP catalogue record for this book
is available from the British Library

Keynesianism vs. Monetarism
ISBN10: 0–415–38212–2 (volume) (hbk)
ISBN10: 0–415–43671–0 (pbk)

ISBN13: 978–0–415–38212–0 (hbk)
ISBN13: 978–0–415–43671–7 (pbk)

ISBN 0-415-37850-8 (subset)
ISBN 0-415-28619-0 (set)

Routledge Library Editions: Economic History
Printed and bound by CPI Antony Rowe, Eastbourne

Keynesianism vs. Monetarism and Other Essays in Financial History

Keynesianism vs. Monetarism and Other Essays in Financial History

CHARLES P. KINDLEBERGER

Routledge
Taylor & Francis Group

LONDON AND NEW YORK

Published by Routledge
2 Park Square, Milton Park, Abingdon, Oxon, OX14 4RN
270 Madison Ave, New York NY 10016

First published in 1985
First published in paperback in 1986

British Library Cataloguing in Publication Data

Kindleberger, Charles P.
    Keynesianism vs. monetarism and other essays in financial history.
1. Economics
I. Title
330   HB171
ISBN 0-04-332104-6
ISBN 0-04-332129-1 Pbk

Library of Congress Cataloging in Publication Data

Kindleberger, Charles P. 1910–
    Keynesianism vs. monetarism and other essays in financial history.
Includes index.
1. Finance – History – Addresses, essays, lectures.
2. Economic history – Addresses, essays, lectures.
3. Keynesian economics – Addresses, essays, lectures.
4. Chicago school of economics – Addresses, essays, lectures. I. Title.
HG171.K56   1985   332'.09   85–3869
ISBN 0-04-332104-6 (alk. paper)
ISBN 0-04-332129-1 (pbk.: alk. paper)

Set in 10 on 11 point Times by Fotographics (Bedford) Ltd

Contents

PART V THE TWENTIETH CENTURY

Introduction

As they contemplate mortality and immortality, many economists of my generation think it useful to gather their scattered academic detritus into packages, organized either chronologically or by subject. Herewith is a series of essays in the field of financial history, assembled from lectures, articles for *Festschriften* and symposia, commissioned articles, and a few papers for the normal run of periodicals, including one or two obscure ones. They form a complement to my *Financial History of Western Europe* (1984), in particular carrying the argument of necessarily condensed passages wider and deeper than could be set out in a synthetic work with limitations of space. In a few cases where I have published a lecture in a truncated version to serve the limitations of the outlet, I offer here the extended original; like virtually all authors, I am infatuated with the sound of my own prose and hate the pruning pencil.

One of the principal themes of *A Financial History...* was the dialectic between monetarism and Keynesianism. If the anachronism can be forgiven, it is an ancient one, going back at least to the sixteenth century when Bodin tangled with Malestroit over the rise of prices caused by, or perhaps independent of, the inflow of gold and silver from the New World. Tension between the two points of view continued through the next centuries in debates between Lowndes and Locke and John Law and his critics, the nineteenth-century clash between the Banking and the Currency Schools in Britain, even to the sharply divergent explanations for the hyperinflation in Germany culminating in 1923. Today the points of view are embodied in Milton Friedman and John Maynard Keynes. But the dichotomy is not between any particular views of those great economists. It is rather far more general, between one school worried about inflation and deflation of prices and the quantity of money, the other more about output and employment, or, in some versions, believing that the quantity of money behaves suitably if it moves up and down with the business cycle. Nothing is implied about the merits of monetary policy and fiscal policy.

Part 1 provides the title of the book as a whole. Its first essay, an Adam Smith Lecture before the National Association of Business Economists, makes clear that to ask whether a good economist is a monetarist or a Keynesian is fallacious – the fallacy of the undistributed middle. Adam Smith was a little vague on macro-economic issues, unable to decide whether he favored banks, credit creation and bank notes to stimulate economic activity, or the safety of limiting the money supply to coin. This indecision seems to me to have been based on a sound instinct.

President Nixon once said we are all Keynesians today, and, if my memory serves, Paul Samuelson has said we are all monetarists, too. Each doctrine has a time and place. The second paper, delivered to a conference at Newport, Rhode Island, to celebrate the Bicentennial of the Franco-American Treaty of Alliance of 1778, emphasizes that Michel Chevalier, the outstanding French economist of the middle of the nineteenth century, was a rabid expansionist in France and a monetarist on his visit to the United States in the 1830s, where he was appalled by wild-cat banking and by the Populism of Andrew Jackson, who vetoed the restraint on money creation of the Second Bank of the United States.

In his review of *A Financial History. . .*, Sidney Pollard calls me a Manichean, a word, I fear, I had to look up; it is derived from the prophet Mani, whose religion combined elements of both God and the devil (1984). Unlike the prime minister of the developing country who asked for a one-armed economic adviser to be spared the counsel of 'on the one hand . . . and on the other hand', I take the view that to be either consistently Keynesian or consistently monetarist is to be wrong. Economics, as Joan Robinson has said, is a box of tools. Both the tools of Friedman and those of Keynes belong in the box to be taken out and applied as the problem and circumstances call for. Economists should specialize and exchange, to be sure, and some economists may wish to specialize in one mode of analysis or another; but the economist with only one model, which he or she applies to all situations, is wrong much of the time. Different circumstances, and sometimes different time horizons in the same circumstances, call for different prescriptions. The art of economics is to choose the right model for the given problem, and to abandon it when the problem changes shape. John Law, foremost perhaps among the French monetary actors with strong views and the subject who leads off in Chapter 3, was an expansionist with a good grasp of the need for pumping credit into the system in depression, and extending it from the financial center to the provinces, but, like the story of the man who knew how to spell 'banana', he did not know when to stop.[1]

Part II represents a continuation of my interest in comparative economic history, or what I prefer to call comparative historical economics, which is set out in *Economic Response* (1978a). Chapters 4 and 5, comparing British and French financial institutions and financial integration, respectively, pursue another theme of *A Financial History. . .* in greater depth – whether economic realities shape economic institutions, as the Coase theorem would have it, or institutions determine outcomes, as institutionalists claim is the more frequent case. Chapters 6 and 7 also relate to Britain and France, but compare responses to circumstances in a single country that are not dissimilar, long periods of time apart. Whereas the cross-national comparisons emphasize differences, the inter-temporal comparisons reveal similarity and consistency of national behavior. Chapter 6, on the return to the gold standard after the Napoleonic wars and World War I by Britain, was called 'pawky' by one reviewer – another word I had to look up, and of which some definitions are pejorative, others not (Supple, 1984, p. 113). The point was that, by and large, Britain in 1925 did not remember the experience of 1819. It is uncomfortably at odds with the theme of Chapter 8, to the effect that collective memory of traumatic financial episodes often shapes policy choices many generations later.

Why some experience is remembered across the generations, and another is not, is baffling to students of economic history. Economists who believe in rational expectations – i.e. the notion that markets respond to information in accordance with the mechanics of some appropriate economic model, and learn from experience – must wonder how the British public could forget financial crises so rapidly that they experienced a new crisis every ten years or so in the nineteenth century – 1816, 1825, 1836, 1847, 1857, 1866, and then a gap to 1890 (Kindleberger, 1978b).

The sceptical reader may want to be reminded in connection with the Franco-British comparisons of Chapters 4 and 5 that in *Economic Response* I was a little worried by comparisons that involved only two countries, on the ground that, in some financial studies covering six countries, extension to another four or five made it necessary to modify the original generalizations (1978a, p. 5). Generalizations that are based on two cases have more validity than those involving only one. They may stop short of universality.

The division of the essays into parts is in great degree arbitrary. Chapter 19 on 'Keynesianism vs Monetarism in the 1930s Depression and Recovery' should perhaps be fitted into Part I with the early economists rather than Part V with the papers on the Great Depression of 1929, though the latter position gives it the effect of a musical reprise. Similarly, Chapter 12 on 'Historical Perspective on Today's Third-World Debt Problem' could as easily be shifted from Part III on Historical Models to Part II with the comparisons. The difference between Part III and Parts IV and V is that the former explores a model across great chunks of historical time, whereas the latter two tell stories in which various models appear. Together they raise questions of methodology.

For my sins, I have to deliver an address on an economic subject in December 1985. When he heard of the circumstance that calls for this, my colleague, Peter Temin, in a passing encounter said 'For heaven's sake, don't discuss methodology'. I think I understand what prompted the remark. There is a strong temptation after a long life to attempt to justify what and how one does what one does and does not, and most people find the result soporific after dinner. However, discontent with today's trends in economics seems on the increase. It is hard not to feel that change is in the air. Melvin Reder's article (1982) on the Chicago school and its 'strong priors', or preoccupations, from which it is willing to be dislodged, if at all, only after heroic battle, makes a case against unalloyed deduction. Edward E. Leamer's 'Let's Take the Con out of Econometrics' (1983), to be followed, I understand by 'Let's Take the Tricks out of Econometrics' (forthcoming), suggests that econometric testing can be carried to excess. Donald N. McCloskey in turn has a paper on 'The Rhetoric of Economics' (1983) that calls for a retreat from the giddy heights of mathematical theory to the pedestrian world of intuition. Joseph Steindel's 'Reflections on the Present State of Economics' (1984) is only the latest in a series of laments by mathematical economists that their lead has been taken too seriously. Economic history continues to be driven out of graduate curricula in economics in the United States to make room for more and more technical tools, including more and more difficult mathematics. It may, none the less, be the darkest hour before the dawn.

My Columbia teacher of the 1930s, Wesley Clair Mitchell, turned to numerical testing because he found theorizing too easy. A theoretical explanation, he thought, could be adduced for virtually any set of facts, and often took on a spurious generality. In consequence, he accumulated numbers, piling them higher and higher. (It is widely remembered that Lionel Robbins, in *An Essay on the Nature and Significance of Economic Science* – 1949, p. 112–13 – said that the only impact of the great depression on the National Bureau of Economic Research, founded by Mitchell, was to require it to change its trend lines.) Although there is a great deal to be said for Mitchell's view that it is deceptively easy to spin *ad hoc* theoretical explanations for economic events, statistical testing is useful, but not always conclusive. A difficulty for economic historians is that systematic gathering of statistical data began for the most part only in the last third of the nineteenth century. Moreover, mechanical testing with excessive reliance on t-statistics, Durbin–Watson tests, coefficients of regression, Granger causality and the like, may be misleading and less helpful than a feel for the data and a finely honed intuition as to how economies work. For these purposes, a search for uniformities in history, as in Part III, or the elaboration of economic 'stories', such as those told in Part IV on the nineteenth century and Part V on the twentieth, strikes me as a vital complement to, and, for one whose professional formation took place in the 1930s, even a substitute for, high-powered theory, mathematical modelling and statistical testing.

Chapter 9 on 'The Cyclical Pattern of Long-Term Lending' tries to make clear that there is not just one pattern of long-term lending in the domestic business cycle, but two, and that the shift from one to the other, which at first blush seems to depend on the experience of the lending financial center, does not always work that way. Some countries start off with the anti-cyclical pattern generally found in experienced lenders, and some experienced lenders on occasion slip back into more adolescent behavior. In 'Key Currencies' (Chapter 10), the pattern is more uniform. In combination, the two papers make one wary of the claims of 'positive economics', which seeks for models that enable the economist confidently to forecast the future. 'The Financial Aftermath of War' (Chapter 11) persuades this economist at least to be modest about the limits of his subject; economic choices appear often to depend more on the socio-political matrix than on the experience and wisdom of the politicians and economic policy makers. The same message

emerges strongly from Chapter 16 on the German inflation after World
War I, which carries the story of the financial aftermath of war to greater
depths in a single classic case.

A few of the papers have closer ties of intellectual consanguinity (to
mix a metaphor) to other books of mine than *A Financial History...*,
especially *The World in Depression, 1929–1939* (1973) and *Manias,
Panics and Crashes: A History of Financial Crises* (1978b). The
economic storm clouds across the world since 1973 and again, more
threateningly, since 1979 make me look prescient in writing these
books. Alas, it was not so. In 1969, Wolfram Fischer, editor of the
Deutsche Taschenbuch Verlag series on world economic history by
decades, offered first Alexander Gerschenkron and then, when he
declined, me a choice of one among a number of decades since the
1890s. I chose the 1930s, not because of any premonition, but because I
had been drawn into economics during, and perhaps because of, the
depression, and still lacked a clear idea of what had happened and why.
From that monograph, finished in 1971 and published in 1973, it was an
easy transition for a teacher of European economic history to other
financial crises, searching for uniformities and differences, and then
only a step or two to European financial history more generally. When
contributions to *Festschriften* were called for, it was natural to see
analogies between earlier crises and today's third-world debt problem
(Chapter 12), to relate the nineteenth-century drive for monetary
reform to the world of today (Chapter 13), or to fill in a major gap in
earlier work, as in the 1888–93 financial crisis (Chapter 14), which is
relatively neglected in *Manias...* The analogies extend even to
personalities: Lord Overstone, the leader of the Currency School in
England – strong monetarist and bitter opponent of the decimalization
of British money – seems very much like Milton Friedman in the
firmness with which his views are held and in his power in debate,
whereas the Walter Bagehot analogue today – brilliant writer, if not a
banker–journalist – would be J. Kenneth Galbraith.

I keep coming back to the 1929 depression. This is largely by
invitation, as the billowing of financial storm clouds makes economic
impresarios think of 1929 and turn to those of us who have written about
it. A symposium to celebrate – if that is the right word – the fiftieth
anniversary of the stock market crash of October 1929 had lead articles
by Samuelson, Friedman and me (*Journal of Portfolio Management*,
1979). Their explanations diverged widely. Samuelson called the 1929
depression 'fortuitous'. Friedman ascribed it almost entirely to one
cause – the failure of the Federal Reserve Board to maintain and enlarge
the money supply. Both these explanations ran largely in terms of events
in the United States. My perspective, set out in Chapter 17, is more
complex and more widely cast. In causation it runs from a liquidity
squeeze caused by the stock market crash that spread to commodity and
asset prices and finally to bank failures and a money decline, the last
being a result rather than a cause. In scope, more was involved than a
depression starting in the United States and spreading to the rest of the
world. Complex interactions in geographic space preceded and followed

the collapse of 1929–33. The literature on the great depression remains to a considerable extent a dialogue of the deaf, with little if any impact of the ideas of one writer on those of others. It is a sad reflection on the state of economic science that, despite all the advances in technical analysis, there is so little convergence in our understanding of a major economic event of the century. I remain interested in the problem, doubtless as deaf as the others, and took on other assignments. Chapter 18 on Latin America and Chapter 20, dealing with the relations between banks and industry in Europe, were assignments eagerly embraced for the purpose of filling gaps in understanding.

Some years ago in a symposium on French planning, where I took a sceptical view of the merits of the system, I confessed to being merely a conversational or literary economist. A more pejorative characterization would be anecdotal. It seems to me, however, that my scepticism about French planning has been proved correct by the gradual subsidence of the vogue for planning and the move to *deplanification*. The papers below belong to the same literary rather than technical mode. So much the worse for them, or, if trends are changing, so much the better.

Note

1   In *A Financial History...* I chose as the monetarist protagonist, opposed to the Keynesian John Law, the Paris brothers who belonged to the financial establishment of the *financiers* and *officiers* threatened by Law's reforms. If I had been a deeper student of the period, I should have chosen Richard Cantillon, an Irish banker operating in Paris and a strong monetarist. Cantillon has been the subject of recent studies by Antoin E. Murphy (1983, 1984), in one of which he states 'The French environment of 1715–20 is not totally alien to the twentieth-century debate between Keynesianism and Monetarism' (1983, p. 45).

References

Journal of Portfolio Management (1979), 'The Great Crash, Causes, Consequences, Relevance: a Fifty-Year Perspective', vol. 6, no. 1 (Fall), pp. 7–21.

Kindleberger, Charles P. (1973), *The World in Depression, 1929–1939* (London: Allen Lane).

Kindleberger, Charles P. (1978a), *Economic Response, Comparative Studies in Trade, Finance and Growth* (Cambridge, Mass.: Harvard University Press).

Kindleberger, Charles P. (1978b), *Manias, Panics and Crashes, A History of Financial Crises* (New York: Basic Books).

Kindleberger, Charles P. (1984), *A Financial History of Western Europe* (London: Allen & Unwin).

Leamer, Edward E. (1983), 'Let's Take the Con out of Econometrics', *American Economic Review*, vol. 73, no. 1 (March), pp. 31–43.

McCloskey, Donald N. (1983), 'The Rhetoric of Economics', *Journal of Economic Literature*, vol. 21, no. 2 (June), pp. 481–517.

Murphy, Antoin E. (1983), 'Richard Cantillon – An Irish Banker in Paris', in Antoin E. Murphy (ed.), *Economists and the Irish Economy* (Dublin, Irish Academic Press), pp. 45–74.

Murphy, Antoin E. (1984), 'John Law and Richard Cantillon: the Mississippi System and the South Sea Bubble' (unpublished manuscript).

Pollard, Sidney (1984), 'A Basic Division', *Times Higher Education Supplement* (May).

Reder, Melvin W. (1982), 'Chicago Economics: Permanence and Change', *Journal of Economic Literature*, vol. 20, no. 1 (March), pp. 1–38.

Robbins, Lionel (1936), *An Essay on the Nature and Significance of Economic Science*, 2nd rev. edn. (London: Macmillan).

Steindel, J. (1984), 'Reflections on the Present State of Economics', Banca Nazionale del Lavoro *Quarterly Review*, no. 148 (March), pp. 3–14.

Supple, Barry (1984), 'Revisiting Rostow', *Economic History Review*, 2nd ser., vol. 37, no. 1 (February), pp. 107–14.

Part I

Keynesianism vs. Monetarism

1

Was Adam Smith a Monetarist or a Keynesian?

The title I have given this talk reminds me of the time in 1930 when I was a deck boy on the S.S. Bird City, a freighter of the Moore–McCormack line, at $20 a month, sailing from New York to Copenhagen, Gdynia, Helsinki and Leningrad, plus three small Finnish paper ports on the return voyage. This was the period of prohibition, but after the ship reached Copenhagen, the crew was privileged to buy liquor from the slop-chest against its pay. One able-bodied seaman, that I remember only as 'Blackie' – I was 'Slim' and my best friend was 'Whitey' – was continuously drunk, owed the ship money so that he could not quit without being blacklisted, and had been converted to membership in the Communist Party on the preceding voyage. One evening he rolled heavily out of his lower bunk in the fo'c's'le, which I shared with him and a dozen others of the deck crew, grabbed a broom and waved it around wildly, asking 'If J. P. Morgan was over there, the Russian Army was over there, and your father and mother there, who would you shoot?' I think I have learned to call this sort of reasoning *ignoratio elenchi*, or the fallacy of the undistributed middle. The question addressed in this talk is of the same sort. It happens, however, that this is to be an Adam Smith lecture, and I have some remarks to get off my chest on Keynesianism and monetarism.

Let me then start by saying that Adam Smith is tops. He started our science off in growth, resource allocation, income distribution and a host of similar aspects of micro-economics. Despite a number of interesting passages, such as that on debt, however, he was not distinguished as a macro-economist. The hagiography tends either to ignore his weakness in money and banking, as does Samuel Hollander in *The Economics of Adam Smith* (1973), or to protest that he is much better on the balance of payments (Eagley, 1970), or on monetary economics generally (Laidler, 1981) than most observers are willing to allow. I yield to none in my admiration for *The Wealth of Nations* – and in fact recommend to students that they, like Bismarck's tariff negotiator for Prussia under the Zollverein, Rudolph Von Delbrück (1905, I), read

Adam Smith Lecture given to the National Association of Business Economists at Detroit, Michigan, on 29 September 1983. Published in abridged form in Business Economics, *vol 9, no. 1 (January 1984), pp. 5–12.*

the hallowed text each night for half an hour before retiring. But it is helpful for Smith's reputation as a human being to acknowledge that he, like the rest of us, from time to time made a mistake or overlooked a significant aspect of the economy of his day – even on the micro-economic side.

I happened to get another vigorous going over from two critics at the Glasgow celebration of the bicentenary of *The Wealth of Nations* when I suggested that Adam Smith was totally unaware of the technological changes taking place in the industrial revolution cooking around him (Briggs, 1976; Hartwell, 1976). His other slips not recited in my paper on that occasion include the remark that Dutch merchants are uneasy at being separated from their capital, which is why they unload goods from East Prussia in Amsterdam to look at them before shipping them on to Italy – when the real reason was to repack the grain more carefully to prevent it from exploding from spontaneous combustion under the hot Mediterranean sun (Book IV, chap. ii, p. 422); or the amateurish and quite unsupported sociology that ascribed French interest in life annuities and tontines to the 'fact' that the farmers general (of tax collections and the like) who accumulate wealth are social upstarts, cut off from marrying into the upper classes and too proud to marry their lower-class equals, hence celibate and without heirs (Book V, chap. iii, pp. 871–2). This is the sort of implicit theorizing to which social scientists are always tempted and against which Wesley C. Mitchell warned us at Columbia in the mid-1930s. Some years ago in a book on the terms of trade, I wrote in the introduction that I would thereafter give up empirical work, disheartened that some of our most fascinating results at the three-quarter mark turned out to rest on computing errors. The statement evoked a warm response from professional friends. But the thrust of all this is to assert that Adam Smith is a marvellous economist even when he proves to be somewhat short of outstanding on money and banking.

Keynesianism and monetarism in what follows are used loosely. I am tempted to paraphrase Gilbert's lyric in *Iolanthe* on Liberals and Conservatives by saying that all economists are either Keynesians who believe in expanding investment or government spending to achieve higher employment, or monetarists who want to restrict bank lending and the growth of the money supply to help fight inflation. In some cases it makes a difference when one came into the profession, whether in the 1930s when unemployment was rife, or in the period after World War II of steady growth and reasonably full employment. In a paper a few years ago on Keynesianism vs monetarism in eighteenth- and nineteenth-century France (1980; see Chapter 3 below), I lined up John Law, Napoleon I, the Saint-Simonian school (including notably Jacques Laffitte, the Pereire brothers who founded the Crédit Mobilier, and Michel Chevalier) among the Keynesians; the Paris brothers (who won out over John Law), François Mollien (Napoleon's Minister of the Public Treasury), and the Bank of France establishment of the *hautes banques* (including especially Baron James de Rothschild) among the monetarists. For England, a generation after Adam Smith, the big division occurred in the Bullionist controversy between the Currency School, which can broadly be identified with monetarism, and the Banking School, which clung to the quasi-Keynesian belief in the real bills doctrine that money can be expanded *pari passu* with underlying actual trade transactions. The same issue in Sweden in the mid-eighteenth century had divided the 'Hats', who had interests in exports and large-scale business and believed in monetary expansion, from the 'Caps', in small business and to a considerable extent import-competing. The Caps ascribed exchange depreciation of the period to excess expansion of the note issue, while the Hats, like the Banking School in England half a century later, attributed it to crop failures that worsened the balance of payments. A similar debate was pursued over the causes of the German hyperinflation of 1923 between monetarists like Bresciani-Turroni and Philip Cagan, who ascribed it to the expansionary policies of the Reichsbank, and the balance-of-payments school including, along with Germans such as Karl Helfferich and Moritz Bonn, such Americans as James W. Angell and John H. Williams, who blamed reparation payments. Outside Europe, the same contentious issue has been met in the Baring crisis of 1890 in Argentina, in which monetarists blamed the changes in Argentine banking laws that led to over-issue, while the Keynesian or balance-of-payments school pointed to the cut-off of British lending to Argentina, the resultant depreciation of the peso, and the necessity, with higher international prices, to issue more banknotes to support the price level (Williams, 1920).

Which side of this perennial debate was Adam Smith on? First of all, he was more interested in real than in monetary analysis. There are such folk about today. In his stupendous book on the *World Economy* (1978), Walt Rostow explicitly states that he is unconcerned with monetary or banking developments, believing in the dominance of real factors such as population growth, discovery and technological change, ordered in cycles of various sorts, including the Juglar eight-to-nine-year business cycle, the 'stages of growth' and the 50-year Kondratieff cycle. Ronald Coase (1937, 1960) holds the opinion that institutions, including financial institutions, adapt to real conditions of demand and supply – except in the rare cases that transactions costs are especially high – so that monetary and banking practice and institutions fall passively into place. Schumpeter's *History of Economic Analysis* (1954, p. 283) observes that real analysis dominated economic thought prior to 1600, after which there was an interlude to 1760 in which monetary analysis was considered important, until real analysis (with Turgot and Adam Smith in the lead) took over once more.

But Adam Smith thought something about money. Of course. Book I, chapters iv and v, explain the exchange functions of money that widen the market and hence extend the limits to the division of labor. Book II, chapter ii, deals with money as part of the capital of society, and with banking in a general way. There are other scattered passages – the long digression on silver, that on banks of deposit, especially the Bank of Amsterdam, the treatment of the public debt. There is, however, no consistent orderly analysis of money and banking, either in the national or in the international dimension, despite the valiant efforts of a number of writers, in their pious defense of the Master, to find them.

Money is the great wheel (Book II, chap. ii, pp. 273, 276), presumably a water wheel that powers the system. Banking goes further. If gold and silver money, which circulates in a country and allows the dead stock to be converted into active stock, may properly be compared to a highway, banking (if he, Smith, may be allowed so violent a metaphor) provides a sort of 'waggon-way through the air' (*ibid.*, p. 305). These are Keynesian metaphors – although, as Bentham complained, from wheels, water and wagons one cannot get a clear idea of money and banking, which need definition and exemplification (Vickers, 1975, p. 301). On the other side of this methodological issue, however, I commend to you a recent paper by Donald McCloskey on 'The Rhetoric of Economics' (1983), which maintains that a penetrating metaphor is worth more than a lot of integrals, differentials and matrices, together with scads of $a + b$. He cites as an illustration 'investment in human capital' (a Chicago metaphor of Ted Schultz and Gary Becker), which illuminates many issues in the economics of labor, of capital and of education. But the metaphors should be apposite and powerful.

To return to the waggon-way through the air provided by banks and the paper money they issue, a monetarist note creeps in when Smith goes on:

> The commerce and industry of the country, however, it must be acknowledged, cannot be altogether so secure, when they are thus, as it were, suspended on Daedalian wings of paper money, as when they travel about on the solid ground of gold and silver. (Book II, chap. ii, 305)

This is the way it goes throughout the great work: passages here that sound monetarist, others there that suggest an interest in expansion.

Before going into further detail, let me pause to note that a young English economic historian has recently noted that financial history can be written in four differing modes: first, the orthodox, in which the story line is how the central bank gradually got control of the money supply, developed appropriate policy instruments. and repressed the tendency of the financial system to what Smith called 'overtrading'; second, the 'heroic', in which great innovations in money and banking give a needed lift to economic growth and development; third, the Populist, with emphasis on how orthodox monetary and banking development have held back the small merchant, small farmer and small industrialist by denying them credit and favoring foreign trade, trusts, and perhaps government; and fourth, the 'statist', in which emphasis rests on the development of money and banking to assist government in carrying out its functions, especially the finance of war (Jones, 1982). The author of this taxonomy was making a point that the central banks of Argentina, Australia and Canada were all created to help finance governments; the same could be said of the founding of the Bank of England in 1694 during the Nine Years' War, of the Bank of France in 1800 in the Napoleonic Wars, and of the National Bank Act of 1863 in the United States, which helped finance the Union in the Civil War. The orthodox mode of writing financial history fits into the monetarist view of money and banking, the heroic into the Keynesian as I loosely use the term, and the Populist into a frustrated Keynesian viewpoint.

On the domestic front, Smith took an orthodox position in so far as he strongly favored convertibility of bank notes into specie, opposed the issue of banknotes of small denominations, worried about chains of discount accommodation bills in which A drew on B, B on C, C on D and M or N back on A, each discounting these accommodation bills after an appropriate interval. He applauded the Bank of Amsterdam, although not for the subtle reasons that later led Henry Simon and Milton Friedman to advocate 100 percent reserves against bank deposits in order to frustrate the expansion and contraction of bank money through the money multiplier, but because of its contribution to 'money-circulating', or monetizing the economy and pushing back the limits on the division of labor. He opposed overtrading. The ideas of John Law are called splendid but visionary and are said to have contributed to the excess of banking that of late had been complained of both in Scotland and in other places (Book II, chap. ii, 303).

And yet, in an earlier passage, he observed that the new banking companies of Scotland of the last twenty-five or thirty years, i.e. since about 1750, in almost every considerable town, and even in some country villages, had produced great benefit:

> I have heard it asserted, that the trade of the city of Glasgow doubled in about fifteen years after the first erection of the banks there; and that the trade of Scotland has more than quadrupled since the first erection of the banks at Edinburgh. . . .

But then he waffles:

> Whether the trade of Scotland in general, or of the city of Glasgow in particular, has really increased in so great a proportion, during so short a period, I do not pretend to know. If either of them has increased in this proportion, it seems to be an effect too great to be accounted for by the sole operation of this cause. That the trade and industry of Scotland, however, have increased very considerably during this period, and that the banks have contributed a good deal to this increase, cannot be doubted. (Book II, chap. ii, p. 281)

It is worth noting, as it bears on a modern debate, that Smith, like most modern monetarists, believed in regulation of banking. His interest was in the convertibility of bank notes into gold and silver on demand, and the prohibition of the circulation of bank notes of small denomination such as £1 and under. But the emphasis on liberty in other fields of economic endeavor, whilst maintaining limitations in money and banking, presents philosophical problems for 'liberals' with a small 'l', or possibly I make myself clearer if I say 'libertarians'. It is a Keynesian position sometimes to want regulation in fields other than money and banking, but to insist on easier entry, more expansion, extension of banking into the provinces, and the like in money and banking. A French monetarist, Louis Wolowski, testifying before the 1867 Inquiry into money and banking pushed by the expansionist (Keynesian) school, kept reiterating that 'free trade in banking is free trade in swindling', a quotation ascribed to Daniel Webster. He also pointed out that Richard Cobden, the leader of the fight for free trade and against the Corn Laws in England, had voted three times against crippling amendments to the Bank Act of 1844, a victory for the monetarist Currency School (Ministère des Finances, *et al.*, 1865–7, II, pp. 205, 230, 383). While Milton Friedman is prepared to deregulate by removing license requirements for all sorts of activities, from brain surgery to teen-age automobile driving, leaving the necessary discipline to prevent abuse to the market, he has been outdone by the Austrian school that is ready to throw banking and the issue of money open to all comers (Hayek, 1972; Vaubel, 1977). Vaubel regards money as a private, not a public good, even in its function as a standard of measurement (unit of account). He believes that Gresham's law need not operate with competitive monies, provided they are traded with flexible exchange rates among them. He maintains, in fact, that the opposite of Gresham's law will result, that good money will drive out bad as banks compete to have their money accepted. This optimistic view seems to fly in the face of a long record of bank failures from John Law's Banque royale to the recent troubles in Nashville and in Penn Square, Oklahoma. Vaubel does not consider the objection that, if different banks' deposits are traded at varying prices, they cease in effect to be money, if we define money as the one asset fixed in price in terms of itself. Adam Smith is far from such a libertarian stance. In his eyes, regulation of banks is not a violation of natural liberty: 'those exertions of the natural liberty of a few individuals, which might endanger the security of the whole society, are, and ought to be, restrained by the laws of all governments, of the most free as well as of the most despotical' (Book II, chap. xi, p. 308).

Further on domestic banking, Smith is generally sharply criticized both by monetarists and by some Keynesians for believing in the real bills doctrine (Checkland, 1975, p. 519; Matthews, 1976, p. 337; Laidler, 1981, p. 195). This doctrine, held by the Banking School, considered that expansion of the money supply was entirely acceptable if the underlying credit transaction was one backed by a bill of exchange drawn on a sale of merchandise by a bona fide seller on a bona fide buyer, rather than on accommodation bills or promissory notes. This is generally regarded as a complete fallacy. With full employment, expanded credit based on a commercial transaction can lead to higher prices, more credit expansion justified by the higher value of the real goods traded, and hence to a cumulative inflationary process. Moreover the attack on accommodation bills, implicit in Smith's discussion of chains of discounts and taught to me in the 1930s by my banking teacher, H. Parker Willis, can go too far, as Hawtrey has pointed out

(1927, pp. 124–5). But there is a kernel of truth in the real bills view when there is widespread unemployment. It does not justify Smith on real bills, however, as his general assumption was one of full employment (Hollander, 1973, p. 207). He never did accept Hume's contention that material advantages may be gained by an economy where money is growing – because of initial unemployment.

On the international front, Smith had an opportunity to accept another of David Hume's position – that of the price–specie-flow mechanism, but he did not. Viner (1937, p. 97) regards this as one of the foremost mysteries in the history of economic thought, since Smith was well-acquainted with Hume and his work, and in fact corresponded with him frequently. In fact Smith went back to an old notion in which each country requires a certain amount of money, and if more is issued than the country requires it ships it abroad to buy foreign goods. Viner calls this an obsolete model, but it comes close to the monetary approach to the balance of payments today as expounded by Frenkel and Johnson (1975) or McKinnon (1979). I must say I find the monetarist model of the balance of payments bizarre. In McKinnon's exposition, for example, if more money is issued than households and businesses want to hold, the money is spent or lent abroad, leading to a deficit that brings domestic demand and supply for money back into balance. In some formulations, where capital flows are excluded by assumption, changes in earning and spending are used to adjust the stock of money to some desired level, rather than, as my generation was taught, using money to equilibrate temporary discrepancies between income and expenditure. The monetarist model of the balance of payments seems to have switched money from an instrument to an objective variable, and vice versa with income and expenditure. Moreover, why employ assumptions that put the burden on changes in income and expenditure? For the most part, with a banking system in existence, changes in the desired stock of money are brought about by borrowing or lending.

Eagley and Laidler, as already mentioned, seek to exonerate Adam Smith from the charge that he unduly neglected Hume's balance-of-payments adjustment mechanism, although their defense, however respectful and even dutiful, fails to persuade. Laidler is more successful in his assertion that Smith had an appropriate insight into what is called today world monetarism – how world discoveries of gold and silver set the world price level, and the mechanism by which paper money can replace precious metals with important savings for society in real resources. It must be remembered, however, that Smith is not certain he wants to trust the Daedalian wings of paper money, as contrasted with the terra firma of gold and silver.

Part of Smith's uncertainty about paper money and banking had its origin in the fact that Scottish banking was undergoing a series of significant changes in the years from the early 1760s (Checkland, 1975). The period was somewhat comparable to the present day when deregulation is going forward in banking at a ferocious pace and analysts have a hard time trying to decide what the net effects on the system are going to be of CDs, NOW accounts, SUPER-NOW accounts, credit

cards, Euro-currencies, money funds, bank holding companies, and the
intrusion of insurance companies, brokerage houses and retail stores
into banking and of thrift institutions into industrial lending. The pace
from 1763 to 1776 was perhaps not so giddy as that of today, but 1763
was the year both that Adam Smith finished the first draft of *The Wealth
of Nations* (revised in two years in France, six in the tiny town of
Kirkcaldy in Scotland, and four in London) and of the start of branch
banking in Scotland. New bank legislation in 1765 gave rise to a debate,
addressed particularly to questions of free entry into banking and the
so-called 'optional clause', which made it possible for banks to postpone
redeeming bank notes for six months after presentation. No sooner had
these controversies been settled when the Ayr Bank was founded in 1770
and failed in 1772 with £200,000 of notes in circulation and £600,000 of
discounts on banks in London which it could not pay. Among the share-
holders who lost some or all of their estates because of unlimited liability
was the Duke of Buccleugh, Adam Smith's patron. Checkland (1975,
p. 515) finds it curious that this failure did not modify Smith's optimistic
view of the merit of free entry into (regulated) banking, which he
thought would require banks to be circumspect in their own interest, a
position paralleled today by Vaubel.

What had brought caution to the Scottish banks earlier in the century
was the device by which the Bank of Scotland and the Royal Bank of
Scotland each accumulated and held supplies of the bank notes issued
by the other, ready to present them for specie when the competition got
particularly rough. Again in 1774 after the Ayr failure, a unified system
of note exchanges was established among all Scottish banks (Checkland,
1975, p. 510). The rapid rate of institutional change in Scottish banking
in this period when *The Wealth of Nations* was being revised perhaps
accounts for the lack of a clear line of thought of banking on the part of
Smith. It is evocative of the view today that changes in banking and
finance are proceeding at too rapid a pace to enable analysts and policy-
makers to figure out how the system is likely to function under different
circumstances, and leading Henry Kauffman (*New York Times*, 3 May
1983) and others to call for a slowdown of deregulation.

Was Smith a Keynesian or a monetarist? My answer to that fallacious
question is not 'none of the above', as in some questions based on
ignoratio elenchi, but, giving him the benefit of the doubt, 'both'. To be
both a Keynesian and a monetarist is the only reasonable position. If it
does not emerge with crystal clarity in *The Wealth of Nations*, I believe
it to be there concealed behind a film of muddle. For a superior
statement of such a balanced position, one should read – perhaps earlier
in the evening than just before going to bed – Henry Thornton's *An
Enquiry into the Nature and Effect of the Paper Credit of Great Britain*,
published in 1802, a short generation after *The Wealth of Nations*.
Thornton was a dedicated philanthropist, an abolitionist regarding
slavery, a banker, and a thoughtful student. In an introduction to the
1939 edition of *Paper Credit*, Hayek points out that Thornton is over-
shadowed by the monetarist Ricardo, but 'It is not too much to say that
the appearance of *Paper Credit* marked a new epoch in monetary

theory'. It is perhaps unfair to add that in some respects we have today retrogressed from Thornton's understanding.

Thornton was both monetarist and Keynesian. He thought that some Currency School adherents such as Boyd were far too simple in criticizing the Bank of England for over-issue. He made allowance in the depreciation of sterling for the effects of bad harvests and of British subsidies to her Continental allies (1802/1939, p. 354). A monetarist in so far as he drafted the Bullion Report of 1810 with William Huskisson and Francis Horner, he applauded Adam Smith's remark about banks being able in the short run to activate the dead stock of the country (*ibid.*, p. 175 n.), and regarded bills of exchange as near money. In this his ideas differed sharply from those of the leading monetarist and bullionist of fifty years later, Lord Overstone, who excoriated Colonel Torrens in 1857 for having briefly regarded anything as money except gold or bank notes that substituted one-for-one for gold. In Torrens' case, Overstone's scorn was heaped on him for having flirted with the idea that bank deposits might be money (O'Brien, 1971, II, pp. 713–17). Thornton opposed too violent a contraction of Bank of England notes in order to attract gold, believing that it would in fact repell it (1802/1939, pp. 122, 153). He further believed that the Bank of England should act as the lender of last resort in crisis (p. 188), while holding that in normal times the Bank should keep its circulation of notes steady, regardless of fluctuations in its gold stock (p. 67).

I am especially interested in Thornton's views of fixing on a certain money aggregate. Bagehot later said apropos of M_1, M_2 and so on:

> Men of business in England do not like the currency question. They are perplexed to define accurately what money is; *how* to count they know, but *what* to count they do not know. (1857/1978, vol. 9, p. 319; italics in original)

In another passage in his early writings on monetary questions, well before the magisterial *Lombard Street* of 1873, Bagehot records a victory of Thomas Tooke, the Banking School leader, over Colonel Torrens of the Currency School on the issue:

> No. Tooke contends that no new purchasers can, under the present law [the Bank Act of 1844], be brought into the market by an undue issue of bank notes, nevertheless other media of interchange can be found, such as bills of exchange and book credits, that will do the work ... (1848/1978, p. 256)

But Thornton had made the point in 1802:

> If bills and bank notes were both extinguished, other substitutes for gold would be found. Men save themselves the trouble of counting, weighing and transporting guineas in all the larger operations of commerce. ... Credit would still exist, credit in books, credit

depending on the testimony of witnesses, or on merely verbal promises. (1802/1939, p. 101)

There is nothing new under the sun. I thought I had done well in attacking the monetarist view that booms can be contained by fixing some money aggregate, arguing:

> Fix any M_i and the market will create new forms of money in periods of boom to get around the limit and create the necessity to fix a new variable, M_j (Kindleberger, 1978, p. 58),

by citing John Stuart Mill and the Radcliffe Commission. Thornton was ahead of them (us) all. And if you want a modern illustration of his insight, I can refer you to the 1982 stock market boom in Kuwait, which was financed by the simplest form of 'money' creation I can think of, the writing of post-dated checks.

The essence is that both monetarism and Keynesianism in their simple formulations are right in their place and wrong if one tries to make too much of them as all-purpose weapons. Michel Chevalier was an unreconstructed Keynesian in France in the middle of the nineteenth century, wanting more bank notes, more banks, an end to the monopoly of the Bank of France, and especially the extension of banking into the provinces. On his visit to the United States in the 1830s, however, he changed his spots, sympathizing with Nicholas Biddle of the Second Bank of the United States and criticizing President Andrew Jackson, who vetoed the renewal of its charter (Chevalier, 1938, I, Letters 4, 5, 6). Chevalier was struck by the resemblances between the attacks on the Bank and the Republican tirades of 1791 and 1792 that led up to the Reign of Terror (*ibid.*, I, p. 72), and went on to say that, if one got rid of the Bank, one would plunge the country into commercial anarchy, which would end up as political anarchy (*ibid.*, I, p. 95). This goes further than most monetarists today.

More contemporaneously, I find the debate between Temin (1976) and Friedman and Schwartz (1963), plus the rest of the monetarist school represented in Brunner's *The Great Depression Revisited* (1981), terribly simple-minded. To wrap up the great depression of the 1930s in a model in which it is critical whether the *IS* curve, representing spending (the Keynesian view), or the *LM* curve, standing for the monetarist explanation, moved first, and to decide which by whether the interest rate moved up or down, is to elevate a useful model in its own place into a fetish at the expense of the complex web of history. Where are the other elements in the intricate mechanism; the fragility of international debts, the seizing up of bank credit in New York as a result of the stock market crash and its propagation of the crisis to trade credits and consumer debt, the fall of prices, the debt deflation process, the appreciation of exchange rates and the like? In *The Great Depression Revisited*, various monetarists finally admitted one international element into a previously purely domestic account of the depression – the Hawley-Smoot tariff act of 1930, although most international trade models regard tariffs as a force for expansion, not contraction. In *The Way the World Works* (1977), Jude Wanniski even tries to explain Black Thursday and Black Tuesday, 24 and 29 October 1929, respectively, by the defeat of some low-tariff adherents in a Senate subcommittee on a minor carbide item somehow foreshadowing the passage of the Hawley-Smoot tariff some nine months later, its signing into law by President Hoover over widespread protest at home and abroad, retaliation by some forty countries, and the world depression that ensued. This is more than rational expectations: it is second sight. I subscribe to the principle of Occam's razor, that one should use parsimony in explanation, the simplest explanation consistent with the facts. My adherence stops short, however, of trying to explain the great depression with a monetarist model – or a simple Keynesian one for that matter – with or without the addition of the Hawley-Smoot tariff.

One conflict between Keynesians and monetarists worth noting is mentioned apropos of Ricardo and his critics by an historian of the debate over the resumption of specie payments in 1819. Keynesianism, states Hilton (1977, p. 70), partly quoting Winch, achieved its success in the 1930s by reason of its advocacy of an interventionist philosophy at a time when politicians were thoroughly frustrated. In 1819, on the other hand, the monetarism of Ricardo appealed to such politicians as Lord Liverpool because it justified inaction. I sympathize with the liberal view that there is a lot of capacity in market economies to recover by themselves, but the notion that government should never interfere, or that all intervention is dysfunctional, is surely an exaggeration. For those who think otherwise, let me ask you to contemplate the German monetary reform of 1948 – to my mind the most brilliant feat of social engineering in historical memory – or such governmental successes as lend-lease in World War II and the Marshall Plan.

Government is an art that sometimes calls for deregulation and laissez-faire, sometimes for intervention. The monetarists and the Keynesians are both right – some of the time. The trick for government, or, less pejoratively, the art of government, is to decide when and how much to intervene, and when and how rapidly to turn away.

After embarking on the outline of this lecture, I ran across an excellent little book by Ralph Bryant, *Controlling Money: The Federal Reserve and its Critics*, which with a somewhat more technical approach comes close to the position here set forth – that putting the fundamental questions of macro-economic policy in terms of monetarism vs. Keynesianism obscures rather than illuminates the issues. Each is correct, some of the time (1983, p. 110), and to focus on a choice limited to these two positions neglects other highly important issues of monetary policy: viz.,

rules vs. discretion,
relations between money and fiscal policies,
preferred macro-economic policies for reducing inflation, and
the interdependence of monetary policy in the United States and that in the rest of the world.

I would modify the list slightly, as Bryant might himself have done if he had developed these themes. In the first place, as earlier noted, the issue of rules vs. discretion is implicit in the debate over monetarism vs. Keynesianism, monetarism favoring rules, Keynesianism discretion. Secondly, I would like to see the interdependence question broadened from a focus on interest rates or world money supplies to include coordinated exchange rates. But surely Bryant is right that the answer to Keynesianism versus monetarism is both, each in its time and place.

If one wants a simple rule which tells when to change rules, try monetarism on trend and Keynesianism in crisis. Friedman and Schwartz (1963, p. 395) come close to articulating this position when they write about the need for a lender of last resort, using the metaphor that one rock held in place may stave off an avalanche, and quoting Bagehot's *Lombard Street* (1873) that a panic is a species of neuralgia and one must not starve it. I am doubtful about the metaphor and the therapy recommended, but have no difficulty with the monetary policy implied.

In the 1930s, the *New Yorker* ran a series of cartoons by Gluyas Williams concerning the so-called Sceptics Society, in which a group of frock-coated men would undertake to test aphorisms that loomed large in folklore. I have quoted them often, and if you have heard me on the subject before, please forgive. One cartoon showed the dignified Sceptics chasing a pig, to decide by scientific experiment whether one could or could not make a silk purse out of a sow's ear. On one occasion, the Society took on two folk-sayings simultaneously. They stood around on a platform while a blind-folded man stood on a board, poised over a precipice, as the Society sought to determine whether 'he who hesitates is lost' or it is better to 'look before you leap'. But of course the one or the other applies in the proper time and circumstances. Equally Keynesianism and monetarism are both right, as on the right occasions are Say's law that supply creates its own demand, the Keynes' law that demand creates its own supply. But not simultaneously, and not inevitably in all circumstances. The task of us economists is to back off from the Pavlovian responses that make the stock market rise or fall on each Friday's announcement by the Fed of the money aggregates, and to explore what circumstances alter what cases, and how and to what extent.

I believe that Adam Smith, if he were to put his mind to macro-economic policy today would agree. He was a superb economist.

References

Bagehot, Walter (1848/1978), 'The Currency Monopoly'; reprinted in N. St John Stevas (ed.), *The Collected Works of Walter Bagehot* (London: *The Economist*).
Bagehot, Walter (1857/1978), 'The General Aspect of the Currency Question', *The Economist*; reprinted in N. St John Stevas (ed.), *The Collected Works of Walter Bagehot* (London: *The Economist*).

Bagehot, Walter (1873/1978), *Lombard Street*; reprinted in N. St John Stevas (ed.), *The Collected Works of Walter Bagehot*, vol. IX (London: *The Economist*).

Briggs, Asa (1976), 'Comment' on C. P. Kindleberger, 'The Historical Background: Adam Smith and the Industrial Revolution', in T. Wilson and A. S. Skinner (eds), *The Market and the State: Essays in Honour of Adam Smith* (Oxford: Clarendon), pp. 25–33.

Brunner, Karl (ed.) (1981), *The Great Depression Revisited* (The Hague: Martinus Nijhoff).

Bryant, Ralph C. (1983), *Controlling Money: The Federal Reserve and its Critics* (Washington, DC: Brookings Institution).

Checkland, S. G. (1975), 'Adam Smith and the Bankers', in A. S. Skinner and T. Wilson (eds), *Essays on Adam Smith* (Oxford: Clarendon), pp. 504–23.

Chevalier, Michel (1838), *Lettres sur l'Amérique du Nord*, 3rd ed. (Paris: Charles Gosselin, 2 vols).

Coase, Ronald H. (1937), 'The Nature of the Firm', *Economica*, new ser., vol. 4, pp. 386–405.

Coase, Ronald H. (1960), 'The Problem of Social Cost', *Journal of Law and Economics*, vol. 3, pp. 1–44.

Delbrück, Rudolph von (1905), *Lebenserinnerungen* (Leipzig: Duncker u. Humblot, 2 vols).

Eagley, Robert V. (1970), 'Adam Smith and the Specie-Flow Doctrine', *Scottish Journal of Political Science*, vol. 17, pp. 61–8.

Frenkel, Jacob and Johnson, Harry G. (1975), *The Monetary Approach to the Balance of Payments* (London: Allen & Unwin).

Friedman, Milton and Schwartz, Anna J. (1963), *A Monetary History of the United States, 1867–1960* (Princeton, NJ: Princeton University Press).

Hartwell, R. M. (1976), 'Comment' on C. P. Kindleberger, 'The Historical Background: Adam Smith and the Industrial Revolution', in T. Wilson and A. S. Skinner (eds), *The Market and the State: Essays in Honour of Adam Smith* (Oxford: Clarendon), pp. 33–41.

Hawtrey, R. G. (1927), *Currency and Credit*, 3rd edn. (London: Longmans, Green).

Hayek, F. A. (1939), 'Introduction' to Henry Thornton, *An Inquiry into the Nature and Effect of the Paper Credit of Great Britain* (London: Allen & Unwin).

Hayek, F. A. (1972), *Choice in Currency: A Way to Stop Inflation*, Institute of Economic Affairs Occasional Paper No. 48 (London: IEA).

Hilton, Boyd (1977), *Corn, Cash, Commerce: The Economic Policies of the Tory Governments, 1815–1830* (Oxford: Oxford University Press).

Hollander, Samuel (1973), *The Economics of Adam Smith* (Toronto: University of Toronto Press).

Jones, Charles (1982), 'The Monetary Politics of Export Economies before 1914: Argentina, Australia, and Canada', a paper presented to the Symposium on 'Argentina, Australia and Canada: Some Comparisons, 1870–1950', at the 44th International Congress of Americanists, Manchester, England, 8 September 1982.

Kindleberger, C. P. (1978), *Manias, Panics and Crashes: A History of Financial Crises* (New York: Basic Books).

Kindleberger, C. P. (1980), 'Keynesianism vs Monetarism in Eighteenth- and Nineteenth-century France', *History of Political Economy*, vol. 12, no. 4 (Winter), pp. 499–523.

Laidler, David (1981), 'Adam Smith as a Monetary Economist', *Canadian Journal of Economics*, vol. 14, pp. 185–99.

McCloskey, Donald N. (1983), 'The Rhetoric of Economics', *Journal of Economic Literature*, vol. 21, no. 2 (June), pp. 481–517.

McKinnon, Ronald I. (1979), *Money in International Exchange: The Convertible Currency System* (London: Oxford University Press).

Matthews, R. C. O. (1976), 'Public Policy and Monetary Expenditure', in T. Wilson and A. S. Skinner (eds), *The Market and the State: Essays in Honour of Adam Smith* (Oxford: Clarendon), pp. 330–50.

Ministère des Finances, *et al.* (1865–7), *Enquête sur les principes et les faits généraux qui régissent la circulation monétaire et fiduciaire* (Paris: Imprimerie impériale, 6 vols).

O'Brien, D. P. (ed.) (1971), *The Correspondence of Lord Overstone* (Cambridge: Cambridge University Press, 3 vols).

Rostow, W. W. (1978), *The World Economy: History and Prospect* (London: Macmillan).

Schumpeter, Joseph A. (1954), *History of Economic Analysis* (London: Allen & Unwin).

Smith, Adam (1776/1937), *An Inquiry into the Nature and Causes of The Wealth of Nations*, Cannan edn. (New York: Modern Library).

Temin, Peter (1976), *Did Monetary Forces Cause the Great Depression?* (New York: W. W. Norton).

Thornton, Henry (1802/1939), *An Enquiry into the Nature and Effect of the Paper Credit of Great Britain* edited with an introduction by F. A. Hayek (London: Allen & Unwin).

Vaubel, Roland (1977), 'Free Currency Competition', *Weltwirtschaftliches Archiv*, vol. 113, no. 3, pp. 435–59.

Vickers, Douglas (1975), 'Adam Smith and the Status of the Theory of Money', in A. S. Skinner and T. Wilson (eds), *Essays on Adam Smith* (Oxford: Clarendon).

Viner, Jacob (1937), *Studies in the Theory of International Trade* (New York: Harper).

Wanniski, Jude (1977), *The Way the World Works* (New York: Basic Books).

Williams, John H. (1920), *Argentine International Trade under Inconvertible Paper Money, 1880–1900* (Cambridge, Mass.: Harvard University Press).

2

Michel Chevalier (1806–1879), the Economic de Tocqueville

This paper is an hors d'oeuvres. It was intended to be a paper on John Law, Jacques Lafitte and the Pereire brothers as Keynesians in 18th and 19th century France. I shall save that dish for another occasion. In the course of my reading, however, it became clear that Michel Chevalier's economic reflections on America and France, based on his visit to these shores in 1834 and 1835, would be more suitable for this occasion. Chevalier was a Keynesian in France, but a monetarist in the United States, where he sided with Nicholas Biddle and the Second Bank of the United States against the Populist Andrew Jackson. His comparisons of France and the United States, however, run far more widely than money and banking, into the full range of Saint-Simonian interests, including public works, education and 'the spirit of association'.

Chevalier is best known in economics for his service under Napoleon III, and especially for his negotiation of the Anglo-French Treaty of Commerce of 1860, often called the Cobden–Chevalier treaty (Dunham, 1930). He was a Saint-Simonian, editor of *Le Globe* in 1831 and 1832, professor of economics (the only such post in France) from 1840 until his death (though inactive after 1852), deputy in 1845–6, Senator from 1860 to 1870, economic adviser to Louis Napoleon, and probably the author of Louis Napoleon's letter to *Le Moniteur*, dated 5 January 1860, laying out the Second Empire's principles on commercial policy – a letter which he, in the manner of bureaucrats who write letters for their betters, calls 'celebrated' (1868, p. cclxxi). His published works are extensive. A full bibliography can be found in a recent biography (Walch, 1975, pp. 492–509). The best known of them consist in *Lettres sur L'Amérique du Nord* in two volumes (1836), *Histoire et description des voies de communications aux Etats-Unis* in two volumes (1840–1), *Des Intérêts matériels en France, Travaux publics, routes, canaux, chemins de fer* (1838), *Cours d'économie politique fait au Collège de France*, in three volumes (1855, 1858, 1866), *La Liberté aux Etats-Unis, Examen du système commercial connu sous le nom de système*

A paper given at the 200th Anniversary of the Franco-American Treaty of 1778 in Newport, Rhode Island, September 1978. Abridged in Society for French Historical Studies, Two Hundred Years of Franco-American Relations, Society for French Historical Studies (October 1983), pp. 121–50.

protecteur, L'Isthme de Panama, etc. He served on the jury of the
Exhibition held in Paris in 1855 and as head of the International Jury at
the Universal Exposition in Paris in 1867, for which he wrote a
500-page introduction to the official report (Chevalier, 1868). The same
year he testified in the investigation of money and banking conducted in
France as part of the struggle between the Keynesians and the
monetarists. His writing is somewhat less impressive when one takes
into account that a considerable number of passages in later books can
be found in the 1836 letters, a practice of self-plagiarism not unknown
today among economists, and perhaps even to practitioners of other
disciplines.

The forces that sent Chevalier to America are of some interest.
Charles Henri de Rouvrez, Comte de Saint-Simon (great-nephew of the
eighteenth-century memorialist duke) died in 1825. His movement
went on under Prosper Enfantin, who in 1830 persuaded Michel
Chevalier, first in his class at the Ecole Polytechnique and member of
the Corps des Mines (as an economist), to undertake the editorship of
the Saint-Simonian newspaper *Le Globe.* So-called 'Père' Enfantin
became more and more mystical, ran a retreat in Paris on the rue
Monsigny, where the faithful met on Tuesday, Thursday and Saturday,
wore blue vestments over white trousers for greater intimacy, ate
together, conducted some religious ceremonies like marriages and
funerals – rather like a modern commune in Vermont in blue jeans.
Bazard wanted to form the movement into a political party. Schism
came in 1831. Chevalier sided with Enfantin, who began to produce
advanced ideas on the liberation of women, who had to be freed from the
law of fidelity in marriage if they were to achieve equality with men.
Some members quit over the issue of sexual liberty. In April 1832, 40
members retired to Ménilmont outside of Paris where couples were
broken up, celibacy required, domestic life suppressed and the blue
habit made obligatory. In August 1832, Enfantin, Chevalier, and several
others were arrested for outrage to morals – Enfantin for his views, and
Chevalier for publishing them in the *Globe.* In due course they were
found guilty, and Enfantin and Chevalier each sentenced to a year in jail
and a fine of 100 francs. Chevalier broke away from Enfantin's
mysticism in the course of their imprisonment. In August 1833, after
seven and a half months of incarceration, they were pardoned. It is of
some interest that, in visiting a penitentiary in Philadelphia in the spring
of 1834, Chevalier found it admirable, 'everything comfortable in
contrast to our abominable prisons in France, dirty, infected, freezing in
winter, humid in summer' (1836, I, p. 105). De Tocqueville and
Beaumont went to the United States in 1831 and 1832 to study prisons,
but Chevalier had a personal interest, rather than a professional one.

On release from prison, Enfantin set off for Egypt to try to obtain a
concession for a Suez canal, and to find a 'mère' for the Saint-Simonian
church. Chevalier set off in the opposite direction. He sought out
leading personalities, especially Adolphe Thiers, LeGrand of Ponts et
Chaussées and others, to obtain some of the money voted by Parliament
to study railroads, especially in Britain, the United States and Belgium.

On the basis of Chevalier's brilliant career in the *grandes écoles*, and his determination to throw off the mystical aspects of Saint-Simonism, LeGrand approved, obtained Thiers' consent and Chevalier was sent to the United States for eight months. Several extensions, one covering virtually six months spent in visiting Mexico and Cuba, brought the total trip to two years.

The combination of public works and banking goes back in Saint-Simonian thought to the visit of Saint-Simon to Spain in 1788. There he met one Francesco Cabarrus, of French origin, who had founded a successful Bank of Saint Charles and made a fortune, which he used in merchant trading with the Philippines. Saint-Simon and Cabarrus planned a canal from Madrid to the sea, to be financed by the bank, but constructed in large part by the Spanish army. The fruit of this operation proved to be entirely intellectual. Saint-Simon made his fortune in speculation in *biens nationaux*, and lost it in social experiments. To his philosophy of public works and credit expansion, he added education and the spirit of association, asserting that they all fit together and interacted in the economic and political development of countries. Saint-Simon, Enfantin and Chevalier were all bemused by connection East and West, first through the Suez isthmus, later through Panama. Writing in the *Globe* in the spring of 1832, Chevalier's *Système de la Méditerranée* foreshadowed Fernand Braudel's preoccupation with that sea as a meeting place for conflict or cooperation between East and West. The same series also laid out the plan for the railroad *étoile* of France, with Paris in the center and lines running out to the great ports and frontier towns, much the same as the LeGrand plan finally adopted in 1842. The theme that communication implies association and peace is found in the first of the *Lettres*, which advocated a train from Paris to London so that French 'speculators, shopkeepers, capitalists, merchants, agriculturalists, workers, engineers', etc., can benefit from seeing how the British do things. In the final pages of his introduction to the reports of the Jury at the Universal Exposition (1868), Chevalier urges a trans-Andean railroad, a trans-Siberian railroad, and a tunnel beneath the English channel.

The Letters on North America are a remarkable work. Essays, rather than letters, they were written when Chevalier was under 30. Walch (1975, p. 114) claims that the letters published in the *Journal des Débats*, of which Chevalier became an editor between leaving prison and his departure, are fresher and more alive than when they were later re-edited. Only a third were so published. Chevalier went up and down the Atlantic coast, more than once, and penetrated to the interior to travel down the Ohio and Mississippi rivers to New Orleans. But Chevalier always had France and her problems in mind. Few descriptions are not comparisons. The thirty-four letters and more than a hundred notes of anything from a few lines to eight or ten pages contain disquisitions on engineering, economics, sociology and political science in the United States, France and England, not neglecting other places such as ancient Greece and Rome plus some socio-cultural comment which ranks with the opinions of Colonel Bramble and Major

Thompson. Reduced from nineteenth-century prose to more aphoristic form these include:

> ... Americans do anything for money, except marry. Frenchmen marry for money [the *dot*] in order to be able to live well. (1836, II, p. 149)

> ... [quoting Talleyrand] I never knew an American who had not sold a dog or a horse ... The clock of his village is nothing more than a clock, and the newer it is the more beautiful. The Yankee would sell the clothes of his father ... house first, then the clothes. (1836, II, p. 133)

> ... America is democratic except in church, where pews are bought and sold and the congregation arranges itself in the order of wealth. In France, the church is the only place where the orders mix. (1836, I, p. 285)

> ... The Englishman is surly and terse in the morning, especially when opening the mail. In the evening he is expansive and full of humanity. The American copies the Englishman's morning manners, both morning and evening; the Frenchman his evening manners, again both morning and evening. (1836, II, pp. 111–12)

> ... American cities specialize. Men work in one place and live in another. In Paris 'the worst arranged city in the universe', people live everywhere, work everywhere and lose time in meeting over business. But time is of no importance to them. (1836, II, p. 109)

> ... Americans keep ancient designations, like King Street and Queen Street, even after the War of Independence. In France each revolution requires a change of street names, and of initials on public monuments (1836, II, pp. 197, 244).

> ... One of the aspects in which the French most differ from Americans: with us, moral and religious life are tolerant and easy, like American political life, whereas the principle of political authority which is vigorous with us at all times – and under all forms of government, monarchy, empire or republic – corresponds to the severe reserve of the manners of Americans (1836, I, p. 215).

One more digression before getting down to business. The *Lettres* are a pleasant source of regional rivalry in the United States at the superficial level. For one who lives near Boston, and who recently discovered that a great-grandfather had been born in Cambridge, it is agreeable to learn:

> The most enlightened and richest inhabitants of the United States are those from Massachusetts. (1858, II, p. 143)

> Nowhere are there more consummate merchants than in Boston (1836, I, p. 157).

The Yankee is the best sailor in the world [this ancestor was in the navy] and does not have the same need as Ulysses to stop his ears when he passes close to the Sirens ... imperturbably faithful. (1836, I, p. 158)

To work in the manner of Boston signifies in the United States to carry something out in perfect order and without words. (1836, I, p. 308)

New Jersey [from which part of my wife's family comes] is a poor state without importance. (1836, I, p. 69)

But my satisfaction with the above was somewhat modified by the view:

Some people claim that Pennsylvania is the most cultivated state in the Union, but the rustic settlers there of German origin [among them my patronymic forebears] were the least intelligent people in North America. (1836, I, p. 246)

Pittsburg, it may be noted, is one of the least diverting cities in the world. There is no interruption of work there six days a week, except for meals, the longest of which is scarcely ten minutes, and Sunday, instead of being a day of distraction and gaiety, is according to the English custom, reinforced by the Anglo-American. (1836, I, p. 256)

Lowell, while proper, and decent, peaceful and wise, is not amusing. (1836, I, p. 218)

I had hoped for a comment on Newport, Rhode Island, for this occasion. The nearest Chevalier comes verbally is Newport, Kentucky (1836, I, p. 293). Geographically, he several times mentions Providence and the boat that brings passengers there from New York, whence they proceed to Boston by train (e.g. 1836, II, p. 66), and in the other direction Point Judith, the swells of which are known to him, as, somewhat less than a century later, to me. It enabled me to learn a new word, *houleuse* (1836, II, p. 69). A list of seven naval arsenals – Portsmouth, Boston, New York, Philadelphia, Norfolk, Washington and Pensacola (1836, I, p. 95) – fails to include Newport, as does a roster of lesser Atlantic ports after Boston, New York, Philadelphia and Baltimore, which did include Portland, Salem, New Bedford, Nantucket and Providence (1836, I, p. 225). Crevecour, the 'American farmer' of the late eighteenth century, had called Newport the Montpellier of America (Bridenbaugh, 1955, p. 368). During the seventeenth and eighteenth centuries down to the Revolution it was one of five leading port cities in the United States along with Boston, New York, Philadelphia and Charleston (Bridenbaugh, 1964, *passim*). But Providence, with its more extensive economic hinterland, overtook Newport after 1770 and it went into the doldrums until the Civil War, cutting off Southern naval facilities, brought it the Naval War College, the training station and the Goat Island torpedo station. Newport started as a resort in the eighteenth century (Bridenbaugh, 1955, p. 368), but came into its own in this capacity after the establishment of the Fall

River line, unmentioned by Chevalier, involving boat from New York to Fall River, and train thence back to Newport. The only resorts that Chevalier does mention are Bedford Springs, Pennsylvania (1836, II, p. 166), of which I confess I have never heard, and Saratoga Springs, New York. His letter from Bedford Springs, dated August 1835, suggests that he is not having much fun there. Europeans enjoy spas because they are exclusive. Americans able to afford them know that there are 20,000 other Americans who could be there as well as they. American democratic relaxation takes the form of camp-meetings and political parades . . .

But my concern is with Chevalier as economist, and I must say I find him good. I come presently to the questions of public works, banking, education and association – the secrets to economic growth in his system of thought – and offer a few more general observations to suggest how his economist's mind works.

The economist today has the well-worn formulation of the second law of thermo-dynamics: there is no free lunch. Chevalier puts this kernel in two different ways: except in fairy stories, there are no seven-league boots (those who want to read the *Lettres* intelligently should bear in mind that a league is 4 kilometers, or about 2½ miles) (1836, I, p. 207); and, with an apology for using a vulgar expression, swallows do not fall from the sky fully roasted (1836, II, p. 218). In these passages and elsewhere, he emphasizes that the Americans of his day had a love of work not conspicuous in France, although it should be noted that, when he was editor of the *Globe*, he worked each day from 9 to 2 the next morning, with scarcely 20 minutes off for dinner (though twice the allowance in Pittsburgh) (Walch, 1975, p. 19).

One modern insight was his treatment of time. The American was preoccupied with saving time, in contrast with the French for whom the problem was how best to spend it. The passionate love affair of the Americans with railroads was to save time (1836, I, p. 104). On a boat going down the Chesapeake Bay, the dining room filled up 10 minutes after the gong sounded, emptied 10 minutes later, and passengers started lining to disembark hours before docking, as in the futile rush to escape from docking airplanes today (1836, II, p. 423). Chevalier's treatment anticipates in general, though not in rigor or in intimacy of illustration, Staffan Burenstam Linder's *Theory of the Harried Leisure Class* (1970), in which the accumulation of consumption goods requires us to consume faster. One of Linder's illustrations deals with the speed-up of courtship, from a hundred requests for a lady's favor before giving up, to one, or at most two; and to the decline in time for lunch from 3 hours to 15 minutes, which time may also include watching television simultaneously.

Steamboats on the rivers of the west cut the round trip from Louisville to New Orleans and back from 300 days, or once a year, to 8 or 9 days down, and 10 to 12 back, making possible, with turnaround time, four trips a year. Chevalier was impressed less with the saving of capital than with that in manpower (1836, II, p. 15). When New York is only 6 or 8 days from New Orleans, moreover, separation is impossible, and a country keeps its unity without effort (1836, II, p. 98). The Erie Canal is the work that Chevalier perhaps admired most in the United States, not for its construction, which was simple without ornament, and in the end proved, like Route 128 in Boston, to be too small so that it was immediately necessary to expand it. Impressive were the speed with which it was built and the speed with which boats were put through it – locks working (for those that paid extra) night and day (1836, II, p. 40).

The high cost of labor in the United States was a stimulant to invention, innovation and speed. It existed because of the frontier, with its cheap, virtually free land (1836, I, p. 218). In modern economic jargon, if Europe grew with the Lewis (Marxian) model of growth with unlimited supplies of labor (off the farm), the United States grew with unlimited supplies of land. Unlimited labor developed the Ricardian theory of rent. The abundance of land in the United States attached the rent to men, rather than land. Chevalier is sensitive enough to notice that American inventiveness not only attaches to production for the market, but also results in improved household utensils. These contribute 'more than one would think' to liberty in the house by economizing on time and trouble in the household tasks. His illustration of butter-making machines that are dog-driven is not one that seems especially apt from an historical perspective, though he liked it so much that he used it a few years later in his Collège de France lectures (1836, I, p. 431; 1858, II, p. 163).

I come now to public works, the central purpose of the trip to North America. The history and description of United States communications are touched on in the *Lettres*, but developed in a separate two-volume book (which I have not read), while the application of his observations to France are contained in *Intérets matériels* (1838). Comparisons abound in costs per kilometer, rates charged per ton/kilometer or passenger/kilometer, speed of canal boat or train, receipts, traffic, types of construction, engineering standards. Some of the discussion is at the technical engineering level, much runs in economic terms. The tension between the engineer who dominates in France and the business man (read economist) who wants the job done cheaply in the United States is effectively evoked throughout. Ponts et Chaussées sets standards on grades, curves of track, double-tracking, types of materials, that are much higher as a rule than those used in the United States, where absolute engineering standards are qualified by a trade-off between technical performance and cost. An interesting comparison is afforded by the size of canals (width and depth, especially of locks, and length of locks). The British adopted standards that proved to be too small, and kept them. The French adopted standards that were originally too large, thus tying up capital that might have better been utilized in more directly productive projects. The Americans started with an economical standard, as noted, and rebuilt when forced to (1836, II, pp. 40–2). Cheap materials were substituted for better within the limits of safety standards, and Chevalier marvels at some of the wooden bridges, one 2,000 meters across the Susequehanna, for example, carrying trains, two roadways, two pedestrian ways. In France, if one recommends such a bridge, of which hundreds have been built in America, the reply is made that it won't stand up, as if the laws of gravity were different in the two hemispheres (1855, I, p. 487 n.). He may not, however, have taken adequately into consideration the relative prices of iron and wood in the two markets.

One point recognized by Chevalier – and lost on many a developing country today – is that the bottleneck in public works in America and in Europe was not capital, or even ordinary labor, but skilled engineers. Chevalier is particularly struck by the success of Ohio in building a canal longer than any in France without trained engineers, but 'with more intelligence and ability than is deployed in Pennsylvania, despite the enlightened people in which Pennsylvania abounds'. One would not dare undertake similar projects in Europe without long preparatory studies. In Ohio, the mysteries of Ponts et Chaussées are explained in bar-rooms with tumblers of whisky, a little like the methods of descriptive geometry perpetuated in workshops by tradition before Monge gave them the sanction of theory (1836, II, pp. 53–4).

Chevalier is not above making mistakes. He is enamored of the Main Line from Philadelphia to Pittsburgh, which goes first by train to Columbia, then by boat to Holidayville, and then by train again, the cars of which are hauled over the Alleghanies on an inclined plane – a grade too steep for locomotives. This was designed by his friend, Moncure Robinson of Richmond, a man who received his early instruction in engineering in France, and who spent two-plus years, 1825–1828, surveying public works in France, England, Wales and the Low Countries before returning for an illustrious career in the United States (*Who Was Who in America*, 1967, p. 520; Chevalier, 1836, II, p. 96). (Robinson pronounced a eulogy of Chevalier after his death, but disassociated himself from Chevalier's free trade views.) But for the reason that the Roissy rail line from Gare du Nord to Charles de Gaulle airport is unsuccessful, the Main Line could not compete with the water-level rail routes to the West on the Baltimore and Ohio, or the later Grand Central (Albion, 1939). Transhipment is boring and expensive, as Chevalier recognizes, and the Main Line had three such (1836, II, pp. 44, 72).

Public works are central in economic development for Chevalier. He wrings his hands that some of the indemnity in France for confiscation of land under the Terror was invested in Pennsylvanian improvements, not French (1836, II, p. 244); calls New York imperial (the Empire State) for the energy deployed in its canalization, and especially the Erie Canal – 'simple as a work of art, prodigious as an economic artery (1836, II, p. 300); and, anticipating the Bordeaux, 'L'Empire, C'est la paix', speech of Louis Napoleon of December 1851, calls for a vast program of public works in France, from

> great railroads to modest country roads, to drain marshes and irrigate the countryside, to open up Brittany and make Rouen, Lille, Calais, Orleans, Troyes and Reims suburbs of Paris . . . give a little life to Bordeaux which is dying and revive Nantes which is dead, restore the

Loire, lost in sands, attaching it to the lively provinces of the interior, and above all bringing it to Paris; place Lyons as near to the Rhine and even the Danube as it is to the Rhone and the Loire; to bring minerals out of the entrails of the earth to the market; and to deliver each village and isolated farm from the blockade of six months of mud each winter. (1836, II, pp. 244–5)

The one bizarre, even fruity, note that Chevalier brings to public works is the suggestion that armies be used to do much of the work of construction (1836, I, p. 20; II, p. 226–9; 1858, II, Lessons 10–18). Part of the motivation is education, part is reduction in cost. A germ of utopianism seems to rest in the view that, if the army were busy digging canals and building railroads, it would not have time to plan wars. The idea, as noted earlier, goes back to Saint-Simon and the projected canal from Madrid to the Mediterranean. Chevalier cites the Roman roads built by the Imperial soldiers, and the lending of army engineers and geodetic survey officials by the United States government to assist the survey staffs of private companies (1836, II, p. 96). To give him the benefit of the doubt, he might be proposing the equivalent of the CCC corp of the New Deal.

Public works thus require credit, and may involve the use of the army, which would spread education. Speed of travel extends the arm of government, and the breaking down of distance makes possible association. To the economist, the foremost benefit is in joining markets, raising the price to producers, and lowering it to consumers. Chevalier takes this almost for granted.

As already indicated, Chevalier is a Keynesian in Europe and a monetarist in the United States. Saint-Simonian thought viewed banks as the stimulator and regulator of industry, the instruments for both impulsion and coordination, the motor and the brake, the exciter and the director (Vergeot, 1918, subtitle and pp. 22, 91, 96 and 128). In France the need was for stimulus, in the United States for brake. But when his mind turns to France, Chevalier is fascinated by the dynamism of banking on the other side of the Atlantic. Scotland, with its depth of joint-stock banks, occasionally comes to mind, especially in the third volume of the *Cours* (1866). Over the thirty-some years of his writing, from 1834 to 1867, Chevalier keeps returning to the ease and speed with which banks are created in the United States in contrast to France. He remarks that when Americans build a town, they start with an inn and a bar-room, then post office, several houses, a church, school, printing establishment and then a bank, to complete the triple representation of religion, science (the school and the printer) and industry (the bank) (1836, I, pp. 262–3). (The British equivalent a century later is suggested by the story of an English prisoner who escaped from the Germans, made his way through the battle lines, and came upon the British army half an hour after they had taken a town. He went straight to the British officers' club, already fully operational.) At least three times in the thirty years, Chevalier uses the story of Port Carbon, Pennsylvania, with only thirty houses, burned tree stumps still standing in the unpaved streets, but a sign saying 'Office of Deposit and Discount, Schuykill Bank' (1836, I, p. 264; 1855, I, p. 84; 1868, p. ccclxxxi). Throughout his writing, he cites the Saint-Simonians, Jacques Laffitte and the Pereire brothers, who turned away from the mysticism of Enfantin but kept faithful to the original message of the need for pressure to expand credit. But in the United States, Jackson's fight against Biddle and the Second Bank of the United States was too much for him, as it was for de Tocqueville in one of his rare discussions of economics (Walch, 1975, pp. 174, 214). He quotes, in a footnote without comment, William Cobbett's letter to President Jackson, congratulating him on his veto message and expressing the hope that soon there would be no banks in the United States (1836, I, p. 73 note). But the blind and unreasoning animosity of the President and the 'democracy' (masses) against the Bank of the United States distracted attention from the real need to reorganize the banking system (1836, I, p. 73). *Bancomania* as Jefferson called it, was worse before the Bank of the United States tried to police the system, and might return when it left the scene (1836, I, p. 55). Letter 25 is entitled 'Speculations' and is devoted to that subject in considerable part, rather more agreement between title and content than is normal. The United States is one immense rue Quincampoix (1836, II, p. 152) from Maine to the Red River. Most of the speculations are imprudent, some are crazy. Public opinion forbids sensual satisfactions: wine, women, luxury, cards and dice. Americans thus demand great emotions from business (1836, II, pp. 156–7). But the direct connection between banking and speculation is not made.

Three further points interested me, who am more a student of the European than of United States economic history. Chevalier is impressed by the New York (state) Safety Fund Act, which was an early forerunner of the Federal Deposit Insurance Corporation of 1934. Banks paid in 0.5 percent of their capital each year, until the accumulated sum reached 5 percent, Commissioners of the Act examined the banks (eighty-seven in all) three times a year (1836, II, pp. 295–7), and the fund was available for use in a panic, which Chevalier characterizes as worse, 'however short a time it lasts, . . . than the most terrible earthquake' (1836, I, p. 37). A second is the sense of solidarity between business and banking. A big fire in Pearl and Wall Streets in December 1835 threatened widespread commercial disaster. The New York bankers, 'who showed as much courage as a soldier on the field of battle', offered loans to those affected to reconstitute their businesses. Chevalier expresses the conviction that, in such an event, French banks would have cut credit off (1836, I, pp. 357–9). The doctrine of a lender of last resort was still to be formulated by Walter Bagehot in *Lombard Street* (1873) forty years later, but was spontaneously put into practice. Third is the role of historical memory in a nation. The world today is troubled by the German memory of the inflation of 1922–3 and the equivalent British paranoia about the unemployment of 1925–9, fifty-year old memories which play strong roles in shaping current macro-economic policies. The French equivalent in Chevalier's day was the memories of John Law and the *assignats*, which made France fearful of banks. But the United States was not bothered by any memory of the Continental currency (1836, II, p. 232). Chevalier has no answer to the question, nor do I, though one can offer the conjecture that young countries may have shorter memories than old.

Finally on credit, one can, as in public works, expect a utopian note. Bankers, says Chevalier, are a gage for peace (1858, II, p. 239). Princes who wish to make war have to arrange lines of credit. The remark foreshadows John Hobson's remark that the Rothschilds could have stopped World War I if they had chosen to do so. The supposition, like so many about the power of the multinational corporation, is far-fetched.

Education in France and the United States is discussed at various levels – primary, apprenticeship (including the use of the army for public works), university, and the *grandes écoles*, for which the United States lacked an equivalent beyond the Military Academy at West Point (1836, I, p. 315 n.). Chevalier touches on primary education in several places, but nowhere as fully as in connection with New York state, which he found a pleasing synthesis of the breadth of the southern states and the spirit of detail of New England. With one-sixteenth of the people of France, New York had one-fifth of the numbers of children in school, and spent on education one-third of the amount of money. This was the result, of course, of higher wages for teachers necessitated by the availability of land at 2 or 3 dollars an acre, along with abundant credit (1836, II, pp. 290–3 and note 59, p. 481). A comparison is also furnished at the college level. Chevalier concludes that since New York and France have the same numbers of students in college per 1,000 persons, and New York is richer per capita, France must value higher education more than New York (*ibid.*, p. 295). The failure to discuss fees, however, or the cost implied in earnings forgone by students, would mark the calculation down in a modern classroom in econometrics. Moreover, Chevalier later raises a question about the value of the university for the bourgeoisie, and argues in favor of industrial instruction. He suggests that France raises the sons of bourgeois families as if they were destined to become members of the Académie Française or of the Academy of Science. Such education is suitable for the sons of grand seigneurs, called upon to enjoy 100,000 francs of *rente*, but the bourgeoise need industrial education, just like the workers, including peasants, need apprenticeship (1838, pp. 17–18).

As for the *grandes écoles*, in these Chevalier was drawing on his own experience and making a fairly commonplace point that the schools were highly theoretical, especially in mathematics, and that their graduates often fail to appreciate the need for a trade-off between engineering beauty and economic practicality. The point is put with especial force in *Intérêts materiels*:

> I do not claim at all to determine with precision at what point it is worthwhile to depart from the rules the engineers [of Ponts et Chaussées] have worked out, only request an inquiry to see that they

are not applied as holy writ, nor solely mathematically, but also economically, financially, and administratively . . . Let us profoundly respect the mathematical sciences. They are an excellent touchstone. But mathematics cannot claim either to govern or to administer the state, and experience, once again, is worth all the $a + b$ in the world. (1838, pp. 277–8)

In the *Lettres*, he proposed modification of the Ecole Polytechnique, wanting it not less wise, but wise in different ways (1836, II, pp. 445–50). These would include calculating how much material for a given railroad would affect the output of coal, iron, even engineers. In a rudimentary form, this is a statement of Input–Output theory for which Wassily Leontief won the Nobel prize in 1971, but the idea goes back to Quesnay and his *Tableau économique*. It has strong overtones of the present-day Commissariat au Plan in the French technocratic tradition, just as Michel Chavalier was the Jean Monnet of his day.

Chevalier is perhaps making an *apologia pro vita sua*, but comes out strongly in the *Lettres*, and other works, for travel to add a practical gloss to a strongly Cartesian formation. I had occasion not long ago to quote on the point a Japanese psychiatrist who had worked in Paris as a business consultant, and hope I will be forgiven if I repeat myself. French education, said the doctor, and especially the *grandes écoles*, teach students to discourse in ways that are brilliant and final. Graduates who had been abroad to work or study were different, however; they had acquired a practical bent which distinguished them from their stay-at-home compatriots. I am not sure I understand why so few French emigrate. Those that did, as Chevalier noticed on occasion, were largely from Alsace and Lorraine (Walch, 1975, p. 139, quoting Rémond). The reason may be contained in a statement repeated frequently in the 1880s by a master of a Paris secondary school attended by my father, who repeated it all his life: '*Paris est France, et France est le monde.*' In any case, Chevalier, like my Japanese psychiatrist, was persuaded that travel, especially to Anglo-Saxon countries, was useful in adding practicality to theoretical competence, and to temper vainglory. Letter 9, written from Philadelphia, asks 'Who is the First People of the World?', and says that, before passing the frontier, Chevalier had thought it was the French:

> not only the most generous and chivalrous, the most spiritual and artistic, the people with the most qualities both lovable and brilliant, but also the people wise, the people industrious, the people administrative, both inventive and practical, unique, perfect, in spite of the rains and fogs of Paris, the people with the best weather . . . When one crosses the border, little by little one downgrades these pretensions. (1836, I, pp. 134–5)

A Frenchman comes back from England ashamed of French agriculture, communications and schools (1836, I, p. 8) and from America humiliated by the state of French housing (1858, II, pp. 371–2).

Travel is a force for practicality, humility, but above all for international association.

Association belongs more to political science, or perhaps better to sociology, than to economics, and in Saint-Simonism it comes close to philosophy. It abounds in dialectic. But the concept may have economic importance, not least in our day. Anglo-Saxons are masters of association, so much so that it enabled them to avoid revolutions (1858, II, p. 600), but the British are exclusive (1836, II, p. 259). Anglo-Saxons associate for business, the French for pleasure (1836, II, p. 475), but the West was won by individuals in isolation, an effort at which the French could never succeed, since their thirst for glory and their spirit of emulation are excited by human contact (1836, II, pp. 117–18). The American spirit of association goes hand in hand with individualism, which favors competition of master against master, worker against master, and worker against worker, each one for himself, with no provision for old age, even for national heros (1836, II, p. 479; I, pp. 298–301). Association is best when it is hierarchical, with royalty, for example, intermediating between the bourgeoise and the proletariat (1836, II, p. 273).

International association will bring peace in Europe, so that Europe can become one family, with every war a civil war, an impious war (1838, p. 156). The progress of commercial and political relations among the peoples of Europe should lead to the creation of an international bank, with a seat in each of the great states (1866, III, p. 653). In another place, he writes of western civilization, rather than European civilization, since it is impossible to separate the two sides of the Atlantic, which have 'the same arts, and the same religions, the same moral, social, political and scientific ideas' (1868, p. xxv, note).

Associations intermediate. Trade unions aid the worker who is otherwise helpless before the employer, and save the employer the necessity of considering the welfare of each separate worker and his family. The same is true, *mutatis mutandis*, of political parties, people's banks, chambers of commerce, industrial associations, etc. In a recent broadcast on the anniversary of the events of May–June 1968, Alain Peyrefitte, the then Minister of Education, said that it was odd that, in France, disorder in Nanterre and the Sorbonne should be a matter for resolution by the Minister of Education, the Minister of the Interior, the Prime Minister and the President, asserting that the President of the United States would not get himself involved in the free speech movement in Berkeley. One hundred and twenty-five years earlier, anything that comes between the individual and the state in France is suspect (1858, II, p. 599). Chevalier is prepared to admit that some associations are formed to irritate (*gêner*) the government. But association in Britain, supported by the greatest of all forces in civilized countries, the reciprocal spirit of moderation, is responsible for the solidarity of British power. Today, when the spirit of association in Britain has run riot, it is ironic to read:

In what country would one find an equal degree of equity, so much spirit of conduct as among the chiefs of the unions [in Britain], or an equal sentiment of social harmony, in the midst of the clash of inflamed interests. (1858, II, p. 602)

Association remains elusive. With the reciprocal spirit of moderation, or perhaps applied hierarchically in the technocratic spirit of benign despotism, it may be a critical element in economic advance. Economic aging, which Chevalier could see in France to some degree, but not in England or the United States, may be marked by associations which dig in, instead of intermediating between the parts and the whole, to such degree that they prevent the whole from functioning. An interesting hypothesis accounting for the economic rebirth of Germany and Japan after World War II, as compared with the relative declines of such countries as Britain and France, is that the network of *positions acquises* in society and in the economy was destroyed by military defeat. Individuals had to go back to determining their own separate fates, rather than leaving their fortunes in the hands of a particular association.

Focusing as it does on Chevalier, the economist, this paper has said nothing about his several other preoccupations – with slavery, in which he saw clearly that manumission was a less difficult problem than integration, and especially in the North (1836, II, p. 263); with women; with self-government; and a host of other questions on which he was always interesting, and sometimes profound, especially for a man under 30. In conclusion, however, let me say a few words about how French he is – wistful over the wars that lost France the opportunity to connect up Quebec with New Orleans and Saint Louis, through Fort Dusquesne and the French settlement of Chicago (1836, II, p. 10); ravished, as they say, by meeting a Frenchman who had lived fifty years in Richmond, remaining there despite the opportunity to better himself elsewhere, because Virginia was the France of the United States (1836, I, p. 228 n.); remarking in the Cincinnati museum along with the mammoth bones, the Indian costumes and weapons, the Egyptian mummy, stuffed birds and pickled snake, a French sword from the battle of Waterloo, a picture of Napoleon, and a picture, among a series of American notables, of Lafayette (1836, I, p. 292); comparing the Alleghanies to the Vosges, and the Rockies to the Pyrenees and the Alps (1836, II, p. 29), and the rise and fall of tides at New York and the Bay of Fundy with those at Brest and Saint Malo (1836, II, p. 35); taking satisfaction in the exposure of Jefferson, the high priest of American democracy, to the principles of eighteenth century philosophy at Paris (1836, II, p. 208) and in the fact that the plans for the Chesapeake and Ohio canal had been drawn by General Bernard of France (1836, II, p. 36). There are passages of hyperbole: 'France is the most beautiful and administrative unit that there is in the world' (1836, II, p. 287), and passages of implied criticism, such as when the French of Lower Canada are described as absorbed in political quarrels, of which one can hardly determine the issue, and neglecting their material interests to pursue the chimerial interest of nationality (1836, II, p. 66).

The Letters evoke in this reader an acute nostalgia for the American past, the American youth:

The United States is a happy people for whom everything succeeds. (1836, I, p. 86); or

The Americans are the most enterprising of men and the most ambitious of nations. If we remain too long absorbed in our sterile disputes, they will be the people to relieve us of the precious charge of the destinies of the human race and to take first place. (1836, I, pp. 142–3); or

America forms a society which marches by instinct rather than according to a preconceived plan. (1836, II, p. 197)

How ironic these statements echo after the difficulties of the last two decades!

Chevalier sometimes despairs for the salvation of 'our old France', for which fourteen centuries of glory should have been enough. But these black thoughts last only as long as a thunderstorm (1836, II, p. 256). Chevalier was an economist, curious as to how other systems worked, anxious to apply their lessons in practice. It is perhaps typical of most social science that he emerged as he started, with the Saint-Simonian precepts of public works, credit expansion, education and, somewhat more elusive, association. The message is none the less worth serious contemplation.

References

Albion, Robert G. (1939), *The Rise of the Port of New York, 1815–1860* (New York: Scribners).

Bagehot, Walter (1873), *Lombard Street. A Description of the Money Market*; reprint edn., London: John Murray, 1917.

Bridenbaugh, Carl (1964), *Cities in the Wilderness, Urban Life in America, 1625–1742* (New York: Capricorn Books); original edition, 1938.

Bridenbaugh, Carl (1955), *Cities in Revolt, Urban Life in America, 1742–1776* (New York: Capricorn Books).

Chevalier, Michel (1836), *Lettres sur L'Amérique du Nord* (Paris: Gosselin, 2 vols).

Chevalier, Michel (1838), *Des Intérêts matériels en France. Travaux publics, routes, canaux, chemins de fer* (Paris: Gosselin).

Chevalier, Michel (1840–1), *Histoire et description des voies de communications aux Etats-Unis et des travaux d'art qui en dépendent* (Paris: Gosselin, 2 vols).

Chevalier, Michel (1844), *L'Isthme de Panama: Examen historique et géographique des différentes directions suivant lesquelles on pouvait le percer et les moyens à y employer; suivi d'un aperçu sur l'isthme de Suez* (Paris: Gosselin).

Chevalier, Michel (1849), *La Liberté aux Etas-Unis* (Paris: Capelle).

Chevalier, Michel (1852), *Examen du système commercial connu sous le nom du système protecteur* (Paris: Guillaumin).

Chevalier, Michel (1855, 1858, 1866), *Cours d'économie politique fait au Collège de France* (Paris, Capelle, 3 vols).

Chevalier, Michel (1968), *Exposition universelle de 1867 à Paris. Rapports du Jury International publiés sous la direction de M. Michel Chevalier. Vol. I: Introduction par M. Michel Chevalier* (Paris: Paul Dupont).

Dunham, Arthur (1930), *The Anglo-French Treaty of Commerce of 1860* (Ann Arbor, Mich.: University of Michigan Press).

Linder, Staffan Burenstam (1970), *The Theory of the Harried Leisure Class* (New York: Columbia University Press).

Who Was Who in America, Historical Vol. 1607–1896 (1967), revised edn. (Chicago: Marquis).

Vergeot, J.-B. (1918), *Le Crédit comme stimulant et régulateur de l'industrie. La conception saint-simonienne, ses réalisations, son application au problème bancaire d'après-guerre* (Paris: Jouve).

Walch, Jean (1975), *Michel Chevalier, économiste, saint-simonien, 1808–1879* (Paris: Librairie Philosophique J. Vrin).

3

Keynesianism vs. Monetarism in Eighteenth- and Nineteenth-Century France

The clash of Keynesianism and 'monetarism' is intense today at the levels of theory and policy. The contention of this article is that it has been so for at least 250 years.[1] Keynesianism is loosely defined as the economic view that, left to itself, the economy may not fully employ the resources available, and that expansionary governmental action may be required to achieve full employment and growth; monetarists, in contrast, think broadly that the principal economic task of government is to regulate the money supply, and in particular to set limits to it, and that achievement of adequate levels of employment and growth can be left to the market. As always in a period of inflation, the monetarists appear to be winning the intellectual debate today; in periods of recession and unemployment, the tables are normally turned. The debate is broadly the same as that between the Banking School, representing the Keynesian point of view, and the Currency School (monetarism) in the first half of the nineteenth century in Britain, although convergence between the French Keynesians and the Banking School is far from complete. It may be noted that the French Keynesians had their American contemporaries of like persuasion: Benjamin Franklin at the time of John Law, Andrew Jackson in the 1830s of Jacques Laffitte, and, considerably later than the Pereires, the perennial Populist candidate for president, William Jennings Bryan.

Law, Laffitte, and the Pereires were alike in more than their economic beliefs. Law is generally characterized as a genius (Lüthy, 1959, p. 269 n. 7, quoting Hamilton; Faure, 1977, p. 182). Laffite was said to have been the best governor of the bank of France in the nineteenth century (Dauphin-Meunier, 1936, p. 129). The Pereires' creation, the Crédit Mobilier, was in the eyes of many responsible for the great economic spurt of France in the middle of the nineteenth century (Gerschenkron, 1962; Hoselitz, 1956). All four were 'thinker–doers' who joined action to a system of thought, unlike the business genius Baron James de Rothschild, who 'left to Laffitte and the Pereires the burden of reflecting

Reprinted with permission from the History of Political Economy, *vol. 12, no. 4 (Durham, NC: Duke University Press, Winter 1980), pp. 499–523.*

on the necessary mechanism' (Bouvier, 1967, p. 155). Law's partisans–defenders ascribe his failure to errors of reasoning. Of Laffitte it is said that he trusted others too much (Courtois, 1875, p. 148). The Pereires were done in by the unremitting hatred of the Rothschilds, whom they offended by resigning from the Rothschild railroad to found a competitor and having the effrontery to buy an estate that James de Rothschild coveted (Cameron, 1961, *passim*; Bouvier and Cameron, 1963). A more general view, addressing especially the Saint-Simonian school (to which Laffitte and the Pereires remained intellectually faithful when most other bankers had turned away because of the extravagance of its ideas; Vergeot, 1918, p. 51), asserts that men of logic find it easy to conceive systems that are models of vain scholastic construction, but that other qualities are needed to make them function (Vergeot, 1918, pp. 287–8).

In the debate in Britain between the Banking School and the Currency School, the latter is judged to have won decisively, first in the Bullion Report of 1810 pointing out the error in Banking School thought that it was safe to issue money in proportion to underlying commerce and industry – on what is known today as the real-bills principle that money can be issued without inflation, on the basis of bills of exchange representing actual commercial transaction; and second, in the Bank Act of 1844 that limited the note issue of the Bank of England, above a low minimum, to the specie reserves of the Bank. During the Napoleonic War, the Bank of England had asserted that in issuing money *pari passu* with the needs of trade it had conformed to good central-bank practice and had in no way caused the depreciation of sterling (agio on gold). Ricardo and the Bullionists made clear that, since the prices of goods rose with inflation, expanding the money supply on the basis of the value of commerce during a boom was a recipe for continuous inflation. The real-bills doctrine nonetheless had tremendous survival value. It was fundamental to the theories of Laffitte and the Pereires, as well as those of Law, persisted well into the twentieth century in the United States (in the view of Laughlin of the University of Chicago and H. Parker Willis, his student), and was incorporated into the Federal Reserve Act of 1913. But the error goes back far and is persistent. Law's *Money and Trade Considered: with a Proposal for Supplying the Nation with Money* (1705) had 24 examples to show that if the money supply were increased by notes issued for productive loans, employment and output would rise proportionately, and the value of money would remain stable (Hamilton, 1968, p. 79). Isaac Pereire insisted that it was not banks that gave credit to commerce, but commerce that gave credit to banks in using their notes (I. Pereire, 1865, p. 150).

The Currency School was guilty of at least one error, too, in thinking that it was possible to limit the money supply. It thought of money as only coin and bank notes, and sometimes as only coin. But the Bank Act of 1844 that fixed the amount of the note issue was circumvented by the growth of bank deposits and of bank clearings and by the rapid run-up of undiscounted bills of exchange circulating in the 1850s as means of payment. What money was, was a matter of great confusion, as Michel Chevalier's book on *Money* shows: he starts contending that bank notes are not money (Chevalier, 1866, ch. 3, § 2) and ends asserting that bank notes, checks, bills of exchange are all capable of substituting for precious metals in circulation, as is 'paper money', i.e. exchequer bills, used by merchants in commercial payments and even by consumers regulating accounts with their suppliers, along with Indian bonds (*ibid.*, pp. 665–6). Today monetarists have difficulty in deciding how to define money; at least seven definitions co-exist in the United States. But John Law stretched matters too far in adding, to his Banking School error of expanding money with business, two more, successively rather than simultaneously. The first error was that it was safe to issue money against land, as later undertaken with the *assignats* issued against the *biens nationaux* in the 1790s, and briefly in Germany in 1924 with the *Rentenmark*. According to Lüthy, Law thought he was getting away from this 1705 view when in 1718 he based the Banque Royale largely on the earning power of the Compagnie d'Occident (Mississippi), but that in an ultimate sense the company really represented the abundant lands of Louisiana (Lüthy, 1959, p. 189). The second error, to which much more attention has been paid, was in thinking of shares and government debt as money, so that it was not dangerous to 'monetize' them (Hamilton, 1968, p. 78).

Let me at this early stage settle the conflict between Law, Laffitte, and the Pereires, on the one hand, and their opponents, between the Banking and Currency schools, and between the Keynesians and the monetarists. Each insists on a different half of the same truth. This Hegelian verdict was rendered by E. Victor Morgan (1943, p. 142) as between the Banking and Currency schools, without, however, much explanation. It is more general. The Saint-Simonian school understood that credit was both 'stimulator and regulator', with the functions of 'impelling and directing', 'exciting and coordinating', acting as 'motor and brake' (Vergeot, 1918, subtitle and pp. 22, 92, 96, 128); Law, Laffitte, and the Pereires emphasized the stimulating, propelling, energizing functions, their proponents the fact that there must be some limit. Wolowski, a monetarist opponent of Chevalier, said that bank notes were like food that could turn into poison (Pose, 1942, I, p. 149). Keynesian analysis applies in depression, at less than full employment, although current stagflation suggests the necessity to complicate the analysis. The expansionists were right in 1716 when, says Hamilton (1968, p. 61), 'No other "Keynesian" economist ever had such a golden opportunity'; and in the 1830s, and in 1849 to 1852. They were wrong in thinking their therapy applied all the time. The monetarists by contrast were right in boom, but too often felt it desirable to hold back when trade and industry were in the doldrums. 'It had been claimed that the *haute banque* had taken a certain pleasure in recognizing the decline in the crisis of 1848 which had the advantage of liquidating an important number of speculators whose maneuvers had hurt the market' (Gille, 1967, II, p. 95).

If each school is half-right; one ought to be able to switch theories as circumstances alter. Robert Mundell once informally suggested that, in world deflation, countries with balance-of-payment surpluses are at fault and should pay interest on their accumulations of reserves; in inflation, on the other hand, deficit countries should be blamed for the disequilibrium and should pay interest on negative balances. The observation is theoretically just, but operationally impossible. Agreement on when circumstances have changed from slack to taut, or back again, is elusive, and changing course takes time.

Moreover, expansion is difficult to stop even when the need for it is recognized. Even if John Law had wanted to stop in May 1719, he could not have done so. He found himself on a 'slope' (a word used twice) on which it was impossible to halt without risking collapse (Levasseur, 1854/1970, pp. 93, 107, 148). James de Rothschild said of the Crédit Mobilier: 'We do not like to encourage societies of this nature, because their direction escapes you. However wisely conducted for a time, they are easily diverted from their original purpose, and it is not always easy for them to stop in time' (*ibid.*, p. 117). As a governor of the Bank of France put it in the debate that raged in France between 1857 and 1868, 'One yields too easily to the spirit of adventure and to the thirst for gain' (Bouvier, 1973, p. 88).

But there are some examples on the other side. Michel Chevalier was a Keynesian in France and a monetarist in the United States, where he supported Nicholas Biddle and the Second Bank of the United States against President Jackson and the masses with their 'blind and unreasonable animosity' (Chevalier, 1838, I *Letters 1*, 2–5, pp. 73, 78), albeit noting that the multiplicity of banks and their liberal ways profited everyone from farmers and mechanics to great merchants (*ibid.*, p. 44). He thought, however, that the Bank of the United States was necessary to save the country from 'commercial anarchy which ends up as political anarchy' (*ibid.*).

Napoleon III shifted allegiance from the expansionist school of the Pereires and Chevalier to the side of the Rothschild banking establishment. Whether this represented seduction by the latter, as such a protagonist as Cameron suggests, or his astute judgment that it was useful to switch from the accelerator to the brake, is not self-evident. As late as 1864 in crisis, however, it was he who insisted that the name of the Société Générale should include 'pour favoriser le commerce et l'industrie en France', echoing, of course, the Belgian Société Générale of the 1830s and Laffitte's Caisse Générale pour le Commerce et l'Industrie of 1837 (Bigo, 1947, p. 179).

It may be thought that a stretch of the imagination is required to equate the Banking School, and expansionists in France like Law, Laffitte, and the Pereires et al., with Keynesianism. Nonetheless the comparison has been made many times. Paul Harsin's magnificent bibliography on Law (1977) contains a number of titles with Keynes specifically included: 'John Law and John Keynes' (Wilson, 1948), his own 'Keynes, Law et Montesquieu' (Harsin, 1952), and an 'Essai sur quelques problèmes économiques et monétaires de J. Law à J. M. Keynes' (Sibert, 1958), quite apart from many titles indicating the

modernity of Law's views. Schumpeter (1954, pp. 321–2) called Law the
'forerunner of managed money'; Hamilton's reference to his Keynesian
'opportunity' has already been noted; and Lüthy (1959, p. 289 n. 7) calls
him an 'ancestor' of Keynes. In discussing the contest between the
Pereires and the Bank of France, Bouvier notes that the struggles of more
than a century ago are not far from us today (1973, p. 211).

Just as Law is readily connected with Keynes, so Laffitte and the
Pereires are easily associated with Law. References to Law are frequent
150 years after the Mississippi Bubble, sometimes quoting him
favorably during the days of the Banque Générale (Chevalier, in
Ministère des Finances, 1865–7, III, p. 80; VI, p. 102) and sometimes
unfavorably, as when Isaac Pereire (1865, p. 223) accuses the Bank of
France of reproducing the error of Law's *système* in associating the
abundance of money with the rate of interest, or in the Chevalier debate
with Wolowski over monopoly banks (Chevalier, 1867a, p. 205). The
Pereire brothers wrote a serious study of Law (1834 and 1868).
Chevalier and Isaac Pereire refer frequently to Jacques Laffitte, both in
support of the Keynesian (depression) view that continued reduction of
the rate of interest conforms to an economic law (I. Pereire, 1865,
p. 132), and of the general proposition that banks are needed to gather the
savings of the country and use them to stimulate commerce and
especially industry.

In defending the comparison of Keynes with Law, Laffitte and the
Pereires, not to mention Michel Chevalier, and in some respects
Napoleon I, an erroneous argument to which I myself once subscribed
must be dismissed: that modern Keynesian macroeconomics were
needed only after World War I – Temin (1971, p. 67) suggests after the
sharp recession of 1920–1 – because prior to that time prices and wages
moved freely down as well as up, with the consequence that there was
consistently full employment. This is gross exaggeration. Depressions
were frequent and often extensive. Complaints of the shortage of money
were virtually continuous. The depression of 1716 has been mentioned.
Before the eighteenth century, scarcity of specie led sometimes to
expansions in the issue of notes and bills of exchange, and payment by
assignments of sums due on open account, and occasionally, in the other
direction to barter and the use of salt as a *numéraire* (Van der Wee, 1977,
p. 30; Meuvret, 1970, p. 145). A persistent lack of liquidity was
characteristic of the regional economy of the sixteenth and seventeenth
centuries as deeper penetration of finance into the local economy
enlarged the need for means of payment faster than the availability of
metal coinage (Van der Wee, 1977, p. 300). The proposals of John Law
and contemporaries, such as Petty, Davenant, Locke, et al., were
directed at a condition rather than a theory (Harsin, 1928, pp. 149n,
154–5). In various passages, Law suggests his interest in full employment of resources (Lüthy, 1959, p. 289 n. 7). The Saint-Simonian school
has a modern ring in its insistence on two essential articles of faith:
instruction for the public and then work for all citizens. 'The State owes
work to the individual' (Vergeot, 1918, pp. 16, 18). The clash between
full employment and inflation embodied in the debate between

Keynesians and monetarists has been under way for at least a quarter of a millennium.

The issues are many and convoluted, and many of the participants in the debate had views that were contradictory, inconsistent, or wrong on one or another aspect of the total question. Moreover, there are many important issues of money and banking of the period – bimetallism, the role of bank capital, the effect of foreign lending on the internal capital market, the three-signature requirement on discounts of the Bank of France, and the like – which time and space do not permit us to explore.[1] In the analysis that follows, the issues are broken down into (1) the importance of paper money and banks to employment and growth; (2) the regional aspects of money and banking – not strictly a Keynesian subject perhaps, but one important at the time, which has achieved new prominence today in the literature of economic development with the research of Shaw (1973) and McKinnon (1973); (3) the role of the rate of interest, including its level and frequency of change; (4) the need for a monopoly of the note issue; and (5) limits on the issue of bank notes. The first two subjects focus on growth and employment; the last two on inflation. The debate over the role of the rate of interest, as indeed over possible limits to the issuance of money, goes in both directions.

Money and banking and employment and growth

The fundamental belief of Law, Lafitte, the Pereires, and such Saint-Simonians as Michel Chevalier is that society needs active banks to push the expansion of commerce, agriculture, and industry, to keep busy, and to achieve growth. Others recognize an identification problem, asking whether industrialization leads to banking or banking to industrialization, although a refined analysis suggest three possibilities: that inadequate finance restricts, permissive finance accommodates, and aggressive finance promotes growth (Cameron and Patrick, 1967, pp. 1, 2). To John Law, credit was the blood of society. 'When blood does not circulate through the body, the body languishes; the same when money does not circulate' (Harsin, 1928, p. 146):

> As Money encreas'd, the Disadvantages and Inconveniences of Barter were remov'd; The Poor and Idle were employ'd, more of the Land was Labour'd, the Product encreas'd, Manufactures and Trade improv'd, the Landed-men lived better, and the People with less Dependence on them. (Law, 1705, p. 11)

Laffitte held that the insufficiency of credit institutions in France was responsible for that country's inferiority to England and thought that his Caisse Générale pour le Commerce et l'Industrie would increase the wealth of the country, render great service, furnish all needs, give great profits, and take risks (Laffitte, 1932, pp. 335–9). 'The thought of the

Crédit Mobilier was born of the insufficiency of credit offered for the great affairs of the country, of the isolation to which financial forces are reduced in the absence of a sufficiently powerful center' (Gille, 1967, p. 110, quoting a Crédit Mobilier statement to the stockholders' meeting of 1854). A Saint-Simonian simile had credit serving like water in the desert, with the role of banks akin to that of the venerable elder who doles out the precious life-giving substance (Vergeot, 1918, pp. 97–8). Today's metaphor would be that of locomotives, needed to propel or rather pull the world's macroeconomic system. Theorists conscious of the need for credit expansion had difficulty in contemplating excesses, just as the dwellers in the desert were unlikely to fear flooding. They thus easily slipped into the real-bills fallacy that the 'employment of fiduciary money has no other limits than the development of business' (Bouvier, 1973, p. 210).

Monetarists attacked the Keynesians for confusing money and wealth, for thinking, for example, that the issue of bank notes beyond the volume of specie deposited with a bank would add to capital. 'Law misunderstood: an augmentation of money does not produce a proportional augmentation of the wealth of the country' (Levasseur, 1854/1970, p. 29). Mollien, Napoleon I's Minister of the Public Treasury, wrote that the terrible example of Law and 87 years of experience had only revealed the problem of confusing the *numéraire* and capital (Mollien, 1845, I, 451n). Adolphe Thiers told the Conseil Supérieur, it is impossible to create more capital than society creates through savings (Ministère des Finances, 1865–7, III, 433). Wolowski offered a version of the modern theory of crowding out: 'Nothing is more false than the idea that credit creates capital. Ricardo exposes this error in 1819. Loans cannot create that which does not exist. Loans create nothing; they displace' (Ministère des Finances, 1865–7, II, 222). The Conseil itself concluded that the issuance of bank notes cannot add to the wealth of the country (*ibid.*, VI, 98). Add to representative values and you do not add to wealth (Cernuschi, 1866, p. 112). But Michel Chevalier correctly put the Keynesian proposition that lower interest rates produced by the issue of notes can stimulate investment and 'place the country as if it had a more considerable capital' (Ministère des Finances, 1865–7, VI, 102). This is the kernel of the Keynesian system, that investment creates savings through raising income with a positive marginal propensity to save. Banks were needed to mobilize savings. As Bagehot told the Conseil, each village in England had at least two banks, thanks to which no shilling of savings was lost (*ibid.*, I, 24). Chevalier's emphasis is more on this function of collecting savings than on creating them. Large numbers of banks in Scotland and in the United States as well as in Britain helped bring down interest rates by collecting savings and directing them into their most effective uses. So impressed was Chevalier at discovering a bank in a small Pennsylvania community of 30 houses, with stumps still standing in the streets, that he mentioned it three times over thirty years – *Lettres*, I (1838), p. 264; *Cours*, I (1855), p. 84; *Exposition universelle* (1868), p. ccclxxxi. But more banks represent not only efficiency in the collection of a given pool of savings;

they also mean an increased issue of fiduciary money – especially bank notes – lower interest rates, greater spending, greater employment and growth. The expansionists were far from articulating the Keynesian model in its rigor – as indeed was Keynes himself – but their intuition grasped it.

Law, Laffitte, and the Pereires, however, went further than the real-bills theorists of the Banking School in wanting banks to provide long-term capital for industry, as well as to validate the short-term credit already implied by commercial transactions. Law's views on credit were vague and changing, linked originally to land, as already noted, and confusing shares and money. In his time the distinction between commerce and industry was less sharp than later. But Jacques Laffitte made no bones about his interest in lending to industry on the basis of the issue of bank notes, or when permission to do so was denied, on the basis of short-term transferable bearer notes. He wanted to start a Bank for Commerce and Industry in 1825, but was turned down. When permission was granted on a subsequent request in 1837, it was on condition that it be called a *caisse*, rather than a bank, and that it issue not bank notes but short-term interest-bearing notes – a limitation later applied to the Crédit Mobilier. Even in the 1820s, with his own funds, Laffitte was involved in investing in insurance, canals, Paris real estate, stone-cutting and glass, a cotton-spinning mill, and (although there is some dispute about it) coal mines and iron works (Cameron, 1967, p. 114; Gille, 1959, pp. 193–4). Redlich (1948) calls him the first French investment banker. Rothschild offered to join Laffitte's proposed bank in 1825. In 1837 he stood aside, saying that 'Laffitte acquired his popularity by the extreme facility with which he advanced money to industry. Other bankers say that his greatest fault is to interest himself in all these enterprises . . . instead of limiting himself to being a simple lender and getting good guarantees' (Gille, 1965, I, 193).

Law was interested in expanding commerce, Laffitte in commerce and industry, and the Pereires mainly in industry, as they claimed, but much of it actually public works of the overhead capital variety rather than manufacturing. The merchants of Bordeaux opposed Law, as did financiers more narrowly interested in farming taxes and floating the public debt (Levasseur, 1854/1970, p. 53). Other Atlantic ports supported him, and his *système* gave a great impulse to maritime and colonial commerce in the rest of the century (Lüthy, 1959, pp. 295, 423). Great claims have been made for John Law's legacy in eliminating the remnants of mercantilist interference in trade and improving French finances by simplifying and reducing waste in the collection of taxes (Hamilton, 1968, p. 61). These have been disputed; Lüthy (1959, p. 423) writes that nothing remained of Law's reforms after 1730, and some bad financial habits even became worse. In one view Lorient was the only benefit of Law's system that survived to the middle of the nineteenth century (Levasseur, 1854/1970, p. 153) – a somewhat bigger residue perhaps than for the South Sea Bubble, for which it was said Guy's Hospital, built with the profits of the speculator Sir Thomas Guy, remains today the best memorial

(Carswell, 1960, p. 138). Law's intellectual bequest, it is claimed, remains substantial.

Law's opponents attacked on all kinds of grounds and, like those of Laffitte and the Pereires, were not above joining with or imitating the objects of their attack. The quarrel between the Pereires and the Rothschilds is illuminated by three letters, two from Baron James de Rothschild to the Emperor, which, Gille says, state the same objections, though the case is difficult to substantiate, and the other from Persigny, French ambassador in London, to the Emperor, setting forth the substance of a conversation with Lionel Rothschild of the London house. In November 1852, before the Crédit Mobilier had gotten started, James de Rothschild argued that it was dangerous, that it would create a mass of paper which in a moment of crisis would lead the public fortune to slide into the abyss. In prosperity it would be obliged to speculate to make money; in crisis it would be in difficulty. With its enormous capital, 60 million francs, plus the power to borrow – first 5 times its capital and ultimately 20 times – it would penetrate into all railroads, mines, and industries and constitute a monopolistic danger, even a calamity for the country (Gille, 1967, II, 100–2). Four years later, in November 1856, before the forecasts of 1852 had been realized in the crisis of 1857, James de Rothschild wrote again to Napoleon III, asserting that the activities of the Crédit Mobilier, the capital of which was insignificant, had had nothing to do with the economic expansion of 1852 to 1856, and that the real cause of the boom had been the interest in securities instilled in the masses by the events of 1848 (*ibid.*, pp. 103–4). The Persigny letter of October 1855 is perhaps not as solid evidence, since he is a partisan of the Pereires and is quoting James de Rothschild at second hand. He does observe, however, that the objections of de Rothschild are contradictory: the baron both derides the significance of the Crédit Mobilier and fears it will become so rich that it will lay down the law to the government (*ibid.*, p. 115). Persigny himself states that the Crédit Mobilier is able to simulate business by forcing people to take money out of their pockets, notes that James de Rothschild kept his money intact by halting investment at the first sign of war or any other difficulty – also inducing other banks to do the same (*ibid.*, pp. 115–16) – and quotes Lionel to the effect that the 60 millions of capital of the Crédit Mobilier, in active hands, is a powerful force for maintaining confidence.

The expansionists were right in believing that with primitive banks and little opportunity to create money, whether by bank notes or deposits, the hoarding of money with inefficient capital markets was likely to lead to underemployment. The monetarists, on the other hand, were right in thinking that the credit mechanism was unstable to a considerable degree, and that the creation of money for loans to industry might become expansionary in a cumulative way that led to 'over-trading' and 'discredit'. The pragmatic and anti-theoretical compromise by which British banks made loans to commerce and for the working capital of business, but not fixed capital, was just that – a practical compromise that could be rationalized only by some erroneous real-bills doctrine.

The regional issue

The overall issue of growth is whether more banks and more bank notes are needed to stimulate commerce and industry, and if, when this is done, it is possible to stop short of some inflationary level. The regional issue is the geographical dispersal of the new banks and issues of bank notes – whether the Bank of France, for example, should have provincial branches or agencies, whether regional banks should be established to issue notes and, in either case, whether the notes of Bank of France branches or those of separate regional banks should be redeemable only locally, especially in Paris, or anywhere throughout the kingdom. As stated earlier, this is not a Keynesian question in a literal sense, though it has its modern counterpart in Shaw (1973) and McKinnon (1973). Shaw and McKinnon realized the necessity for developing countries to break down the financial isolation of geographical regions. The point was evident to the founders of the Federal Reserve System, who created a network of 12 regional banks. In Britain, the Bank of England operated with a monopoly of the note issue within 65 miles of London from 1825, and after 1826 began a policy of establishing branches outside that limit. The Keynesians in France were continuously urging the establishment of branches of the Bank of France in the provinces, and/or independent regional banks of issue. The Bank of France had the final say in whether or not such banks were started. Application was made to the Minister of Finance, who, following custom, would seek the advice of the Conseil of the Bank of France (Gille, 1970, p. 37). Statutory authorization was required of Parliament, but this followed the Minister and the Bank of France when it came to laying down stipulations and conditions, as well as on the question of yes or no.

John Law wrote of the need for credit 'in the provinces' to circulate like blood throughout the body (Harsin, 1928, p. 14). The conversion of the Banque Générale to a Banque Royale, which Hamilton (1968, p. 80) dismisses as 'only a formality since the crown had already bought 100 percent of the stock', was followed by the establishment of branches in La Rochelle, Tours, Orléans, and Amiens (Levasseur, 1854/1970, p. 87). Law won the right to establish a branch also in Lyons, but it was resisted. The July 1719 acquisition by the Compagnie des Indes added '25 virtual branches', including this time Lyons (Hamilton, 1968, p. 80). 'In the summer of 1716 custodians of public revenue in the provinces were instructed to accept and redeem' Banque Générale notes, and 'on October 7 they were ordered to remit to Paris exclusively in these notes. Consequently, even in the Bank's first year, notes were circulating in distant provinces' (*ibid.*, p. 79). As thinker and doer, Law was interested in spreading the circulation of money and easing credit conditions, both in the financial center and out to the periphery.

After Law's bankruptcy, the issue may have arisen in the Caisse d'Escompte of 1776, but it comes to the forefront of policy with the establishment of the Bank of France. In the eighteenth century, French banking had existed in Paris and in the ports. The Revolution drove many Swiss bankers away, and after it they returned not to the ports but to Paris. Napoleon sought to bring banking to the provinces, especially when he was pestered on visits through France by delegations of merchants and manufacturers who complained that they could not get credit as cheaply as did those in Paris. In 1810, especially in May, Napoleon I entered into a long correspondence with Mollien, his Minister of the Public Treasury, and directed him to issue instructions to the regents of the Bank of France on the establishment of Bank of France branches at Amiens, Saint-Quentin, Lille, Valenciennes, Cambrai, and Lyons (Mollien, 1845, III, pp. 137–46). Mollien understood the problem, bluntly calling the Bank of England the Bank of London, and not objecting when Napoleon referred to the Bank of France as the Bank of Paris (*ibid.*, I, pp. 186, 452–5; III, p. 155) – as two economist witnesses also did in the 1867 Enquiry, one with emphasis, the other matter-of-factly (Ministére des Finances, 1865–7, II, pp. 164, 347). In the view of Mollien, a Bank of Paris was theoretically preferable to a Bank of France, as well as more practicable (Wolowski, 1864, p. 51). Mollien and the Regents argued that the branches did not pay for themselves, lacking both businessmen, to put up the necessary capital to qualify as local directors, and sufficient discountable paper to cover the costs of the branch (Mollien, 1845, III, pp. 155–6). Liesse (1908, p. 115) calls Mollien 'completely wrong' on centralization, but does not explain why. Presumably better credit facilities throughout the country are a public good which should be centrally subsidized, rather than insisting on each branch or *comptoir* paying its own way, much in the manner of justifying branch lines on railroads. Mollien trained Napoleon to ask the delegations to furnish a list of men prepared to tie up their capital to qualify as stockholders and of merchants who would discount several millions of good letters of exchange annually (Mollien, 1845, I, p. 157). A branch was opened at Lille in 1811 and closed down in 1814 (Gille, 1970, p. 36). *Comptoirs d'escompte* (agencies) were established in place of branches at Rouen and Lyons. With the fall of the Empire, these too were closed.

Jacques Laffitte served as governor of the Bank of France from 1814 to 1820. Under his leadership the Bank withdrew its objections to local banks of issue, and these were established in Rouen (1817), Nantes (1818), and Bordeaux (1818) – all ports, to be sure, as contrasted with the manufacturing towns that Napoleon wanted to help. Laffitte sought to convert the Bank of France into a simple commercial bank, free of governmental control and without a monopoly of the note issue (Cameron, 1967, pp. 103–4). He perhaps tolerated, rather than pushed, the regional banks in the 1820s. After his term, the issue of regional banks rose again, and six more were created, notably in Marseilles and Lyons (1835), Lille (1836), Le Havre (1837), and Toulouse and Orléans (1838) (Pose, 1942, I, p. 149). A bank was planned for Dijon but never got under way (Gille, 1970, p. 84). The Bank of France argued strongly against giving these local banks powers to issue small-denomination notes and to redeem their notes in specie in Paris; it sought to keep them local and small rather than to integrate them into a national network. Such may in fact have been impossible before the advent of railroads and the telegraph. In 1838 the circulation of credit nationally was limited. Some communities like Lyons had a plethora of funds (although the city had a wide seasonal pattern and ran short when silk was purchased from Italy in the spring). Others had a dearth, Dijon had to pay 9 to 10 percent for discounts, when Paris paid 4 (Gille, 1970, p. 77). Napoleon I's second letter from Le Havre on 28 May 1810 said, 'My intention is to establish without delay a branch at Lille. There is no objection to such an establishment in a place so large which has money at 6 percent, when by means of a branch, it will be 4 per cent' (Mollien, 1845, III, p. 145).

In the crisis of 1848 the Bank of France permitted all the regional banks to fail and turned them from independent issuers of their own notes to *comptoirs d'escompte* of the Bank of France. To get a third name on paper for discounting, it assisted with the creation of 60 more *comptoirs* to add their names to those of merchants and local private banks. After the crisis had been resolved, many of these regional creations were converted into *caisses d'escompte*, including the Paris Caisse, which became a great national bank (Bouvier, 1973, p. 84). But as late as 1863, three-quarters of the area of France lacked access to banking facilities (Bigo, 1947, p. 42).

The Pereires' views on regional banking are complicated by their particular concern, at the time of the Enquiry, of retaining the note-issue privilege for the Bank of Savoy which they had acquired in buying the bank, after Savoy had been added to France. At times they argue in favor of virtually free entry into banking. In his testimony to the Conseil Supérieur in 1867, Emile Pereire recalled his 1834 views on reform of the Bank of France, when he demanded two signatures on discountable paper instead of three, the establishment of current accounts, the issue of notes in the amount of 100 francs in contrast with the existing minimum of 250, and new *comptoirs d'escompte* in Lyons, Marseilles, Lille, Strasbourg, Saint-Quentin, Orléans, Tours, Limoges, La Rochelle, Bayonne, Toulouse, Montpellier, Grenoble, Amiens, Rennes, etc., in addition to banks then existing at Bordeaux, Nantes, and Rouen. No place should be without a bank within 20 to 30 leagues' (80 to 120 kilometers') distance. The Bank of France should triple its note circulation, popularize its credit throughout France, and bring capital it could not employ in Paris to the provinces. The spread of capital throughout the country was the secret of the industrial and political power of Great Britain (Ministère des Finances, 1865–7, I, pp. 602–5). Isaac Pereire did not deal with the issue in his testimony (*ibid.*, III, 248–309). In his earlier treatise (1865, p. 25) he argued that the nine departmental banks competed with the Bank of France to the satisfaction of everyone before 1848, but that if it was impossible to adopt a good solution (to the regional and the monopoly questions), there was no other remedy than the creation of a new establishment to rival the Bank of France and to make it admit the necessity of reform (*ibid.*, pp. 212, 232). But this modest, self-interested vision is overwhelmed at other stages by a grandiose scheme of an integrated European capital market, each national market run by a monopolized group of credit institutions (Gille, 1967, II, p. 112).

Wolowski, a monetarist, states that Leon Faucher, a free-trader and an expansionist friend of Chevalier, and the banker d'Eichtal excoriated regional banks because of the embarrassments they created and the faults they committed (Wolowski, 1964, p. 238). Liberty of banking at the regional level was called by Faucher a 'château of cards' (*ibid.*, p. 269).

The discussion of branches of the Bank of France in the Enquiry is particularly illuminating. In the renewal of the charter in 1857, a requirement was laid down that the Bank have at least one branch in each department at the end of ten years. In asking questions of officials in 1865, Michel Chevalier, who was the one Keynesian on the Conseil Supérieur, observed that the Bank had only 54 branches. He thought, moreover, that 90 branches would not be enough and that some departments would need more than one, so that not 200 or 300 branches, but more nearly 1,000 would be required (Ministère des Finances, 1865–7, III, 130–2). The Bank of France Regent de Waru observed dryly that the Bank was interested in the question, but that Chevalier's view struck it as more theoretical than practical. A problem with additional branches was the necessity of dispersing specie reserves widely if bank notes were redeemable elsewhere than only in Paris, although the advent of railroads and the telegraph improved the situation (*ibid.*, VI, pp. 125–6, 165–8). Bank of France officials were re-interviewed just before the Conseil Supérieur reached decisions on various issues, going down the line for the most part against the expansionists and in favor of the monetarist Bank of France view. On branches, the Bank representatives said laconically 'when we have one in each department we will consider more . . . We start by executing the law' (*ibid.*, V, p. 222). The Conseil refused to put further pressure on the Bank, and it was not until the charter renewal of 1894 again required extension of branches, and the expansionist governor George Pallain took office, that a policy of covering France more fully with branches was undertaken (Dauphin-Meunier, 1936, p. 129).

The rate of interest

The rate of interest played a rather confused role in the monetary debates of the eighteenth and nineteenth centuries, and in practice in the nineteenth. Law, Laffitte, and the Pereires, plus Napoleon, Chevalier, and other expansionists, wanted to hold the rate of interest down and keep it stable for the purpose of making credit available to commerce and industry and stimulating employment and growth. For the most part favoring free entry into banking, as into commerce and industry, they were unwilling to contemplate the movement of the rate of interest up and down in response to conditions of supply and demand, often arguing that since the Bank of France in the nineteenth century was a monopoly, it should be regulated. In the debates of the 1860s, the monetarists argued that the expansionists were acting like those who would fix the thermometer at 35 degrees, claiming that it was then impossible to suffer from hot and cold (Ministère des Finances, 1865–7,

III, pp. 75–6, 305). In fact the discount rate of the Bank of France was fixed at 4 percent from 1820 to 1848, and then again, after an interval of roughly ten years of intense discount-rate policy – the discount rate having been changed 50 times between 1855 and 1864 (Lévy-Leboyer, 1976, p. 424) – returned to low rates with infrequent changes as the expansionists demanded.

Law tended to think in terms of capital values, *rentes*, annual interest, or other payments, rather than explicitly in terms of rates of return, and used rates far too low for the conditions of his day (Viner, 1937, p. 150, quoting Henry Thornton). He adjusted the dividend sought for the value of the shares of the Compagnie d'Occident to actual earnings, rather than letting share prices find their market level (Levasseur, 1970, p. 149). But he urged the establishment of the Banque Générale in a crisis when the discount rate on bills of exchange, as he said, was 2½ percent a month or 30 percent a year (Faure, 1977, p. 105), and later claimed credit for reducing the rate of interest as required for prosperity (Levasseur, 1854/1970, p. 124). At the same time he opposed laws to fix the rate of interest (Harsin, 1928, p. 154).

Much of Saint-Simonian theory ran in terms of availability of credit rather than its cost, using expressions such as the 'union of credit and industry' (Vergeot, 1918, p. 51). But Laffitte was concerned about the cost of capital to the state and to industry. In the 1820s he participated in the conversion of state debt. In the prospectus for his Caisse Générale in 1837 he observed that 'industry can obtain capital only at a high price. Its products are expensive, and consumption is limited in the interior, and sales difficult abroad' (Laffitte, 1932, p. 340). He went further in anticipating Keynes by enunciating an 'economic law of the successive reduction of the rate of interest' that Isaac Pereire quoted with approval, adding that 'he was profoundly persuaded that one of the greatest gains it is possible to procure for a country is to reduce its rate of interest' (I. Pereire, 1865, p. 132, quoting a pamphlet written by Laffitte in 1824).

Like Law and Laffitte, the Pereire brothers participated in a massive refunding of state debt that lowered the rate of interest more generally in the early days of the Second Empire. They helped to found the Caisse d'Escompte used to meet the crisis of 1848, and to found the Crédit Foncier in 1852.

In his testimony before the Conseil Supérieur, Emile Pereire said he had worked with his brother for 33 years to lower interest rates. He quotes from Turgot, who called the rate of interest a thermometer of the scarcity and abundance of money: 'a country with a 2 percent rate of interest can do things impossible to do at 5 percent'; and then developed a metaphor of his own. The price of interest sets a level at which all work, culture, industry, commerce ceases. A sea over a vast country: summits, mountains, lift themselves up and form fertile islands. If waters recede, as far as they fall, slopes are turned into plains and valleys. If it rises or falls a foot, it inundates or makes available immense shores (Ministère des Finances, 1865–7, I, pp. 607–8). All this was preliminary to the assertion that the establishment of the Crédit Mobilier had lowered the rate of interest to 3 percent. Isaac Pereire claimed he did not demand a fixed rate of interest, but rather limits and narrower oscillations. The Bank of France had a monopoly and, like a railroad, should be subject to rate regulation. He demanded a maximum of 4 percent: raising the rate of interest since 1855 was a calamity, against which he protested with all his might (*ibid.*, III, pp. 302–4). But neither Pereire nor Michel Chevalier, who was voted down in the Conseil (*ibid.*, VI, p. 146), handled the question well. They would fix maximum rates irrespective of existing conditions of demand and supply; they especially made analytical messes of a number of related questions: whether capital exports from France raised interest rates in the interior of France, whether low rates of interest raised capital values and encouraged speculation, whether, if London raised its discount rate, pressure was put on Paris, and whether there was any need for the Bank of France to defend its reserves (*ibid.*, I, pp. 636–42; III, pp. 270, 306). A theme that runs through the Pereires' testimony is that if the Bank of France would convert its capital from *rentes* into specie, there would be no need to defend its reserves – 'an expression which should be banned from the dictionary' (ibid., III, p. 306) – but they are unclear what would happen to the credit base and the rate of interest if the 180 millions of *rentes* were sold, nor do they explain why they assume that the open-market sales would be made against specie instead of bank notes. To Emile Pereire, the rate of interest is no indication of the abundance or scarcity of money (*ibid.*, I, p. 645).

On this issue the Bank of France and the monetarists had the intellectual edge by a wide margin, in current views, unless one adheres entirely to a rationing theory of credit. They threw it away after 1870 by going back to the Bank's 1820–48 habit of a pegged rate.

A monopoly bank

Among the more interesting aspects of monetary theory in the eighteenth and nineteenth centuries was the question whether there should or should not be a monopoly of the note issue. On the whole, the expansionists were against, though exceptions were important, whereas the monetarist spoke up for solid control in the hands of an official agency. The subtle differences, however, among the views of Law, Laffitte, Pereire, and Chevalier call to mind that today the monetarists of the Chicago School want monopoly, while the ultra-liberals, like Hayek (1972) and Vaubel (1977), call for 'free currency competition'.

A monestarist like Wolowski (1864, p. 58n) strongly favors monopoly of the note issue in the Bank of France and chides Chevalier for having changed his mind that 'artificial and conventional money to offer more of a guarantee must come from the same factory'. Wolowski (*ibid.*) quotes an early article of Chevalier criticizing Perregaux, first governor of the Bank of France, for not seeing that a great bank is not purely private but partakes of the character of a public institution. This view of money as a public good echoes the views in the third letter on the *système* attributed to Law. Money is a good of society on which the State has sovereign authority, but which it can use only in the public interest. Money belongs to the king like the roads, not to enclose them in his own domain, but to prevent others from doing so in theirs. Just as the king can change the roads for the public convenience, of which he is the sole judge, so he can alter money. His goods belong to him only on the condition that he makes of them a use convenient to society (Harsin, 1928, p. 153). Laffitte, when he became governor of the Bank of France in 1814, proposed a reorganization of the bank which would have involved the loss of its monopoly, but it failed to gain approval (Palgrave's *Dictionary*, 1925–6/1963, II, p. 553).

The Pereires vehemently opposed the monopoly of the Bank of France, though for private rather more than for public-policy purposes. Saint-Simonians exhibited a monopolistic tendency along technocratic lines which Vergeot (1918, p. 243) criticizes. In the Enquiry before the Conseil Supérieur, Michel Chevalier was the only member to speak out in favor of competition for the Bank of France. His talk in the final voting session covered ten pages, reciting the usual arguments about Scottish, American, and English banks, asking for liberty for banks as well as for industry. D'Eichtal having already noted that the American system had changed from wild-cat banking in the 1830s when Chevalier first visited the country to the restrictive National Bank Act of 1863, no member of the Conseil bothered to reply to Chevalier after he finished talking, and he was voted down without a word (Ministère des Finances, 1865–7, VI, p. 128). Thomas Tooke, the Banking School leader, also opposed free banking, repeating the slogan of Daniel Webster that 'free trade in banking is free trade in swindling' – as quoted by Wolowski (1864, pp. 188, 324), citing Tooke's *History of Prices*, but different places – Ministère des Finances, III, p. 298; II, p. 206; and (1867a, p. 397), Ministère des Finances, III, p. 207. See also Ministère des Finances, II, p. 302.

Monopoly and competition in banking are concepts which do not run parallel to Keynesianism (expansion) and monetarism (restriction). In the eighteenth century, monopoly in the hands of a Banque Royale was congruent with expansion, as perhaps in Chevalier's first view, attacked by Wolowski, and in the modern views of Hayek and Vaubel. Free entry, on the contrary, is regarded by the later Chevalier and by Laffitte and the Pereires as expansionist. In between, there are many muddled views, such as that of Garnier-Pagès, the 1848 governor of the Bank of France, who told the Enquiry that of the three possible systems of banking – complete liberty, state control, and a monopoly bank subject to conditions, like the Bank of France – he would subscribe to complete freedom if he were a theorist; but given past facts, traditions, customs, and his unlimited confidence in the Bank of France, he was content to proceed by the third path, modifying the terms of the Bank of France agreement from time to time in unspecified ways (Ministére des Finances, 1865–7, II, p. 68).

Michel Chevalier and Louis Wolowski debated one another, and fenced, in the *Journal des Economistes*, the *Revue des Deux Mondes*, in the Enquiry before the Conseil Supérieur, and presumably elsewhere.

The exchanges were polemical, tinged with irony, sarcasm, and mock honorifics. Each fought to obtain the sanction of authority for his point of view. Neither covered himself with glory. In particular, Chevalier failed to make adequate distinction between the liberty of banking which prevailed in England and an expansive money supply, which did not; and Wolowski had a difficult time defending the Bank Act of 1844 in England and explaining away its suspensions, for lack of distinction between trend and crisis liquidity (Chevalier, 1867a, b, c; Wolowski, 1867a, b).

Limits to the note issue

In early modern times, there were two sorts of banks: deposit and lending banks. The former, like the Bank of Amsterdam, could not create money. They credited depositors only up to the limit of specie left with them, charging a small rate of interest or premium for the convenience afforded by the bank notes that were easier to handle, transport, count, divide, and guard than coin or specie. The modern equivalent of the deposit bank is 100 percent money, sometimes advocated by monetarists. Deposit banks changed the form of money, but by and large did not create it. Lending banks, on the other hand, did create money by issuing liabilities of notes or deposits. A muddled issue between Keynesians and monetarists in the eighteenth and nineteenth centuries was whether there should be a limit to the notes issued by lending banks.

The Banque Générale of John Law acted like a deposit bank. It assisted economic expansion not by expanding the money supply but by increasing the effectiveness of its circulation. Conversion of the Banque Générale to the Banque Royale led to a critical change in the limits to the note issue. Notes were limited not by specie deposited, nor even by discounted bills of exchange representing underlying commercial transactions, but by royal decree. The system called for operations both prudent and sure (Lüthy, 1959, I, p. 308). In theory, Law believed convertibility of notes into coin desirable and thought that restricting note issues to loans on commercial transactions would maintain confidence in the capacity of the bank to sustain convertibility. In another of his views he said that specie reserves of 25 to 33 percent would be enough to assure convertibility. In the event, he was unable to stop at these multiples and obtained the Regent's consent to keep raising the ceiling on note issues and lower the reserve ratio (Harsin, 1928, p. 149). The notes of the Banque Royale were made legal tender (Levasseur, 1854/1970, p. 88). When the Mississippi Bubble was fully distended, Law had to keep on supporting the stock with new note issues to forestall collapse. In this fashion the limits to the note issue that would sustain confidence in convertibility were quickly passed.

In the nineteenth century, the debate was confused by the fact that Keynesians and monetarists alike for the most part believed in convertibility, opposed the restrictive provisions of the Bank Act of

1844 in Great Britain, and supported the potentially much more expansive French 3:1 *de facto* ratio of notes to specie as it developed over time, but without wanting to see the ratio or any other limitation written into law. There were a few all-out monetarists. Cernuschi (1866) inveighed against paper money altogether, and Wolowski admired the limitations of the Bank Act of 1844, insisting that everyone in England belonged to the metallic school and was a bullionist (Ministère des Finances, 1865–7, II, pp. 358, 381–2). In his opinion, echoed in that of Rueff in our day, precious metals introduce a common language into the relations of international commerce (*ibid.*, II, p. 372). D'Eichtal, a banker on the Conseil Supérieur conducting the 1865–7 Enquiry, urged the adoption of a rule limiting note issues, on the ground that the public was incapable of reading balance sheets and that, without a rule, one evildoer, financial or political, could unleash a panic that the Bank would be unable to prevent (*ibid.*, VI, pp. 114, 117). The Conseil turned him down. On the whole, both expansionists and monetarists were Frenchmen first and analysts second, criticizing the restrictions of the English Bank Act as unsatisfactory in one way or another because it limited the note issue either too much or in the wrong way, and clinging to the 3:1 expansion ratio of the Bank of France as it evolved in practice, without wishing to hamper the Bank's freedom by imposing it strictly by law.

Both groups defended convertibility. Rothschild stated that the goal of his life was to preserve the Bank and to prevent it from having recourse to paper, or rather, to forced note circulation. As a young man he had accompanied his brother in the 1825 London crisis and witnessed the inquietudes of that time. Constant convertibility of notes is the essential condition of a bank of issue (*ibid.*, I, pp. 457, 462). In his youth, Chevalier had said, 'A collapse of credit, however short a time it lasts, is more fearful than the most terrible earthquake' (Chevalier, 1838, I, p. 37). Conversion of bank notes into coin, he said almost 30 years later, was 'indispensable', for in a panic (*sauve-qui-peut*) the whole system founded on credit was likely to collapse (1866, III, sec. 2, ch. 4, esp. p. 67). Magne, the Minister of Finance at the last session of the Enquiry, called suspension of convertibility a 'dishonor' (Ministère des Finances, 1865–7, VI, p. 157). The monetarists who tried had a hard time defending the Bank Act of 1844 in Britain, at which the expansionists scoffed because of its suspension in 1847, 1857, and 1866. Wolowski called it 'an imaginary remedy for an imaginary illness' (*ibid.*, II, p. 233n). But both groups had difficulty with the fact that the Bank of France had suspended convertibility in 1848, and the Regents had asked the government for permission to do so on two later occasions, 1856 and 1864, and had each time been refused (*ibid.*, VI, pp. 113, 156–7). The expansionists failed to indicate how larger note issues, lower interest rates, stable interest rates, and more banks of issue would avoid forced circulation when the restrictive policies they opposed had led to it or come close. The monetarists, in their turn, expressed satisfaction with the performance of the Bank of France, its monopoly, and its interest-rate policies, without suggesting how close they had come to disaster.

That there was a limit, the expansionists knew. In discussing the *système* of Law, Chevalier attacks the notion of land as collateral for bank notes: 'If the emission exceeds the quantity of money which would be necessary in the service of transactions, even when it is far from exceeding the collateral, depreciation will not be less inevitable' (1866, III, p. 676). Mention of the quantity of money is significant, although the real-bills fallacy is mixed with the same thought.

Nowhere is the confusion abounding in the discussion better illustrated than in the testimony of the banker, Bischoffsheim. (i) He is against joint-stock banks. He recognizes that they have done good as well as bad. Having been solidly established, and their shares having gone to premia, they often engage in less solid operations, successively moving to the worst, which disappear, leaving large losses. On the whole it would be better not to have the good or the bad that they produce (Ministère des Finances, 1865–7, II, p. 102). (ii) As for the utility of paper money, one is tempted to wonder whether it is not better to renounce the advantages in order to escape the sad results. He would not go so far as to prohibit bank notes. He finds them agreeable and would not dream of suppressing them. When he lived in Holland, people looked down on payment in *écus sonnants* (money that rings). On the one hand, paper money is agreeable and costs nothing; on the other, there may not be enough advantage to compensate for the evil it can produce. It is perhaps better to renounce paper money. People claim that it does much good for little evil, and that nothing is perfect. 'As for me, I suggest that the benefit is not demonstrated' (*ibid.*, II, pp. 111–12).

The agonizing of banker Bischoffheim summarizes the position fairly well. If the expansionists are right in depression, but the monetarists right that it is difficult to stop before going too far and ending in speculative excess, plus crisis, the cost–benefit calculation is complex and subjective. Law, Laffitte, and the Pereires came into their own in depressed periods. All overshot the mark, Laffitte and the Pereires less than the genius Law. Both Keynesians and monetarists wanted a simple rule (Viner, 1937, pp. 232–3) and there is none. The judgment of Solomon that each is half-right is correct.

I suggest that the rule they were looking for and could not find is to expand bank lending and the money supply in depression with low rates of interest, to raise rates when full employment is approached, the balance of payments turns adverse, or confidence in the maintenance of convertibility sinks, and to restrict money rigorously in periods of excited speculation until the virtually inevitable crisis, when the lender of last resort should make it available again to sound borrowers. Each portion of this prescription calls for subtle distinctions. There is no workable Keynesian or monetarist rule.

Notes

1   This article started as a study of John Law, Jacques Laffitte, and the Pereire brothers, Emile and Isaac, and remains such to a considerable degree, despite the more general

title. The extension is largely directed to the nineteenth-century debate, especially in the Enquiry (Ministère des Finances, 1865–7, 1867) into monetary circulation and fails to cover the views of Turgot or Necker in the *ancien régime*, or the experiences with the *assignats* in 1792. It has benefited greatly from a vigorous dissent with a number of views, expressed by Professor Earl J. Hamilton, not all of whose suggestions for improvement, however, have been accepted.

2   On inconsistency, observe that Populism in the United States in the 1830s, in contrast to expansionism in France, opposed all banks and favored payments in gold (Chevalier, 1838, I, p. 223). Cobbett even wrote to Jackson from England, expressing the hope that his attack on the Bank of the United States would be the first step in the general abolition of banks (*ibid.*, p. 73n). Cernuschi and Wolowski, monetarists, were strong for bimetallism (Cernuschi, 1876; Wolowski, 1869), whereas Chevalier, the expansionist, favored silver over both bimetallism and gold, because of instability, in the first instance, and the inflationary consequences of gold discoveries in California and Australia, in the second (Chevalier, 1859). For a hyperbolic Populist statement comparable to Bryan's Cross of Gold speech, see Cobbett's claim that one million would die of hunger in Britain if gold payments were resumed in 1819, that resumption could on this account never be carried out, and if it were, 'he would suffer Castlereagh to broil him alive while Sidmouth stirred the coals and Canning stood by to make a jest of his groans (Doubleday, 1847, p. 49).

References

Bigo, Robert (1947), *Les Banques françaises au cours du XIXe siècle* (Paris: Sirey)

Bouvier, Jean (1967), *Les Rothschilds* (Paris: Fayard).

Bouvier, Jean (1973), *Un Siècle de banque française: Les Contraintes de l'Etat, et les incertitudes des marchés* (Paris: Hachette Littérature).

Bouvier, Jean and Cameron, Rondo E. (1963), 'Une lettre inédite de Persigny à Napoléon III', *Revue historique*, 467 (July–September), pp. 91–5.

Cameron, Rondo E. (1961), *France and the Economic Development of Europe* (Princeton, NJ: Princeton University Press).

Cameron, Rondo E. (1967), 'France, 1800–1875', in Rondo E. Cameron *et al.*, *Banking in the Early Stages of Industrialization: A Study in Comparative Economic History* (New York: Oxford University Press).

Cameron, Rondo E. and Patrick, Hugh T. (1967), 'Introduction' to Rondo E. Cameron *et al.*, *Banking in the Early Stages of Industrialization: A Study in Comparative Economic History* (New York: Oxford University Press).

Carswell, John (1960), *The South Sea Bubble* (London: Cresset Press).

Cernuschi, Henri (1866), *Contre le billet de banque* (Paris: A. Lacroix, Verboeckhoven).

Cernuschi, Henri (1876), *M. Michel Chevalier et le bimétallisme* (Paris: Guillaumin).

Chevalier, Michel (1838), *Lettres sur L'Amérique du Nord*. 3rd edn. (Paris: Gosselin, 2 vols).

Chevalier, Michel (1855), *Cours d'économie politique fait au Collège de France.* Vol. I: *Tous les discours d'ouverture, 1840 à 1852* (Paris: Capelle).

Chevalier, Michel (1859), *On the Probable Fall in the Value of Gold, the Commercial and Social Consequences Which May Ensue and the Measures Which it Invokes*, 3rd edn., translated from the French by Richard Cobden (Manchester: Alexander Ireland).

Chevalier, Michel (1866), *Cours d'économie politique*. Vol. III: *La Monnaie*. 2nd edn. (Paris: Capelle).

Chevalier, Michel (1867a), ' "La Liberté des banques", Lettre à Louis Wolowski', *Journal des Economistes*, 3rd ser., 5–6, pp. 191–229.
Chevalier, Michel (1867b), 'Postscriptum à la lettre addressé à M. Wolowski', *Journal des Economistes*, 3rd ser., 5–6, pp. 414–16.
Chevalier, Michel (1867c), ' "La Question des banques" I. Réponse à M. L. Wolowski', *Journal des Economistes*, 3rd ser., 5–6, pp. 66–72.
Chevalier, Michel (1868), *Exposition universelle de 1867 à Paris. Rapports du Jury International publiés sous la direction de M. Michel Chevalier*. Vol. I: *Introduction par M. Michel Chevalier* (Paris: Paul Dupont).
Courtois, A., fils (1875), *Histoire de la Banque de France et des principales institutions françaises de crédit, depuis 1716* (Paris: Guillaumin).
Dauphin-Meunier, A. (1936), *La Banque de France* (Paris: Gallimard).
Doubleday, Thomas (1847), *A Financial, Monetary and Statistical History of England, from the Revolution of 1688 to the Present Time* (London: Effingham, Wilson).
Faure, Edgar (1977), *La Banqueroute de Law, 17 juillet 1720* (Paris: Gallimard).
Gerschenkron, Alexander (1962), *Economic Backwardness in Historical Perspective* (Cambridge, Mass.: Harvard University Press).
Gille, Bertrand (1959), *La Banque et le crédit en France de 1815 à 1848* (Paris: Presses universitaires de France).
Gille, Bertrand (1965, 1967), *Histoire de la Maison Rothschild*. Vol. I: *Dès origines à 1848*; Vol. II: *1848–1870* (Geneva: Librairie Droz).
Gille, Bertrand (1970), *La Banque en France au XIXe siècle. Recherches historiques* (Geneva: Librairie Droz).
Hamilton, Earl J. (1968), 'John Law', in *International Encyclopedia of the Social Sciences*, Vol. 9 (Chicago, Ill.: Macmillan & Free Press), vol. IX, pp. 78–81.
Harsin, Paul (1928), *Les Doctrines monétaires et financières en France du XVIe au XVIIIe siècle* (Paris: Alcan).
Harsin, Paul (1952), 'Keynes, Law et Montesquieu', *Bulletin de la Classe des Lettres et Sciences morales et politiques de l'Académie Royale de Belgique*, 5th ser., 38, pp. 27–36.
Harsin, Paul (1977), 'Essai de bibliographie critique', in E. Faure, *La Banqueroute de Law* (Paris: Gallimard), pp. 691–722.
Hayek, F. A. (1972), *Choice in Currency: A Way to Stop Inflation* (London: Institute of Economic Affairs).
Hoselitz, Bert F. (1956), 'Entrepreneurship and Capital Formation in France and Britain Since 1700', in National Bureau of Economic Research, *Capital Formation and Economic Growth* (Princeton, NJ: Princeton University Press).
Laffitte, J. (1932), *Mémoires de Laffitte (1767–1844)*, edited by Paul Duchon (Paris: Firmin-Dutot).
Law, John (1705), *Money and Trade Considered: With a Proposal for Supplying the Nation with Money* (Edinburgh: Heirs and successors to A. Anderson).
Levasseur, E. (1854/1970), *Recherches historiques sur le système de Law*, reprint edn. (New York: Burt Franklin).
Lévy-Leboyer, Maurice (1976), 'L'Affermissement du système capitaliste: les transformations structurelles', in Fernand Braudel and Ernest Labrousse (eds), *Histoire économique et sociale de la France*. Vol. III: *L'Evénement de l'ère industrielle, 1789–1880* (Paris: Presses universitaires de France).
Liesse, André (1908), *Portraits des financiers: Ouvrard, Mollien, Gaudien, Baron Louis, Corvetto, Laffitte, de Villèle* (Paris: Alcan).
Lüthy, Herbert (1959), *La Banque protestante en France de la révocation de l'édit de Nantes à la révolution*. Vol. I: *Dispersion et regroupement (1685–1730)* (Paris: SEVPEN).

McKinnon, Ronald I. (1973), *Money and Capital in Economic Development* (Washington, DC: Brookings Institution).

Meuvret, Jean (1970), 'Monetary Circulation of the Sixteenth and Seventeenth Centuries', in Rondo Cameron (ed.), *Essays in French Economic History* (Homewood, Ill.: Irwin), pp. 140–9.

Ministère des Finances et Ministère de l'Agriculture, du Commerce et des Travaux Publics (1865–7), *Enquête sur les principes et les faits généraux qui régissent la circulation monétaire et fiduciaire* (Paris: Imprimerie impériale, 6 vols).

Mollien, Francois Nicholas (1845), *Mémoires d'un ministre du Trésor Public, 1780–1815* (Paris: Fournier, 4 vols).

Morgan, E. Victor (1943), *The Theory and Practice of Central Banking, 1797–1913* (Cambridge: Cambridge University Press).

Palgrave's *Dictionary of Political Economy* (1925–6/1963), revised edn., edited by Henry Higgs (New York: Kelley. 3 vols).

Pereire, Emile and Pereire, Isaac (1834, 1868), *Du Système des banques et du système de M. Law*, 1st and 2nd edns. (Paris); cited in Harsin (1977).

Pereire, Isaac (1865), *Principes de la constitution des banques et de l'organisation du crédit* (Paris: Paul Dupont).

Pose, Alfred (1942), *La Monnaie et ses institutions* (Paris: Presses universitaires de France, 2 vols).

Redlich, Fritz (1948), 'Jacques Laffitte and the Beginnings of Investment Banking in France', *Bulletin of the Business Historical Society*, vol. 22 (December), pp. 137–60.

Schumpeter, Joseph A. (1954), *A History of Economic Analysis* (London: Allen & Unwin).

Shaw, Edward S. (1973), *Financial Deepening in Economic Development* (New York: Oxford University Press).

Sibert, J. (1958), 'Essai sur quelques problèmes économiques et monétaires de J. Law à J. M. Keynes', thesis, University of Lyon.

Temin, Peter (1971), 'Three Problems in Economic History', *Journal of Economic History*, vol. 31, no. 1 (March), pp. 58–75.

Van der Wee, H. (1977), 'Money, Credit and Banking Systems', in E. E. Rich and C. H. Wilson, *The Cambridge History of Europe. Vol. V: The Economic Organization of Early Modern Europe* (Cambridge: Cambridge University Press), pp. 290–392.

Vaubel, Roland (1977), 'Free Currency Competition', *Weltwirtschaftliches Archiv*, vol. 113, no. 3, pp. 435–59.

Vergeot, J. B. (1918), *Le Crédit comme stimulant et régulateur de l'industrie: La conception saint-simonienne, ses réalisations, son application au problème bancaire d'après-guerre* (Paris: Jouve).

Viner, Jacob (1937), *Studies in the Theory of International Trade* New York: Harper).

Wilson, Edwin B. (1948), 'John Law and John Keynes', *Quarterly Journal of Economics*, vol. 62 (May), pp. 381–95.

Wolowski, Louis (1864), *La Question des banques* (Paris: Guillaumin).

Wolowski, Louis (1867a), ' "La Question des banques", réponse a M. Michel Chevalier', *Journal des Economistes*, 3rd ser., 5–6, pp. 387–413.

Wolowski, Louis (1867b), ' "La Question des banques". II: Observations de M. Wolowski', *Journal des Economistes*, 3rd ser., 5–6, pp. 72–3.

Wolowski, Louis (1869), *La Question monétaire*, 2nd edn. (Paris: Guillaumin).

Part II

Compare and Contrast

4

Financial Institutions and Economic Development: A Comparison of Great Britain and France in the Eighteenth and Nineteenth Centuries

I

It has long been a conventional view that Great Britain had a higher level of income per capita than France in the eighteenth and nineteenth centuries. Gregory King put the difference in 1688 as 10 to 30 percent (Deane and Cole, 1967, p. 38 n. 1). Angus Maddison is the latest of economic historical statisticians to compare the two (among others) and reached the conclusion that the levels of living were about equal in 1700, but that the United Kingdom had pulled ahead by 1820, increased its lead to 1870, and slipped thereafter to be widely outclassed by 1979. His (Maddison, 1982, p. 8) data for gross domestic product per head at US 1970 prices show

	1700	1820	1870	1950	1979
France	275[a]	377	627	1693	4981
United Kingdom	288	454	972	2094	3981

[a] 1701–1710.

This conventional numerical evidence was supported by the qualitative testimony of contemporary travelers, notably Adam Smith (1776/1937, pp. 6, 91, 187, 394–5), Arthur Young (1790/1969), Alex de Tocqueville (1833/1958, pp. 94–116), Johan Conrad Fischer (Redlich, 1968), John Bowring (1840, p. 50), Michel Chevalier (1838, I, Letters 1, 2) and others (E. Jones, 1930, especially ch. VI), though not Friedrich Engels (1892). In his magisterial *History of Economic Analysis* Schumpeter asserts that description by travelers of the conditions they observed forms an important part of the economic literature in the prestatistical period and that neglect of this is apt to distort seriously our picture of the economies of those centuries and to hide the full extent of

Reprinted with permission from Explorations in Economic History, *vol. 21 (Academic Press Inc., 1984), pp. 103–24.*

the fact-finding work actually done (1954, p. 158). The conventional
view was presumably reflected in the inability of French industry to
compete with exports from Britain, either in the French market after
tariffs were reduced in 1786 in the Treaty of Vergennes (until the French
revolution three years later) (Gouraud, 1854, II, pp. 21–7, 45–6) or in
third markets such as the United States. French exports to the United
States consisted of luxuries such as wine, brandy, and silk, whereas
British goods were for the most part necessities such as textiles,
hardware, iron, coal, and the like (Fohlen, 1978, *passim*). Further
support for the view comes from such simple tests as the proportion of
the labor force engaged in agriculture – 51.4 percent in France in 1856
after a considerable movement off the farm into the city, compared to 29
percent for Britain in 1851 (INSEE, 1957, p. 3; Mitchell and Deane,
1963, p. 60). Even after correction for the amount of food subtracted by
exports or furnished through imports by exports of manufactures, these
data show through Engel's law that Britain had a considerably higher
level of living than France. Still another test was furnished by the
anxiety of French entrepreneurs to steal British industrial secrets, to buy
British machinery, and to import British workmen and businessmen
(Ballot, 1923). The conventional wisdom regarded the Englishman as a
big man who ate meat while the smaller Frenchman ate bread and wore
clogs (Braudel, 1977, p. 91).

So ingrained was this view that a small army of scholars sought to
explain it. France's economic retardation has been variously attributed
to lack of coal (Kindleberger, 1964, pp. 17–23), the family firm (*ibid*, ch.
6), aristocratic values (Pitts, 1957, 1963), the failure of the family farm
to release labor in adequate amounts for transfer into industry
(Gerschenkron, 1953, p. 11), the traditional resistance to technical
change in agriculture (Augé-Laribé, 1950, *passim*, but especially
pp. 54–5, 80, 157), and the backwardness of French banking until the
establishment of the Crédit Mobilier in 1852. The retardation, in fact,
was close to being overexplained, with more equations than there were
unknowns (Kindleberger, 1964, ch. 15).

Like so much other, this conventional wisdom has been attacked by
revisionists and stood on its head, in this case by Patrick O'Brien and
Cagler Keyder (1978), who have sought to prove in an econometric
exercise that France was richer per capita in 1786, and, apart from the
years of the Napoleonic wars, grew faster up to about 1870. The authors
dismiss the contemporary travelers, and the simple tests just noted,
relying rather on estimates on the volume and value of physical product
worked out by Marczewski (1961), Markovitch (1964–6), and Toutain
(1961). They explicitly do not include services in their measurements
on the ground that much of the services should be included as
intermediate product, used up in producing final product (O'Brien and
Keyder, 1978, p. 31). It is not completely clear that they are aware of the
dangers implicit in ignoring *a priori* information in econometric
testing,[1] or in using time series for cross-sectional analysis (Fisher,
1962). Another observer, François Crouzet, who is skeptical of the more
threadbare versions of Franco-British comparisons of real income, is

disposed to regard the Marczewski benchmark of 1786, on which most of the econometric comparison rests, as far too high (Crouzet, 1970, especially pp. 271–3; Crouzet, 1972, p. 99²). Nor do O'Brien and Keyder seem adequately cognizant of the wide regional differences in levels of development and rates of growth in 18th-century France. Edward Whiting Fox wrote of two Frances, one of Paris, Lyons, and Strasbourg (on the inland trade routes) and the coastal cities, which grew rapidly in the eighteenth century, and the other inland that was relatively stagnant except for the island of farmland around Paris which had been drained of excess labor and forced to adopt improved agricultural methods (1971). Braudel speaks of three Frances, one of rich merchants, using gold to settle its balances, another of middle-class producers and traders using silver, and a third in the countryside, heavily dependent on the exchange of goods and services in barter, with only a small part of its economy monetized and that using copper (Braudel, 1977, *passim* and p. 100). An interesting methodological exercise for economic historians would be to compare the aggregative econometric approach of O'Brien and Keyder with the historian's reliance on archival evidence, set out in Eugen Weber's *Peasants into Frenchmen, The Modernization of Rural France, 1870–1914* (1976). This latter shows in detail, from police, prefect, and other records, the ignorance, hunger, and poverty of the French peasant, who was not brought fully into French society on an integrated basis until after 1870. Despite the adoption of the metric system during the French revolution and the *franc germinal* in 1803, the peasant was still reckoning in *pieds* and *livres* 70 years later (*ibid.*, ch. 4, entitled 'The King's Foot').

The purpose of this exercise, however, is not to attack the O'Brien and Keyder thesis head on, but to pose another rough test for it. It should be said in their defense that their conclusions are put forward tentatively and with frequent recognition of the limitations of their statistical method. It seems to me nevertheless that the fact that French financial institutions lagged behind those of Great Britain by about a century should be added to the other qualitative demonstrations – the share of agriculture in the labor force, travelers' opinions, the flow of technological information, and a considerable amount of direct measurement – to buttress the conventional view that Britain was richer than France for most of the eighteenth and nineteenth centuries.

II

The most careful work in the realm of financial institutions has been done by Raymond W. Goldsmith, who notes their development in the terms shown in Table 1 (1969, p. 34). Table 1 is necessarily summary, but it may be noted that the third and fourth categories are alternative paths to financial development. There were lone central banks, for example, in Sweden (established 1668), in Norway (1816), and in Denmark (1818) down almost to 1850 (Hovde, 1943, p. 242), while in Holland and Hamburg there were over the same period (as Sweden) deposit banks – the Bank of Amsterdam (1608–1782) and the Bank of Hamburg (1609–1873) – but no central bank (Van Dillen, 1934; Sieveking, 1934). Parenthetically it is ironic that Goldsmith writes of a 'full complement of financial instruments' in 1969 before the flowering of such institutions as the Euro-currency market, credit cards, money-market funds, repurchase agreements ('repos'), negotiable orders of withdrawal ('NOW accounts'), bank holding companies, and, in Kuwait, trade in securities with post-dated checks.

Table 1   *Types of Financial Institutions*

	Characteristic	Historical sample (Europe only)
1	Only commodity money, no financial institutions, but occasional credit transactions.	Early antiquity
2	Metallic money, bills of exchange and indigenous small-scale financial institutions (moneylenders)	Classical antiquity; most parts of medieval Europe and large parts of Europe through the 18th century
3	Central bank the only, or predominant, financial institution	France and Russia (early 19th-century)
4	Deposit banks, and no central bank and no paper money	Medieval Italian cities (from 13th century on)
5	Multiplicity of note issuing and deposit banks, beginning of other financial institutions	Scotland in first half of 19th century; United States to 1913
6	Central bank, modern deposit banks; indigenous small-scale financial operators	
7	Central bank, deposit banks, beginnings of other financial institutions (particularly savings banks, mortgage banks, development banks and insurance companies	Western Europe from mid-19th century to World War I
8	Full complement of financial institutions and instruments	

The pattern laid out by Goldsmith is of course not one of tight coupling between economic growth and financial development. At most he finds (among his twelve conclusions) 'rough parallelism . . . in most countries' (1969, p. 48). He notes that in some countries financial institutions are ahead of economic development because of the 'strong influence of the more advanced countries' (*ibid.*, p. 47) but does not call attention to the opposite condition, where economic development has a long lead on money and banking.

While the presumption against France having a lag of roughly a century between its economic development and its financial institutions is only a presumption, it is a strong one. To have achieved such a position would have required some substitute for the normal relationship of rough concurrence, either

(a) an enormous superiority of France over Britain in industry and agriculture, accompanied by inferior commerce matched by inferior monetary and banking institutions (this would have been at variance with Adam Smith's dictum that division of labor is limited by the extent of the market);

(b) broadly the same degree of comparative development in production and commerce in the two countries, but substitution of other means of payments in France for the bank notes and bank deposits that lagged; or

(c) parallel production and distribution mechanisms in the two countries, lagging monetary and banking institutions in France, but much greater efficiency in such French institutions than the equivalent British.

None of these possible explanations is supportable by evidence. That French productive methods in industry were inferior to British is attested by the flow of technology. In agriculture, Dutch methods penetrated southeast England rapidly in the eighteenth century, northeast France slowly. In commerce, both France and England struggled to free themselves from dependence on Amsterdam's entrepot trade. British success was more striking than that of France, which suffered from major losses in the colonial trade due to wars, but in the 18th century at least the French made great progress against Holland (Crouzet, 1968, pp. 250–6). The inland bill of exchange was perhaps more developed in France than in Britain up to the 1860s when it began to disappear in the latter in favor of the more efficient lower-cost system of payment by check. The international sterling bill went on of course to world dominance. And in the boom of the 1850s even the inland bill in England showed great vitality (Hughes, 1960, pp. 258–65), at a time when the Bank of France was discounting railroad bonds to sustain the boom (Dauphin-Meunier, 1936, pp. 97–101). The possibility that French bank notes and bank deposits were used more efficiently than those in Britain is hard to countenance. Abundant evidence testifies to the fact that French banks were slow and inefficient, giving poor service for high commissions as compared with British institutions (Pose, 1942, I, p. 341).

There is thus little basis for believing that France had an adequate substitute for lagging financial institutions which would enable it to have a higher level of living than Britain with inferior money and banking. If then it can be demonstrated that France did lag behind Britain in financial development by approximately a century, the case that French economic development was equal to or superior to the British – by whatever path – is seriously if not fatally weakened.

Unfortunately for our purposes, Goldsmith's study of financial institutions relies on statistical demonstration and is therefore limited, for the period of our interest, to the last quarter or fifth of the nineteenth century and the years to 1913. On the whole, data extracted for France and Great Britain from the rich tables for many countries show that France was well behind Great Britain in financial development from 1860 to 1913, but had been catching up. The central statistic in Goldsmith's analysis is the financial interrelation ratio (FIR), which compares the volume of all financial assets, including those of financial institutions, households, and government bodies, with gross national product. On Goldsmith's findings this starts at some low level such as 0.20 and rises with development until about 1 or 1½ when it levels off (Goldsmith, 1969, p. 45). In 1913 the French FIR was 0.79 as compared with 1.04 for Britain on the basis of observed values, or 1.30 on calculated values (*ibid.*, Table 7-10, p. 338). Within the FIR as a whole, the ratio of the assets of financial institutions to gross national product developed as follows:

Assets (%) of Financial Institutions/GNP
(Goldsmith, 1969, Table 4-13, p. 209)

	1860	1880	1900	1913
France	19	50	96	104
Great Britain	57	95	93	103

which shows French financial institutions reaching the leveling-off stage at the end of the nineteenth century, but well below those of Britain in 1860. The variety of financial institutions for the same dates is given by the numbers of different kinds:

Varieties of Financial Institutions (Goldsmith, 1969,
Table 8-1, p. 345): Number of Types of Financial
Institutions in Operation

	1860	1880	1900	1913
France	9	9	11	11
Great Britain	13	14	16	17

As financial sophistication grows, the weight of central banks among the totality of financial assets diminishes, and that of deposit banks rises for a certain distance. This is illustrated by data for France and Britain again showing the wide gap in the early part of the period covered by comparable data and its narrowing:

Net Issue Ratios of Central Banks (Goldsmith, 1969, Table
5-2, p. 218) in % of period's gross national product

	1861–1880	1881–1900	1901–1913
France	0.45	0.30	0.35
Great Britain	0.09	0.06	0.02

Net Issue Ratios of Deposit Banks (Goldsmith, 1969,
Table 5-6, p. 227) in % of period's gross national product

	1861–1880	1881–1900	1901–1913
France	0.46	0.45	1.42
Great Britain	1.61	1.06	0.97

These data and others presented by Goldsmith show a rapid convergence of financial institutions in most respects by the end of the nineteenth century or 1913, but something of a gap – often a wide one – in 1860. In the main portion of the paper, we start at the other end of the modern era with the early development of particular institutions, and demonstrate that for many institutions the gap in time was close to a century.

III

The Bank of England was established in 1694, the Bank of France in 1800 – a gap of 106 years. Proposals for the creation of a major bank had been put forward in Britain continuously through the seventeenth century, for the most part patterned after the Bank of Amsterdam, a deposit bank that did not issue notes (Richards, 1965). When it came to the event, however, the founders – financed by the liquidation of stocks of wine that could not be replenished because of the Nine Years' War (D. W. Jones, 1972) – loaned the government £1,200,000 in a purchase of debt in exchange for the right to issue bank notes. The earliest issue of bank notes by a central bank in Europe was that of the Swedish Riksbank in 1668, patterned after the copper notes issued by copper mines because the copper money itself was so awkward to handle because of its bulk and weight (Heckscher, 1954, pp. 88–91). In theory, but not in practice, these notes were backed by metallic reserves to the extent of 100 percent. In Britain, government payment orders designating the priority in which certain bills would be paid had circulated late in the seventeenth century as hand-to-hand currency (Richards, 1965, p. 60). The Bank of England note issue, backed by government credit, however, represented a major innovation.

The long lag in the creation of the Bank of France behind the Bank of England was the result of the unhappy experience of France in the Mississippi bubble when the Banque Royale collapsed in 1720, having issued notes that proved to be worthless (Levasseur, 1854/1970); in the relative failure of the Caisse d'escompte, formed in 1776, reorganized when it overloaned to Louis XVI (Harsin, 1933, pp. 88–9); and in the *assignats*, which exploded as paper money in 1795 (S. E. Harris, 1930). Napoleonic finances were peculiarly chaotic at the end of the century. Two of the steps designed to restore order were the establishment of the Bank of France and the issue of a new currency, the *franc germinal*, in 1803, to replace the *livre*. French collective memory of the Law period and his *Banque générale* and *Banque royale* was so sharp that almost no institutions known as banks were formed until the second half of the nineteenth century, but rather *crédits, caisses, comptoirs*, and *sociétés*. The Bank of France, the guess may be hazarded, was named a bank after the pattern of the Bank of England, which was highly regarded by the French for its century of successful experience (Liesse, 1909, p. 12).

The development of the Bank of England earlier than the Bank of France was evidently responsible for the earlier development of central banking theory in England, although the Bank of France had an opportunity to catch up by studying the Bank of England's experience. E. V. Morgan and F. W. Fetter have studied the development of central-bank theory in the first half of the nineteenth century, and this period is rich in learning with its controversies, crises, and legislation (Morgan, 1943; Fetter, 1965). But the Bank of England learned intuitively in the eighteenth century how to behave as a lender of last resort (Ashton, 1959, p. 111), and Thornton had an excellent understanding of the function in 1802, even though the better-known rationalization of the process had to wait for Bagehot's *Lombard Street* in 1873. In France, the Bank of France cut down on lending to the market in the crisis of 1818, although the governor, Jacques Laffitte, offered private assistance to the Bourse (Gille, 1959, pp. 293–300; Lévy-Leboyer, 1964, p. 483 n.). It did far better in the crisis of 1825, but then forgot the technique of acting as lender of last resort until ultimately it defeated the regional banks in 1848 and secured a monopoly of the note issue (Bouvier, 1973, p. 80).

For a time, the Bank of France was readier to emulate the Bank of England's discount policy, developed for the most part in the troubles of the 1830s and early 1840s after the failure of Palmer's rule (Lévy-Leboyer, 1982). From 1856 to 1865 the Bank of France departed from its initial policy of holding the discount rate steady at 4 percent, and sought to control the money market by varying the rate. At the end of the period, however, it returned to a rate that was virtually fixed and used a very different technique of varying the proportions of bullion and foreign coin, and of gold and silver, when it wanted to affect external drains (Liesse, 1909, pp. 86, 120). The Bank of France's ratio of specie to liabilities was far higher than that of the Bank of England, suggesting a reluctance to expand the ratio of financial claims to national product and hence a lower stage of economic development.

Substitutes for coin before bank notes have been noted in Britain about the 1670s, when treasury orders were used in payments. French rescriptions served the same purpose in the second half of the eighteenth century (Bosher, 1970, pp. 14, 94–5). Bank notes proper were issued by the Bank of England and the country banks. The former were originally issued in a minimum denomination of £20, reduced to £10 in 1754, and to £5 in 1794 during the crisis caused by the canal mania and the Reign of Terror in Paris. Notes of £2 and £1 were put out in 1797 after suspension of gold convertibility, withdrawn in 1817 prior to the resumption of 1819, but put back into circulation once more in the crisis of 1825. Bank of England note circulation was assisted by petitions of merchants and investors, asserting their own willingness to receive the notes in payment and urging the public to do the same, the first in 1745 when the Young Pretender marched on Derby, invading from Scotland, the second in 1797 when panic broke out as the French landed a small detachment at Fishguard (Andréadès, 1909, p. 151; O'Brien, 1971, I, p. 13).

Bank of England notes circulated mainly in London in the eighteenth century. Elsewhere there were various substitutes – domestic bills of exchange in Lancashire (Ashton, 1953), and notes of country banks more widely. The country banks flourished in several waves, followed by collapse and shrinkage, the first in the 1750s, the next in the canal mania of the early 1790s, and a third major one in the 1820s (Pressnell, 1956). With the establishment of Bank of England branches in 1826, and ultimately the Bank Act of 1844, the Bank of England acquired a monopoly of the note issue, just about the time that the Bank of France did.

In France, bank notes had a limited circulation before 1850. The Bank of France was reluctant both to expand itself and to encourage other note-issuing banks outside Paris or its own branches. Efforts were made by Napoleon, by Jacques Laffitte, and by the regional banks, established over the opposition of the Bank of France in the 1830s, to expand note circulation in the provinces, but the Bank persuaded the Conseil d'Etat to limit the regional banks, first in setting a high minimum denomination for the notes they could issue, and second by refusing them the right to redeem their notes in Paris, which permission would have extended the area in which the notes would have circulated (Gille, 1970, pp. 1–101). Bank of France notes themselves were initially set at a minimum denomination of 500 francs (roughly £20) in Paris, 250 francs in the provinces (Bigo, 1947, p. 75). A proposal to reduce the denomination to 100 francs was resisted by the Bank of France in 1846 and defeated. In the financial crisis of 1848 a more extreme proposal to go to Ff50 (roughly £2) was accepted, just under a century after the denomination of the British bank notes had been reduced from a minimum of £20 to £10. One rough estimate suggests that the use of bank notes in France rose from 7 percent of all transactions before 1850 to 20 percent in 1856 and 70 percent by 1885 (Bigo, 1947, p. 59). Other transactions, it should be noted, were carried out almost entirely in coin and bills of exchange, and hardly at all in checks drawn on bank deposits.

Bank notes were thus used to a limited extent as a medium of exchange. For store of value the peasant used the wool sock (*bas de laine*) and gold coin. Even businessmen continued to keep large amounts of ready cash in coin on their premises. Wicksell quotes a witness to the English Gold and Silver Commission of 1887 who thought it remarkable that a hotel owner in Southern France with a turnover of 1 million francs annually should point to his safe and say 'that's my bank'. Wicksell compares this with the father of Alexander Pope who was said by Macaulay in his *History of England* to have retired from business at the end of the seventeenth century with a hoard of £20,000 in gold and silver coins on which he drew for household expenses for the rest of his life (Wicksell, 1935, p. 9). If the two cases are in any way representative, perhaps of the last remnants of the practice, the time difference, it should be noted, is almost two centuries.

The use of bank deposits as money began slowly in Britain, but picked up speed in the first half of the nineteenth century. It is significant that the London and Westminster Bank stockholders thought it worthwhile to establish a bank in London in 1836 when it could do so only if it renounced the right of note issue and relied entirely on deposits (Gregory, 1936, I, p. 67). By the time the Bank Act of 1844 limited the amount of bank notes the Bank of England could issue, the use of deposits was spreading rapidly. The National and Provincial Bank, organized as a joint-stock company in 1833 entirely outside the 65-mile zone centered on London in order to be able to issue bank notes, moved into London in 1866, giving up the note-issue privilege, at a time when it had 122 branches (Withers, 1933, p. 67).

France was not a century behind in the early use of deposits, as the major deposit banks sprang up at the end of the 1850s and in the early 1860s. It is difficult to find comparable dates for the ratio of bank deposits to notes in circulation which in 1913 was said to be 3:2 in France, 7:1 in Great Britain, and 20:1 in the United States.

As implied in the last paragraph, the spread of joint-stock banks was less than half of a century apart in the two countries. The Bank Act of 1826 permitted joint-stock banks with the right of note issue outside a circle of 65 miles from London, and from 1833 banks were formed as joint-stock corporations within the circle without the note issue but relying on deposits. As early as 1847 Lord Overstone excoriated Colonel Robert Torrens who had said that he was contemplating regarding bank deposits as money, and drew from Torrens an object surrender: 'I throw deposits to the dogs' (O'Brien, 1971, II, p. 717). But Lord Overstone's intransigence on this and other monetary issues (such as the decimalization of the British money) was notorious. By the 1850s, deposits dominated bank notes in Britain at a time when bank notes were just getting going in France.

French deposit banking can perhaps measure its start from 1848 when the Comptoir de Paris that later developed into the Comptoir National d'Escompte was set up in crisis, along with a great many other *comptoirs* in the provinces to provide a third signature for bills of exchange so that they could be discounted at the Bank of France. A more secure starting point, however, is the formation of the Crédit Industriel et Commercial in 1859, closely followed by the founding of the Crédit Lyonnais in 1863 and the Société Générale pour favoriser le commerce et l'industrie in 1864, on the average perhaps 30 years or a generation behind the major British joint-stock banks such as Barclays, Lloyds, the Midland, the National Provincial, and the London and Westminster. In 1855, England and Wales had 409 banks with 1,185 banking offices (Nishimura, 1971, pp. 80–1). In 1863, whether before or after the formation of the Crédit Lyonnais is not clear, it was said that three-quarters of French towns lacked access to banking, access being defined as a bank within 30 km. France had 115 'bankable places' in 1881. By 1913 the number had risen to 585 (Bigo, 1947, p. 116). It is not clear to me whether 'bankable places' should be equated to banks or to bank offices, although presumably the latter is meant. If the expression means banks, there were 42 percent more banks in France in 1913 than England and Wales had in 1855; if on the other hand it refers to bank offices, France in 1913 had half the number that England and Wales had almost 60 years earlier.

Summing up his study of French, English, and Scottish banking in 1967, Rondo Cameron stated:

> Comparison with English and Scottish data reveals that the complaints of French businessmen were justified: bank facilities were too few, and bank resources pitifully inadequate. At the end of its 'take-off' period, the French economy had approximately the same bank density as Scotland had had in the middle of the eighteenth century. France had fewer bank assets per inhabitant in the mid-nineteenth century than England or Scotland had had in 1770, and in 1870 had not yet reached the position that they held before the beginning of the nineteenth century. (Cameron, 1967, p. 110)[3]

These gaps of 70 years are roughly three-quarters of a century. It should be noted, however, that Cameron has changed his position. In a recent paper with Charles Freedeman he distinctly sides with O'Brien and Keyder and other revisionists, though he is willing to grant that O'Brien and Keyder exaggerate the position, holding that France vies with England for the title of 'First Industrial Nation', and even citing scholarly contributions since 1961 that point to significant contributions to French industrialization by banks in the first half of the nineteenth century (Cameron and Freedeman, 1983, especially pp. 19–21). This finding, however, is not reconciled with those of the 1967 study.

The gap can be stretched from a generation back to a century by noting that the London clearing house was established in 1775, the Paris clearing house in 1872 (Lévy-Leboyer, 1976, p. 347). The comparison is unfair, however, since the London clearing house was created by private banks only for the exchange of notes – the London joint-stock banks were not admitted for the clearing of deposits until the 1850s – whereas the Paris clearing house began with deposits from the beginning.

A similar comparison that is tempting but must be rejected concerns the date for adoption of the gold standard in the two countries. Both countries fixed the price of gold that lasted for almost 200 years, Britain with Isaac Newton as master of the mint in 1717 that lasted with interruptions for the Napoleonic Wars and World War I until 1931, France in 1726 that lasted with more frequent and longer interruptions *de jure* until 1928. But Britain in 1717 was on a bimetallic standard and used largely silver. The gold standard was adopted *de facto* in 1774 when silver was demonetized, France a century later in 1875. It is not self-evident, however, that the gold standard represented a stage in advance of the bimetallism which prevailed in France to 1875; in fact the gold standard with subsidiary silver coinage in England and bimetallism in

France coexisted effectively over the period from 1815 to 1865, when the discovery of the Comstock lode in silver in Nevada, the development of the cyanide process, and later the German switch to the gold standard involving massive sales of silver destroyed silver as a monetary metal. It is true that England ran the gold standard with greater economy of investment in reserves than France, and could on this count be said to have been more highly developed. The dates of adoption of the gold standard cannot be used to measure the gap.

We shift from money and banking to financial integration, or the extent to which the money and capital markets of a country stretch from the financial corner into the far corners of the nation. Here the appropriate criterion is the extent to which the rate of interest on money and the yield on bonds are the same throughout the country, but historical data on a consistent basis are lacking for the period. One could also track the movement of funds in response to changes in demand and supply, whether of rents which move from countryside England to London in May and October, or the seasonal movements from Paris to the provinces after the harvest, and the reverse in the spring. In France, the emphasis in the literature has consistently been how disparate were various localities financially. Marseilles was chronically short of specie because of its trade with the Levant, which drained it of silver (Gille, 1970, pp. 67–8). Dijon, lying between rich Lyons with its silk and rich Paris, the financial center, groaned under a 9 percent interest rate in the first half of the nineteenth century when Lyons enjoyed 3 percent and Paris 4 percent (*ibid.*, pp. 55, 57). John Law, Napoleon, Jacques Laffitte, and Emile Pereire continuously harped on the need to extend the financial institutions of Paris to the countryside, or to build new ones there (Levasseur, 1854/1970, p. 51; Mollien, 1845, III, pp. 137–8; Liesse, 1908, pp. 276–8; Ministère des Finances, 1865, I. p. 604). The Bank of France was attacked as the 'Bank of Paris' as late as the formal inquiry into money and banking published in 1865–1867 (Ministère des Finances, 1865, II, pp. 164, 347), though it should be noted that the Bank of England was characterized as the 'Bank of London', though by a Frenchman and in 1810 (Mollien, 1845, I, pp. 453–5). Some bankers such as LeCoulteux of Rouen and Depont of Nantes maintained residences and counting houses both in the ports and in Paris; but many others like Ouvrard pulled up their local roots completely, or, having left the ports during the Revolution, returned to Paris only when things settled down (Lévy-Leboyer, 1964, p. 434).

In Britain, such a banker as Smith of Nottingham established a London branch in 1758, one year after founding the house, and then branches in Lincoln and Hull in the 1770s and 1780s, respectively (Leighton-Boyce, 1958, p. 20). He was prepared to move money about. A bill broker in London testifying before the Bullion Committee in 1810 observed that the savings of the agricultural areas of East Anglia were transmitted to Lancashire by way of London, a remark quoted by Bagehot in *Lombard Street* at a time (1873) when it was no longer true (Bagehot, 1873/1978, p.53). Lloyds Bank tried to keep its deposit rates fixed in Birmingham and variable (following bank rate) in London but after time was unable to do so as Birmingham depositors transferred their accounts to London when the rate there rose significantly above the Birmingham level (Sayers, 1957, pp. 165, 270). Full equality of rates was not reached, however, until 1920. Adequate historical studies of the process of integration of French and British financial markets have not been produced along the lines of the analysis of McKinnon (1973), who is concerned about the repression of financial markets in developing countries, or of Shaw (1973), whose somewhat different emphasis is on financial deepening, but the impression remains that the English market was financially integrated, or well on its way to financial integration, long before the French. It is true that the filling out of the national structure of branches by the major deposit banks took place virtually simultaneously, beginning in the 1850s for England and the 1860s for France, with spurts in the 1890s and just before the war. The process was associated with the development of railroad networks which were at most 20 years apart for the main lines.

It is true that there remained some considerable differentiation between the City and the provincial capital markets in England, and between Paris and the countryside in France. In neither case was integration complete. In both countries, moreover, there was a strong suspicion of the Populist type that the financial center sucked funds to it to pour abroad in search of commissions, at some cost to the capital needs of industry in the provinces, which had to rely primarily on internal funds (see, e.g., Lewis, 1978, p. 176ff). Since London started to lend abroad on a major scale after 1817 to 1825, and France a few years later, initially to Belgium, and more widely in the 1850s, this possibility, which is not an established fact, might have occurred, if at all, 30 years earlier in England than in France. The peak of the criticism against foreign lending, however, occurs more nearly simultaneously in the 1880s and 1890s.

Finally, on the question of integration, it should be observed that the provincial capital markets that sprang up in England in the 1830s and 1840s were unmatched, as far as I am able to ascertain, by anything as vigorous in the furnishing of equity capital to industry in France (Thomas, 1973).

So much – perhaps not very much – for money and banking. We turn briefly to insurance. Historical accounts are full for Britain, meager, in easy access, for France. It is an interesting sidelight on the Coase theorem that the Hanseatic league failed altogether to produce financial insurance (or for that matter banking and the bill of exchange) even though they were in position to learn from the Italians. To finance trade they relied on a sort of barter – selling for local money in export markets and spending that money for imports to take with them – and settling imbalances on a bilateral basis in specie. To reduce the risks of trade their merchants owned one-tenth of ten different ships in short-term partnerships, rather than an entire ship covered by an insurance contact. Cargoes were divided among ships in a similar way (Dollinger, 1970, p. 156). They relied, in effect, on clumsy and costly real rather than financial insurance. Early forms of insurance lying between the real and the financial were bottomry and respondentia, loans on ships and cargoes, respectively, that were not to be repaid if the item borrowed against was lost.

In 1601 Britain passed a statute permitting insurance on the Italian model, but the first writing of insurance policies took place among individuals congregating informally in coffee houses after the London fire of 1666. The group gradually settled on the meeting place of Lloyds' Coffee House in 1688. A few years before that date, in 1680, a joint-stock insurance company, the Sun Assurance, was founded (Dickson, 1960). Two more major insurance companies were formed in 1720 at the time of the South Sea bubble – the Royal Exchange and the London Assurance (Supple, 1970). Further companies were formed later in the boom of 1823–25. These dates run about 100 years before the comparable institutions were established across the Channel.

For France there was informal insurance written by individuals along the lines of Lloyds' coffee house in Rouen in 1727–40 (Dawson, 1931), and somewhat later in Nantes and La Rochelle (Clark, 1971, ch. 9). *Armateurs* (ship owners and outfitters) in the last two places not only took out policies locally, but also placed insurance in Paris, in London and in the Netherlands, indicating that the facilities of the ports were inadequate. One account of a London marine underwriter in the eighteenth century stated that British insurers were able to write French policies at one fee in France, and reinsure for 100 percent in London at a much lower rate, to make a certain profit without risk (Sutherland, 1933, p. 51); the amounts cannot have been large or arbitrage would have equalized the rates. A financial corporation entered the insurance field briefly in France in 1780, formed by a Swiss financier named Clavière. This was 100 years after Sun Assurance. The company collapsed in the French revolution (Lüthy, 1961, II, pp. 352n, 712–13). In 1816, after French defeat in the Napoleonic wars, the first successful insurance was formed, Royale d'assurances maritimes. This was virtually a century after the Royal Exchange and London Assurance.

Perhaps the most significant difference in time between the development of British and French financial institutions occurred in the shift of royal and national finances from private enterprise to a bureaucratic system. The difference between the two countries lay not only in timing but also in method. In Britain, it was accomplished after the 'Glorious Revolution' of 1688 when the Stuarts, monarchs with the divine right of kings, were replaced by William and Mary whose powers were limited by Parliament (Dickson, 1967). In France, the transformation took place in 1794 and required a bloody revolution in which, among others, 28 *financiers* were guillotined (Bosher, 1970).

Tax farming and the parallel disbursement of royal revenues by individuals who bought the rights made sense at a time when kings had very little staff outside the royal household and when it was difficult in a venal society to trust civil servants, often at a distance from the capital, with the handling of monies that were frequently dealt in small sums (Ehrenberg, 1928, p. 37). For the system to work effectively, the monarch should auction off the rights – to farm taxes and customs duties, spend royal monies, operate monopolies in such goods as tobacco and sweet wine – at frequent intervals and for brief periods of time only. In theory, such a practice would give the king the revenues he was entitled to, and spend them efficiently, while earning the successful bidders a normal rate of return. In fact, however, the various tax-farmers, receivers-general, royal agents in France, having acquired their positions by purchase, tended to regard the offices as permanently theirs, private property that could be bequeathed or alienated through sale. Moreover, the several agents often invested or loaned the king's money in their possession for their own account, including lending it to another *officier*, so that the king was paying interest to lend money to himself. There were calls for reform of the system in the 1640s in England, and in the eighteenth century in France where Law, Turgot, and Necker – the first and last foreigners and outside the inner circle of *officiers* and *financiers* – sought vainly to change the system. The circumstances in which each was frustrated in his proposals for reform were complex as they involved, respectively, the Mississippi bubble (Levasseur, 1854/1970, p. 173ff; Lüthy, 1959, I, p. 414ff), the regulations in commerce in wheat (Lodge, 1931/1970, ch. 12), and fundamental errors in war finance (R. D. Harris, 1978). Contributing to the defeat in each case, however, was the unremitting opposition of the financial establishment. In Britain the transition took place quietly and smoothly after the Glorious Revolution as the new monarchs and the Parliament converted poachers into gamekeepers. Venality persisted in eighteenth-century Britain in other fields – the buying and selling of military commissions and parliamentary seats of rotten boroughs (Plumb, 1963, pp. 37–48). A crucial difference in the financial development of France and Britain, however, was that the change from private management of national finances to bureaucratic administration took place 100 years earlier in Britain than in France, and peacefully, without the necessity to destroy the existing apparatus.

The other important aspect of the 'financial revolution' in Britain was the development of a capital market for government debt. This is one area in which the French had been far in advance of the British, having worked out a system of *rentes* of many sorts from lifetime to perpetual that were bought and sold as early as the fifteenth century. Seventeenth-century Britain still had an antiquated system of different sorts of debt for different government branches: treasury orders, tallies (hazel sticks that were notched and split, with foil given to the purveyor and counter-foil kept by the department to be matched up when payment was made), soldiers' pay bills, seamen's tickets, and the like. The exchequer bill was developed as an instrument of general short-term debt in the 1690s, and the system of funding various obligations into long-term debt from the mid-1690s until the development of the perpetual consol in the 1740s. The histories of both the Bank of England and the South Sea Company were intimately bound up with this major reform in financial methods. Through the eighteenth century the four major securities traded on the London stock exchange were government stock and the shares of the Bank of England, the East India Company, and the South Sea Company.

In 1725 the prices of 14 securities were reported in the London press. By 1740, the number had risen to 40 (Cope, 1978). By comparison, the French Bourse in 1820 quoted only six securities (Freedeman, 1979).

Before summing up, it is important to observe that one financial institution came simultaneously to France and Britain: general incorporation. In both countries it arrived in two stages, in England in 1856 and 1863 (Cottrell, 1980, ch. 3), in France in 1863 and 1867 (Freedeman, 1979). General incorporation had existed in Britain up to 1720 when the Bubble Act was passed requiring royal assent for forming a limited-liability company. While the Bubble Act was repealed in 1824, general incorporation waited until Parliament became overwhelmed with petitions for charters in the railway mania of 1845 and 1846. All other business had to use partnership. French financing of private enterprise had had the advantage over British in that early provision was made for companies with silent partners of limited liability – the *société en commandite*. Generalized incorporation occurred in both countries as a powerful exception to the more usual pattern of a lag in French institutions ranging from a generation to a century behind the pattern in Britain.

IV

One can appeal not only to the facts set forth, but also to the perception, although this runs the risk of subjectivity, the score on which O'Brien and Keyder dismissed the evidence of travelers. French observers consistently thought of Britain as well in advance of their country in terms of financial capacity. Isaac Panchaud (Lüthy, 1961, II, p. 425, n21), Jacques Necker (R. D. Harris, 1978, p. 87) – the two Swiss to be sure, but intimately concerned with French finance – François Mollien (Mollien, 1845, I, p. 460), and at the turn of the last third of the nineteenth century Baron James de Rothschild (Ministère des Finances, 1865–7, I, p. 463) all thought that British credit institutions were more developed and effective than those of France. Rothschild was a monetarist. A Keynesian, Courcelle-Seneuil, said in the same inquiry that free entry into banking was currently needed to provide credit to agriculture in France, and quoted an unnamed Englishman to the effect that France was 150 years behind England and Scotland in banking (Ministère des Finance, 1865–7, III, pp. 38–9). As early as 1833, Emile Pereire, who had strong views on the need for financial reform in France, wrote that the British financial system was the 'secret of the industrial and political power of Britain' (quoted by Cameron, 1967, p. 128). The conclusion of Dickson's study of the 'financial revolution' in England was that British financial capacity enabled that country, with one-third the population, to defeat France in a series of wars in the eighteenth century (Dickson, 1967, pp. 9, 12). Again at the turn of the century, the British defeated a larger country, although the margin had shrunk after the British population explosion of the eighteenth century. British financial capacity enabled the country to subsidize allies and hire mercenaries (Sherwig, 1969). while French armies lived – while they could for a time – off *assignats* and victories, but ultimately depended on squeezing a defeated enemy after such battles as Jena and Austerlitz for indemnities to keep the Grand Army going (Thiers, 1895, I, p. 6). Jean-Baptiste Say on the French side said that England had been able to sustain the war by virtue of its credit system (E. Jones, 1930, p. 127).[4]

The lead of British over French financial institutions, extending up to a century in many particulars, surely does not prove that Britain had a higher per capita level of living and an equal or faster growth rate over most of the eighteenth and nineteenth centuries. In combination with the other evidence, however – of travelers, of the technological flow, the proportions engaged in agriculture, and competition in trade – it builds a strong case that Britain's economic development started in the eighteenth century, ahead of that of France, and remained ahead at least to the end of the nineteenth century.

A final point: the development of financial institutions may be necessary to economic development. It is not sufficient. The proof: the Netherlands in 1750 boasted the most highly developed financial institutions in the world, including such sophisticated features as futures markets, but failed to make the transition from commercial preeminence to industrialization for more than 100 years.

Notes

1   On the same point. J. H. Plumb (1963, p. 143) quotes Arthur Young who calls Richard Price's theory of England's depopulation in the eighteenth century absurd: 'Move your eye and you will behold nothing but great riches and greater resources. It is vain to talk of tables of births and lists of houses and windows, as proof of the loss of our people; the flourishing state of our agriculture, our manufactures, and our commerce, without general wealth, prove the contrary.'
2   The moderate revisionism of Crouzet is shown in the latter reference by his statement that per capita income in France was not half that in Great Britain, as some claimed, but more nearly 80 percent.
3   The overall conclusion of the essay runs in the same direction (Cameron, 1967, pp. 127–8).
4   One witness. Louis Wolowski, an economist of strong monetarist and pro-Bank of France views, quoted William Huskisson, the postwar Chancellor of the Exchequer, as saying that James Watt alone helped England fight France in the Napoleonic wars, and that the Bank of England in Pitt's lifetime did not (Ministère des Finances *et al.*, 1865–7, vol. II, p. 206).

References

Andréadès, A. (1909), *History of the Bank of England* (London: P. S. King).
Ashton, T. S. (1953), 'The Bill of Exchange and Private Banks in Lancashire, 1790–1830', in T. S. Ashton and R. S. Sayers (eds), *Papers in English Monetary History* (Oxford: Clarendon Press), pp. 37–49.
Ashton, T. S. (1959), *Economic Fluctuations in England, 1700–1800* (Oxford: Clarendon Press).

Augé-Laribé, Michel (1950), *La Politique agricole de la France de 1880 à 1940* (Paris: Presses universitaires de France).

Bagehot, Walter (1873/1978), *Lombard Street*; reprinted in N. St John Stevas (ed.), *The Collected Works of Walter Bagehot* (London: *The Economist*), vol. IX.

Ballot, Charles (1923), *Introduction du machinisme dans l'industrie française* (Paris: Reider).

Bigo, Robert (1947), *Les Banques françaises au cours du XIXe siècle* (Paris: Sirey).

Bosher, J. F. (1970), *French Finances, 1770–1795, from Business to Bureaucracy* (Cambridge: Cambridge University Press).

Bouvier, Jean, 1973), *Un Siècle de banque française* (Paris: Hachette Littérature).

Bowring, John (1840), 'Report on the German Commercial Union, 1840', *Parliamentary Papers, 1840*, vol. 21 (London: HMSO).

Braudel, Fernand (1977), *Afterthoughts on Material Civilization and Capitalism*, translated by Patricia M. Ranam (Baltimore, Md.: Johns Hopkins University Press).

Cameron, Rondo (1967), 'France 1800–1875', in Rondo Cameron *et al.* (eds), *Banking in the Early Stages of Industrialization. A Study in Comparative Economic History* (New York: Oxford University Press).

Cameron, Rondo and Freedeman, Charles E. (1983), 'French Economic Growth: A Radical Revision', *Social Science History*, vol. 7, pp. 3–30.

Chevalier, Michel (1838), *Lettres sur l'Amérique du Nord*, 3rd edn. (Paris: Gosselin).

Clark, John G. (1971), *La Rochelle and the Atlantic Economy during the Eighteenth Century* (Baltimore, Md.: Johns Hopkins University Press).

Cope, S. R. (1978), 'The Stock Exchange Revisited: A New Look at the Market in Securities in London in the Eighteenth Century', *Econometrica*, vol. 45, pp. 1–22.

Cottrell, P. L. (1980), *Industrial Finance, 1830–1914: The Finance and Organization of English Manufacturing Industry* (London: Methuen).

Crouzet, François (1968), 'Economie et société (1715–1789)', in F.-G. Pariset (ed.), *Bordeaux au XVIII siècle* (Bordeaux: Fédération historique de Sud-Ouest).

Crouzet, François (1970), 'An Annual Index of French Industrial Production in the 19th Century', in Rondo Cameron (ed.), *Essays in French Economic History* (Homewood, Ill.: Irwin).

Crouzet, François (1972), 'Western Europe and Great Britain: "Catching up" in the First Half of the Nineteenth Century', in A. J. Youngson (ed.), *Economic Development in the Long Run* (London: Allen & Unwin).

Dauphin-Meunier, A. (1936), *La Banque de France* (Paris: Gallimard).

Dawson, W. R. (1931), *Marine Underwriting at Rouen, 1727–42* (London: Lloyds).

Deane, Phyllis and Cole, W. A. (1967), *British Economic Growth, 1688–1959* (Cambridge: Cambridge University Press).

Dickson, P. G. M. (1960), *The Sun Insurance Office* (London: Oxford University Press).

Dickson, P. G. M. (1967), *The Financial Revolution in England: A Study in the Development of Public Credit, 1688–1756* (New York: St Martin's Press).

Dollinger, Philippe (1970), *The German Hansa*, translated and edited by D. S. Ault and S. H. Steinberg (Stanford, Calif.: Stanford University Press).

Ehrenberg, Richard (1928), *Capital and Finance in the Age of the Renaissance*, translated from the German by H. M. Lucas (New York: Harcourt Brace).

Engels, Friedrich (1892), *The Condition of the Working Class in England in 1844* (London: Allen & Unwin); reprinted 1950.

Fetter, Frank W. (1965), *Development of British Monetary Orthodoxy, 1797–1875* (Cambridge, Mass.: Harvard University Press).

Fisher, Franklin M. (1962), *A Priori Information and Time Series Analysis: Essays on Economic Theory and Measurement* (Amsterdam: North-Holland).

Fohlen, Claude (1978), 'The Commercial Failure of France in America', in *Two Hundred Years of Franco-American Relations, Bicentennial Colloquium of the Society for French Historical Studies at Newport, R.I.*

Fox, Edward Whiting (1971), *History in Geographic Perspective: The Other France* (New York: W. W. Norton).

Freedeman, Charles E. (1979), *Joint-Stock Enterprise in France, 1807–1867* (Chapel Hill, NC: University of North Carolina Press).

Gerschenkron, Alexander (1953), 'Social Attitudes, Entrepreneurship and Economic Development', *Explorations in Entrepreneurial History*, vol. 6.

Gille, Bertrand (1959), *La Banque et le crédit en France de 1815 à 1848* (Paris: Presses universitaires de France).

Gille, Bertrand (1970), *La Banque en France au XIXe siècle. Recherches historiques* (Geneva: Librairie Droz).

Goldsmith, Raymond W. (1969), *Financial Structure and Development* (New Haven, Conn.: Yale University Press).

Gouraud, Charles (1854), *Histoire de la politique commerciale de la France et son influence sur le progrès de la richesse depuis les moyens âges jusqu'à nos jours* (Paris: August Durand), vol. 2.

Gregory, T. E. (1936), *The Westminster Bank through a Century* (London: The Westminster Bank), vol. I.

Harris, R. D. (1978), *Necker, Reform Statesman of the Ancien Régime* (Berkeley, Calif.: University of California Press).

Harris, Seymour E. (1930), *The Assignats* (Cambridge, Mass.: Harvard University Press).

Harsin, Paul (1933), *Crédit public et Banque d'Etat en France du XVIe au XVIIIe siècle* (Paris: Librairie Droz).

Heckscher, Eli K. (1954), *An Economic History of Sweden*, translated from the Swedish by Goran Ohlin (Cambridge, Mass.: Harvard University Press).

Hovde, B. J. (1943), *The Scandinavian Countries, 1720–1865: The Rise of the Middle Classes* (Ithaca, NY: Cornell University Press).

Hughes, J. R. T. (1960), *Fluctuations in Trade, Industry and Finance: A Study of British Economic Development, 1850–1860* Oxford: Clarendon Press).

INSEE (Institut National de la Statistique et des Études Économiques) (1957), *Annuaire statistique de la France* (Paris: Imprimerie nationale).

Jones, Ethel (1930), *Les Voyageurs français en Angleterre de 1815 à 1830* (Paris: Baccard).

Jones, D. W. (1972), 'Merchants, Financiers and Interlopers: the London Mercantile Community and the Nine Years' War, 1688–1697', preprint of a paper delivered to the Economic History Society at Canterbury, England, April.

Kindleberger, C. P. (1964), *Economic Growth in France and Britain, 1851–1950* (Cambridge, Mass.: Harvard University Press).

Leighton-Boyce, J. A. S. L. (1958), *Smith, The Bankers, 1658–1958* (London: National Provincial Bank).

Levasseur, E. (1854/1970), *Recherches historiques sur le système de Law*, reprint edn. (New York: Burt Franklin).

Lévy-Leboyer, Maurice (1964), *Les Banques européennes et l'industrialisation internationale dans la première moitié du XIXe siècle* (Paris: Presses universitaires de France).

Lévy-Leboyer, Maurice (1976), 'Le Crédit et la monnaie: l'évolution institutionelle', in Fernand Braudel and Ernest Labrousse (eds), *Histoire économique et sociale de la France*. Vol. III: *L'Événement de l'ère industrielle (1789–années 1880)* (Paris: Presses universitaires de France), Part I, ch. 4.

Lévy-Leboyer, Maurice (1982), 'Central Banking and Foreign Trade: the Anglo-American Cycle in the 1830s', in C. P. Kindleberger and J.-P. Laffargue (eds), *Financial Crises: Theory, History and Policy* (Cambridge: Cambridge University Press), pp. 66–110.

Lewis, W. Arthur (1978), *Growth and Fluctuations, 1870–1913* (London: Allen & Unwin).

Liesse, André (1908), *Portraits des financiers: Ouvrard, Mollien, Gaudien, Baron Louis, Corvetto, Laffitte, de Villele* (Paris: Alcan).

Liesse, André (1909), *Evolution of Credit and Banks in France* (Washington, DC: US Government Printing Office, for the National Monetary Commission).

Lodge, Eleanor C. (1931/1970), *Sully, Colbert and Turgot. A Chapter in French Economic History*, reprint edn. (Port Washington, NY: Kennikat Press).

Lüthy, Herbert (1959, 1961), *La Banque protestante en France de la révocation de l'édit de Nantes à la révolution*. Vol. I: *Dispersion et regroupement (1685–1730)*; Vol. II: *De la banque aux finances (1730–1794)* (Paris: SEVPEN).

McKinnon, Ronald I. (1973), *Money and Capital in Economic Development* (Washington, DC: Brookings Institution).

Maddison, Angus (1982), *Phases of Capitalist Development* (Oxford: Oxford University Press).

Marczewski, J. (ed.) (1961), *Histoire quantitative de l'économie française*, series published from time to time in *Economies et sociétés* (formerly *Cahiers de l'Institut de Science Economique Appliquée*).

Markovitch, T. J. (1964–6), *L'Industrie française de 1789 à 1964*, *Cahiers de l'ISEA*, 4 vols.

Ministère des Finances et Ministère de l'Agriculture, du Commerce et des Travaux Publics (1865–7), *Enquête sur les principes et les faits généraux qui régissent la circulation monétaire et fiduciaire* (Paris: Imprimerie impériale, 6 vols).

Mitchell, B. R. with the collaboration of Deane, Phyllis (1963), *Abstract of British Historical Statistics* (Cambridge: Cambridge University Press).

Mollien, François Nicholas (1845), *Mémoires d'un ministre du Trésor Public, 1780–1815* (Paris: Fournier, 4 vols).

Morgan, E. Victor (1943), *The Theory and Practice of Central Banking, 1797–1913* (Cambridge: Cambridge University Press).

Nishimura, Shizuya (1971), *The Decline of Inland Bills of Exchange in the London Money Market, 1855–1913* (Cambridge: Cambridge University Press).

O'Brien, D. P. (ed.) (1971), *The Correspondence of Lord Overstone* (Cambridge: Cambridge University Press, 3 vols).

O'Brien, P. K. and Keyder, C. (1978), *Economic Growth in Britain and France, 1780–1914: Two Paths to the 20th Century* (London: Allen & Unwin).

Pitts, Jesse (1957), 'The French Bourgeois Family and French Economic Retardation', unpublished thesis, Harvard University.

Pitts, Jesse (1963), 'Continuity and Change in Bourgeois France', in Stanley Hoffman *et al.*, *In Search of France* (Cambridge, Mass.: Harvard University Press), pp. 235–304.

Plumb, J. H. (1963), *England in the Eighteenth Century* (Harmondsworth, Middx: Penguin Books).

Pose, Alfred (1942), *La Monnaie et ses institutions* (Paris: Presses universitaires de France, 2 vols).

Pressnell, L. S. (1956), *Country Banking in the Industrial Revolution* (Oxford: Clarendon Press).

Redlich, Fritz (1968), 'Frühindustrielle Unternehmer und ihre Probleme in Lichte Selbstzeugnisse', in W. Fischer (ed.), *Wirtschafts- und sozialgeschichtliche Probleme der frühen Industrialisierung* (Berlin: Colloquium Verlag), pp. 339–413.

Richards, R. D. (1965), *The Early History of Banking in England* (London: Frank Cass).

Sayers, R. S. (1957), *Lloyds Bank in the History of English Banking* (Oxford: Clarendon Press).

Sayers, R. S. (1978), 'Introduction' to N. St John Stevas (ed.), *The Collected Works of Walter Bagehot* (London: The Economist).

Schumpeter, Joseph A. (1954), *History of Economic Analysis*, edited from manuscript by Elizabeth Moody Schumpeter (London: Allen & Unwin).

Shaw, Edward S. (1973), *Financial Deepening in Economic Development* (New York: Oxford University Press).

Sherwig, John M. (1969), *Guineas and Gunpowder: British Foreign Aid in the Wars with France, 1793–1815* (Cambridge, Mass.: Harvard University Press).

Sieveking, Heinrich (1934), 'The Hamburger Bank', in J. G. Van Dillen (ed.), *History of the Principal Public Banks* (The Hague: Martinus Nijhoff), pp. 125–63.

Smith, Adam (1776/1937), *An Inquiry into the Nature and Causes of the Wealth of Nations*, Cannan edn. (New York: Modern Library).

Supple, Barry (1970), *The Royal Exchange Assurance. A History of British Insurance, 1720–1970* (Cambridge: Cambridge University Press).

Sutherland, Lucy Stuart (1933), *A London Merchant, 1699–1774* (London: Oxford University Press).

Thiers, Louis Adolphe (1895), *History of the Consulate and the Empire under Napoleon* (Philadelphia: J. B. Lippencott).

Thomas, W. A. (1973), *The Provincial Stock Exchanges* (London: Frank Cass).

Thornton, Henry (1802/1939), *An Enquiry into the Nature and Effect of the Paper Credit of Great Britain*, edited with an introduction by F. A. Hayek (London: Allen & Unwin).

Tocqueville, Alexis de (1833/1958), *Journeys to England and Ireland* (New Haven, Conn.: Yale University Press).

Toutain, J.-C. (1961), 'Le Produit de l'agriculture française de 1700 à 1958', *Cahiers de l'ISEA*, série AF, nos 1–2.

Van Dillen, J. G. (1934), 'The Bank of Amsterdam', in J. G. Van Dillen (ed.), *History of the Principal Public Banks* (The Hague: Martinus Nijhoff).

Weber, Eugen (1976), *Peasants into Frenchmen. The Modernization of Rural France, 1870–1914* (Stanford, Calif.: Stanford University Press).

Wicksell, Knut (1935), *Lectures on Political Economy*. Vol. II: *Money* (London: Routledge).

Withers, Hartley (1933), *National Provincial Bank, 1833–1933* (London: privately printed).

Young, Arthur (1790/1969), *Travels in France during the Years 1787, 1788 and 1789* (Garden City, NY: Doubleday Anchor Books).

5

Integration of Financial Markets: the British and French Experience

I am honored to be asked to Karachi to celebrate the life and work of a distinguished statesman, educator, planner, and central banker, Mr Zahid Husain, Minister of Finance in the Government of the Nizam of Hyderabad before partition, Chancellor of Aligrah University, Member of the Commission distributing assets between Pakistan and India in 1947, first chairman of the Pakistan Planning Commission, first Governor of the State Bank of Pakistan. I am honored but at the same time I am considerably embarrassed. It is hard to know what if anything I can contribute to the edification or interest of a central-banking audience in a developing country in this part of the world when my recent research has been almost entirely confined to the economic history of Western Europe. The subject of economic development is one that I had a brush with in the 1960s, but it has become too subtle, complex and ramified for me to keep up with. I have become aware, however, of the interest in the development literature in financial institutions, and in particular in the research of McKinnon (1973) on financial repression, and of Shaw (1973) on financial deepening. While I fear I know nothing of the past, present, or future state of financial institutions and their structure in Pakistan, it occurred to me that it might be of interest to you to offer a contrast of the experience of financial integration in the eighteenth and nineteenth centuries of England on the one hand and France on the other. To give the comparison somewhat greater generality, I propose to add a highly compressed account of the issue in the United States from which I come.

I

Financial repression in McKinnon's phrase consists in setting a price for external finance (the interest rate) below the equilibrium level, and discriminating in favor of the government, firms engaged in foreign trade, and perhaps a few others, at the expense of other would-be

The Zahid Husain Memorial Lecture No. 6 given in Karachi on 16 May 1983, and published by the State Bank of Pakistan. Reprinted with permission of the State Bank of Pakistan.

borrowers who are either excluded from the market altogether and made to depend on internal finance, limited to high-priced credits from money lenders, or unable to find any capital with which to grow. The position can be illustrated in Figure 1 from Maxwell Fry's (1982) discussion of financial repression. Given the initial schedules of savings and investment, the equilibrium interest rate should be r_1, but has been set by the government or central bank at r_0, limiting investment to I_0. At that interest rate the excess demand for savings is $I_d - I_0$. With no discrimination and savings limited to I_0, the interest rate would tend to r_2 and the rectangle $O - I_0 \times r_0 - r_2$ would be either the profits of a monopolized banking system or a sum spent by competing banks in building branches to attract deposits. In the usual McKinnon case of discrimination, there is strong rationing and some $O - I_d$ favored borrowers will get bank loans at rates at or below what they would be willing to pay. Many others will be frustrated.

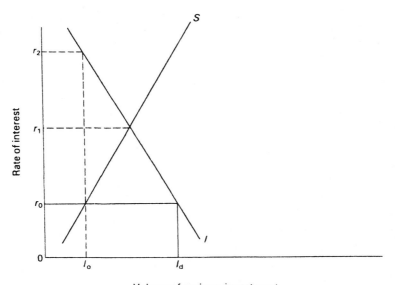

Volume of savings, investment

Figure 1 *Repressed Financial Market (after Maxwell J. Fry, 'Models of Financially Repressed Developing Countries', World Development, vol. 10, no. 9, September 1982, Figure 1, p. 733)*

My interest is slightly different – in the fragmented or compartmentalized market that requires a somewhat different but equally simple diagram. McKinnon and Fry sometimes call repressed markets 'fragmented', meaning that the demand for savings is divided by discrimination. Interested especially in regional discrimination, I

prefer to use the 'back-to-back' partial-equilibrium diagram of international trade in a single commodity, where barriers of some sort – high
transport costs, tariffs, lack of knowledge, or forceful discrimination by
traders or government – keep markets apart. In Figure 2, investment
demand and savings supply in the provinces run from left to right in the
normal fashion on the right-hand side of the diagram, but oppositely in
the financial center on the left. With an impenetrable barrier between
center and periphery, the rate of interest would be r_p in the provinces
and r_c in the center. If the barrier were completely removed, the rate of
interest would rise in the center and fall in the periphery to a new
national level r_n. McKinnon focuses on the removal of repression and
the rise in interest rates from r_c ro r_n. In the historical literature
especially in France, however, more attention is paid to the possibility of
credit creation – called by Schumpeter 'the essential part of the capitalist
engine' (1954, p. 312) – which is diagrammed in Figure 3. This is done
by the introduction of new curves for savings on the provinces' portion
of the diagram as a result of the establishment of new banks or the
issuance of newly created banknotes in the countryside. I leave open for
the most part whether new country or provincial banks add to the total
supply of money and credit, or somewhat reduce that available for the
financial center because of the need to transfer reserves from London
and Paris, the centers I shall be largely talking about, to the rest of the
country.

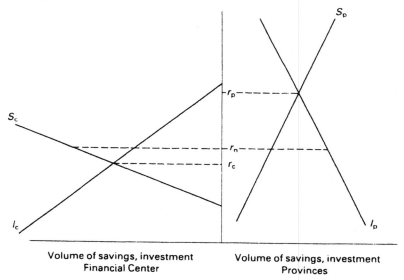

Volume of savings, investment   Volume of savings, investment
Financial Center   Provinces

Figure 2   *Fragmented Financial Markets*

So much for simple geometric analysis. But I am not through with the
appetizers or ready for the main course. A bright young British
economic historian, Charles Jones (1982), has stated that there are four

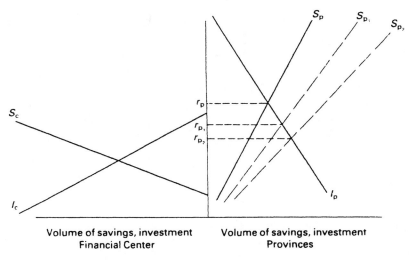

Figure 3   *Fragmented Market with Credit Creation in Provinces*

ways to write financial history, or possibly four different kinds of such history: the 'orthodox', the 'heroic', the 'populist', and the 'statist'.[1] The orthodox suggests that the problem through time is to curb the tendency of banks in the system to overissue banknotes, to lend to excess. The task, that is, is for the central authority, usually the central bank, to get potential wildcat banking under control by monopolizing the issue of banknotes and by developing central-bank techniques for assuring stability such as manipulating the discount rate, undertaking open-market operations, and the like. The heroic view focuses on major innovations such as the Crédit Mobilier of the Pereire brothers in France, which in 1852 altered the character of the French banking system by a quantum jump in lending for public works. The Populist position is the antithesis of the orthodox insofar as it resists the control of the authorities over independent and sometimes wildcat banking outside the major financial centers. It is especially illustrated in the history of banking in the United States, as succinctly described below, with Populists in the South and West of the United States warring against Philadelphia, Boston, and New York, the financial centers that allegedly limited their access to money and credit. Finally the statist explanation holds that banks were created to serve the needs of government. Jones stated that this applied to Argentinian, Australian, and Canadian central banks. It also clearly explains the origins of central banking in England, when the Bank of England was granted a charter in 1694 to help finance the Nine Years' War against France, and in France where the Bank of France was created in 1800 to regularize Napoleonic finances in the war against England. After statist beginnings, however, the financial histories of England and France diverged. That in Britain became largely orthodox after the middle of the eighteenth century as the Bank of England and the City tried to bring the ebullient country banks to heel. There were orthodox elements in French financial history, too, as the Bank of France tried to limit the spread of independent note-issuing banks in the provinces. At the same time there was continuous pressure from a group of Paris intellectuals, among them bankers, who thought it was vital for French economic growth to extend banking and credit in various forms beyond the confines of the capital. A small amount of Populism existed in the provinces themselves, but the main source of agitation in this direction came from the Saint-Simonian opposition to the financial establishment on largely theoretical grounds rather than a strongly felt demand for external finance.

The fragmentation of financial markets I shall be talking about is largely geographical, with ports, and to a lesser extent market towns, lying between the principal financial center and the remoter countryside. In Britain, fragmentation calls for analysis of the City of London, of ports, the agricultural counties of the South and East, and the industrial agglomerations of the Midlands and North. Distinctions in France run along lines that have been noted time and again. Edward Whiting Fox (1971) wrote of two Frances, divided between the major centers, including ports, and the rest, and Fernand Braudel (1977), with an eye to finance, of three, one using gold and banknotes, centered on Paris, one in the market towns with silver coin, and the material life of the countryside where little money at all was seen, and that mostly copper. Eugen Weber (1976) notes that it took seventy years for the monetary vocabulary adopted by Paris in 1800 to reach the peasantry. French provinces outside the major inland centers and ports, moreover, should probably be divided into the agricultural departments of the West and South and the industrial departments of the North and East. The manufacturing towns especially differed from the market cities in their credit needs.

But the breakdown was by no means exclusively geographic. It was also functional. Finance may be dominated by government and by foreign trade, the sectors regarded by McKinnon as favored enclaves, but there are also public works – canals, turnpikes, and railroads – agriculture, sometimes divisible into small holdings and large estates, the mortgage market, large industry, small industry, shipping, etc. Within industry, financial requirements and therefore institutions differed as between, for example, iron and steel on the one hand and textiles on the other. Financial markets at the informal level may be fragmented by social class: the intermediation of banks is necessary to allow aristocrats to lend to middle-class entrepreneurs or borrow from middle-class savers, operations of great difficulty if conducted face to face (Mathias and Joslin, quoted by Cameron, 1967, p. 23, n. 13). Further fragmentation runs along lines determined by risk, affecting the term structure of loans on the one hand and such distinctions as debt vs equity or domestic against foreign lending on the other. The famous Macmillan gap was by size of firm, with large firms having access to the formal capital market of London, and small firms acquiring capital informally in provincial towns, but great difficulty for a middle-size class of firms between (Frost, 1954).

II

The differences between English and French experiences are striking. In England, 'country banks' sprang up in the middle of the eighteenth century, after 1750, and especially during the industrial revolution. Over the first century of its existence, the Bank of England operated almost exclusively in the City of London, and was referred to from time to time, in a Populist way, as the 'Bank of London' (Mollien, 1845, I, pp. 186, 453–5). Outside London, Bank of England notes were rare, but the needs of trade and industry found a more or less spontaneous response. Business men issued their own tokens and coins, sometimes even guinea notes. In Lancashire, bills of exchange of all sorts of denominations including odd amounts passed from hand to hand as money. But as the demand for circulating media grew, the major response was a rise in country banks. These were partnerships with no more than six partners, and unlimited liability. From 12 in 1750, numbers doubled to 1770 and reached 400 by 1800 (Pressnell, 1956, p. 11). There were widespread bankruptcies in financial crises, new upsurges in subsequent booms. Some like Smith's of Nottingham went in for branching, including the establishment of an office in London. Most country banks had correspondents among the private banks in London, and the role of the London private banks gradually grew into that of clearing country-bank transactions. J. H. Plumb states that the industrial revolution was initially held back by lack of transport and lack of finance (1963, pp. 80–1, 146). The construction of canals and turnpikes, and, after 1830, of railroads, took care of transport. The working-capital needs of industry were largely met by the country banks.

In the eighteenth century, the London securities market was limited to government debt and a few equities, notably the stock of the Bank of England, the South Sea Company and the East India Company. Bank of England notes which circulated in London were initially available only in large denominations, which gradually declined during the century down to the Napoleonic wars. Not everyone was satisfied with the system, and people found especially trying the propensity of the country banks to fail in crisis. One reformer, Thomas Joplin, a Newcastle timber merchant, agitated for permitting joint-stock, i.e. incorporated, banks on the Scottish model in England. The Act of 1826 responding to this pressure and to the rash of failures in the crisis of 1825 authorized the establishment of joint-stock banks beyond 65 miles from London, but within that distance preserved a monopoly of joint-stock banking and note issue for the Bank of England. Joplin came from Newcastle, a city notorious for its appetite for capital for the coal industry As coal mining grew, its capital requirements mounted beyond the ability of informal markets and sleeping partnerships to satisfy. All this time, however, there were the beginnings of a regular national flow of savings from the agricultural counties of the South and East to the North through the country banks and their London correspondents. The distance of 65 miles was presumably drawn so as to include some towns of financial significance and exclude others. It may be observed, however, as of interest to the geography of finance, that the cost of money in 1734 was much higher 'outside 60 to 70 miles of London' than in that city, and that 'two-thirds of the Nation's Cash are the property of those who reside in and about the City' (Dickson, 1967, p. 477).

The Act of 1826 further provided for the branching of the Bank of England into the countryside to spread the use of its notes in competition with those of the country banks in an orthodox attempt to centralize control. Banknotes continued to replace coin. The £1 and £2 notes issued during the suspension of convertibility from 1797 to 1819 were withdrawn during the process of resumption but reissued again in the financial crisis of 1825.

Among the joint-stock banks created under the 1826 Act was the National Provincial, which combined existing and newly created banks in nine cities beyond the 65-mile limit into a single institution. The cities were Gloucester, Exeter, Stockton, Darlington, Kingsbridge, Manchester, Ramsgate, Newcastle, and Emlyn. To create a sprawling organization of this sort is said to have required courage in an era of slow communication (Withers, 1933, pp. 61–2). It marked a striking innovation in financial integration. The bank maintained an office for administration in London, but performed no banking operations there until the 1860s when it gave up the right of note issue. An analogous much earlier proposal for a series of banks – actually more nearly pawnshops – in a series of English cities had been put forward a century and a half earlier in 1571 at a time when there was little if any banking in England but many proposals to emulate those of the Continent. This called for seven principal 'banks' in London, York, Norwich, Coventry, West Chester, Bristol, and Exeter – all cathedral towns it may be noted. The capital of each of these banks was to be provided by people leaving their best garments to be sold by church wardens in the bank's area (Richards, 1965, pp. 93–5).

A loophole had been found in the banking legislation of 1826 and 1833 under which joint-stock banks could be established within 65 miles of London provided that they did not issue banknotes and thus challenge the Bank of England's geographical monopoly. The first such bank was the London and Westminster of 1836 combining offices in the City of London with another in Westminster or Mayfair where the aristocracy maintained its London residences. This social group did some borrowing, typically on mortgages for consumption or construction, but also moved rents from the provinces to London twice a year in May and November, and invested its savings in government stock, equities, and in due course foreign bonds.

Markets outside London were highly fragmented until about 1830, by borrowers, by lenders and by institutions. There had been demands for land banks in the seventeenth century, but these had not come to fruition. Schumpeter has remarked that landed gentlemen in the House of Commons, no more than other agrarians, were unable to 'see why they should not borrow as cheaply as traders or financiers, and they did not take kindly to arguments about the difference between a bill and a mortgage' (1954, p. 295). The provincial mortgage market was largely in the hands of scriveners whose services were needed in the conveyance of property. Finance of ships was carried out in highly informal markets in the ports where shipowners, captains, merchants, families, and friends and neighbors dealt in shares of ships on a binary basis, down as a rule to 64ths. This system lasted until about 1840 when the coming of the steamship and the iron-clad vessel raised the size of the capital needed, which outgrew the confines of the primitive arrangements.

Most industrial equity capital was also dealt in on an informal basis with family acquaintances. It is now recognized that the early emphasis of Thomas Ashton (1948), W. W. Rostow (1960), and W. A. Lewis (1955) on the capital needs of the industrial revolution was misplaced (see Crouzet, 1972). The requirements for fixed capital in Lancashire and the Midlands were small: buildings were rented, machinery bought with mercantile credit. Working capital was obtained by buying for credit and selling for cash to the extent possible, and beyond that from short-term bank finance. Growth was financed through plowed-back profits. Banks furnished some long-term capital, for the most part involuntarily through successive renewals of short-term credit.

The major exception was the iron industry with its large capital requirements, initially financed by London merchants and then by the sale of securities. With the passage of time and the increase in firm size, the shift from informal provincial markets to London continued, in ships as already noted, and beginning about 1870 even in such an industry as cotton textiles for those firms building plants of 70,000 spindles.

The London market was of course needed for government stock, for the great chartered companies, and gradually for public works such as railroads. London was also the gateway for international lending, toward Britain in the eighteenth century, almost entirely from Amsterdam and Geneva, and from London to the Continent from the Baring loan to finance the French indemnity after the Napoleonic War in 1817 to the revolution of 1848. That episode frightened British investors who turned their attention to the Empire, the United States, and Latin America.

The coming of the railroad gave rise as well to the establishment of provincial stock exchanges. These got their start in such cities as Manchester and Liverpool in auctioning off securities accumulated in estates, and gradually developed into organized exchanges for continuous trading (Thomas, 1973).

Th culmination of orthodox efforts to get the country banks and their note circulation under control was the Bank Act of 1844. From the 1850s the joint-stock banks spread into national networks, partly by absorbing country banks, partly by the establishment of new branches. Banks outside the metropolis set up head offices in London; those in

London filled out the gaps whether north or south. Lloyds Bank of Birmingham for a time maintained one deposit rate outside the City, another in London that tracked the Bank of England discount rate. With the passage of time it found it less and less possible to do so as depositors would move funds back and forth in search of the higher rate (Sayers, 1957, pp. 110, 165, 270). At this stage the money and capital market could be said to be virtually integrated. There were flaws in that integration: the Macmillan gap for firms of an awkward size, and perhaps the tendency of the City to favor foreign investment in government bonds and railroad securities over domestic industrial enterprise. The history of the English money and capital market, however, was less one of eliminating repression than of the 'orthodox' task of getting widespread spontaneous financial forces under discipline and control.

III

In France the drawn-out history of financial integration was intimately linked to the continuous running battle between two schools of thought in finance, which may be called, with some license, Keynesians and monetarists (Kindleberger, 1980). The Keynesians were expansionists who wanted to establish more banks, use credit to stimulate industry and agriculture, as well as commerce, and especially to spread banking and the use of banknotes from the financial capital – Paris in the period of our interest, though Lyons was the larger financial center prior to 1700 – to the provinces. The monetarists were orthodox, fearful that note-issuing banks in the countryside would get out of hand in speculative excess. That there was some merit to their fears is illustrated not only by the sporadic financial crises in England, but even today by experience in Latin America where the end of repression has led to financial excess and caused McKinnon to back away from the strong implication of his initial analysis, that banking should be freed of regulation, to a second-best position that calls for ending repression with great circumspection (McKinnon and Mathieson, 1981).

The list of Keynesians in French financial history in our period starts with John Law, Turgot, and Necker in the eighteenth century, and continues with Napoleon, Jacques Laffitte, and the Saint-Simonists, especially Michel Chevalier and the Pereire brothers in the nineteenth. The monetarists, on the other hand, consisted in the *anti-système*, opposed to the System of John Law, and the *officiers* and *financiers* of the royal court who defeated the financial reforms of Turgot and Necker; of Francois Mollien, who argued against Napoleon's Keynesianism, the Bank of France, the Rothschilds, and indeed the monetary and banking Establishment of the Parisian *hautes banques*. Time does not permit more than the sketchiest account of the action over 200 years.

John Law's Banque générale and successor Bank royale, which blew up spectacularly in 1720 in the Mississippi bubble, were both interested in extending the use of their banknotes into the countryside. To Law and to other thinkers going back a century or two, money and credit were compared with blood which needed to circulate throughout the body economic (Levasseur, 1854/1970, p. 20). Hamilton (1968, p. 78) observes that the Banque générale lowered interest rates first in Paris in 1716 to which its operations were initially confined, but then achieved a national circulation far more quickly than did any other public bank before the nineteenth century. A decree of April 1717 providing that Banque générale notes be accepted in payment of local taxes was said by Levasseur to make finance bureaus throughout the country into branches of the Banque: 'Money stayed in the provinces. The notes, flowing through thousands of canals, inundated France with its benefaction' (Levasseur, 1859/1970, p. 52). The receivers of taxes in the provinces resisted Law's changes because they lost the profits on bills of exchange used to remit taxes to Paris (*ibid.*, pp. 53, 56).

After the collapse of the Banque royale, the issue of financial integration took fiscal form. It could hardly operate through money and banking since there were no major banks. The subsistence peasant economy contributed through the *corvée*, or taxes in labor, largely building roads, which Turgot tried to reform into money payments; the economy of the ports paid through taxes and the purchase of *offices* by means of payment to the court. The state is said to have skimmed off money from the economy on the coast, the rivers that served each other, the colonies and foreign nation (Clark, 1971, p. 17). Turgot and Necker both warred against the centralization of royal finances at Paris and Versailles and lost out. The task remained to be accomplished by the French revolution (Bosher, 1970).

With the establishment of the Bank of France in 1800, and later with Napoleon as Emperor, the financial integration of the country could once more proceed by the spread of money and credit to the provinces. The road was a rocky one. There were two principal means: creation of branches of the Bank of France in the provinces and the founding of independent local note-issuing banks. Under Napoleon, the Bank of France started three branches at Rouen, Lyons, and Lille. Napoleon wanted a much wider program of branching but met resistance from the Bank of France itself, and especially from Mollien, his Minister of the Public Treasury, on whom he relied for financial advice. Napoleon would write Mollien letters asking whether it was not wise to do this and that, especially push for a program of branches of the Bank of France, as he was under pressure from delegates from various cities, asking for branches for the purpose of bringing down the local rate of interest. Mollien opposed him with a variety of arguments: if Bank of France notes were to circulate through France and be redeemable at many branches, one would have to have the equivalent of the Bank's reserve at each such branch to assure convertibility of banknotes into specie (1845, III, p. 157). In addition, each branch should have its own capital and be able to earn its way by an adequate annual volume of discounts. Mollien urged Napoleon to turn away delegations of petitioners seeking branches by asking them to furnish lists of potential stockholders and of merchants able and willing to discount several million francs annually in bills of exchange (*ibid.*, I, pp. 463–4). But Mollien's real objection was monetarist. Banks produce artificial money, not supported by real values. Stockholders sometimes forget their obligations to the holders of their notes (*ibid.*, III, p. 143). Napoleon, he complained, took no notice of abuses of discounting (*ibid.*, p. 138). In trying to persuade Napoleon against the establishment of branches in the industrial towns of Amiens, Cambrai, Saint-Quentin, and Valenciennes, Mollien offered to draft a statute changing the name of the Bank of France to the Bank of Paris (*ibid.*, I, p. 470). When Napoleon fell, a force for expanding credit in the countryside was lost, and the Bank of France closed down the existing branches.

With the Restoration of the monarchy in 1815, initiative shifted to the provinces. No bank could be created in France without the approval of the Paris government's Conseil d'Etat, which in its turn sought the advice of the Bank of France. When the expansionist Jacques Laffitte became governor in the postwar period new note-issuing banks were approved for Rouen, Nantes, and Bordeaux. With Laffitte's resignation in 1819, there was a relapse. After the July monarchy of 1830, however Laffitte came back into favor briefly. There began the formation of a series of provincial banks, admirably studied by Bertrand Gille in a series of papers, describing the credit conditions in which the banks were each sought, the negotiations with Paris to gain, or in the case of Dijon not to gain, permission, and the terms on which permission was granted. Gille describes provincial credit in the 1830s as a vacuum, rudimentary and primitive, in contrast to Paris, some centers well provided, especially the ports and several manufacturing cities, but for the rest large sections blank or almost blank (Gille, 1970, pp. 15, 35, 76, 87, 105). The fragmentation of the national capital market is illustrated by citing interest rates: 9 to 10 percent for Dijon as contrasted with 4 percent for Paris and 3 percent for Lyons on either side of it (*ibid.*, pp. 57, 77). In the same decade a partisan Saint-Simonian, Michel Chevalier, described fragmentation by the interest rates available to different borrowers. The treasury could borrow at 4 or even 3 percent when it did not need to, and so could privileged merchants in their prosperous moments. Landlords almost everywhere pay 6 percent. Little proprietors and little industrialists pay 8, 9 and 12 percent. 'As one descends the social scale, the interest rate mounts. For the worker in the city in his retail purchases for household needs, it is 50 and even 100 percent. For the peasant in his relations with the bailiff, the publican, and the merchant of the village, 100 percent a month' (Chevalier, 1838, II, p. 241). This statement of course takes no account of the costs and risks of lending to different groups.

In the space of a few more years to 1836, six more departmental note-issuing banks were formed, making nine in all, in Rouen, Lyons, Lille, Marseilles, Le Havre, Toulouse, Orleans, Bordeaux, and Nantes, all ports or entrepot towns except Lille in manufacturing and Orleans and Toulouse as major market towns. At that stage the Bank of France turned to acquire control over the note issue through a monopoly rather than through negotiated conditions. It set out deliberately to create its own branches, to resist further independent banks, and to stand ready to take over the existing ones. The opportunity presented itself in the financial crisis of 1847 when the departmental banks got into trouble but were not rescued by the Bank in a lender-of-last-resort capacity. On the contrary, it absorbed them and achieved a monopoly of the note issue. The problem, however, did not go away. In the late 1840s, there was more information on discount rates and the variation remained wide. The Bank of France discount rate was maintained at 5 per cent in those days and never varied. The position in the provinces, states Gille (1970, p. 147), was 'infinitely worse' (*sic*), with interest rates varying between 3 and 3½ percent in Lyons and 18 to 30 percent in Eure et Loir. Between the extremes were found Chateauroux at 6 to 8 percent according to some, 7 to 12 for others; Grenoble 8½ percent, Besançon more than 6, Mulhouse 5 to 6, Angoulème 6 to 8, Nîmes 8, Agen 6, Caen 6 to 10.

Larger firms had access to credit in Paris, no matter where in the country they were located, usually as a result of close association with a private bank. The Anzin coal company in the North was in fact owned by the Perier bank in Paris, which also owned a large machine shop at Chaillot. Schneider of the Schneider-Creusot steel company had worked for the Seillières bank in Paris and maintained an association with it. Georges Dufaud of Fourchambault in the Nivernais to the south of Paris relied for capital expansion primarily on plowing back profits, but in 1829 raised 6½ million francs from a Paris bank under the control of his partner Boigues, plus the help of a deposit of 4 millions from Boigues' relatives (Thuillier, 1959, pp. 38–40). Thuillier observes that banks in the Nivernais played practically no role in developing local industry, maintained very high liquidity, and reserved their resources for agriculture and expansion and equipment of large estates (Thuillier, 1955, pp. 511–12). What leadership there was in banking for industry was in Paris. In his account of Georges Dufaud, however, Thuillier mentions a failed forge which local banks tried to restart with 1 millions of capital, calling it 'a rare example of direct intervention of local bankers in the life of a factory' (Thuillier, 1959, p. 53). Finally in this brief catalogue may be mentioned the complex financial life of Les Fonderies et Forges d'Alais, which raised its initial capital in the 1820s among two distinct groups, the local notables of the Gard deep in the countryside and financial interests in Paris. In the difficulties of 1837 it was obliged to sell 30 percent of the firm to a Paris banker and managed to raise 1.2 million francs in the same year in Marseilles. In 1856 it put out a 2 million franc bond issue, subscribed to more than two-thirds in the Midi, but failed in an attempt to raise 1½ millions through a bond issue in 1858. In 1866, it managed to borrow 600,000 francs from the Crédit agricole in Paris (sic!). Talabot's Paris–Lyons–Marseilles railroad and its constituent elements had been Alais' largest customer, and Drouillard, Benoist d'Azy & Co. lent it their political weight in 1836 when Talabot borrowed 6 million francs from the French government on a bill that passed the Chamber of Deputies by but six votes (Locke, 1978, pp. 16, 43, 77, 83).

In renewing the Bank of France charter in 1857, the Chamber of Deputies required it to establish a branch in each of the 90 departments in France by 1867. At the beginning of the 1850s, the Bank had 24 such branches, of which 7 made losses and 17 profits (Saint-Genis, 1896, p. 61), a criterion of success adduced by Mollien with an implicit philosophy that appealed to many students of finance at the time but not to the Saint-Simonians. The latter regarded bank branches that brought credit to the countryside as public goods, needed to stimulate commerce and industry, and akin to the branch lines of railroads that may be unprofitable in themselves but justified because of external economies.

In addition to this pressure from the legislature, the monopoly of the Bank was threatened when the Pereire brothers bought the Bank of Savoy in a province previously Italian which had become French when Savoy was ceded to France in 1860 to enlist the support of Louis Napoleon for Italy in its war against Austria. The Saint-Simonians managed to organize a formal inquiry into money and banking, ostensibly to discuss the financial crisis of 1864, but in reality to deal with questions of the Bank of France monopoly of the note issue and the need for more banks and banking throughout the country. These were the questions raised time and time again by Michel Chevalier who served on the Conseil Supérieur conducting the Inquiry in his rather hostile cross-examination of the banking establishment. In his testimony, Emile Pereire said that no place should have a bank more than 20 or 30 leagues (60 or 90 miles) away, that the Bank of France should triple its note circulation, popularize the use of credit and bring the capital it could not employ in Paris to the provinces (Ministère des Finances *et al.*, 1867, I, pp. 603–4). The first witness to testify was the English editor of *The Economist*, Walter Bagehot, who found the banking system of France inferior to that of England in transferring the nation's savings to industry: 'In England each village has at least two banks. Thanks to them, no shilling of savings is lost' (*ibid.*, I, p. 24). In questioning de Waru of the Bank of France, Chevalier noted that the Bank had only 54 branches, well short of the 90 due by 1867 by law, but even that number far short of needs, put by Chevalier as not 200 or 300, but 1,000 (*ibid.*, III, p. 131).

It should be noted that, in creating branches in the provinces, the Bank of France to a considerable extent was serving a clearing rather than a credit function, by making it possible for merchants in the countryside to collect sums due to them by discounting bills drawn on buyers. In this effort, required because of the rudimentary development of payment by checks, the Bank of France was a competitor of the commercial banks. The expansionists applauded the establishment of more branches; Georges Palladin, who became governor in 1897 and stepped up the branching effort, was hailed by one 'Keynesian' as the greatest governor since Jacques Laffitte (Dauphin-Meunier, 1936, p. 129). A twentieth-century monetarist observes somewhat disdainfully that by 1897 everyone in France had adequate discount service and that the important service of collecting drafts did not require the costly apparatus of Bank of France branches. The Bank of France would have developed from an operating br nk into a bankers' bank, he thought, had it not been for the ignorance of Parliament on the one hand, and that of the authorities on the other (Pose, 1942, I, pp. 256, 286).

By the 1860s, French banking put on a substantial push. The last of the four great deposit banks was the Société générale, established in 1864 after the Crédit Lyonnais of 1863, the Crédit industriel et commercial of 1859 and the Comptoir d'escompte. This last with a number of regional banks grew out of the *comptoirs d'escompte* established by the French monetary authorities in the crisis of 1848 to provide a third name for bills of exchange to make them eligible for discount at the Bank of France. The deposit banks spread rapidly, creating branches in what has been described as a logistic curve, from 170 bank offices (*guichets*, literally 'wickets') for the three largest to 1,400 for the same three in 1927 and 1,496 in 1939 (Divisia, 1942, p. 36). The Crédit industriel et commercial acquired a network by buying 11 existing regional banks, while the Crédit Lyonnais and the Société générale struck out both to absorb local banks and to create new branches (Bouvier, 1961, esp. I, ch. 5; Labasse, 1955). We have more detailed information on the Crédit Lyonnais than on any other. It was particularly interested in acquiring deposits in the countryside for investment in Paris or abroad. When the railroad came to a town it would try to estimate whether the town, with a newly established branch, would create deposits or demand loans, and tend to avoid it in the latter instance. The head office gradually moved from Lyons to Paris. On occasion the bank called loans to local clients in order to be able to participate in foreign security operations (Bouvier, 1961, I, pp. 305, 350–1). McKinnon (1973, p. 84) and Shaw (1973, p. 147) make the point that more branches of banks may not be conclusive evidence of financial integration, as they may be built in cities or suburbs to gather deposits – the word in French is 'drainage' – rather than to make credit available to borrowers. The description well fits the history of the Crédit Lyonnais.

France has been a highly centralized society in many respects since at least the time of Louis XIV in the seventeenth century who drew the aristocracy to Versailles. Labasse at the end of the 1960s observes that the world presents three geographical models in finance: the 'centralized', the 'spread', and, between these extremes, the 'median'. He illustrates these types with tables showing the percentages of total clearing that go through the financial capital. In the centralized case, Paris has 91.3 percent of the clearings of France, the nearest city being Lyons with 0.65 percent. Canada furnishes an example of the spread model, which applies particularly to federal states, with Toronto having 37.3 percent of Canadian clearings, as compared with Montreal's 25.5 percent and Vancouver's 6.5. Between them stands Japan, representing the median, with Tokyo having 51.2 per cent and Osaka in second place with 19.7 (Labasse, 1974, p. 144). Paris is not far different from London in this respect, however, because London has 87 per cent of British clearings, and, again like Paris with the highest percentage in the world, has 100 times the clearings of its nearest rival, Liverpool (*ibid.*, p. 145).

Labasse's research unfortunately does not compare France and Britain and their financial centers in terms of deposits and credits. In France, Paris has 19 percent of the French population, 42 percent of total deposits and 46 percent of credits. This profile, Labasse holds, illustrates the exceptional concentration of the French capital in the country's economic and social life, and reflects the fact that Paris has attracted to it the head offices of the country's most important companies. In the provinces one finds the opposite condition – of the sort frequently encountered in Third World countries at the beginning of their financial development, though not at the end – with the percentage of population exceeding that of deposits, which in turn exceeds that of credits (*ibid.*, p. 164).

The disparity between the financial history of England, where it was necessary to restrain the animal spirits of country banks, and France, where a significant intellectual movement sought to stimulate them, is of course no accident and lies deep in the social matrixes formed by the two countries' respective histories and national characters. It is important for economic theory to observe that comparative financial history teaches that the model and the policies deriving from it appropriate to one country may not have general applicability.

IV

A purer Populist experience than that of France is presented by the United States, where the Eastern seaboard sought continuously to get money and credit under control and the South and West strained to break the bonds. One struggle in the East was for financial supremacy, with New York winning out over Philadelphia, Baltimore, and Boston. The East as a whole then tried to restrain the uninhabited expansion of wildcat banking in the rest of the country. Traveling in the country in the 1830s, Michel Chevalier remarked that newly founded towns tended to establish a bank almost before the streets had been laid out and the stumps of felled trees had been uprooted (1838, I, p. 263).[2] The Second Bank of the United States was vetoed by the Populist president, Andrew Jackson, for fear that it would unduly limit bank expansion, this in the 1830s. In the 1850s, a number of states sought to prevent banks in their jurisdictions from holding their reserves in New York funds.

The National Bank Act of 1863 passed in the North during the Civil War had a statist aspect as it provided for the issuance of national bank notes with Union bonds as collateral. It further provided, however, that required reserves of national banks could be held either in cash or in deposit claims on nine different cities, of which New York was only one, and banks in these cities had to switch from holding deposits on New York to holding currency. The anti-New York provisions of this legislation were moderated the following year by allowing half the 25 percent reserve of the reserve cities – the number being increased from nine to eighteen – to be held in New York funds. This in effect made New York a central reserve city.

The crisis of 1907 revealed that the banking system was far from stable. After a prolonged investigation by the National Monetary (Aldrich) Commission, the Federal Reserve Act was passed in 1913, providing not for one central bank, but for twelve, one for each of twelve Federal Reserve districts. The purpose once again was to downgrade New York's financial position, through the creation of eleven other Federal Reserve banks and the coordination of all by a Board of Governors in Washington, the political capital at a distance from the money powers. The effort proved vain. The enormous requirements of government finance during the World War called for a single financial center with its economies of information and scale, so that New York emerged as the apex of the system. Some of the regional Federal Reserve banks have prominent roles to play, notably those of Chicago and San Francisco with their somewhat differentiated money markets.

The experience of the United States is thus contrary to the McKinnon model of repression, unless one thinks of the rest of the country trying unsuccessfully to repress New York. Populism is rather like today's *dependencia* theory in Latin America in which the periphery fears it is being throttled by the center. The South and West struggled against the money interests not only in banking but in trying to sustain bimetallism, to gain free coinage for silver, special agricultural price supports, and the like. The hierarchical structure of banking demonstrated its inherent efficiency by the fact it survived more than a century's continuous efforts to alter it.

V

This lecture has covered too much ground to lend itself to easy summary, and I must try at this late hour to be brief. What I think I have demonstrated is that there are no easy generalizations about financial repression, fragmentation, or integration that are good for all countries, times and places. Consistency, as Ralph Waldo Emerson remarked, is the hobgoblin of little minds. It was a mistake, McKinnon recognizes, to apply the lessons of repression from South Korea without modification to the banking systems of Latin America. Michel Chevalier deserves credit for having been a monetarist in his views on banking in the United States, while he was a Keynesian in the circumstance of France (1838, I, Letters 3, 4, 5), but he may be faulted for his cross-examination of witnesses in 1865–67 for having implied that the lessons of Scottish banking were applicable everywhere in the world (Ministère des Finances *et al.*, 1865–7, II, pp. 394ff; III, pp. 39ff). Populist policies in the United States ran up against the hard fact that even in a federal system there is some residue of hierarchical ordering that is impervious to policy. Careful adjustment to shift systems to correct obvious excess in any direction is clearly desirable.

I wish I knew enough to apply the conclusions of this study to conditions in Pakistan, but I do not. In my ignorance I must state them in highly general terms, and allow you to see which, if any, fit:

1   The banking history of any country is not likely to fall consistently
    into one of Jones' categories as orthodox, heroic, populist, or statist,
    but to swing among them from time to time, now one, then another
    in emphasis, but with different emphasis in different countries.
2   The history of the development of banking in a country is likely to be
    strongly affected by the nature of the commodities in which it has a
    comparative advantage, including the technology and scale.
    Comparative advantage, technology and scale, moreover, all change
    with the unfolding of history, so that the nature of banking remains
    in continuous evolution.
3   There is no one pattern that all countries must follow in a series of
    stages. Much of the structure of money and banking at a given stage
    of economic development – if you will forgive the expression –
    depends upon such elusive considerations as the social matrix and
    national character. Strong individualism in Britain led to ebullient
    country banking – the same in the United States to wildcat banking,
    from which followed in both cases the orthodox necessity to get
    banking under control. The French predisposition to centripetal
    gathering of economic force at the capital in Paris gave rise to the
    opposite necessity – at least as seen by a series of outsiders and astute
    intellectuals – to spread the sources of initiative in financial
    questions to some considerable degree into the provinces.
4   In all societies there must be some balance – difficult to find and
    maintain – between the economies of scale from centralized finance
    and the gains in information from local knowledge that can be
    acquired – at the present stage of technology at least, and certainly in
    the past – from a local presence in the countryside.
5   All this leads me to great skepticism that there are any iron laws as to
    how the geography of finance should or must be ordered. At the
    same time I remain persuaded on general grounds based on Pareto-
    optimality in favor of some degree – probably some considerable
    degree – of national, and yes, international financial integration.

Notes

1   For a contrast between orthodox British commercial banks operating in Latin America
    and the native banks with a style more like that of the Crédit Mobilier, see Jones (1977).
2   Chevalier repeats this story of finding a bank at Fort Carbon before the streets have
    been laid out at least twice. See Chevalier (1868), p. ccclxxxi; (1855), p. 84.

References

Ashton, Thomas S. (1948), *The Industrial Revolution, 1760–1830* (London:
    Oxford University Press).
Bosher, J. F. (1970), *French Finances, 1770–1795, from Business to
    Bureaucracy* (Cambridge: Cambridge University Press).
Bouvier, Jean (1961), *Le Crédit Lyonnais de 1863 à 1882. Les Années de
    formation d'une banque de depôts* (Paris: SEVPEN).

Braudel, Fernand (1977), *Afterthoughts on Material Civilization and Capitalism* (Baltimore, Md.: Johns Hopkins University Press).

Cameron, Rondo (1967), *Banking in the Early Stages of Industrialization: A Study in Comparative Economic History* (New York: Oxford University Press).

Chevalier, Michel (1838), *Lettres sur l'Amérique du Nord*, 3rd edn. (Paris: Gosselin, 2 vols).

Chevalier, Michel (1855), *Cours d'économie politique fait au Collège de France*. Vol. I: *Tous les discours d'ouverture, 1840 à 1852* (Paris: Capelle).

Chevalier, Michel (1868), *Exposition universelle de 1867 à Paris. Rapports du Jury International publiés sous la direction de M. Michel Chevalier*. Vol. I: *Introduction par M. Michel Chevalier* (Paris: Paul Dupont).

Clark, John G. (1971), *La Rochelle and the Atlantic Economy during the Eighteenth Century* (Baltimore, Md.: Johns Hopkins University Press).

Crouzet, Francois (ed.) (1972), *Capital Formation in the Industrial Revolution* (London: Methuen).

Dauphin-Meunier, A. (1936), *La Banque de France* (Paris: Gallimard).

Dickson, P. G. M. (1967), *The Financial Revolution in England. A Study in the Development of Public Credit, 1688–1756* (New York: St Martin's Press).

Divisia, F. (1942), 'La Géographie des banques en France'. *Collection Droit Social*, vol. 15 (May).

Fox, Edward Whiting (1971), *History in Geographic Perspective: The Other France* (New York: W. W. Norton).

Frost, Raymond (1954), 'The Macmillan Gap, 1931–53', *Oxford Economic Papers*, vol. 6, pp. 181–201.

Fry, Maxwell. J. (1982), 'Models of Financially Repressed Developing Countries', *World Development*, vol. 10, no. 9 (September), pp. 731–3.

Gille, Bertrand (1970), *La Banque en France au XIXe siècle* (Geneva: Droz).

Hamilton, Earl J. (1968), 'John Law', *International Encyclopedia of the Social Sciences*, vol. 9 (Chicago, Ill.: Macmillan and Free Press), pp. 78–81.

Jones. Charles (1977), 'Finance', in D. C. M. Platt (ed.), *Business Imperialism. 1840–1930. An Inquiry Based on British Experience in Latin America* (Oxford: Clarendon Press), pp. 17–52.

Jones, Charles (1982), 'The Monetary Politics of Export Economies before 1914: Argentina, Australia and Canada', a paper presented to the Symposium on 'Argentina, Australia, and Canada: Some Comparisons, 1870–1950', at the 44th International Congress of Americanists, Manchester, England, 8 September.

Kindleberger, Charles (1980), 'Keynesianism vs Monetarism in Eighteenth- and Nineteenth-Century France', *History of Political Economy*, vol. 12, no. 4, pp. 499–523.

Labasse. Jean (1955), *Les Capitaux et la région. Etude géographique. Essai sur le commerce et la circulation des capitaux dans la région lyonnaise* (Paris: Colin).

Labasse, Jean (1974), *L'Espace financier, analyse géographique* (Paris: Colin).

Levasseur, E. (1845/1970), *Recherches historiques sur le système de Law*, reprint edn. (New York: Burt Franklin).

Lewis, W. Arthur (1955), *The Theory of Economic Growth* (Homewood, Ill.: Irwin).

Locke, Robert R. (1978), *Les Fonderies et forges d'Alais à l'époque des premiers chemins de fer, 1829–1874* (Paris: Riviers).

McKinnon, Ronald I. (1973), *Money and Capital in Economic Development* (Washington, DC: Brookings Institution).

McKinnon, Ronald I. and Mathieson, Donald J. (1981), 'How to Manage a

Repressed Economy', *Princeton Essays in International Finance*, No. 145 (December), pp. 1–26.

Ministère des Finances et Ministère de l'Agriculture, du Commerce et des Travaux Publics (1865–1867), *Enquête sur les principes et les faits généraux qui régissent la circulation monétaire et fiduciaire* (Paris: Imprimerie impériale, 6 vols).

Mollien, François (1845), *Mémoires d'un ministre du Trésor Public* (Paris: Fournier, 4 vols).

Plumb, J. H. (1950), *England in the Eighteenth Century* (Harmondsworth, Middx: Penguin Books).

Pose, Alfred (1942), *La Monnaie et ses institutions* (Paris: Presses universitaires de France, 2 vols).

Pressnell, L. S. (1956), *Country Banking in the Industrial Revolution* (Oxford: Clarendon Press).

Richards, R. D. (1965), *The Early History of Banking in England* (London: Frank Cass).

Rostow, W. W. (1960), *The Stages of Growth* (Cambridge: Cambridge University Press).

Saint-Genis, Victor Bénique Flour de (1896), *La Banque de France à travers le siècle* (Paris: Guillaumin).

Sayers, R. S. (1957), *Lloyds Bank in the History of English Banking* (Oxford: Clarendon Press).

Schumpeter, Joseph A. (1954), *History of Economic Analysis* (London: Allen & Unwin).

Shaw, Edward S. (1973), *Financial Deepening in Economic Development* (New York: Oxford University Press).

Thomas, W. A. (1973), *The Provincial Stock Exchanges* (London: Frank Cass).

Thuillier, Guy (1955), 'Pour une histoire bancaire régionale: En Nivernais de 1800 à 1880', *Annales*, vol. 10 (October–December).

Thuillier, Guy (1959), *Georges Dufaud. Les Débuts du grand capitalisme dans la metallurgie, en Nivernais, au XIXe siècle* (Paris: SEVPEN).

Weber, Eugen (1976), *Peasants into Frenchmen. The Modernization of Rural France, 1870–1914* (Stanford, Calif.: Stanford University Press).

Withers, Hartley (1933), *National Provincial Bank, 1833–1933* (London: privately printed).

6

British Financial Reconstruction, 1815–22 and 1918–25

It may be regarded by some as ill-mannered to argue with Walt Rostow in honouring him. A superficial defence can be found in the modern statement that it doesn't make any difference what you say about a person as long as you mention him frequently and spell his name correctly. More fundamentally, Professor Rostow has posed an interesting and profound interpretation of a classic issue that is worth illuminating.

In the first place, in *The World Economy* (1978, pp. xlii, xliii), he states:

> For some, at least, monetary affairs will appear to have been slighted. In the analysis of the pre-1914 era monetary affairs appear only when I believe they left a significant impact on the course of events, e.g. transmitting the effects of bad harvests in the eighteenth and nineteenth centuries; in helping create the settings for cyclical crises and then (in Britain at least), cushioning their impact; in stimulating, under the gold standard, the inflationary diversion of resources to gold mining. In the post-1918 world of more conscious monetary policies, they emerge on a stage in the 1920s with the French devaluation and the British return at the old rate, as well as the failure of the United States to accept its responsibilities for the trade and monetary structure of the world economy. After 1945, the rise and fall of the Bretton Woods system forms (*sic*), of course, part of the narrative.
>
> Nevertheless it should be underlined that the view taken here of the course of production and prices – in cycles, trend periods, and in the process of growth itself – would regard the non-monetary factors as paramount . . . Men and societies have devised and evolved monetary systems which more or less met their deeper needs and purposes as they conceived them. Different monetary policies, at different times and places, might have yielded somewhat different results than history now records. The same could be said with equal or greater

Reprinted with permission from Charles P. Kindleberger and Guido di Tella (eds). Economics in the Long View: Essays in Honour of W. W. Rostow. *Vol 3:* Applications and Cases, Part II *(London: Macmillan, 1982), pp. 105–20.*

strength about fiscal policies. But down to 1914 modern concepts of monetary and fiscal policy did not exist, except perhaps in a few unorthodox minds; and prevailing notions reordered the monetary system substantially passive and responsive.

In a subsequent essay reviewing the new monetarism, he defends this position at length, insists that pre-1914 monetary systems were passive and flexible, and sides once more with the Thomas Tooke position, against David Ricardo, that price changes emanate from the supply side through costs and output changes (1980).

I have a difficult time with these propositions, and especially with the notions: (1) That there was a major discontinuity in 1914; and (2) the pre-1918 world was less conscious of monetary problems than the post-1918 and that the modern concepts of monetary and fiscal policy did not exist theretofore. The more usual view is that monetary orthodoxy goes back at least to 1797, or, if you prefer, to Thornton and Ricardo in 1802 and 1809 (Fetter, 1965; Morgan, 1943). But the inspiration of this paper comes secondly from Rostow's sharp reaction to a remark I made in his seminar at the University of Texas at Austin, shortly after having read A. W. Acworth's *Financial Reconstruction in England, 1815–1822* (1925), suggesting close parallelism between Britain, 1815 to 1822 and 1918 to 1925. Analogues run between the Bullion Report (1810/1978) and the Cunliffe Report (1925/1978); the postwar booms of 1814 and 1919, followed by collapse in 1816 and 1920, and then recovery for a couple of years in both cases; the Parliamentary committee report favouring resumption in 1819 and the Chamberlain–Bradbury report of 1924; the Peterloo 'massacre' of 1819 and the coal strike of 1925 plus the General Strike of 1926; deflation following for four more years to 1823 after resumption in 1819, for six years until the 1931 depreciation in the case of 1925. Rostow denied that the troubles of 1815 to 1822 were anything like those of 1918 to 1925 or 1931. The latter were monetary, the former non-monetary. One could cite weightier authority than Acworth who says in his preface that he has 'refrained from pointing comparisons, contrasts with the last seven years' (1925, p. v.), for example T. E. Gregory in his introduction to Tooke's *History of Prices* (1928), who states:

If the economic and, in particular the monetary problems we are facing today have a startling resemblance to those which were the subject-matter of contention for two generations a century ago, the experience of the Napoleonic and post-Napoleonic days has an interest for us in two respects. The two periods illumine one another, and we can pass from the depreciated exchanges of 1797–1819 to those of 1914–1925 . . . with the feeling that our comprehension of the past and present is increased by comparing one with the other.

But these volumes have a renewed interest in another . . . respect. The interpretation of the events of the period . . . gave rise to an intellectual conflict in which now one side, now the other seemed for a time to have carried off the final victory.

It is true that the major participants in the decision to stabilise the pound seem not to have thought about the analogy – *pace* Acworth. I recall no reference to it in Keynes (1930, 1932, 1933), Leith-Ross (1968), Grigg (1948), the Moggridge accounts (1969, 1972), the Norman biographies – Clay (1957/1978), Boyle (1967) – or Howson (1975). A peek is worth two finesses, however, so I wrote to Moggridge and asked. He kindly replied that only Hawtrey evoked the analogy between 1919 and 1925, and he did so several times. Nonetheless there seems to be enough evidence to reopen the question, to indict, if not at this stage to convict.

If I were more ambitious, I might try to extend the analogy to the British recoinage of silver in 1696, which involved appreciation and depression (Hawtrey, 1927, pp. 290 ff), or that of Demaretz in France in 1715 when the *livre* was raised from 20 to 14 to the *louis d'or* (Lüthy, 1959, I, p. 281). I urge these extensions on the reader, not excluding Professor Rostow.

Apart from the closeness of the 1815/1918 analogy, it is hard to accept the suggestion that money and banking were passive and accommodating. Resumption was subject to 'extremely heated controversy', particularly as it was accompanied by sharp deflation, probably intensified by the decision in 1821 to return to a full gold-coin standard instead of Ricardo's bullion plan (O'Brien, 1971, I, p. 71). The decision to resume gold payments was postponed at least six times. Nor did all but a few unorthodox minds agree on policy choices. There were clearly many who were unorthodox – William Cobbett who detested paper money, the national debt and banks; Sir John Sinclair, who 'went off in all directions at once, as he so often did', wanted a large note issue but was concerned about the 'coinage of paper money' (Fetter, 1965, pp. 22, 29); the eighth Earl of Lauderdale, an advocate of silver money, or at best bimetallism, a perpetual Cassandra of the economic situation in England (*ibid.*, p. 15). In his review of a book by Lord King, Francis Horner, the chairman of the Committee that wrote the Bullion Report of 1810 stated: 'In great commercial cities, opinions have been avowed by persons who ought to be acquainted with the money trade that precious metals are unnecessary and that the provisions of the law of 1797 should be made permanent' (*ibid.*, p. 56). On the other side of the debate, Wheatley was, if penetrating and original, an extreme bullionist who held that monetary expansion had no effect on output, and foreign payments no impact on the exchange rate because of frictionless real transfer (*ibid.*, p. 38). Most participants in the discussion, however, were prepared to concede some merit to the opposite case. Ricardo would have advocated devaluation if the pound had been depreciated in 1819 by 30 per cent, as it had been in 1813 (Viner, 1937, p. 205n.). 'Even so ardent a disciple of Ricardo as McCulloch thought the old par a mistake' (*ibid.*, p. 175). Thomas Attwood of the Birmingham School, who resisted resumption and wanted monetary expansion, would halt such expansion whenever it was sufficient to call every labourer into action;

any further stimulus would be nugatory or injurious (*ibid.*, p. 212 n.).
Even Tooke, says Gregory, was *never* (his italics) an extreme bullionist
(1928, p. 16). He was however a good hater (*ibid.*, p. 120), a magnificent
controversialist, with a thesis to uphold and an enemy to vanquish.

Rostow, of course, has been over this ground years ago. He wrote Part
I of Volume I of the classic Gayer, Rostow and Schwartz, *Growth and
Fluctuations of the British Economy, 1790–1850* (1953, I, p. vi). In this
work he broke down restriction from 1797 to 1819 into a series of short
periods, largely, for our purposes, 1803 to 1806, 1807 to 1811, 1812 to
1816, and 1817 to 1821, and submitted each one to an identical period-
by-period analysis of prices, foreign trade, investment, industry and
agriculture, finance and labour. Finance was only one factor out of six,
and that taken up penultimately. Moreover, he follows Tooke closely. I
counted 10 long quotations from that authority in the 110 pages, in
addition to 60-plus citations. Tooke's time periods are somewhat
different, 1799–1803, 1804–8, 1809–13, 1814–18, and 1819–22, and his
schema is divided in three: the effect of the seasons, which discusses the
harvest; the effect of war, dealing largely with the need to finance British
and foreign troops fighting the French; and finally currency, which in
his view essentially has nothing to do with prices or the exchange rate.
Rostow follows him and Silberling (1924) in the analysis of the exchange
rate. Extraordinary expenses abroad consist of bills and specie remitted
for British armies, subsidies and loans for allies, and grain imports of
more than £2 million in any year. The sum of these tracks very well with
the price of silver and the exchange rate on Hamburg, as Viner shows
(1937, p. 143), and the depreciation of the pound is not markedly
different whether one takes the premium of the market above the mint
gold price, the premium on silver, or the Hamburg exchange rate. Tooke
and Rostow have a solid victory in this over many of the bullionists,
including especially Ricardo and Wheatley, who dismissed extraordinary foreign expenditures as a source of depreciation because they
assumed a frictionless transfer mechanism. The directors of the Bank of
England on the other hand were also wrong in telling the Bullion
Committee that foreign payments led to a 100 per cent loss of specie. But
the division of the period into short subperiods leads to overemphasis of
the short run and neglect of the truths of the long.

Tooke has little difficulty in indicating a whole series of years at the
beginnings and ends of his mini-periods when currency issues and prices
were going in different directions. In some of his more ironic passages,
he goes down into quarters and months, finding, for example, that the
gold premium and the exchange rate were improving in the spring of
1814 when the circulation was rising, and that prices collapsed in the
spring of 1819 when the Bank of England circulation was still
unchanged (1838, II, pp. 80–1, 96–7). I shall have something more to say
about these speculative periods later. For the moment, however, one
should observe that if 1797 to 1822 is divided into one expansionary and
inflationary period from 1797, and particularly from 1808 to 1814,
followed by deflation to 1822, as Viner does (1937, chs iii, iv), it would
have been evident that the sum of Bank of England commercial paper

under discount and advances to the government rose from a low of £14.1 millions in 1798 to £41.4 millions in 1815 (*ibid.*, p. 167); and that thereafter total advances (a somewhat different concept) declined from £42.9 millions in 1814 (£42.5 million in 1815) to £14.8 millions in 1824. To focus on the short run and leads and lags neglects long-run truth. Bank of England circulation is not a good measure of the money supply for a number of reasons – the debated question whether the note issues of the country banks are substitutes or complements for notes of the Bank; the even more hotly debated issue whether or not to count £1 and £2 notes, issued for the first time to conserve gold early in the war, and replaced by gold coin at an unknown rate beginning in 1816; and the gradually evolving role of deposits at the Bank.

It is none of our tasks to resolve these questions and decide by how much the money supply rose to 1814, and fell thereafter, or whether in fact the Bank responded passively, as Tooke and his Banking School believe it should and did, or whether the Bank behaved perversely in following the real-bills doctrine erroneously up to 1814, and then, beginning to get ready for resumption, withdrawing money and stock-piling gold. It is enough to point out the analogy between the two periods, 100-plus years apart, and to suggest that, if anything, economic analysis of the resumption issue was more sophisticated after the peace of Vienna than after Versailles.

Modern monetary theory may have been said to have begun with Henry Thornton's *An Enquiry into the Nature and Effect of the Paper Credit of Great Britain* in 1802 rather than in 1936 with Keynes' *General Theory*. Thornton not only developed the doctrine of the lender of last resort, well before Bagehot, but he also had a nice sense of the long run and the short. Much of the work is devoted to the quantity theory which he later brought to his shared authorship of the Bullion Report (1810/1978), but he also warned against too-precipitous contraction of the Bank of England circulation which may well produce convulsions leading to outflows of specie, rather than the inflow predicted by the monetary theory of the balance of payments (1802/1962, pp. 116, 122, 226–7). Tooke admired *Paper Credit*, he asserted, and called Thornton profoundly acquainted with the principles and details of banking, adding, however, that he had not necessarily, from his occupation as a banker, any knowledge of markets (1838, I, pp. 313–14). The remark could be turned against Tooke, who was a merchant and business man, in insurance and docks, but whose understanding of banking came from the perspective of a customer, rather than the inside.

Unlike 1925, when there was little or no organised opposition to the return of sterling to par, and only the somewhat chaotic and unconvincing arguments of Keynes and McKenna (Moggridge, 1972, pp. 42 ff), two groups opposed resumption in 1819 and earlier, and wanted it reversed in subsequent years. In numbers and position they were so prominent that it is hard to characterise them as 'a few unorthodox minds'. The Birmingham School was interested in employ-ment, maintaining an embryonic Keynesian view (of the 1930s, not

1920s) that expansion of bank circulation was necessary to increase employment and that it was impossible to achieve such expansion with resumption. The agriculturalists had what was close to a Populist position, with emphasis on higher prices to lighten the burden of debt, both mortgage and national debt, the service of which required high taxation. It even contained a bimetallist, who sometimes appears to be in favour of the silver standard, the Earl of Lauderdale (Smart, 1911/1964, I, pp. 478, 622) who was the sole member of the 1819 Lords Committee to vote against resumption (Fetter, 1965, p. 93 note). In this he was a precursor of the Junkers who favoured bimetallism for Germany at the end of the century (Williamson, 1971, p. 21), and of course the American Populists of William Jennings Bryan's day.

It does not seem to me to be entirely correct to say that the Birmingham School had no interest in the inequity between creditor and debtor from inflation and deflation (Fetter, 1965, p. 75; Checkland, 1948, p. 3). Checkland himself notes that Thomas Attwood conceded the case for resumption, provided all debts and obligations would be adjusted (1948, p. 5; Viner, 1937, p. 186). He further talked in terms of stabilising money in terms of wheat, all prices, the rate of interest, or the wages of agricultural labour, all but the third of which comes close to the agricultural position. But the main interest of Birmingham was employment.

There was no doubt that Birmingham was hurt by real factors. War expenditure had been cut, particularly affecting the city that manufactured small arms, hardware, and the 'toy trade'. Machinery was displacing handwork. Exports had been reduced not only by the miscalculations of 1814, comparable to those of 1919, but by tariff increases in the United States and on the Continent. Britain had made rather feeble efforts to guarantee entry of her products in the territory of her wartime allies, seeking, like the United States in the Lend-Lease settlements nearly a century and a half later, to use its bargaining power for trade advantage. It did not succeed (Sherwig, 1969, p. 311). The failure was complained of contemporaneously by Brougham and in 1835 by Cogden (Acworth, 1925, pp. 121–2). A Birmingham petition of labourers, with 11,000 signatures collected in 48 hours, was presented by Brougham to Parliament in 1817, complaining that the city was unemployed or down to 2 to 3 days work a week. Another petition of Birmingham citizens in 1820, drafted by the banker Thomas Attwood, called for a reconsideration of resumption. (These petitions have left a less lasting impression in history than the well-known petition of the Merchants of London for freer trade, presented in 1820 too, written by Thomas Tooke, and presented to Parliament by Alexander Baring (Smart, 1911/1964, I, pp. 744–7).) A motion for repeal was introduced into the House of Commons by Baring, and was defeated twice, the second time on a roll-call vote of 141–27. In the course of the debate, Edward Ellice said he would have preferred resumption at £5 10s for gold, compared to the parity price of £3 17s 10½d. This would have been a depreciation of more than 40 per cent (Fetter, 1965, pp. 100–1). Lord Folkestone for the agriculturalists would have settled for £4 0s 6d in

1819. Tooke states that undertaking resumption at the market price of 1819 'however *palpably unjust*, would have least have been *intelligible*' (1838, II, p. 65, his italics). In 1828 Mr Denison said the proper course to be taken in 1819 was not widely agreed. He held to £4 10s or £4 15s while a colleague in the House of Commons, agreeing with a noble Lord in the other House (Lord Lauderdale?) thought that it ought to be £5 5s or £5 10s (*ibid.*, II, pp. 67, 68). Thomas Attwood himself wanted abandonment of the gold standard altogether, but failing that he sought devaluation by raising the price of gold to £8, qualified to £6 in 1821 and to £5 in 1826 (Checkland, 1948, p. 15). The first number qualifies as unorthodox.

Here was a sharp contrast with 1925 when the issue was never posed in terms of alternative exchange rates but only resumption or no resumption at the price for gold set by Isaac Newton in 1717. It will also be remembered that, when Britain finally went off the gold standard in September, 1931, Tom Johnson, an ex-Labour minister, is said to have remarked 'They never told us we could do that' (Moggridge, 1969, p. 9).

The problem of money as a standard of deferred payment for contracts came to national attention early when Lord King in 1811 for political reasons wrote a letter to his tenants giving them notice that he wanted his rents paid in gold equivalents because of the depreciation of paper currency. Paper currency had not been made legal tender officially because of the frightening example of the *assignats* in France, but the government responded to Lord King's initiative by legislation preventing Bank of England notes being received for a smaller sum than specified on the notes passed (Levi, 1880, pp. 123–33; Fetter, 1965, p. 59). When inflation turned to deflation, 'one William Cobbett' (*sic*, Smart, 1911/1964, I, p. 739) petitioned Parliament for relief by reducing his debt to its 1813 value. He had bought and improved an estate to the extent of £30,000, of which £13,000 was borrowed. With prices less than half their 1813 level 'on account of the Resumption Act' he was about to be ruined. The petition was ignored, and he did lose his farm at Botley in Southampton (*Encyclopaedia Britannica*, 1970, V, p. 989). But Cobbett was more interested as a Radical in the problems of farm labourers and factory workers. He did not 'hate Peel like Castlereagh and Pitt, but held him primarily responsible for severe distresses of common people. Returning to gold without any liquidation of debt charges or reduction of other burdens had been the main cause of semi-starvation . . .' (Cole, n.d., p. 396).

A short digression on Cobbett may be worthwhile, even though he is assuredly one of the few minds that Rostow characterises as unorthodox. In 1819 he had written from the United States, where he had taken refuge from the 1817 act repealing Habeas Corpus, that 'resumption would result in a big fall in prices which would be universally ruinous . . . ruin to all who held stocks of goods or who owed large sums or who had heavy mortgages'. Later, when the Resumption Act passed (and he had returned to Britain), he wrote saying that at least one million would die of hunger, that the act would never be completely carried out, and that, if it were so, he 'would suffer Castlereagh to broil him alive while

Sidmouth stirred the coals, and Canning stood by to make a jest of his groans' (Doubleday, 1847, pp. 248–9). A gridiron became his symbol and logograph for his newspaper, the *Political Register*. The key word in his promise is the word 'completely', meaning the need to eliminate the note issues of the country banks and the Bank of England (Fetter, 1965, p. 108) and do something about the burden of the national debt. A Feast of the Gridiron was promised to his Radical followers and held in April, 1826 (Cole, n.d., pp. 280–3). But by this time Cobbett had returned to his hatred of paper money, inspired by his reading of Thomas Paine's *Decline and Fall of the English System of Finance* (1796), and embodied in his *Paper against Gold* (1815), written when he was in Newgate prison for sedition. When prices were rising in 1824 and 1825, he tried to bring them down by urging trade unionists to convert paper money into gold at every opportunity, and trade unions to appoint a 'gold man'. In August 1832 he debated Thomas Attwood, the Birmingham expansionist, who wanted larger issues of paper money while Cobbett wanted to eliminate both paper money and debt. Attwood opened the debate before 1,400 people in a speech lasting four and a half hours, and Cobbett came back the next day with a moderate two hours of rebuttal (Cole, n.d., pp. 223, 263, 396–7). E. P. Thompson notes that it is not difficult to show that Cobbett had some very stupid and contradictory ideas but he quotes with approval Raymond Williams' attribution to Cobbett of an 'extraordinary sureness of instinct' (1963, pp. 749, 758), and Cole calls him 'largely right' (Cole, n.d., p. 280). Both men write, to be sure, from a leftist perspective.

The classical writers were by no means unaware of the problem of equity between creditor and debtor. Thornton said that the question of whether resumption should be undertaken or not turned on whether depreciation had lasted a long time, such as 15 or 20 years, during which bargains had been made in depreciated currency, or merely two or three years (1802/1962, p. 345). In 1802 when *Paper Credit* was written there had been but two years of 10 per cent or so depreciation (premium on the mint price of gold). This then subsided until 1809 when it rose to 40 or 50 per cent until 1814. What Thornton would have thought about the equity of resumption in 1819 in the light of this uneven record is an interesting puzzle but academic. He died in 1815. Ricardo and McCullogh were concerned less with mortgages and private bargains than with the national debt, as was a wide section of opinion in the 1810s. There was no such issue, so far as I am aware, in public opinion in the 1920s. Ricardo advocated a capital levy to restore equity. In 1817 the income tax had been abandoned, and in any case had not been progressive (Acworth, 1925, ch. v, esp. p. 57). In his first tract in economics, J. R. McCulloch proposed reduction of interest on the national debt because much of it had been advanced in depreciated currency (Smart, 1911/1964, I, p. 510). This would not have affected the capital value of repayment of short-dated issues. Tooke was scornful of all such talk, especially in agricultural land: 'What it has since been the fashion to call an equitable adjustment of contracts means in reality an indemnification of bad speculations' (1838, I, p. 326). Nor did his heart bleed for the industrialists who suffered losses from the fall in prices of industrial goods, some running as high as 50 per cent upon the return of Napoleon from Elba:

> That rise of prices of exportable produce and manufactures which proved so ephemeral as being founded upon the most unwarranted expectations of demand *in consequence of the peace* [his italics], and of the renewal of commercial intercourse with the Continent, has been the occasion of the most absurd conclusions conceivable . . . The disastrous effects of these ill-judged and extravagantly extensive speculations began to manifest themselves in numerous failures which took place toward the end of 1814. (*ibid.*, vol. II, pp. 6–8)

The analogue, of course, is with the boomlet of 1920–1 when a great number of industries in Britain, notably cotton textiles, steel and shipping, went into debt at very high prices of output and capital assets that could not be sustained, and piled up interest charges that were a heavy burden for the rest of the decade (Pigou, 1948, p. 12; Youngson, 1960, pp. 25–6).

Speculation ran the prices of agricultural produce and exports up and down. It did the same with gold, silver and foreign exchange. Once resumption was in the offing, the premiums on gold, silver and Hamburg exchange declined sharply, so that the depreciation of sterling from par was less than 5 per cent. In 1924 after the change of government from Labour to the Conservative party, the pound sterling rose against the dollar to a depreciation of the order of 10 per cent. In these circumstances, the temptation to go the rest of the way is strong indeed. Tooke calls the gap a 'trifling' distance or divergence (1838, II, pp. 65, 76). In commenting on Peel's view that failure to undertake resumption would have been a fraud on creditors Hawtrey uses the same word: 'It would have been a mean-spirited course to go back on the century-old standard on account of so trifling a premium on gold' (1927, p. 351).

'Fraud' and 'mean spirited' introduce into the question the moral issues which were present both in 1819 and in 1925. 'Defenders of the metallic standard contented themselves with an appeal to arbitrary dogmas and moral issues' (Viner, 1937, p. 216). Fetter quotes Brougham: 'To tamper with the public faith; to sully the honour of the country; to declare a national bankruptcy? Good God! Who in his senses would recommend it?' (1965, p. 105). Compare Sauvy on resumption in 1925: 'A question of prestige, a question of dogma, . . . almost a question of honor' (1965, p. 121). Another French view states that it came from the need to look the dollar in the eye . . . 'an affair of *amour propre* rather than monetary policy' (Perrot, 1955, p. 35).

Tooke initially held to the view that the elimination of the 3 or 4 per cent premium on gold or discount on sterling could not have reduced prices by more than that percentage (1838, I, p. 4). He later admitted that, by drawing gold from the Continent, Britain could have raised the price of gold, or lowered commodity prices on a world-wide basis. Ricardo had tried to limit the British demand for gold by urging that resumption take place on the bullion standard, so that convertibility would not be made into coin. This raises the issue of the £1 and £2 notes again, and how much gold was required to retire them from circulation. Tooke admits the possibility of deflation from this source but argues that the amounts of British gold and silver lost to or gained from the rest of the world never amounted to more than £12 to 15 million as contrasted with a world money supply of gold and silver somewhere between £1,200 and £2,000 million, or close to 1 per cent and surely no more than 2 per cent (1838, I, pp. 131–5). The counter to this contention is that the world was, for the most part, on the silver standard, and British gains and losses in gold were a much higher percentage of the world gold supply. Soetbeer's tables of the average ratio of gold to silver in Hamburg goes from 15.11 in 1817 to 15.95 in 1821 (US Senate, 1879/1978, p. 709), which suggests an increasing scarcity of gold, above that of world money in general. From the modern theoretical views of Mundell and Laffer embodied in the expression 'World Monetarism', some pressure on the world money supply, more in gold currency than in silver, thus came from British gold acquisitions from 1819 on. Ricardo put this effect at 5 per cent, and agreed with Tooke that it was the result of Bank mismanagement, that is acceptance of the decision to redeem in coin as well as bullion (Viner, 1937, p. 175).

Insistence of the Banking School that it was real factors that produced these drastic up and down swings in prices, and especially series of crop failures or gluts in a row, encounters another serious objection, that all prices rise and fall more or less together. This is true in Britain, as between agricultural and industrial prices, and between Britain and the Continent, where general price levels rise and fall in wider swings than can be accounted for by exchange-rate differences, which in their turn, on the Banking School showing, were generated by extraordinary foreign payments – another real factor. On the other hand, the classical explanation is probably not much help here either. It was not that prices rose and fell with Bank of England policies of monetary expansion and contraction, although there was some of that as far as the government was concerned. There was some expansion up to 1814 to finance government, and some contraction when the government, in connection with resumption, acceded to the Bank's request to pay down its advance by £10 million. For the most part, however, and particularly for private discounts, the Bank was passive, as indeed the Banking School and the real-bill doctrine believed it should be. Speculation drove prices and prices drove money. As Temin explains in his discussion of the depression in the United States in 1929–33, it was not the LM curve which moved independently and reduced nominal income; it was the shift in spending, the IS curve, which reduced income and led to a decrease in the money supply (1976). A Currency School approach under which the attempt would have been made to limit fluctuations in money to those dictated by the state of the specie reserve would have moderated the swing of prices responding to speculation, but not eliminated them. Speculation in agricultural produce, agricultural land and export commodities responding to variations in harvest and to changes in the fortunes of war could be financed for some considerable distance on the up-side and without limit on the down by the possibility of monetising personal credit. The country-bank note issues responded in this way. Bills of exchange could equally do so. The fact that agricultural and industrial prices rose and fell together suggests that it was not variations in crops alone that affected prices, but that there were important forces working on the side of money as well, despite the passiveness of monetary policy.

The same issue arises with Europe. European prices rose and fell with British ones. Tooke attempts to rebut the argument that this bespeaks the primacy of monetary over real factors, advanced by Matthias Attwood, a London banker and brother of the Birmingham banker, Thomas Attwood, in debate on 10 July 1822 on Mr Western's motion to reconsider resumption, by stating that the same real factors were operative on the Continent as in Britain, and that in fact the decline of prices in 1819 originated on the Continent not England (1838, II, pp. 87, 89, 95). The charge has a familiar ring to those who recall the debate as to whether the financial crisis of 1836 originated in the United States or Britain, and the similar issue over 1929. It is evident that variations in weather can leap the Channel with little difficulty and that one can have long and short crops simultaneously in England and the Continent. The coincidence that the same real factors in industrial products would move non-agricultural prices in similar directions is hard to credit, unless speculation financed by monetised personal credit be regarded as a real instead of a monetary factor.

On these scores I find it hard to accept the view that

(a)   monetary policies were more conscious after 1918 than before;
(b)   that non-monetary factors are paramount in economic history (I propose to say more on this question at another time and place);
(c)   that modern concepts of monetary policy did not exist down to 1914;
(d)   that the monetary system was substantially passive and responsive; and
(e)   that economic reconstruction after 1815 was altogether different from that after 1918.

I should perhaps go further, and suggest here, as I have in the case of eighteenth- and nineteenth-century France (1980), that the clash between monetarism and Keynesianism is an ancient one, going back at least to John Law a century before Henry Thornton. I expect it will still be around a century hence.

Perhaps I should give the last word to the Rostow of about 1941 who wrote:

During these years (1819–21) and in the following three decades there was much controversy on the allegedly deflationary consequences of the Act of 1819. These speculations (along with those of 1810) evoked perhaps the most fruitful monetary discussion of the nineteenth century. (Gayer *et al.*, 1953, p. 165)

This would seem to dispose of the 'few unorthodox minds'.

References

Acworth, A. W. (1925), *Financial Reconstruction in England, 1815–1822* (London: P. S. King).

Boyle, Andrew (1967), *Montagu Norman* (London: Cassell).

Bullion Report (1810/1978), *Report from the Select Committee on the High Price of Gold Bullion*, Ordered by the House of Commons to be printed 8 June 1810; reprint edn. (New York: Arno Press, 1978).

Checkland, S. G. (1948), 'The Birmingham Economists, 1815–1850', *Economic History Review*, 2nd ser., vol. 1, no. 1, pp. 1–19.

Clay, Sir Henry (1957/1978), *Lord Norman* (London, Macmillan); reprint edn. (New York: Arno).

Cole, G. D. H. (n.d.), *The Life of William Cobbett* (New York: Harcourt Brace, preface dated 1924).

Cunliffe Report (1925/1978), British Parliamentary Reports on International Finance, *The Cunliffe Committee and the Macmillan Committee (1931) Reports* (New York: Arno Press).

Doubleday, Thomas (1847), *A Financial, Monetary and Statistical History of England from the Revolution of 1688 to the Present Time* (London: Effingham, Wilson).

Fetter, Frank Whitson (1965), *Development of British Monetary Orthodoxy, 1797–1875* (Cambridge, Mass.: Harvard University Press).

Gayer, Arthur D., Rostow, W. W. and Schwartz, Anna Jacobson (1953), *The Growth and Fluctuation of the British Economy, 1790–1850. An Historical, Statistical and Theoretical Study of Britain's Economic Development* (Oxford: Clarendon Press; largely unchanged from the MS. of 1941).

Gregory, T. E. (1928), 'Introduction' to Thomas Tooke and William Newmarch, *A History of Prices and of the State of Circulation from 1792 to 1856* (New York: Adelphi, 6 vols; reproduced from the original; first 2 vols originally 1838).

Grigg, P. J. (1948), *Prejudice and Judgement* (London: Jonathan Cape).

Hawtrey, R. G. (1919/1927), *Currency and Credit*, 3rd edn. (London: Longmans, Green).

Howson, Susan K. (1975), *Domestic Monetary Management in Britain, 1919–38* (Cambridge: Cambridge University Press).

Keynes, John Maynard (1930), *A Treatise on Money* (New York: Harcourt Brace, 2 vols).

Keynes, John Maynard (1932), *Essays in Persuasion* (New York: Harcourt Brace).

Keynes, John Maynard (1933/1951), *Essays in Biography*, new edn. with three additional essays (London: Hart-Davis).

Keynes, John Maynard (1936), *The General Theory of Employment, Interest and Money* (New York: Harcourt Brace).

Kindleberger, Charles P. (1980), 'Keynesianism vs. Monetarism in Eighteenth- and Nineteenth-Century France', *History of Political Economy*, vol. 12, no 4 (Winter), pp. 499–523.

Leith-Ross, Sir Frederick (1968), *Money Talks. Fifty Years of International Finance* (London: Hutchinson).

Levi, Leone (1880), *The History of British Commerce* (London: Murray).

Li, Ming-Hsun (1963), *The Great Recoinage of 1696 to 1699* (London: Weidenfeld & Nicolson).

Lüthy, Herbert (1959), *La Banque protestante en France de la révocation de l'édit de Nantes à la révolution*. Vol. I: *Dispersion et regroupement (1685–1730)* (Paris: SEVPEN).

Moggridge, D. E. (1969), *The Return to Gold, 1925. The Formulation of Policy and its Critics* (Cambridge: Cambridge University Press).

Moggridge, D. E. (1972), *British Monetary Policy, 1924–1931. The Norman Conquest of $4.86* (Cambridge: Cambridge University Press).

Morgan, E. Victor (1943), *The Theory and Practice of Central Banking, 1797–1913* (Cambridge: Cambridge University Press).

O'Brien, D. P. (ed.) (1971), *The Correspondence of Lord Overstone* (Cambridge: Cambridge University Press, 3 vols).

Paine, Thomas (1796), *The Decline and Fall of the English System of Finance* (Paris: Hartley Adlard & Son).

Paine, Thomas (1815), *Paper against Gold* (London: J. M'Creery).

Perrot, Marguerite (1955), *La Monnaie et l'opinion publique en France et en Angleterre, 1924–36* (Paris: Colin).

Pigou, A. C. (1948), *Aspects of British Economic History, 1918–25* (London: Macmillan).

Rostow, W. W. (1978), *The World Economy* (Austin, Tex.: University of Texas Press).

Rostow, W. W. (1980), 'Money and Prices: An Old Debate Revisited', in *Why the Poor Get Poorer and the Rich Slow Down: Essays in the Marshallian Long Period* (Austin, Tex.: University of Texas Press).

Sauvy, Alfred (1965), *Histoire économique de la France entre les deux guerres*. Vol. I: *1918–31* (Paris: Fayard).

Sherwig, John M. (1969), *Guineas and Gunpowder. British Foreign Aid in the Wars with France, 1793–1815* (Cambridge, Mass.: Harvard University Press).

Silberling, N. J. (1924), 'Financial and Monetary Policy in Great Britain during the Napoleonic Wars', I, II, *Quarterly Journal of Economics*, vol. 38, pp. 214–23, 397–439.

Smart, William (1911/1964), *Economic Annals of the Nineteenth Century*. Vol. I: *1801–1820*; Vol. II: *1821–1830*, reprint edn. (New York: Kelley).

Temin, Peter (1976), *Did Monetary Forces Cause the Great Depression?* (New York: W. W. Norton).

Thompson, E. P. (1963), *The Making of the English Working Class* (New York: Knopf).

Thornton, Henry (1802/1962), *An Enquiry into the Nature and Effect of the Paper Credit of Great Britain, together with the Evidence*; edited with an introduction by F. A. Hayek (London: Frank Cass; reprint of 1939 edn., London: Allen & Unwin).

Tooke, Thomas and Newmarch, William (1838/1928), *A History of Prices and of the State Circulation from 1792 to 1856*, reproduced from the original with an introduction by T. E. Gregory (New York: Adelphi, n.d.; introduction dated 1928; 6 vols, first 2 vols originally 1838).

US Senate (1879/1978), *International Monetary Conference of 1878, Proceedings and Exhibits* (Washington, DC: USGPO); reprint edn (New York: Arno Press).

Vilar, Pierre (1976), *A History of Gold and Money, 1450–1920*, translated from the 1969 Spanish original by Judith White (London: New Left Books).

Viner, Jacob (1937), *Studies in the Theory of International Trade* (New York: Harper).

Williamson, John (1971), *Karl Helfferich, 1872–1924, Economist, Financier, Politician* (Princeton, NJ: Princeton University Press).

Youngson, A. J. (1960), *The British Economy, 1920–1957* (London: Allen & Unwin).

7

The International Monetary Politics of a Near-Great Power: Two French Episodes, 1926–1936 and 1960–1970

I

Students of international monetary relations have lately learned that their subject has, along with its technical intricacy, a high content of pure politics, and political scientists have begun to explore inter-national relations beyond the usual confines of diplomatic and security questions into areas of technology and high finance (see, for example Rolfe, 1966; Kindleberger, 1967; Strange, 1970, 1971).[1] The production of testable hypotheses as to how various powers will behave politically in monetary affairs has hardly begun, however. Miss Strange has offered a taxonomy which divides currencies into 'Top Currencies, Master Currencies, Passive or Neutral Currencies and Political or Negotiated Currencies' which combines elements of economic and political analysis (1971, p. 217). A number of historians have blamed the British crisis of 1931 on the small powers which converted sterling into gold in self-protection and helped to bring about the departure of the pound from gold (see, for example, Born, 1967; Hurst, 1932).

The hypothesis submitted to testing in this paper is that the inter-national monetary politics of great powers and little powers are relatively simple compared with those of countries in between. Great powers, typically one great power, have responsibility for the stability of the international monetary system. Small countries with no power separately to affect the system have no such responsibility and are free to pursue the narrow national interest. In between, near-great powers face a difficult problem since they have power to hurt the system, generally insufficient power to steady it in the face of disruption on a wide scale, but are tempted to pursue national goals which diverge from the interest of the system. The parts of the hypothesis applying to the great and the small powers are evidently widely challenged. The near-great powers especially contend that the great power purporting to act in the interest of the stability of the system is in reality motivated by self-interest which

A paper presented to the Economic History Society meeting at the University of Kent, Canterbury, England, 1972, and published in Economic Notes, *vol. 1, no. 2–3 (Siena, 1972), pp. 30–44. Reprinted with permission of Monte dei Paschi di Siena.*

it confuses, deliberately or with self-hypnosis, with the broader world interest. On a high ethical plane, the small countries should adopt the Kantian Categorical Imperative, acting in ways which can be generalized, rather than pursue their national interest by means, which, if many small countries used them, would undermine the system. Since present interest attaches to such a near-great power as France, however, the validity of these parts of the hypothesis can be put aside, except insofar as it affects the behavior of near-great powers. The problem is the course of behavior of a country not strong enough to stabilize the system, but with ambitions and purposes of its own and sufficient strength to disturb it.

The question is examined historically with concise accounts of two periods when a case could be made that France rocked the international monetary boat for purposes of its own, in one case helping to capsize it. The first of these periods runs from the *de facto* stabilization of the French franc by Poincaré in 1926 to the Blum devaluation ten years later. The second covers the approximate decade from the de Gaulle stabilization of 1958 to the Pompidou devaluation of August 1969. In the first period, French national goals were largely of a security nature, although the economic aim of securing reparation from Germany played a significant role. In the second, French purposes included a change in the international monetary system itself, with a downgrading of the role of the dollar, a central place for gold, and a change in procedure for making international monetary decisions.

II

After World War I, the pound sterling was stabilized at its pre-war par in 1925, whereas the French franc, halted in its continuous depreciation by an heroic effort by Poincaré in July 1926, was stabilized *de facto* in the fall of 1926 and *de jure* in June 1928 at one-fifth of its pre-war value. The return to par overvalued the pound, weakened the British balance of payments and produced unemployment.[2] In the short run, however, it conveyed prestige on sterling. Poincaré thought long and hard when the French franc recovered in the fall of 1926 about letting it go all the way to par (Moreau, 1954, pp. 61, 94, 166, 184, etc.). Complaints from the automobile industry and from Léon Jouhaux, the leader of the CGT, as appreciation proceeded, turned the decision against any such course. The rate of 125 to the pound (roughly 4 cents) left the franc undervalued, although the decision was made with care.[3] In arriving at the rates, both Britain and France thought about national interests, rather than the impact of a disequilibrium cross-rate on the international monetary system. In the light of the pre-war position, however, there was more obligation on Britain to contemplate the wider interest than on France.

The overvaluation of the pound and undervaluation of the franc resulted in an accumulation of sterling (and later dollars) by France which altered the balance of financial power, weakened the international monetary system, and ultimately contributed to the world depression. A small part of the difficulty was the result of a technical point; beginning in the summer of 1927, the Bank of France held some sterling in the form of forward contracts with the Paris money market, which held sterling balances sold forward to the Bank of France. This made it appear that Bank of France (official) sterling was less than it really was, and further enabled the Bank of France, when the contracts ran off, to appear to convert into gold newly acquired rather than existing holdings of British exchange. The main problem was, however, first, that the French were somewhat antipathetical to Britain; second, that they chose to use their economic power for political purposes; and third, that in the final analysis, it was the British, not they, who were responsible for the stability of the system.

On the first score, the memoirs of Governor Moreau are highly revealing. As the apex of the hierarchical organization of the world economy, Governor Montagu Norman of the Bank of England thought it appropriate that the Bank of England organize the return to the gold standard of the other central banks in Europe. Governor Moreau was interested in competing for satellite central banks, and resented the efforts of the Bank of England. On frequent occasions, Governor Benjamin Strong of the Federal Reserve Bank had to be called in to lead a consortium to offer a stabilization loan to, for example, the National Bank of Poland. Moreau was conscious of the power which the Bank's sterling gave him over the Bank of England, and remarks on it frequently (1954, pp. 246, 250, 336, 488–9, etc.).

More significant was the difference between the British and the French over the use of the power of the lender to achieve political ends. The record is full of allegations of threats and calling of loans in the light of political rather than economic considerations. By no means all can be verified.

The French were hardly alone in attaching political conditions to economic loans. The Department of State had urged Wall Street not to lend to countries which failed to settle their war debts (Feis, 1950. pp. 20ff). Germany conditioned its participation in the Belgian stabilization loan on a rectification of the border at Eupen and Malmedy (Moreau, 1954, p. 76). Moreover, as noted, many of the accusations against France are debatable or unproved. The record, nonetheless, is a full one.

It is widely claimed, inconclusively, that the French threatened to withdraw credits from Germany when Schacht raised the questions of the return of German colonies and of the Polish corridor at the Young Plan discussions of Paris in April 1929 (Schacht, 1 ˙ 1, pp. 88–91).⁴

Leith-Ross of the British Treasury recounts in his memoirs that Quesnay of the Bank of France, supported by Francqui of Belgium and Pirelli of Italy, had reacted to Snowden's characterization of French demands for the division of reparations as 'ridiculous and grotesque' by threatening to withdraw all French sterling from London (£240 million). Leith-Ross states that he rang for a messenger and directed him 'Kindly show these gentlemen out', knowing that the Bank of France would certainly not want to see the collapse of sterling (1968, p. 124). This was in August 1929. Tight money in London, especially after the Hatry crisis of September 20, the day after the New York stock market peak, drew funds from New York and precipitated the crash. French opinion allows for the possibility that the spark that set off the explosion was the reaction to Snowden's abusive remark (Néré, 1968, p. 78).[5]

In the fall of 1930, the French press threatened the withdrawal of credits from Germany over a fancied slight – Germany hinting that it needed a loan to meet the withdrawals of capital which followed the National Socialist victory in the September elections, and then contracting it with Lee Higginson alone (Bennet, 1962). In the following spring, the accusation was made that France withdrew credits from Austria and Germany, over the Bruening initiative of Zollunion, a domestic political counter to the Nazi electoral gains. The facts of matter are in some confusion, and a recent investigator is doubtful (Bennet, 1962, p. 100).[6] But the French record on rescue loans for Austria and Germany is clear. They participated in the first Austrian credit, but insisted on political conditions. In the case of the second Austrian loan, Montagu Norman became angered at the French attitude, which he deplored, and went forward with a 50 million schilling loan to Austria for one week. It was not sufficient. A rescue loan for Germany did not get far. The French conditions of abandonment of the customs union with Austria and of the construction of the Panzerkreuzer were unacceptable to Bruening, looking desperately for foreign-policy successes to fend off the rising tide of National Socialism at home. While Stimson was for a loan, President Hoover and Secretary of the Treasury Ogden Mills felt that, with the Moratorium, they had gone as far as they could, and in particular were opposed to sending good money after bad, the essence of rescue operations. The British, weakened by withdrawals, explained that the 'Bank of England had already lent quite as much as is entirely convenient' (Federal Reserve Bank of New York files, telegram, Norman to Harrison, 3 July 1931). There was no rescue loan and Germany joined Austria in blocking foreign credits.

There is no evidence that French officialdom contributed to the pressure on Britain which pushed that country off the gold standard in September 1931. On the contrary, the Bank of France joined the Federal Reserve Bank of New York in a rescue loan in August. Leith-Ross asserts that Moret, the governor of the Bank of France (successor to Moreau as of October 1928) was 'very helpful', and the latter was in fact awarded a KBE in October 1931 (1968, p. 139). This may have been part compensation for the fact that the Bank of France lost heavily on the £62 million it had on deposit in London on September 21.

The loss on sterling converted the attitudes of France into those of a small country, concerned little with the stability of the monetary system and anxious about the safety of its dollar holdings. On September 21, Moret asked Governor Harrison of the Federal Reserve Bank of New York whether the Fed would object to the conversion of Bank of France dollars into gold. He was told that it would not. The next day the Bank of

France converted $50 million (and the Bank of Belgium $106.6 million). Virtually daily thereafter the conversions continued. Moret explained politely the reasons for his concern – the British losses – and asked continuously whether his actions bothered the United States authorities. The loss of $775 million to all countries in the first three weeks did bother the Federal Reserve Bank, which was short of 'free gold', but it proudly refused to acknowledge any inconvenience. Conversions died down only to be revived in January of 1932 in response to two events, the legislation indemnifying the Bank of France by the French government over the losses in Britain which awakened acute political concern, and a dispatch to the *Agence Economique* by Professor H. Parker Willis of Columbia University, characterizing the establishment of the Reconstruction Finance Corporation in the United States as inflationary. The Glass–Steagall bill passed in February relieved the gold situation in the United States, but only after the crisis had brought the United States, as Hoover said in the 1932 presidential campaign, within two weeks of going off the gold standard. A third flurry of conversion was started in March 1932, suspended briefly, resumed in April at $12.5 million a week. At the end of May when Moret indicated to Harrison that he wished to speed up the conversion, while avoiding 'mischievous interpretations', it was suggested to him that he convert it all at once, and be done with the process. This he did on June 11, 1932. It was the bottom of the depression. (Federal Reserve Bank of New York files.)

One can argue, as do Friedman and Schwartz (1963, *passim*), that the responsibility for the world depression rests on mistaken monetary policy in the United States. The case in my judgement is thin. One can more readily blame the United States for cutting off foreign lending in 1928 just as the boom petered out, and putting strong deflationary pressure on Germany, Central Europe and the less developed countries – though it is difficult to imagine what positive steps this country could have undertaken to sustain lending. One can also fault the United States for raising tariffs as the depression began and for refusing to make rescue loans in time and in requisite amounts. The United States was far from ready to take responsibility for stabilizing the world economy. But the French actions in destabilizing for political advantage, in refusing rescue loans without impossible political conditions, and finally in cutting and running in the manner of a small country with no responsibility for the system compounded the felony.

III

After World War II French national finances were rather chaotic until de Gaulle came to power again in 1958 and devalued the franc for the second time, but successfully. The factors making for that success need not detain us, but the consequences were a positive balance of payments, rising claims in foreign currencies, largely dollars, and an interest in taking a significant role in shaping the evolving international monetary system.

As early as 1958, Professor Robert Triffin of Yale had been criticizing the gold-exchange standard, in which countries held reserves in currencies convertible into gold, as an absurdity (Triffin, 1960). In brief, his point was that holding reserves in the strongest currency induced the country that issued it to issue too much, with the result that the currency became weaker. This led to withdrawals and crisis. The view was well suited to French political interests. Sterling had been top currency, to use Susan Strange's not altogether suitable phrase, and now the dollar was. The French franc served a former colonial area, but enjoyed little international use outside it. French experts, and de Gaulle. attacked the gold-exchange standard, and especially the dollar standard. From the first 'dollar crisis' of the fall of 1960, to the 1969 devaluation of the French franc, French policies were directed to offering an alternative to a dollar-exchange system, and on occasion, to direct attack on the system.

It was recognized at the outset by Triffin and others that, if the dollar no longer served along with gold as an international asset, there would be a world shortage of international liquidity. Triffin proposed a new world central bank issuing a new international currency – an idea which had been advocated during the depression by Keynes and others. This would replace the International Monetary Fund, which did not issue permanent international money but rather made short-term loans which were repayable. The French view, expressed initially by Rueff. was that the price of gold should be raised to meet the liquidity need. In 1963 Giscard d'Estaing proposed the issuance of an international Currency Reserve Unit (CRU), the forerunner of the Special Drawing Right (SDR) which was ultimately adopted. Between the CRU as proposed by the French, and the SDR as adopted worldwide, however, there was this significant difference: the CRU, Giscard suggested, should be issued to every holder of gold in some proportion to his gold holdings. The alternative system, later adopted, and akin to the establishment of quotas in the IMF, was that countries should be issued the new international reserve unit in some proportion to their financial and trade strength. The French proposal was akin to raising the price of gold for central banks and had the disadvantage of encouraging central banks to convert exchange reserves into gold. In 1965 the French began exchanging dollars into gold as if in preparation for the issuance of CRU on the basis they suggested.

On February 4, 1965 President de Gaulle declared war on the dollar standard. He praised gold as 'immutable, impartial and universal' and denounced the benefits which the United States derived from the use of the dollar as a reserve currency – the capacity to finance deficits, and in particular to buy foreign plants with money provided by the foreigners themselves.[7] The Bank of France began a rapid conversion of outstanding dollars into gold. In 1964, the French had been taking incremental increases in reserves in the form of gold rather than dollars, and these reserves increased from $3.4 billion at the end of May 1964 to

$3.7 billion at the end of the year. Then began conversion of infra-marginal dollars into gold to put pressure on the dollar-exchange standard. $1 billion in gold was gained in 1965 and another $500 million in the first nine months of 1966 before the French balance of payments turned adverse.[8] It was announced that henceforward Bank of France reserves would be published in francs, not dollars. In the fall of 1967, in the British crisis, the Bank of France withdrew from the gold pool supplying the hoarders, which had been created after the dollar troubles of 1960 (and in which the French contribution was very small), and further refused to participate in the rescue operations organized by the Group of 10 in behalf of the pound sterling. It is too much to say that France oiled the waters of British devaluation, but she fished them hard to obtain a change in the international monetary system along the hard-money lines already laid out. The effort failed. Britain's devaluation occurred without any change in the system, and when a change occurred in March 1968 it was taken without French participation, and in a direction contrary to French proposals. November 1967 was the peak of French efforts to remake the international monetary system along French economic and political lines.

In March 1968, a burst of gold hoarding led to the decision to institute a two-tier system for gold, with one price, $35 an ounce, for central banks, and a free market for hoarders where prices could rise in full as demand and supply willed, without intervention by the monetary authorities of the Club. The French were unable to denounce the scheme, since this would have committed them not to join the Club, and without membership it was not clear what the gold of the Bank of France was worth. As it turned out, this hesitation was wise, since the events of May and June led to sharp gold losses in July which were compounded by a capital outflow from France in the fall. At the end of March 1968 Michel Debré argued at Stockholm against the arrangements for issuing SDRs, which had been agreed in principle in Rio de Janeiro in September 1967. While he was speaking, the first student riots were taking place in Nanterre.

Successive strikes, first by students, then workers and in September by the middle class led to a crisis in November 1968, one year after the crisis in sterling. The French government cut back on nuclear tests, stretched out the *force de frappe* and the policy for all azimuths, but, in confrontation with the Germans who were unwilling to revalue upward, accepted the rescue operations organized by the Group of 10 and then refused to devalue. President de Gaulle characterized devaluation as absurd. The crisis it was said was international, not national, and the difficulty lay not in the French franc rate but in the whole international monetary system created at Bretton Woods, which was sick and headed for disaster. Reform was needed in the impartial gold standard. But in March 1969, the French government no longer thought it useful to raise the price of gold, which would only give windfall profits to gold speculators, and President de Gaulle, who repeated on March 6, 1969 that the franc would not be devalued, resigned at the end of April. During the period of holidays in August, the franc was devalued from

20.255 to 18.004 cents, or by 11 percent. France accepted her share of SDRs. The attack on the international monetary system, and its use of the dollar, was perhaps not ended. It was at least packed away into cold storage.[9]

IV

While there are broad similarities between the two experiences – extending as far as those between the Accord de Matignon of June 1936 and the Accord de Grenelle of June 1968, representing governmental capitulation to internal forces which made devaluation inevitable and ended the hope of international monetary success – there are significant differences as well. In the 1920s and '30s, the politics involved in monetary politics were low-level, conducted by Moreau, Quesnay, Rist and similar technical people. In the 1960s, the politics had moved higher to the level of the chief executive. Moreau kept in touch with Poincaré in 1926–28, as his diary makes clear, but it was he who issued the threats, or the Minister of Finance who withheld the loans, not the Prime Minister. President de Gaulle, on the other hand, discoursed freely on international monetary theory, not always, one suspects, with complete approval of his experts.

Secondly, the conversion of dollars was undertaken for economic reasons in the 1930s and for political in 1965 and 1966. The challenge to the dollar in the later period was comparable to the challenge to sterling in 1929, but for higher political stakes. Like that challenge, moreover, it is likely that de Gaulle was conscious of the dangers of pulling down the international monetary system, without achieving his positive ends. Just as Leith-Ross could stare down Quesnay, Franqui and Pirelli, confident in the conviction that France did not want to see the collapse of sterling, so the United States must have surely known that the French dollar conversions of 1965 were undertaken only because France believed that the United States could resist them. The episode represents maneuvering, not warfare.

The near-great power finds itself in a cleft stick. If it cooperates in international monetary matters, as do Japan and Germany, it perpetuates the domination of one or more great powers; if it attacks the system *à l'outrance*, it threatens to bring it down around its ears. Isolation is an inadequate strategy, as the United States demonstrated persuasively in 1929 to 1931, and early intervention to produce change in the system either fails as in 1968 or destroys the world economy. The intermediate policy of cooperating until a country is strong enough to change the system and sustain a new one in the face of opposition requires a servility which proud nations find difficult to accede to. In international monetary matters, it would seem to be better to be dominant and accept the responsibility for making the system work, or small and able to ignore the public in favour of the private interest, rather than in between.

Notes

1 Straight historians as distinguished from economic historians have not ignored the politics of monetary problems. See, e.g., Bennet (1962) and Schwartz (1969).
2 For an account of the return to par, see Moggridge (1969).
3 Sauvy (1965, p. 99) calls the decision 'an island of reason in an ocean of errors'. For a defense of the rate and a discussion of its choice, see Rueff (1954, 1959).
4 Schacht's account is supported by remarks of Pierre Quesnay quoted in Clarke (1967, p. 165) and Lüke (1958, pp. 171–2). But the contemporary *Economist* (vol. 108, no. 4470, 4 May 1929, p. 966) is very doubtful.
5 Paul Einzig, the well-known English financial journalist, is another who believes that French withdrawals from Britain because of the Snowden–Cheron affair precipitated the Wall Street Crash. See Einzig (1935), pp. 172–4 and esp. p. 185. Note that 'ridicule et grotesque' is much more abusive than 'riduculous and grotesque'. Paul Schmidt, who was later Hitler's interpreter and who was present both for the Paris and the first Hague Young Plan conference, calls the former a poor translation for the latter (1949, p. 178).
6 But see Born (1967), pp. 56, 65, 66, who denies the allegation. Leith-Ross (1968, p. 144) suggested to Professor Charles Rist that France should lend to Austria on the condition that the government reformed the budget and added that France was always vaunting her financial power but seemed disinclined to use it except for political purposes. 'Professor Rist . . . did not disagree with me.'
7 For a fuller statement on this point, see President de Gaulle's press conference of 27 November 1967, in e.g. *The New York Times*, 28 November 1967.
8 It is not without interest that when the French balance of payments did turn adverse, instead of selling gold, as implied by the statements praising the discipline furnished by the gold standard, France acquired dollars by borrowing them in Euro-dollar bond market through nationalized companies. $30 million of Euro-dollar bonds were sold in January, June and October 1967 by Electricité de France, the Société Nationale des Chemins de Fer Français and the Caisse Nationale des Télécommunications, respectively.
9 The foregoing account has been put together from the contemporary press since there has been insufficient time to get an inside story from memoirs and documents. For an account of some of the French participants, see Fabra (*Le Monde*'s financial correspondent) (1968).

References

Bennet, Edward W. (1962), *Germany and the Diplomacy of the Financial Crisis, 1931* (Cambridge, Mass.: Harvard University Press).
Born, Karl Erich (1967), *Die deutsche Bankenkrise, 1931, Finanzen und Politik* (Munich: R. Piper & Co. Verlag).
Clarke, S. V. O. (1967), *Central Bank Cooperation, 1924–31* New York: Federal Reserve Bank of New York).
Einzig, Paul (1935), *World Finance, 1914–35* (New York: Macmillan).
Fabra, Paul (1968), 'The Moneymen of France', *Interplay*, January, pp. 37–40.
Feis, Herbert (1950), *The Diplomacy of the Dollar, 1919–1932* (New York: W. W. Norton).
Friedman, Milton and Schwartz, Anna Jacobson (1963), A Monetary History of the United States 1867–1960 (Princeton, NJ: Princeton University Press).
Hurst, Willard (1932), 'Holland, Switzerland and Belgium and the English Gold Crisis of 1931', *Journal of Political Economy*, vol. 40, no. 3 (June), pp. 638–60.
Kindleberger, C. P. (1967), 'The Politics of Money and World Language', *Essays in International Finance*, No. 61 (Princeton, NJ, August).

Leith-Ross, Sir Frederick (1968), *Money Talks, Fifty Years of International Finance* (London: Hutchinson).

Lüke, Rolf E. (1958), *Von der Stabilisierung zur Krise* (Zurich: Polygraphischer Verlag).

Moggridge, D. E. (1969), *The Return to Gold, 1925: The Formulation of Economic Policy and its Critics* (Cambridge: Cambridge University Press).

Moreau, Émile (1954), *Souvenirs d'un gouveneur de la Banque de France. Histoire de la stabilisation du franc (1926–1928)* (Paris: Genin).

Néré, J. (1968), *La Crise de 1929* (Paris: Colin).

Rolfe, Sydney E. (1966), *Gold and World Power* (New York: Harper & Row).

Rueff, Jacques (1954), 'Préface' to Emile Moreau, *Souvenirs d'un gouveneur de la Banque de France* (Paris: Genin).

Rueff, Jacques (1959), 'Sur un point d'histoire: le niveau de la stabilisation Poincaré', *Revue d'économie politique*, 69e annee (March–April), pp. 168–78.

Sauvy, Alfred (1965), *Histoire économique de la France entre les deux guerres*. Vol. I: *1918–1931* (Paris: Fayard).

Schacht, Hjalmar H. G. (1931), *The End of Reparations* (New York: Jonathan Cape and Harrison Smith).

Schmidt, Paul (1949), *Statist auf diplomatischen Bühne* (Bonn: Athenäum-Verlag).

Schwartz, Jordan (1969), *1933: Roosevelt's Decision, the United States and the Gold Standard* (New York: Chelsea House).

Strange, Susan (1970), *Sterling and British Policy: A Political Study of an International Currency in Decline* (London: Oxford University Press).

Strange, Susan (1971), 'The Politics of International Currencies', *World Politics*, vol. 23, no. 2 (January), pp. 215–31.

Triffin, Robert (1960), *Gold and the Dollar Crisis* (New Haven, Conn.: Yale University Press).

8

Collective Memory vs. Rational Expectations: Some Historical Puzzles in Macro-Economic Behavior

Modern macro-economists have developed the theory of rational expectations to explain how people forecast important variables in an uncertain world. In place of the naive assumption used in some macro-economic models in the 1960s – that tomorrow will be like today or yesterday – so-called adaptive expectations – the theory of rational expectations holds that people respond to economic events through forming expectations based on standard economic models, and do so in an optimal way within the restrictions imposed by limited information and uncertainty. According to one exponent, 'Practically all theorists and many practitioners accept the validity of the rational expectations hypothesis applied to financial markets' (Poole, 1980, p. 245). No claim is made that it is accepted by economic historians. It may be of interest to contrast this theory with at least two others: that people respond to economic stimuli – at least on occasion – in ideological fashion, or on the basis of some collective memory of past events and outcomes. Ideology, to be sure, is likely to be merely collective memory internalized into a rule of thumb or 'lesson of history'.

To sharpen the distinction between the alternatives, let me cite Jude Wanniski (1977, pp. 133–6), who finds the explanation of the stock-market crash of October 1929 in the action of the United States Senate, amending a draft bill, in defeating the forces resisting an increase in the tariff on carbides, reported in the inside pages of the daily press. In the Wanniski view, this defeat was taken by the stock market as an indication that the Hawley–Smoot tariff would be passed – as proved to be the case nine months later, signed into law by President Hoover, and would be strongly deflationary. Tariffs were later regarded as expansionary in economic models, provided there was no retaliation. With retaliation they could be deflationary. The defeat of the forces opposed to the carbide tariff increase was, in Wanniski's eyes, despite the unimportance of the item, a symbol of forthcoming deep world

Reprinted with permission from Svend Andersen, Karsten Laursen, P. Nørregaard Rasmussen and J. Vibe-Pedersen (eds), Economic Essays in Honour of Jørgen H. Gelting *(Copenhagen: Danish Economic Association, 1982), pp. 118–28.*

depression, and it was this that, by rational expectations, brought about the stock-market crash.

To Schumpeter (1939, II, p. 915), the tariff response of Hoover was merely the 'household remedy' of the Republican party. I was brought up in a Republican household which confirmed this ideological position: my father firmly believed that tariff reductions engineered by the Democratic party from time to time led to depression, while tariff increases produced by Republicans ushered in periods of prosperity.

The same clash between rational expectations and ideology can be seen in European tariff history of the nineteenth century. France, Germany, and (belatedly) Italy responded to the fall in the price of wheat brought about by the decline in transoceanic shipping costs by imposing tariffs. Britain was resolutely committed to free trade, had been since 1846 and was to continue to be for another half century. Not only did Britain not impose a tariff; no single proposal for such a tariff was made in the Parliament. In Denmark, by contrast, there were numerous proposals for tariffs on grain, all of which were rejected.

My interest, however, is less in ideology than in collective memory as it affects some economic responses, but not others, and over periods of time which seem to controvert the simple hypothesis that collective memory in economic questions fades monotonically with the passage of time. I have in mind five examples on which it may be worth-while expatiating:

1   fear of banks, or of institutions named 'banks', that the French derived from the collapse of the Mississippi bubble of John Law in 1720, and the 75-years later hyperinflation and collapse of the *assignats*. Such fear lasted well past the middle of the nineteenth century;
2   fear of inflation generated in the Germans by the hyperinflation of 1923, which extended irrationally to exchange depreciation in the midst of acute deflation (in 1931) through a sort of metonymy that associated exchange depreciation with hyperinflation and its trauma;
3   British paranoia about unemployment for 50 years or so after the 1920s, leading it to choose policies of brimful employment, and inflation;
4   the failure of the British, with few exceptions, to recall the difficulties associated with the restoration of the pound to par in 1819 when they undertook a comparable restoration in 1925;
5   the inability of markets, from at least 1550 to 1866, and in some instances quite a bit earlier to quite a bit later, to learn how to handle efficiently a ten-year cycle of euphoria leading to financial crisis from overextended credit.

Examples 1, 2 and 3 illustrate the Maginot Line complex in which analogies are drawn between circumstances which are superficially similar but are in significant respects different. Examples 4 and 5, on the other hand, furnish a different kind of antithesis to rational expectations, for, in them, markets fail to draw parallels between conditions that are fundamentally the same.

(1) John Law's Banque Générale of 1715 was succeeded in 1718 by the Banque Royale, which exploded in 1720 in the Mississippi bubble's burst, shortly before the related collapse of the South Sea bubble in London. The reasons are well understood. Whereas the Banque Générale had been a private bank which never circulated notes of more than a fifth of its authorized issue of 60 million livres, the Banque Royale had an authorized issue of 110 millions, not guaranteed, redeemable only in current or debased coin, and made compulsory for various payments, which was issued in ever-increasing amounts when Law sought to promote the stock of the associated (Mississippi) Compagnie d'Occident by establishing a forward price for it well above the current price. There was a pell-mell rush to borrow from the Banque Royale and buy shares in the Compagnie d'Occident, followed, as the latter rose to giddy heights, by a pell-mell rush to get out of the stock of the Compagnie and the notes of the Banque Royale. The bubble of Law's *système* was pricked and burst by old-line merchant bankers organized into an *anti-système*. But the effect of the collapse was to discourage French enthusiasm for all banks – except intimate private ones. In 1776 Isaac Panchaud organized a Caisse d'Escompte, a semi-official bank for discounting trade bills (Lüthy, 1961, p. 434). It failed when the Comptrollers of Finance in the last days of Louis XV's reign forcibly borrowed from it for the government. It became moribund until it was reorganized after the failure of the *assignats*, as the Caisse des Comptes Courants. Liesse (1909, p. 12) explains that the Caisse des Comptes Courants was not called a 'bank' because that name still terrified people three-quarters of a century after John Law. It was incorporated into the Banque de France in 1800. The Bank of France presumably could be called a 'bank' because it was thought to be the analogue of the Bank of England – an institution which had enormous prestige in France, based on what Mollien called in his memoirs '108 years of success'. Mollien was Napoleon's Minister of Public Treasury, and adviser on banking questions. In his first note to the First Consul sent in 1802, he cautioned against a general bank which sought to establish offices in France outside Paris, as the Banque Royale had done, and devoted a long footnote to the 'terrible example' of John Law: 87 years of experience since Law's time had only underlined the dangers of confusing capital and money (Mollien, 1845, I, pp. 451, 451 n., 455, 460).

Regional banks were formed after the Bank of France, and called 'banks' – in Le Havre, Lille, Lyons, Marseilles and Dijon (Gille, 1970). They were allowed or helped to fail by the Bank of France in 1848. Private banks continued to be formed, and at the end of the nineteenth century so-called *banques d'affaires*, or industrial banks, many of which had the word 'bank' in their name. But the major commercial banks of the nineteenth century were euphemistically called otherwise: *caisses*, as in the two banks proposed by Jacques Laffitte, one rejected and one formed; *sociétés*, as in the 1822 Société Générale de Belgique and the

1864 Société Générale pour favoriser le commerce et l'industrie en France; *crédits*, of which the Crédit Mobilier, the Crédit Foncier, the Crédit Agricole and the Crédit Lyonnais are the most illustrious; *comptoirs* such as the Comptoir d'Escompte. The word *banque* seemed for more than a century to give rise to misgivings.

Moreover the French Inquiry into Money and Banking of 1867 brought forth four mentions of John Law and the experience of a century and a half earlier, one from Louis Adolphe Thiers, then finance minister and later president of the Third Republic, who was a witness, and three from Michel Chevalier, a member of the inquiring panel. Thiers made merely a perfunctory allusion to the disastrous character of the experience. Chevalier, who was an expansionist, suggested that, despite the outcome, the principles of Law were sound even if he had gone too far (Ministère des Finances *et al.*, 1867, VI, pp. 102, 121). All witnesses acknowledged that the development of French monetary and banking institutions lagged behind those of Britain, with the strong impression left that French caution in financial questions rested on a traumatic collective memory of John Law and the *assignats*.

(2) German inflation in 1923 was a similar experience that affected macro-economic behavior for at least half a century more. There has lately been a tendency to underplay the damage done to the economy and the society by that inflation. Gerald Feldman (1977) has shown that the iron and steel industry took advantage of the inflation to make gains, and Carl-Ludwig Holtfrerich (1980, pp. 218 ff) has demonstrated that the lowest income groups were not hurt relative to 1913 by hyperinflation. But the memory of the experience affected German macro-economic policy both a decade later at the depth of the depression, and especially in the years after World War II when unemployment seemed to West Germans much less to be feared than rising prices.

One historian claims that German policies during World War I and its aftermath were shaped by the memory of the near-century of relatively uninterrupted deflation from 1817 to 1896 (Feldman, 1977, p. 7). The same passage suggests that the Weimar Republic was unable to limit 'speculative fantasizing about unhistorical alternatives' – a considerable distance from rational expectations.

A defender of rational expectations might insist that the German refusal to depreciate the Reichsmark after the British went off gold in 1931 could be justified on the ground that there was no adequate model widely accepted in economics to explain the deflationary consequences of a 40 percent appreciation of the currency against sterling. A present-day econometric study suggests that a 20 percent depreciation would have raised national income in Germany by 18 percent (Schliemann, 1980). In addition to lack of an accepted model on which to base expectations, German freedom of action was circumscribed by the terms of the Young plan, by the Bank Law of 1924/30, and by anticipation of French objection to any currency change (Borchardt, 1980). The main basis for rejection, it would seem, however, was the collective memory of 1923. Depreciation was identified with inflation, and inflation was abhorred.

A subtle form of rational expectations might argue for Communist opposition to depreciation on the ground that the existing appreciation after September 21, 1931 would destroy capitalism in Germany – as indeed it did – and that Communism would inherit the pieces – which it did not. Like Wanniski's explanation of the 1929 crash, such a rationalization would violate the principle of Occam's razor, being too subtle and involute by half. Socialists, Communists, labor-union leaders, politicians, bankers – all but a few heretics – responded instinctively 'No tampering with the currency', which was the slogan of the Socialist financial expert, Rudolph Hilferding, as well as of Schacht, Luther, Brüning and the rest. In November 1931, Brüning stated that a number of people had recommended that, once the pound had fallen, Germany should make a dash for it and devalue. His reply was 'I shall defend to the end against taking any inflationary measure of any kind' (1954, ch. 5 and Anlage IV).

(3) It is hardly necessary to make the point that British economic authorities in the post-war period were guilty of Maginot Line thinking, trying to manage demand when the problem lay in unresponsive supply. As expansionary fiscal and monetary policy produced inflation rather than growth, the reaction of most of the Keynesians was that the difficulty came from insufficient determination in expanding demand, i.e. in stop–go policies which discouraged business men from embarking on time-consuming investments (for an example of the 'stop–go' criticism, see Dow, 1964). If Germans were paranoid about inflation, the British were paranoid about unemployment. Having experienced unemployment rates as high as 22 percent of the labor force (1933), and rates above 10 percent in all but one year in the 1920s, the Labour Party kept the post-war rate down close to 1 percent in the 1950s, presumably well below the desirable level of unemployment needed to provide for entry and exit from the labour force and normal transition between jobs. When unemployment reached 2 percent, expansion programs went into high gear. Since persistent structural unemployment prevailed in distressed areas in Scotland, Wales and Northern Ireland, the pressure in England and especially Southern England was intense. Tight labor markets, moreover, led to labor-hoarding, with firms reluctant to discharge workers in recessions brought on by 'stops' for fear they would be unable to get them back when the lights turned to 'go'. Recessions thus produced declines in output without declines in employment, leading to sharp setbacks in labor productivity. Only belatedly, at the end of the 1970s and in the early 1980s, under pressure of inflation has preoccupation with unemployment begun to fade in Britain, as that with inflation has weakened in Germany under pressure from unemployment. In the two cases, divergent national experience and collective memories have led to substantial differences in policies and macro-economic outcomes, without much influence, for most of the half century, of rational expectations.

(4) In contrast to this experience in which memory of the 1920s shaped economic policies for the subsequent fifty years, there is the failure on the part of the British to draw an analogy between the return of

the pound to par after 1815 and that after World War I. I have written a paper on the subject so that I can be brief (1982).[1]

In writing in 1925 about the post-Napoleonic war period, Acworth stated in the preface that he refrained from pointing out comparisons and contrasts with the last seven years (1925, p. v). Similarly, T. E. Gregory, introducing a new edition of Tooke and Newmarch's *History of Prices* in 1928, pointed to the 'startling resemblance between the 1797–1819 period and that of 1914–1925' (p. 3). For a time I thought that these were the only two observers who were aware of the parallel. A French scholar has found a number of ephemeral references to the earlier period, however – in the *Economist*, the *Times*, and a remark by Keynes (Perrot, 1955, pp. 35–6). And, while Moggridge's authoritative book, *British Monetary Policy, 1924–1931* (1972) covering the 1925 restoration makes no reference to the earlier experience, in a private letter the author has told me that Hawtrey in the British government alone of officials referred to 1819, but that he was not listened to.

Whether one regards the restoration of the pound to par in 1819 as a success, as most scholars including Rostow do, or failure, depends upon whether one takes a long- or a short-run view on the one hand, and the exact period under scrutiny on the other. It is true that recovery had been achieved by 1823, and those taking the long-run point of view probably thought it desirable for British financial stability and reputation in world markets to maintain the price of gold set by Isaac Newton in 1717 for as long a period as possible. In fact that price lasted with interruptions for the Napoleonic war and World War I from 1717 to 1931.

From the short-run point of view, however, the deflationary process leading up to and immediately following restoration was as painful as that of 1925. Sidney Buxton said in 1885 that the first seven years of peace were among the darkest in modern English history (quoted in Acworth, 1925, p. 115). Agriculture, manufacturing, shipping and trade were all depressed. Habeas corpus was suspended in 1817. The Peterloo massacre took place in 1819, William Cobbett, who felt that return to the gold standard without liquidation of debt charges or reduction in other public burdens had been the main cause of semi-starvation of farm laborers and factory workers, agitated in favor of rick-burning in the countryside (Cole, n.d.). The conclusion one draws from the episode may differ from observer to observer. There is enough of a parallel, however, that it is curious that 1815 to 1822 were so largely ignored from 1918 to 1925.

(5) Perhaps a century is too long for collective memory to remain sharp, although the John Law experience continued to be chewed over for 150 years after the event. Consider, however, a collective memory or rational expectations – whichever fits – that is able to repeat financial crises over 10 or 20 years or so over a number of centuries. In his exposition of rational expectations, Poole contrasts it with the 'popular view that speculative markets were semi-rational casinos beset by speculative bubbles and waves of optimism and pessimism', a view ascribed to J. M. Keynes. He asserts that in the 1950s a growing body of

careful statistical work on the stock market failed to uncover evidence of speculative bubbles and irrationalities. Given uncertainty, the stock market makes mistakes, but on the theory of rational expectations it cannot make mistakes that are systematic (Poole, 1980, pp. 245–7). The same is said to be true for prices in all markets – of commodities, of assets such as land, buildings, shopping malls, etc.

As far as I am aware, the theory of rational expectations has never tried to explain the fact of recurring financial crises, waves of what the classical economists called 'overtrading, followed by revulsion and discredit', or, as Hyman Minsky – one of the few monetary economists today who believes in the instability of the financial system – calls them, autonomous shocks followed by euphoria, credit expansion, distress, financial collapse and deflation. There is some debate as to when the last of the 10-years series of crises took place, whether in 1937 or 1866. In the United States in the twentieth century there were financial crises in 1907, 1921, 1929 and 1937. There is a British claim that the last systematic financial crisis took place in 1866, but this overlooks the Baring crisis of 1890, and a bubble of foreign lending in 1910–1914 would probably have ended in crisis if it had not been for the outbreak of World War I. Prior to 1890 there were the French crisis of 1882 and the German–Austrian–American crisis of 1873, together with a string of British crises – frequently extended to other markets – in 1866, 1857, 1847, 1836, 1825, 1813, 1808, 1797, 1792, 1782, 1773, 1763, etc. Ashton takes the series back through the eighteenth century to the South Sea bubble of 1720 and to 1710 and 1701 (1959, p. 67 and ch. 5, esp. p. 112). One can find 10- or 20-year crises in Spain in the sixteenth and seventeenth centuries – largely caused by default of the royal exchequer – in 1552, 1557, 1597, 1607, 1647, 1653 and 1680 – a series of financial disasters from which markets failed to learn (these dates were communicated to me in a private letter by Rondo Cameron).

It is bizarre that financial markets do not learn from these experiences, since the financial crises are remembered. The crisis of 1857 in Hamburg, for example, kept coming back into discussion among Hamburgers and non-Hamburgers alike whenever the discussion of foreign-exchange markets came up, and those reading on the subject could feel the hair on their necks standing up (Böhme, 1968, p. 274). Panics were compared: the crisis of 1866 in Britain was wilder than any since 1825 (Morgan, 1943, p. 177) and in Germany in 1873 it was said that no such protracted crisis had occurred for 56 years (Stern, 1977, p. 189, quoting a letter of October 1875 from Baron Abraham von Oppenheimer to Bleichroeder; a partial collection characterizing separate crises is presented in Kindleberger, 1978, p. 216). Crises were remembered, but the information was not assimilated in useful form capable of guarding against repetition.

The theory of rational expectations treats all participants in markets as equally intelligent. It is a familiar trick of historical analysis that insists on the necessity to disaggregate. Speculators may be divided into insiders and outsiders, the former professionals who devote their time exclusively to financial markets, who are rational, do learn, and move in timely fashion between money and other assets; the latter less experienced, dealing in financial markets as a sideline, given to excitement when they see others get rich from speculation. They enter late, stay too long, and lose money. Perhaps they learn and stay out next time, but it seems to be the case that a new group of outsiders comes along to enable an almost exact replica of the earlier game to be played.

The hypothesis that all participants in financial markets are rational maximizers is evidently false when one contemplates savings banks (or savings and loan associations, or credit unions) in the United States today. No intelligent maximizer would keep savings in a bank limited to paying depositors $5\frac{1}{4}$ percent when he or she could earn more than double that rate in other money-market instruments. Savings banks with a blue-collar clientele tend to have about half their assets covered in regular savings deposits, while those in financially more sophisticated areas have ratios that fall as low as 25 percent, and have to buy their money outside at rates from 14 to 18 percent, which is more than they can earn on long-term mortgages. The first set of banks can still earn profits after a considerable amount of disintermediation. The second is in trouble.

Even sophisticated speculators in financial markets may not be completely rational at all times. While unsophisticated households leave money in savings banks earning real returns that are negative and well below what they could earn elsewhere on assets of equal safety, highly sophisticated speculators in recent years have increasingly been buying real estate with borrowed funds to earn capital appreciation. Many of them today are in difficulty as interest rates remain high, real estate prices have leveled off, and the quantity of sales has declined drastically. Equally or more sophisticated banks are deeply in debt to Eastern European countries and to developing countries which in the state of world trade are forced to borrow to pay the interest as it accumulates. In the recent historical past in foreign lending, the collective memory of bankers and investors in foreign bonds has produced a 30-year cycle with booms and busts in lending commencing in Britain in 1825, 1855 and 1885 for example, with a boom in 1910 headed for a bust that never materialized.

Why 10 years for the usual financial crisis, 30 years for those in foreign lending, 50 years for British unemployment and German inflation, and 100 to 150 years for the French public to have the memory of John Law wear off? On trend, markets may be efficient and investors rational. On occasion, however, and frequently on occasions with periodicity, theories less flattering to the intelligence and learning capacity of authorities, banks, firms, citizens and to capitalism itself seem to hold sway. Rational expectations may serve normally as a pregnant hypothesis of the *als ob* variety, and be useful for prediction most of the time. But not invariably.

Note

1 Professor Rostow does not agree with me that the two periods present a parallel. In a private letter dated May 21, 1981, before he had seen the article, he wrote: 'As for 1819 and 1925 . . . don't believe it. 1819 . . . was followed by one of the strongest booms in British economic history. Read pp. 140–219 in Gayer *et al.* [1953], vol. i. The issue of the alleged depressing effects of resumption is addressed explicitly on pp. 164–167. You might wish to note the general observation on pp. 656–657, vol. ii'.

References

Acworth, A. W. (1925), *Financial Reconstruction in England, 1815–1822* (London: P. S. King).

Ashton, T. S. (1959), *Economic Fluctuations in England, 1700–1800* (Oxford: Clarendon Press).

Böhme, Helmut (1968), *Frankfurt und Hamburg. Des Deutschen Reiches Silber- und Goldloch und die allerenglischste Stadt des Kontinents* (Frankfurt-am-Main: Europäische Verlagsanstalt).

Borchardt, Knut (1980), 'Zur Frage der währungspolitischen Optionen Deutschlands in der Weltwirtschaftskrise', in K. Borchardt and Franz Holzheu (eds), *Theorie und Politik in der internationalen Wirtschaftsbeziehungen* (Stuttgart: Gustav Fischer Verlag), pp. 165–81.

Brüning, Heinrich (1954), 'Keine Reparationen mehr', in Wilhelm Vernehohl (ed.), *Reden und Aufsätze eines deutschen Staatsmannes* (Munster: Verlag Regensburg).

Buxton, Sidney (1885/1966), *Finance and Politics: An Historical Study, 1789–1885*, reprint edn (New York: Augustus M. Kelley).

Cole, G. D. H. (n.d.), *The Life of William Cobbett* (New York: Harcourt Brace, preface dated 1924).

Dow, J. R. C. (1964), *The Management of the British Economy, 1945–1960* (Cambridge: National Institute of Economic and Social Research).

Feldman, Gerald D. (1977), *Iron and Steel in the German Inflation, 1916–1923* (Princeton, NJ: Princeton University Press).

Gayer, Arthur D., Rostow, W. W. and Schwartz, Anna Jacobson (1953), *The Growth and Fluctuation of the British Economy, 1790–1850. An Historical, Statistical and Theoretical Study of Britain's Economic Development* (Oxford: Clarendon Press, 2 vols).

Gille, Bertrand (1970), *La Banque en France au XIXᵉ siècle, Recherches historiques* (Geneva: Droz).

Gregory, T. E. (1928), 'Introduction' to Thomas Tooke and William Newmarch, *A History of Prices and of the State of Circulation from 1792 to 1856*, reproduced from the original (New York: Adelphi, 6 vols; first 2 vols originally 1838).

Grotkopp, Wilhelm (1954), *Die grosse Krise, Lehren aus der Überwindung der Wirtschaftskrise, 1929–1932* (Düsseldorf: Econ-Verlag).

Holtfrerich, Carl-Ludwig (1980), *Die deutsche Inflation, 1914–1923* (Berlin: Walter de Gruyter).

Kindleberger, C. P. (1978), *Manias, Panics and Crashes, a History of Financial Crises* (New York: Basic Books).

Kindleberger, C. P. (1982), 'British Financial Reconstruction, 1815–22 and 1918–25' in C. P. Kindleberger and Guido di Tella (eds), *Economics in the Long View: Essays in Honour of W. W. Rostow* (London: Macmillan).

Liesse, André (1909), *Evolution of Credit and Banks in France: From the Founding of the Bank of France to the Present Time* (Washington, DC: US Government Printing Office, for the National Monetary Commission).

Lüthy, Herbert (1961), *La Banque protestante en France de la révocation de l'édit de Nantes à la révolution*. Vol. II: *De la banque aux finances (1730–1794)* (Paris: SEVPEN).

Ministère des Finances et Ministère de l'Agriculture, du Commerce, et des Travaux Publiques (1865–1867), *Enquête sur les principes et les faits généraux qui régissent la circulation monétaire et fiduciaire* (Paris: Imprimerie impériale, 6 vols).

Moggridge, D. E. (1972), *British Monetary Policy, 1924–1931: The Norman Conquest of $4.86* (Cambridge: Cambridge University Press).

Mollien, François Nicholas (1845), *Mémoires d'un ministre du Trésor Public, 1780–1815* (Paris: Fournier, 4 vols).

Morgan, E. Victor (1943), *The Theory and Practice of Central Banking, 1797–1913* (Cambridge: Cambridge University Press).

Perrot, Marguerite (1955), *La Monnaie et l'opinion publique en France et en Angleterre, 1924/36* (Paris: A. Colin).

Poole, Wiiliam (1980), 'Understanding Monetary Policy: The Role of Rational Expectations', in *The Business Cycle and Public Policy, 1929–1980, A Compendium of Papers Submitted to the Joint Economic Committee, Congress of the United States, November 28, 1980* (Washington, DC: US Government Printing Office).

Schliemann, Jürgen (1980), *Die deutsche Währung in der Weltwirtschaftskrise 1929–1933, Währungspolitik und Abwertungskontroverse unter den Bedingungen der Reparationen* (Berne: Verlag Paul Haupt).

Schumpeter, Joseph A. (1939), *Business Cycles: A Theoretical, Historical and Statistical Analysis of the Capitalist Process* (New York: McGraw-Hill).

Stern, Fritz (1977), *Gold and Iron: Bismarck, Bleichröder and the Building of the German Empire* (London: Allen & Unwin).

Wanniski, Jude (1977), *The Way the World Works* (New York: Basic Books).

Part III

Historical Models

9

The Cyclical Pattern of Long-Term Lending

I

For the most part, Sir Arthur Lewis solves puzzles for us; this time he has reset an old one. In writing on international investment in the period 1870 to 1913, he states: 'The main puzzle which international investment has posed has been its timing' (Lewis, 1978, p. 178). His solution, adding French, German and British capital exports, and subtracting capital imports into the USA to form an overall view of lending, is one that I find less than completely satisfactory. To a certain extent, it hides what is taking place, just as the average height of a family of two adults and four children under 10 years of age would do. Aggregation reveals how much net foreign lending from the core is available for investment at the periphery, but it fails to uncover the secret of the cyclical pattern of long-term lending. That secret, in my judgment, calls for the analysis of separate historical patterns of lending by different countries, and by the same country at different periods of time, rather than an aggregative technique. And it is a secret that may be of consummate importance for world economic stability.

Let me return to a paradigm I used some years ago in a textbook, contrasting lending by the United Kingdom from 1870 to 1913, as illuminated by Cairncross, with that of the USA in the interwar periods, studied by Bloomfield (Kindleberger, 1958, pp. 373–5; Cairncross, 1953; Bloomfield, 1950). British lending was anti-cyclical. In boom, foreign lending slowed down; in depression it picked up. At turning points there were brief periods of positive correlation: foreign and domestic lending soared together from 1871 to 1875, and collapsed simultaneously in 1890. There are also peculiarities about 1910–14, to be discussed below. On the whole, however, foreign lending was counter-cyclical.

The mechanism that produced this result, according to Cairncross, was the terms of trade (the same analysis was developed simultaneously by Rostow, 1948). The terms of trade were regarded as a proxy for relative profitability at home and abroad, as would be true if all changes

Reprinted with permission from Mark Gersovitz, Carlos F. Diaz-Alejandro, Gustav Ranis and Mark R. Rosenzweig (eds), The Theory and Experience of Economic Development: Essays in Honor of Sir W. Arthur Lewis *(London: Allen & Unwin, 1982), pp. 300–12.*

in the terms of trade emanated from the demand side. High import prices reflect profitability in the production of primary products at the periphery and give rise to faster capital exports; rising domestic and export prices relative to import prices in this analysis mean that domestic production can earn good profits and divert investment from overseas primary production to domestic industry. Sir Arthur himself is partial to this sort of explanation. While I found little evidence that the terms of trade actually behaved in the manner implied, and have serious doubts that they are an adequate measure for the relative profitability of home and foreign investment, it is true that, on the whole, British capital moved counter-cyclically. The exceptions are the second half of the 1880s, which Sir Arthur calls 'the real puzzle' (Lewis, 1978, p. 180), and the years 1910–14.

American lending, in contrast, rose and fell in the 1920s and 1930s with domestic investment and the domestic business cycle. The movement at the turning points was anti-cyclical. In 1923 and 1928–9 foreign investment fell because of a pick-up in domestic business that raised interest rates (Lary, 1943, p. 92 ff). In 1930, after the stock-market crash, foreign lending recovered for the first two quarters of the year, actually reaching a ten-year high in the second quarter, as interest rates fell to new, very low levels. It then dried up precipitously as investors lost confidence in the credit-worthiness of potential borrowers. The 1924 success of the Dawes loan lifted overall foreign lending in the second half of the 1920s to 1928. And in the depression of the 1930s, long-term capital moved toward the USA, rather than away from it, although direct foreign investment abroad remained barely positive.

My explanation for this contrast, leaving aside the minor issue of the turning points, has been that there are two cyclical models of foreign lending, one emphasizing relative demands for savings, foreign and domestic, the other domestic supply of savings in the presence of constant demands. In the British case a relatively steady flow of savings was directed now abroad, now to domestic industry, depending upon the relative state of the two demands. In depression at home, savings go abroad; in boom, they are directed at the margin to home investment.

In contrast to this 'demand model', the supply model, applying to the interwar USA, assumes unused opportunities for both foreign and domestic investment in something akin to a rationing situation. A rise in the supply of savings permits increases in both home and foreign investment. This model is helpful, particularly after some event that widens investors' horizons and gives them a view of unexploited opportunities. Unexpected successes of particular loans have served to produce such shifts in horizons, especially the Baring loans of 1816–17 to recycle the French indemnity after the Napoleonic War, the Thiers *rentes* of 1871–2 to recycle the Franco-Prussian indemnity, the French loan to Russia in November 1887 that enabled Russia to refund its 1878 borrowings from Germany to finance the Russo-Turkish war, and the aforementioned Dawes loan of 1924.

Newly awakened interest of US investors in foreign loans after the success of the Dawes loan – the US tranche being eleven times oversubscribed – both conforms to the supply model of foreign lending, and lends support to the widely held contemporaneous view that London was an experienced lender, the USA an inexperienced one with, in the latter case, deleterious effects on the world economy. Part of the indictment was based on US commercial policy, exemplified in the Fordney–McCumber tariff of 1919 and the Hawley–Smoot tariff of 1930. This is not compelling. One can object to US policies after the First World War on microeconomic grounds of resource allocation, but the suggestion that they made it difficult or impossible for creditors to pay debt service is largely partial-equilibrium analysis unacceptable in a general-equilibrium situation. It is true, however, that old foreign lenders are likely to behave differently than new – to eschew the pejorative expressions 'experienced' and 'inexperienced'. This is not so much learning by doing as it is having settled down to a steady scanning of wider investment opportunities. The German case of the late 1880s to be cited below makes it dangerous to be unduly categorical.

The harm of pro-cyclical lending, of course, is that it destabilizes the world economy. For historical reasons, the argument can be constructed in terms of fixed exchange rates. (To extend it to flexible exchange rates would require a host of assumptions about exchange risk, speculation, and the like, and is left to the interested reader.) In upswing, US imports rise to stimulate income abroad and, with it, investment opportunities that evoke a flow of capital imports from the USA. Direct investment may, in fact, respond to the accelerator effect of rising exports in foreign countries. When the downturn occurs in the lending country, imports and investments dry up at the same time, dealing a double blow to foreign balances of payments. It was on this account that League of Nations experts in 1945 recommended that capital flows be made counter-cyclical in the postwar world (League of Nations, 1945, pp. 285, 303).

A number of observers have commented that the United Kingdom was not involved in financial crises from 1866 to 1920 – although this may make too little of the Baring crisis of 1890. This is explicable by her anti-cyclical pattern of lending which served greatly to stabilize the world economy. The crisis of 1873 ran mainly between the USA and the Continent, especially Germany and Austria, and was precipitated in the USA by the halt in Central European pro-cyclical lending. In 1907 financial crisis in New York was linked to that in Italy through short-term capital flows passing through London and Paris, though those two centers did not become involved. But the notion that stable British lending helped to dampen fluctuations in the British economy and the rest of the world overlooks the second half of the 1880s, and the burst of lending from 1910 to 1914. This last was pro-cyclical and would have ended up, in my judgment, in a typical pattern of 'overtrading, revulsion and discredit', had the outbreak of war not produced a very different kind of crisis. In the last spurt before the war British foreign lending, notably to Canada, partook exactly of the pro-cyclical, positive feedback, learning variety that fits the USA after the war. It is inappropriate to regard 1913 lending as a norm for postwar

comparisons as, for example, Cairncross does in the introduction to
Home and Foreign Investment, 1870–1913 (1953, p. x). 1913 was an
outlier, part of a cyclical movement which was sharply at variance with
1870–1910 experience.

A recent paper by Serge-Christophe Kolm also contrasts capital flows
that are correlated positively and negatively with domestic business
cycles, and uses an analysis extending beyond the demand and supply
models above (Kolm, 1979). Three domestic elements affect capital
flows: the supply of savings, which works in the direction of positive
correlation; the domestic demand for savings, which presses in the
counter-cyclical direction; and diminishing returns to scale, which lead
to foreign investment as fuller and fuller utilization of domestic capacity
is reached and domestic costs rise faster than those abroad. Kolm was
seeking to explain that world business cycles under floating exchange
rates were becoming positive coordinated and capital movements in the
1970s increasingly pro-cyclical. His analysis was addressed to the
possibility of different cyclical patterns of foreign direct investment in a
given country at different stages of factor utilization. and is not
concerned with horizon shifts or capital-market learning.

Finally, by way of introduction, it should be mentioned that capital
(and migrants) flow in channels dug by accumulated information and
experience, rather than moving evenly over broad surfaces. In a world of
rational expectations and generalized information with similar objective
functions and aversion or indifference to risk, French, German
and British investors would be expected to respond to the same stimuli
in roughly the same ways. In these circumstances it would be
appropriate to aggregate their respective capital flows. But French
capital exports in the prewar period were directed to Russia, south-
eastern Europe and Africa, British lending to the Continent was cut off
abruptly by the revolutions of 1848 and, apart from some competitive
lending in Italy and the Middle East, thereafter went to the USA, the
Empire and regions of recent settlement such as Argentina. In 1914
France had 60 percent of its investment in Europe; in 1900 Britain had 5
percent (Pollard, 1974, p. 73). French investments in 1910–13 earned
3.87 percent in Russia, while much safer British foreign investments
returned 5.3 percent (Lévy-Leboyer, 1977, p. 113). It is difficult to
imagine the British investors lending 1.25 billion francs (£50,000,000)
to Russia in April 1906 to save the tsar from bankruptcy after the
Japanese defeat and the revolution of 1905 – an expensive French
political gesture (Girault, 1977, pp. 251–2). With different patterns of
domestic activity, different behavioural models, capital flowing in
different channels to different recipients in turn, the suggestion that
there should be one general timing for capital flows of most countries
over the world cycle is difficult to accept.

II

More insight can be obtained into cyclical patterns of foreign lending if
we move out from the British (1870–1910)–US (1920–39) comparison

to include other periods in the nineteenth century and other countries. Maurice Lévy-Leboyer's masterly essay on the French balance of payments in the nineteenth century has a diagram that shows the vast differences between French and British patterns, except in the 1850s when both countries followed a modest pro-cyclical pattern (1977, p. 80). On Imlah's figures, British lending declined from 1859 to 1861, again in pro-cyclical fashion, and recovered from 1862 all the way to 1872, with the pattern changing from pro- to anti-cyclical during the crisis of 1866 as foreign lending continued upward, while domestic business turned down. The United Kingdom switched patterns once again in 1885, with a pick-up in domestic business and foreign lending leading up to the Baring crisis. This last is Lewis's 'real puzzle'. Real income was rising, even though nominal income and the profitability of industry declined. There was something of a stock-market boom at home from a change in the company laws of 1856 and 1863 that led many companies to go public in anticipation of restrictions. In particular, a boom took place in brewing shares as investors anticipated increased profits from the shortage of wine arising from the phylloxera disease attacking French vineyards (Wirth, 1893, p. 200). French lending to Russia picked up in 1887, and especially in 1888 (Girault, 1973; Kennan, 1979, p. 343).

What was particularly interesting at this time was the German anti-cyclical pattern, achieved without much maturing experience during the 1871–9 pro-cyclical period. It resulted from a peculiar mixture of political and economic motives. The political element consisted of steps taken in Bismarck's economic warfare against Russia. The German loan to Russia of 1883 had not gone well. Russian securities were falling in price in Berlin after March 1886. A dubious character by the name of Elie de Cyon suggested that the time had come for Russia to detach itself from economic dependence on Germany and transfer the market for its securities to Paris. In May 1887 Russia confiscated German properties in Russian Poland. In July Bismarck issued an instruction to the Orphans' Courts to discriminate against Russian securities in the portfolios of their wards, and in November the *Lombardverbot*, forbidding banks to lend on Russian securities. The political aim is clear from a quotation of a high German civil servant: 'the intention is to deprive a hostile government of means for the development of armaments against us. Let the Russians, we thought, get money, if they had to, from their friends, the French' (Kennan, 1979, ch. 18, esp. p. 343 and note). Beginning in that year Russian bonds coming due on the German market were increasingly converted into French securities (Girault, 1977, p. 253). And in 1888 the great conversion referred to earlier took place. Russian, German and British banks all took part, but the lion's share went to the French, followed by a Rothschild conversion of 1,702 million francs of railroad bonds. The miniscule relation between gross French exports to Russia and French lending to that country (White, 1933) – in defiance of transfer theory – is accounted for by the fact that French lending was for recycling German loans, not provision of fresh capital.

In addition to selling off their Russian bonds to the French, German investors in this same period dumped some Argentine bonds, largely in London, thus contributing to the weak market in Argentine issues that collapsed in 1890. One reason given for these sales was uneasiness over what was taking place in Argentina (Lauck, 1907, pp. 59–60); another was that the investors disapproved of instability of the exchange rate for the Argentine peso (Morgenstern, 1959, p. 523). It is hard to avoid the conclusion, however, that the strong demand for capital inside Germany played a substantial role in inducing German investors to sell the foreign securities they thought weakest, Kolm's diminishing returns as capacity gets used more fully to the contrary notwithstanding. Reduced profits at home in boom from diminishing returns are one possibility; another is higher profits from demand-led expansion. The character of the boom at home may differ from cycle to cycle, as well as the nature of foreign lending. In Germany at this time, the boom in steel, chemicals and electricity was exigent. Gross foreign lending took place, as exemplified in Bleichroeder's elaborate operations in Mexico (Stern, 1977, pp. 427, 433, 442). By 1900 Germany had joined again in the boom in foreign lending, seeking especially to rival the United Kingdom in the Middle East. The decade after 1885, however, led to a sharp reduction in capital exports, and capital imports from France, via Russian recycling, and Britain, via Argentina.

While Britain and Germany for a time after 1885 swapped accustomed lending models, Germany adopting the anti-cyclical one and the United Kingdom the pro-cyclical, they differed in more than their experience in foreign lending. The British had old wealth, the Germans by and large new. Old wealth is risk-averse. Trustee investments grow as a proportion of total traded securities. Widows and orphans, so often mocked in accounts of the defenseless members of society, are the wives and children of men who have accumulated wealth. Safe securities to the French are those appropriate for 'un père d'une famille' ('the father of a family'). Others thought to need a particular brand of safe investments have been noted from time to time as spinsters, retired clergymen, retired merchants, magistrates, civil servants, admirals, even 'young men about to marry' (Kindleberger, 1978, p. 31n). A substantial incentive on the demand side for the British 'financial revolution' of the first half of the eighteenth century (Dickson, 1967) may well have been the rise in the nuclear family, detected by Lawrence Stone as having occurred in the years 1700–20, calling for new arrangements by heads of families for the protection of their prospective widows and orphans, when less reliance could be put on the extended family to take care of collateral relatives (Stone, 1977). Dutch investment in the United Kingdom in the eighteenth century, largely in East India, Bank of England, South Sea Company shares and government stock (US translation, bonds) took place largely as accumulated wealth sought outlets less risky than mercantile ventures. Many of these investments were made for institutions like orphanages and by (or for) women (Wilson, 1941; Carter, 1975, p. 139). British women subscribers to government stock rose from 18 percent of the total in 1723–4 to 29 percent in 1750 (Dickson, 1967, p. 325), 'partly due to greater longevity, partly to the increasing practice of investing widows', dowers', and spinters' legacies', but there may also have been changes in practice with respect to the use of nominees.

Foreign securities, and especially foreign government and, in the second half of the nineteenth century, railroad securities, were frequently regarded as more suitable for trustee investments, especially in France, and Commonwealth securities in Britain, guaranteed as to debt service by the Colonial Office after the 1850s. This was not particularly rational in the light of widespread defaults of Latin American countries after the pro-cyclical lending boom of the 1820s, or defaults on the part of individual states of the USA, nine in all, in the depression of the early 1840s, following the boom of the 1830s. Sir Arthur regards the tastes of clergymen, widows and orphans as following a bandwagon effect, since they had little hard information (Lewis, 1978, p. 180) and the diversion of 'trustee' investments from 'risky' domestic investments to 'safe' investments abroad as giving rise to unexploited opportunities (*ibid.*, p. 177). Rational or irrational, the predilection of even professional investors for overseas securities seems to have been a fact.

A further source of trustee investments, to be sure, was the moneys disinvested by owners of businesses, or their heirs, as private firms went public. Not all owners of companies, converted to public form after the incorporation acts of 1856 and 1863, or the wave of the late 1880s, disinvested. In some cases change was one of form, not ownership. But going public gave owners, and especially their heirs, with little appetite or capacity for running the business a chance to diversify portfolios, with securities thought to be less risky. One can, of course, argue that, for every share of a private company sold and the proceeds invested abroad, new savings must be used to buy the same share. The rise of the public company, however, provided means by which these new savings were channeled abroad in domestic depression when new company formation at home was limited, and favored foreign investment through furnishing an escape route for reluctant investors in industry (Jeffrys, 1938/1977, pp. 112, 134).

There is one exception to the notion that foreign lending to governments and railroads is less risky than domestic industrial investment. This is the wave of investment in southern and central Europe and in Egypt and Turkey undertaken by the Crédit Mobilier and, following it, other French and some British banks in the third quarter of the nineteenth century and some years thereafter. Crédit Mobilier and Rothschild investments in infra-structure in Italy, Spain and Austria were competitive and known to be risky. Government guarantees were sought and obtained, where possible. French governmental banks established to aid agriculture and to improve the mortgage market joined in making loans to the Khedive of Egypt (Jousseau, 1884, p. lxv). Some of these were eventually sold off in London in 1879 at a loss (*ibid.*, p. lxxiv). Large profits of banks such as the Crédit Lyonnais and the *banques d'affaires* (established for lending to industry) in the Thiers *rentes* of 1871 and 1872 whetted the appetite for speculation in foreign government bonds, issued at low prices and expected to be bid up as the finances of the country in question improved (Bouvier, 1961, I, pp. 214–17). But the French investor who was sold Russian bonds after 1887 did not have fat profits dangled before him. Commissions for the issuers were high, to be sure, but yields were low. The investor was beguiled into thinking that because the bonds were issued by a government, they were safe like *rentes*. Journalists and the French and Russian governments combined to keep this thought alive.

To the extent that investors in foreign securities were looking for safety – truer, I believe, of old money in France and the United Kingdom than of new money in Germany – the foreign and domestic markets were structurally noncompeting. Domestic debt was not rising in France (after 1872) and the United Kingdom. An investor who wanted government or railroad bonds had to go abroad. If the foreign and domestic markets were noncompeting, the notion that foreign lending starved domestic industry – except to a limited extent at the margin – cannot be supported. France, Sir Arthur says, was technologically backward and clearly in need of much larger home investment. 'The case of Britain ... is more complicated but its failure to invest adequately at home clearly belongs in the area of unexploited opportunities' (Lewis, 1978, pp. 176–7). It is hard to detect a shortage of capital as one contemplates the low interest rates prevalent in France, for example.

There is the possibility that present-day observers are misled by nominal rates of interest up to 1896, whereas real rates of interest were much higher because of falling world prices. It is possible even that there was interest-rate illusion on the part of some borrowers, such as the Russians, who were ignorant of the prospect that they would have to repay French francs borrowed in 1887–96 with francs of much greater value. A recent thesis by L. Dwight Israelsen has disposed of this possibility. Refined econometric analysis shows that a perfect foresight real interest-rate model explains Russian borrowing for all major periods, 1800–1914, better than three alternative borrowing models (1979, ch. 3 and p. 362). Similar analysis indicates that the British lender was fully aware of the Gibson paradox relating real and nominal interest rates (Harley, 1977). But observe in Lévy-Leboyer's table of French and British interest rates that these rates were lower from 1895 to 1904, when prices were rising, than in 1885 to 1894, when prices were falling (Table 1). While yields rose in the last period recorded in the table, the level for foreign bonds in both countries is lower in 1900–4, than it had been in 1890–4. It is also relevant that the spread between domestic and foreign yields was narrower in France than in the United Kingdom.

In Germany, domestic industry and foreign borrowers competed more directly than seems to have been true in France and the United Kingdom. This is likely to have been due to the prominent role of the German banks in directing the flow of private savings for the uninitiated public. The conflict between domestic and foreign outlets is clearly visible in banking history: the Deutsche Bank was founded in 1872 for

Table 1   *British and French Yields on Various Securities by Subperiods,*
1885–1904 (in percent per annum)

| | British | | | French | | | |
| | | Foreign | | | | | |
Period	Railroads	bonds	Bonds	Shares	Foreign	Suez	Russian
1885–1889	3.29	5.04	3.79	4.27	4.49	3.92	4.93
1890–1894	2.97	4.74	3.25	4.00	4.11	3.72	4.13
1895–1899	2.61	4.38	3.06	3.56	3.80	2.95	3.84
1900–1904	2.98	4.48	3.28	3.91	3.96	3.32	3.92

Source: Lévy-Leboyer (1977, p. 113).

the purpose of competing with the United Kingdom in the finance of
foreign trade, but found itself so caught up in the *Gründerjahre* boom
that it severely neglected its original purpose for the first decade
(Helfferich, 1956, pp. 32–4, 58–66, 111). The width of competition
between domestic and foreign investment in Germany, as compared
with the United Kingdom, made the anti-cyclical pattern of lending
after 1873 far more sensitive than that in the United Kingdom. What is
not clear is why, with a fairly limited experience in foreign lending in the
pro-cyclical vein over 1850–72, the pattern should have reversed itself
with the boom after about 1879. How much experience is enough?

III

It may be of interest to observe an analogy in migration in Germany
which was anti-cyclical in pattern in the 1850s and again in the early
1890s. Some years ago in a bantering discussion, Per Jacobsson, the
Swedish economist, then at the Bank for International Settlements, and
I found ourselves on different sides of a debate as to whether migrants to
the USA were the more vigorous members of European society, anxious
to leave decadent Europe and to strike out in new challenges, or whether
they were the riffraff, the anti-social who got into trouble, the shiftless
who could not make their way at home, while the vigorous members of
society were caught up into the expanding economy at home. Both, of
course, are true, with a cyclical pattern at work, as Dorothy Swaine
Thomas proved (1941). A steady stream of humanity leaves the
European farm. In prosperity it is directed to the city and industry; in
domestic depression abroad. Regional differences exist: in the United
Kingdom, south of the Trent, the movement was to London or abroad;
north, to the Midlands or stay at home.

In Germany the movement off the farm to 'regions of recent settlement'
was particularly heavy after 1846, given the potato famine and the
Revolution of 1848 in which the dissolution of the guilds played a part;
and in the mid-1880s. In both cases it was arrested abruptly, in 1854 and
1893, respectively, as expanding domestic demand for labor diverted
excess agricultural population into domestic industry (Walker, 1964,
ch. 6; Inoki, 1981, p. 45). In both cases it was late in the cycle; for the first
years, the pattern was pro-cyclical as channels were dug, information

was spread and a positive feedback mechanism developed, with relatives following pioneers. Some prosperity at home, moreover, was needed to cover the costs of moving, which were greater trans-Atlantic than within Germany. Only when the boom became taut did domestic demand pull the migratory movement up sharply. Note in all this that while the French followed the same cyclical pattern, with a peak going abroad (to Algeria) because of the agricultural troubles from 1846 to 1853, the movement was on a highly dampened level. On the whole the French did not emigrate, but stayed in France.

The migratory movement is cyclical in another sense, based on what is happening in the country of immigration. In world depression in the 1930s British subjects returned to the United Kingdom on balance from all over the world, and city dwellers in the USA returned to the farm. It was not necessarily thought that jobs could be found in the United Kingdom or on the farm, so much as that, given unemployment, it was desirable to be at home where the marginal cost of maintenance was less than in an independent household. In these cases the push overwhelmed the pull.

An important difference between migration and capital movements is found in migratory lags. ('Man is of all pieces of luggage the most difficult to be removed' – Bagehot, 1880/1978, XI, p. 313.) Another is probably in the supply response after emigration and capital outflows take place. With more room at home, population increase may pick up after emigration, especially in countries that have not experienced Malthusian revolution. It is not clear that savings respond as elastically to the relative rise in the rate on capital as net reproduction rates do to the relative rise in wages and salaries.

IV

The counter-cyclical movement of migrant workers today, viewed from the standpoint of the receiving country, has highly negative social consequences, especially for Mediterranean workers in northern and central Europe, whose contracts expired after 1973 and who were returned to their homes. A fixed amount of unemployment should be equitably shared, rather than dumped by the core on the periphery. In the absence of offsetting transfers of aid or investments, the country of emigration is destabilized in terms of employment, income and balance of payments. From present appearances, the pattern is unlikely to continue in future, as the receiving countries, especially Germany, are resolved not to become dependent on imported labor, because of social disadvantages which are thought to outweigh economic benefits.

With capital lending, the counter-cyclical pattern makes for world stability, the pro-cyclical one for instability. The stabilizing effect of broadly anti-cyclical lending by the United Kingdom from 1866 to 1910 has been referred to. More interesting for the position today is the anti-cyclical movement of capital from the Euro-currency market in the recession of 1974–5.

Which of the two models of foreign lending obtains at a given time is probably not open to policy choice. The League of Nations recommendation mentioned earlier was incorporated in the articles of agreement of the International Bank for Reconstruction and Development (IBRD). Among its purposes were to 'conduct its operations with due regard to the effects of international investment on business conditions in the territories of its members'. At a very early stage, the bank asserted that counter-cyclical lending would conflict with its primary concern for economic development, holding that the responsibility for anti-cyclical action must devolve on the major industrial countries, on the International Monetary Fund and on any international agency set up to stabilize commodity prices (IBRD, 1949). Given the difficulties of formulating and carrying out domestic discretionary anti-cyclical spending policies, moreover, it is difficult to reach the conclusion that the Bank is wrong. Decision and execution lags probably force discretionary investment policies to have awkward timing. The primary contribution of the Bank, and an important one, is to keep the flow of project lending steady, or steadily rising, and to prevent its falling into a pro-cyclical profile.

If it be accepted that governments of industrial countries have the responsibility of stabilizing the world economy, there is little they can do through international private lending. Foreign government-to-government aid is probably like World Bank lending in that the best that can be done is to stabilize it over time and prevent it from developing a pro-cyclical pattern. Private foreign lending is much more difficult to regulate cyclically. It can be restrained; a number of countries have sought from time to time by devices such as the Capital Issues Committee in the United Kingdom to ration or to eliminate foreign lending. It is much more difficult to stimulate it at all, much less differentially over time, as various devices such as investment insurance demonstrate. To make the foreign investment of a particular country conform to one particular cyclical pattern rather than another seems hopeless. Foreign lending responds to shifts of horizon, to learning and to profit opportunities at home and abroad in ways which thus far do not seem to lend themselves to policy manipulation.

In the early 1970s the switch from one to the other cyclical model occurred very rapidly. An anti-cyclical pattern had been in operation in 1971–2, when the Federal Reserve System lowered interest rates as part of policy steps taken to bring about an upswing in business prior to President Nixon's candidacy for reelection in the fall of 1972. This was an example of what Assar Lindbeck calls the political business cycle. Lowering interest rates at a time when the Bundesbank was trying to hold interest rates high in Germany to restrain inflation led to an enormous outflow of capital. As economic recovery took place in the USA, the capital flow continued, converting the model to a pro-cyclical one. The rise in the price of oil engineered by OPEC in 1973 and 1974 brought about a sharp recession in the USA. The capital outflow continued, resulting once again in a switch in cyclical models, back to the counter-cyclical one. In this instance, with lending taking place through the Euro-dollar market to developing countries, notably Brazil, Mexico, South Korea and to various members of the Socialist bloc, it seemed as though the major banking institutions, especially the money-market banks, were continuing to lend less from a mindless, or perhaps better, unconscious pursuit of income, than from a sense of responsibility for the stability of the world economy. In previous localized recessions in lending on aircraft, on oil tankers and on Real Estate Investment Trusts (REITs), these same banks had kept on lending when planes were mothballed, tankers laid up 'on the mud', REITs had difficulties, to ensure a soft landing rather than crash. The possibility exists that the banks kept on lending because of ample reserves, despite worsening capital–deposit ratios, and in ignorance of rising debt–service ratios among borrowers and growing 'country risk'. An academic observer is in no position to make a definitive judgment, but the evidence on balance seems to indicate that continued lending was a deliberate policy – a sort of lender-of-last-resort, responsible policy to forestall crisis. Slowdown in lending took place only as recovery, especially in the USA, strengthened world commodity prices.

Whether the anti-cyclical pattern of lending can be maintained as a new OPEC price rise takes place in 1979 and the prospect for recession in 1980 becomes increasingly likely is an open question. A serious cutback in lending to the developing countries, however, would seriously threaten to deepen the world depression on the lines of the cutback of lending by the USA in 1829.

V

The conclusion of this exegesis on Sir Arthur's questions about lending in 1885–90 is that there is no one model of the cyclical pattern of foreign lending that can be used to forecast the future and estimate the impact of capital flows on world output and income distribution. Anything can happen and often does. The day of positive economics, useful for prediction, is still some distance away.

References

Bagehot, Walter (1880/1978), *Economic Studies*, reprinted in Norman St John-Stevas (ed.), *The Collected Works of Walter Bagehot*, Vol. XI (London: *The Economist*, 11 vols).
Bloomfield, Arthur I. (1950), *Capital Imports and the Balance of Payments, 1934–39* (Chicago: University of Chicago Press).
Bouvier, Jean (1961), *Le Crédit Lyonnais de 1863 à 1882. Les Années de formation d'une banque de dépôts* (Paris: SEVPEN, 2 vols).
Cairncross, Alexander K. (1953), *Home and Foreign Investment. 1870–1913* (Cambridge: Cambridge University Press).
Carter, Alice Clare (1975), *Getting, Spending and Investing in Early Modern Times, Essays on Dutch, English and Huguenot Economic History* (Assen: Van Forcum).

Dickson, P. G. M. (1967), *The Financial Revolution in England, A Study in the Development of Public Credit, 1688–1756* (New York: St Martin's Press).

Girault, René (1973), *Emprunts russes et investissements français en Russie, 1887–1914* (Paris: Colin).

Girault, René (1977), 'Investissements et placements français en Russie, 1880–1914', in M. Lévy-Leboyer (ed.), *La position internationale de la France, Aspects économiques et financiers, XIXe–XXe siècles* (Paris: Editions de l'Ecole des Hautes Etudes en Sciences Sociales), pp. 251–62.

Harley, C. Knick (1977), 'The interest rate and prices in Britain, 1873–1913: a study of the Gibson Paradox', *Explorations in Economic History*, vol. 14, no. 1, pp. 69–89.

Helfferich, Karl (1956), *Georg von Siemens, Ein Lebensbild aus Deutschlands grosser Zeit*, abridged edn (Krefeld: Serpe).

Inoki, Takenori (1981), *Aspects of German Peasant Migration to the United States, 1815–1914: A Reexamination of Some Behavioral Hypotheses in Migration Theory* (New York: Arno).

International Bank for Reconstruction and Development (1949), Press Release No. 134 (11 May).

Israelsen, L. Dwight (1979), 'The determinants of Russian state income, 1800–1914: an econometric analysis', unpublished doctoral dissertation (Massachusetts Institute of Technology).

Jeffrys, J. B. (1938/1977), *Business Organization in Great Britain, 1856–1914* (London School of Economics); reprint edn (New York: Arno Press).

Jousseau, J. B. (1884), *Traité due Crédit Foncier*, 3rd edn (Paris: Marchal, Billiard).

Kennan, G. F. (1979), *The Decline of Bismarck's European Order: Franco-Russian Relations, 1875–1890* (Princeton, NJ: Princeton University Press).

Kindleberger, Charles P. (1958), *International Economics*, 2nd edn (Homewood, Ill.: Irwin).

Kindleberger, Charles P. (1978), *Manias, Panics and Crashes: A History of Financial Crises* (New York: Basic Books).

Kolm, Serge-Christophe (1979), 'The Suicide of Bretton Woods', unpublished paper.

Lary, Hal B. (1943), *United States in the World Economy* (Washington, DC: US Department of Commerce).

Lauck, W. Jett (1907), *The Causes of the Panic of 1893* (Boston, Mass.: Houghton Mifflin).

League of Nations (1945), *Economic Stability in the Post-War World* (Geneva: League of Nations).

Lévy-Leboyer, Maurice (1977), 'La Balance des paiements et l'exportation des capitaux français', in M. Lévy-Leboyer (ed.), *La Position internationale de la France, Aspects économiques et financiers, XIXe–XXe siècles* (Paris: Editions de L'Ecole des Hautes Etudes en Sciences Sociales), pp. 75–142.

Lewis, W. Arthur (1978), *Growth and Fluctuations, 1870–1913* (London: Allen & Unwin, 1978).

Morgan, E. Victor (1952), *Studies in British Financial Policy, 1914–1925* (London: Macmillan).

Morgenstern, Oskar (1959), *International Financial Transactions and Business Cycles* (Princeton, NJ: Princeton University Press, for the National Bureau of Economic Research).

Pollard, Sidney (1974), *European Economic Integration, 1815–1870* (New York: Harcourt Brace Jovanovitch).

Rostow, Walt W. (1948), *British Economy of the Nineteenth Century* (London: Oxford University Press).

Stern, Fritz (1977), *Gold and Iron: Bismarck, Bleichröder and the Building of the German Empire* (London: Allen & Unwin).

Stone, Lawrence (1977), *The Family, Sex and Marriage in England, 1500–1800* (New York: Harper & Row).

Thomas, Dorothy Swaine (1941), *Social and Economic Aspects of Swedish Population Movements, 1756–1933* (New York: Macmillan).

Walker, Mack (1964), *Germany and the Emigration, 1816–1885* Cambridge, Mass.: Harvard University Press).

White, Harry Dexter (1933), *The French International Accounts, 1880–1913* (Cambridge, Mass.: Harvard University Press).

Wilson, C. H. (1941), *Anglo–Dutch Commerce and Finance in the Eighteenth Century* (Cambridge: Cambridge University Press).

Wirth, Max (1893), 'The Crisis of 1890', *Journal of Political Economy*, vol. 1, no. 2 (March), pp. 214–356.

10

Key Currencies and Financial Centres

The subject of key currencies would seem to be more closely associated with the work of John H. Williams than with Herbert Giersch. It is nonetheless an appropriate subject for this volume since Professor Giersch is a key economist in a key country with what may well be the next key currency. I propose in this essay to discuss the question of whether the arrangements for international money should be organised hierarchically, with a single key currency standing at the apex of a world system – whether two or more such currencies can serve effectively if no single currency stands out following the weakening of the dollar – and to explore a bit of European financial history in search of insights, analogies or contrasts with the present.

In 1944, John Williams (1947, *passim*) testified in the Congress of the United States against the Bretton Woods proposals on the grounds that it was a superior strategy in restoring a well-functioning world monetary economy to focus on key currencies, presumably one or at most a few, and one at a time, instead of seeking to construct a convertible world at one swoop with a worldwide organisation such as the International Monetary Fund (IMF).[1] The concept, which went back to a phrase he had used as a member of the Preparatory Commission of the League of Nations for the World Economic Conference of 1933 – 'key country' – underlay the Anglo-American Financial Agreement of 1946, the so-called 'British loan', designed to restore the pound to financial health first, and through it other currencies, starting perhaps with the sterling area. As it happened, the British loan failed to provide durable sterling convertibility – exchange restrictions were reimposed in the summer of 1947, a few weeks after the pound had been made convertible – and the IMF itself was sidetracked after a wobbly start in 1946, spending its time, until convertibility was finally achieved in 1958, largely in tendering advice to less developed countries. The task of monetary and economic reconstruction in Western Europe was assigned to the European Recovery Programme, also known as the Marshall Plan.

It is not widely known that the United States had an opportunity to apply the key-country approach to European recovery. When the Ambassador to Britain, Lewis Douglas, and the Under Secretary of State for Economic Affairs, William L. Clayton, visited Europe in June 1947,

Reprinted with permission from Fritz Machlup, Gerhard Fels and Hubertus Müller-Groeling (eds), Reflections on a Troubled World Economy. Essays in Honour of Herbert Giersch *(London: Macmillan, for the Trade Policy Research Centre, 1983), pp 75–90.*

less than three weeks after Secretary Marshall's speech, they called on Britain's Foreign Secretary, Ernest Bevin, who suggested that the United States undertake a large programme of aid to Britain and thereafter that Britain and the United States together turn their attention to recovery on the Continent. The 'special relationship' between the United Kingdom and the United States proved not to be sturdy enough to support this proposal and Britain became another recipient of Marshall Plan aid to Europe along with the Continental states (*Foreign Relations of the United States, 1947*, 1972, III pp. 268–70).

Whatever the immediate postwar experience, the insight of John Williams and the question of key currencies are still unresolved. Questions remain open whether a key-currency approach to international monetary arrangements is valid; if so, whether there should be a single key currency, or a series; if more than one, whether these should be arranged hierarchically or on an equal level; and finally, if it be efficient to have a single key currency – or one key currency *primus inter pares* – what Susan Strange (1971), of the London School of Economics, might call from her political-science perspective a 'top currency' or a 'master currency' – how a change can be made from a tired and worn-out top currency to a youthful and more capable one.

In the immediate postwar period at the Massachusetts Institute of Technology (MIT), all social sciences were gathered into a single department and economists would sometimes find themselves more or less unintentionally edified by having to listen to practitioners from other and not always closely allied fields. One experimental social psychologist used to organise small groups in various ways for problem-solving and was persuaded that when task forces were grouped in circles, each connected only with members of the group to his or her right and left, communicating by writing on slips of paper in some constrained way and unable to see the faces of the group, the problem – the nature of which now escapes me – could be solved in many fewer steps than if the group were forced to communicate in hierarchic fashion, through a centralised message centre. I no longer recall whether time constraints played a role. In crisis, it is reasonably clear that strong leadership without extended discussion is desirable. Goodman's novel, *Delilah*, suggests what may happen when enlisted men converse freely with their officers and believe themselves in a position to discuss and question orders in a crisis. Examples more apposite for international economics are the three weeks of discussion insisted upon by the French at the time of the Hoover Moratorium of 19 June 1931, raising the question whether it applied to the unconditional payments provided under the Young Plan of 1929 or only to the conditional ones – a valid legal point, which, however, delayed the rescue of the German money market for so long that its banking system collapsed (Kindleberger, 1973, pp. 154–5). Or again, years of discussion and what seemed interminable delays were required by the point, raised by the French on 'disparities' (*écrètements*) in the Kennedy Round of negotiations under the General Agreement on Tariffs and Trade (GATT), whether it was equitable for a country with a narrower range of customs duties, that is, less disparities, to be required to reduce tariffs by the same percentage as one with the same average level, but a wider range of duties (Curzon and Curzon, 1969, pp. 34–6). The point remains a fascinating conundrum for economists, but came within an ace of ruining the Kennedy Round by exhausting the five years of lee-way given by the Congress to the executive branch before the presidential powers under the legislation lapsed. Equality of participation may be best in the production and exchange of ideas under normal, unstressful times, but it is likely that strong leadership and docile followership are optimal in crisis.

Financial centres and economies of scale

Some years ago in a paper on financial centres (Kindleberger, 1974/1978), I concluded that there were strong economies of scale associated with centralisation in a single financial centre in a country and presumably, by extension, in a region like the European Community and in the world as a whole. These economies are similar to those in an agglomeration of markets, that is, the reduction of transactions costs, especially those of search. A lesser region with excess savings finds it effective to send them to a financial centre where demanders for savings gather. Conversely, demanders are attracted to a central source of excess supply. Local financial institutions cannot be altogether dispensed with, to be sure. One of the most important requirements in finance is credit information; and this is available in detail about small participants in the market only in the village, town or provincial city. Central stapling markets for goods – Antwerp, Amsterdam, Hamburg, London – lost their eminence as trade relays when knowledge of what goods were produced and wanted where became widely diffused and when the cost of transporting from producers to the centre and from the centre to consumers could be reduced by direct dealings. The costs of transferring money to and from a central place, however, are far less, which argues in favour of retaining financial centres and their economies of scale. On the other hand, as computers and the cost of electronic communication become drastically cheaper, and reduce search costs in the field of money to trivial levels, there may be an argument for direct trade in money and securities as in goods, with supply and demand unified worldwide by electronic bands without assembly in geographic centres. (At the moment, it should be noted, new issues of Euro-bonds are marketed worldwide, whereas the secondary market, where search costs have to be absorbed by small transactions, tends to locate in a single place.) For the time being, the $N-1$ argument for money as a unit of account, rather than each good being priced in terms of every other, applies both to currencies and to financial centres. It is more efficient to pick a single (or perhaps a limited number of financial centres) and deal with all transactions above some considerable size in it (or them) than to search the world for outlets or available supply. The same argument applies to selecting one currency as international money and, to shift to another medium of exchange, to conducting international discourse for the most part in a single language. The currency should be one already in use, like the dollar, rather than an artificial one like the Special Drawing Right (SDR), just as the language used as a medium of exchange cannot be Esperanto or a dead language such as Latin.

One puzzle in the study of financial centres was why Canada and Australia were so slow in converging on Toronto and Sydney, respectively, and why Montreal and Melbourne hung on for so long as doughty rivals. Considerations of history, geography and especially the association of a given centre with a certain industry, as St James Street in Montreal was the financial centre for Canadian railroads, each doubtless played a part. Professor S. H. Butlin, the Australian economic historian, suggested in a private letter, however, that there might be a significant difference between federal and unitary states, a difference inherent less in constitutional arrangements, I should think, than in sociology. That this is so is demonstrated, I believe, by German and United States experience, where the formation of a single financial centre took place in the face of national policies directed at preventing it. The Federal Reserve System was set up in 1913 with twelve regional banks which were intended to serve as foci for twelve regional money markets. It was quickly evident after World War I, however, that the system was unified with a dominant financial market in New York and subsidiary markets in Chicago, San Francisco and Los Angeles. In Germany, the occupation authorities after World War II sought to diffuse monetary and banking direction to the *Länder*, and especially to build up Hamburg and Düsseldorf as rivals to Frankfurt, which was the heir-apparent to Berlin's pre-war eminence. The gesture was futile as the centripetal tendencies of money and capital markets in unified states asserted themselves and the main capital market gravitated towards Frankfurt.

The rise and decline of financial centres

Key countries and key currencies are by no means new, although historians tend to illustrate their importance by reference to the contemporary scene. Pierre Vilar asserts that the Florentine florin and the Venetian ducat were the dollars of the Middle Ages, and the Dutch currency the dollar of the seventeenth century (1976, pp. 2–5). (Analogously with English, Italian was the commercial language of the Mediterranean (Braudel, 1973, p. 131), and Dutch prevailed as the commercial language in the Baltic ports and elsewhere in the seventeenth and eighteenth centuries (de Jong-Keesing, 1939, p. 220).) World financial markets were dominated successively by Florence, Venice, Genoa, Bruges, Antwerp and London, but there have always been strong pulls in other directions. From time to time it appears that there have been financial axes, Florence–Lyons, Venice–Augsburg–Bruges, Augsburg–Antwerp, Amsterdam–London and London–Hamburg. Financial distinction appears to have followed temporally after supremacy in trade and to have been causally connected with the decline in trade. Men with fortunes made as merchants chose to reduce their risks by shifting into loans and securities. In one city after another the lament was voiced that merchants were turning their backs on the sea and commodities in favour of money, bills of exchange, securities and country estates, to reduce both trouble and risk.[2] The shift from trade to finance appears to be largely an internal process, associated with accumulation of wealth by merchants.

The decline of financial centres and their supersession by others is more complex: it may come from some inner weakness or decay of the sort that seems to afflict the dollar today; it may reflect an aggressive challenge; or both may apply. Until about 1670 the Dutch considered themselves superior to the British in ability, energy, capital and material resources and the British admitted their inferiority (Boxer, 1970, p. 245). But by then the position had begun to change. After a false start early in the century, the Navigation Acts were passed in 1651 and strengthened in 1660. The British coveted Dutch trade: as his country prepared aggressively for the second Anglo-Dutch War, the Duke of Albermarle stated that 'What we want is the trade the Dutch now have' (Williams, 1970, pp. 44, 484). The Dutch trade advantage went down first – various sources debate exactly when – but between the last quarter of the seventeenth century and 1730. The Dutch advantage in finance declined sometime after the fourth Anglo-Dutch War in 1784, perhaps with Napoleon's occupation of the United Provinces in 1795. Without making a distinction between trade and finance, Braudel states that between 1780 and 1815 the economic centre of Europe, which had remained for two hundred years in Amsterdam, moved to London (and in 1929 crossed the Atlantic to New York) (1977, p. 86). The occupation of the United Provinces of Holland by Napoleonic armies underlines the fact that military power can play an important role in shifts of currencies and financial centres. The shift from Bruges to Antwerp was slow in the latter part of the fifteenth and early sixteenth centuries as Portuguese pepper and German copper came to be traded in the latter and Flemish cloth spread from Bruges to many places visited by the Hanseatic League (see Bergier, 1979, pp. 107–8; Dollinger, 1970, p. 203). Antwerp's yielding of place to Amsterdam (and to a lesser extent to Hamburg and Frankfurt) occurred suddenly as the Spanish invaded the Scheldt in 1585 and cut off its access to the sea. Both rise to financial eminence and decline from it can occur either rapidly or slowly.

It is not inevitable that any financial centre that tries to displace another in the world hierarchy can do so. The Deutsche Bank was started in 1872 with the express purpose of challenging British leadership in world finance. It got caught up in the domestic boom associated with the founding of the German Reich and the receipt of the Franco-Prussian indemnity (Helfferich, 1956, pp. 32–4, 41, 56). Paris challenged London's supremacy several times in the nineteenth century, but especially in the 1850s. In some views, it achieved success.[3] For the most part, however, scholars agree with Walter Bagehot, who concluded that the abandonment of convertibility in 1870 at the outbreak of the Franco-Prussian War spelled the end of French hopes to dominate the finances of Europe (1873/1978, p. 63).

Key currencies or key financial centres?

Should one say key currency or key financial centre? Is New York the world financial centre or is it London with its enormous business in Euro-dollars? In a sense the market for the dollar has no location, as it travels around the world each weekday, starting out west of the international dateline (to be arbitrary) in Singapore, moving thence to Bahrain and on to Europe, before crossing the Atlantic to New York and ending up in San Francisco (see Stigum, 1978, ch. 6, esp. pp. 108–10, 427). This fact complicates the management of a leading currency which is now a 24-hour-day affair during the week which starts on Sunday afternoon in the United States as Singapore is opening on Monday morning. Most financial authorities work from 9 to 5, but news of the sort to disturb the market, such as that of President John F. Kennedy's assassination, can occur in any place in the world and at any time (see Coombs, 1976, pp. 96–8).

A financial centre has certain functions and, I would add, certain responsibilities, notably that of acting as a lender of last resort in crisis. Financial integration may be said to be a good thing if the trouble starts at home and integration into a world market diffuses it over space – a bad thing if it arises abroad and is communicated to a given centre from the outside. In either event, the world centre presiding over a key currency presumably has the function of trying to halt it. The lender-of-last-resort function is generally associated with the name of Bagehot, who articulated a rationale for it in *Lombard Street*, although he left some residual ambiguity by writing from time to time that the system by which the Bank of England held the reserves for the London money market as a whole was an 'unnatural' one that would not have been constructed *de novo* had it not happened to have evolved that way (Bagehot, 1978, IX, pp. 197, 377, 428, 444, 451, 453; XI, pp. 109, 135, 139).[4] I demur from this line of argument, believing that the insurance principle dictates great economies from centralised reserves, although one must recognise that moral hazard is implicit in any system having ultimate responsibility yet divorced from operating units. Revealed historical preference, however, seems to show that the dangers of moral hazard from relieving banks of too much responsibility are less than those in having no lender of last resort. Where there is no clear financial centre, there may be failure to discharge the duty of halting spreading collapse in the international monetary system, such as occurred, in my judgment, in 1929–33, in the midst of the transfer of financial leadership from London to New York (Kindleberger, 1973).

There is a complex disability to the system if the failure starts with the dominant financial centre itself. Paris came to the rescue of Britain at least four times between 1815 and 1914. In 1825 it swapped gold for silver to help the Bank of England meet a run that was ultimately checked by finding some of the £1 and £2 notes left over from the period of inconvertibility that halted with resumption of specie payments in 1819. It did so again on two occasions between 1836 and 1839, when the Bank of England drew on Paris for £400,000 the first time and £2 million, along with £900,000 from the State Bank of Hamburg, the second. In 1890, when the Bank of England was about to announce the collapse of Baring Brothers, it sought assurance from the Russian Government that it would not withdraw its deposit of £2.4 million at the Bank, and arranged for loans of £3 million from the Bank of France and £1.5 million from the State Bank of Russia. Yet again, the Bank of France helped the Bank of England by selling gold to the London market in the crisis of 1907, although British historians assert that this was not a rescue operation, since the Bank of England did not ask for help, and did not need it. (For details of these operations and sources, see Kindleberger, 1978, ch. 10 'The International Lender of Last Resort'.)

Sometimes a government or its central bank acts as the lender of last resort. Sometimes it merely opens its market to permit a foreign institution in trouble – government, central bank, outstanding banker acting as a chosen instrument of the government – a Rothschild or a Baring – to borrow in the private capital market. Many lender-of-last-resort loans in the nineteenth and twentieth centuries were of this type. In these cases governments proposed, the market disposed – and not always favourably. Italy sought a stabilisation loan in 1881 as she was prepared to return to gold following the depreciation of the lira from 1866 – the so-called *corso forzoso*, or forced circulation. The loan was opened in Paris and failed miserably, to such an extent that it was transferred to London (see Lévy-Leboyer, 1977, p. 129). The French capital market happened to be bemused by the boom that collapsed the next year with the failure of the Union Générale. Moreover, French investors were in the process of turning their attention away from involvement with Italy, Spain and Austria, to shift their interest to Russia and South-eastern Europe (*ibid.*, p. 251).

The dollar as a key currency

We come shortly to the problem of the financial difficulties of the dollar. First, however, it may be observed that, historically, financial centres have been aided by winning the role of distributing additions to world monetary reserves. German silver moved to Venice during the Renaissance. African gold went originally to the Levant and then to Europe via Venice or Genoa, often exchanged for silver which was more highly valued in the East. When Spanish treasure arrived at Seville, it was already owed to German, Genoan and later Flemish and Dutch bankers, and had to be shipped out. Small amounts stayed in Spain; a trickle went into France by way of Biarritz (Spooner, 1972, pp. 5, 125). The silver of Spanish America went largely to Flanders in the second half of the sixteenth century, along the Atlantic route. From 1568 it became diverted to Genoa and the so-called Besancon fair at Piacenza

(Braudel, 1977, p. 87; Silva, 1969, pp. 38–40). With the collapse of Genoa as a financial centre after 1620 'for a multitude of causes that occurred simultaneously' (Braudel, 1977, p. 25), the flow went to Amsterdam, which carried off up to 25 per cent of the treasure brought in by the *flota* and redistributed it to the Far East and Europe (Barbour, 1966, p. 50). Portuguese discoveries of gold in the 1680s – which Spooner is bold enough to ascribe to the causes of the Industrial Revolution a century later – led the British to conclude the Treaty of Methuen and helped divert gold to London. In the mid-1850s, the yield of California and Australia arrived in London to be redistributed to the Continent, much of it to be exchanged by France against silver for shipment to the Far East (Hughes, 1960, pp. 243 *et seq.* and esp. p. 247).[5]

The contrast, of course, is with the dollar standard after World War II, when gold production was first cut by retaining a fixed price when mining costs had risen sharply owing to the war and then went into hoarding rather than being distributed by the leading financial centre. A number of economists, notably Milton Gilbert, wanted to raise the price of gold to correct what he saw as an anomaly (see Gilbert's posthumous study, 1980). The world was not short of liquidity, as economists such as Robert Triffin thought would occur; on the contrary, world liquidity was produced on demand by borrowing dollars in New York up to the imposition of the Interest Equalisation Tax in 1963 and then in the Euro-dollar market. The difficulty was that the United States reserve ratio was continuously in decline. It was not in 'deficit', lending long and borrowing short as banks normally do, but, with a fixed and later a declining amount of gold in the face of mounting dollar liabilities, its reserve ratio dwindled. United States assent in 1965 for the adoption and distribution of SDRs was dictated, in my judgment, by the necessity seen to add to United States quick assets. In the process, other countries including those with excess dollars gained reserves as well, in the absence of recognition of the principle that the leading financial centre is different.

The problem of lender of last resort

But to return to the lender of last resort. The function is normally discharged by the key-currency centre. What if it is that centre which finds itself in trouble and it cannot be helped with gold as Paris helped London? What especially if the leading centre committed a blunder of monetary policy, as the Federal Reserve System did in 1971, in trying to lower interest rates (to help President Richard Nixon's chances for re-election) when the next largest monetary power, West Germany, was trying to hold interest rates up, or raise them, to restrain inflation, both at a time when the two money markets were joined through the Euro-dollar market? Money created to lower interest rates in the United States would flow to the Euro-dollar market centred in London. German firms finding local interest rates high and rising would replace loans from German sources by borrowing in dollars in London and selling the dollars to the Bundesbank. The 'liquidity deficit' of $2,000 to $4,000 million a year experienced from the mid-1950s to the end of the 1960s, and tolerable despite the downward path of the reserve-to-foreign-deposits ratio, rose to $20,000 and $30,000 million yearly.

When the dollar was strong and countries in trouble needed dollars, they could be provided in leisurely fashion by the IMF or, if the crisis was more exigent, by the General Agreement to Borrow (GAB) and ultimately by the swap lines. Swaps were devised at the time of the March 1961 British crisis in the Basle agreement and used later for Canada, Italy, a second time for Britain, and for France. The United States spearheaded the operation. But when the crisis was that of the dollar, rescue called not for a single or leading lender of last resort, or many lenders operating in a single currency, but for a whole variety of other currencies sought by the entities quitting the dollar – German marks, Swiss francs, sterling – especially those sought by some countries belonging to the Organisation of Petroleum Exporting countries (OPEC) which at one time had given allegiance to the sterling area – not to mention yen, French francs, *et cetera*. When the leading centre is in trouble, and there is a variety of assets into which its currency might be converted, the lender-of-last-resort function becomes more complex.

A further important complication arises if the secondary centres do not share the sense of responsibility of the primary one. This is partly a question of conditionality, in which it is difficult to distinguish technical economic and financial conditions – what the country in trouble needs to do to correct its position – from ideological and political ones. In addition there may be conditions of a purely foreign-policy nature, such as those demanded by the French as a *quid pro quo* for acceding to the second tranche of the Bank for International Settlements (BIS) led loan to the Creditanstalt in May 1931 – that Austria withdraw from the Zollunion with Germany – or the demand that the Germans abandon construction of the Panzerkreuzer (armoured cruiser), then under way, before the French could consider a stabilisation loan in June 1931.

Political considerations may of course dictate the granting of a rescue loan which could not be justified on economic and financial grounds. In April 1906, the French market was opened to a loan of FR. 1,500 million for Russia, immediately after the defeat of Russia by Japan in war, a failed revolution and the prospective bankruptcy of the Czar (Girault, 1977, p. 251). And even when the supporting centres come to the rescue without hesitation, the possibility of last-minute holding back gives rise to nervousness. Britain felt humiliated by the need to appeal to France in 1839, and the French found vainglory in having helped, albeit resolving never to do so again. In 1873, flushed with pride of victory in the Franco-Prussian War, the Germans offered to help the Bank of England through a gold loan and were thought insulting. In 1890, when Britain needed the help of France and Russia, the appeal gave rise to great uneasiness: 'Suppose for some political–financial reason, they had been unwilling to oblige' (Clapham, 1958, II, pp. 170, 291–4, 329–30, 344; Viner, 1937, p. 273).

It is sometimes suggested that the IMF should act as the lender of last resort, and remove that necessity from private financial centres and their national monetary authorities. For the less developed countries this has the obvious advantage that there is at least the superficial appearance of no imperialistic tutelage. Less developed countries do chafe at the conditions laid down for their borrowing by the IMF, and tend from time to time to penetrate the international form to detect the imperialist guidance of the major powers. They accept these conditions – and those of the Euro-currency bankers – more readily, however, than they would those of national governments.

For the major financial powers, however, the IMF is typically too slow and too limited in size. The slowness arises from the voting procedure and the need to consult domestic monetary authorities, often of a long list of countries. The process takes three weeks at a minimum, and financial crises may blow up in hours. The size limitation had its origin in the initial view that IMF borrowings would meet deficits on current account because capital movements would be subjected to controls. In the event, financial crises are associated with large capital movements, permitted under convertibility, and in any case uncontrollable because of leads and lags. The IMF cannot perform the other functions of a financial centre and in crises operates best in mopping-up operations in the rear rather than at the vortex.

On the national front, an important step was taken at the BIS in Basle in 1975, following the Herstatt and Franklin National bank crises, in the agreement that each major financial country in case of trouble would take care of its own banks, no matter where they operated abroad, and would prevent any failure from spreading to banks or firms of other nations. The agreement spreads responsibility widely: it does not eliminate completely the need for some direction to the system by a leading financial centre. There remains a small and declining problem of consortium banks, owned by other banks in a number of countries for which, in time of trouble, rescue methods would have to be devised *ad hoc*. And there remains, too, the need for international help in cases of sudden switches of hot money from one to another financial centre which it is thought unwise to handle through exchange-rate changes because of irreversible effects on prices, costs and hence on inflation – a problem which the newer generation refers to as 'currency substitution' by contrast with the pre-war expression 'hot money'.

But it is time to conclude. History shows, at least in my judgment, that financial centres and national currencies – no longer completely congruent as national currencies are traded worldwide – tend to organise themselves in hierarchical order, with one key currency serving as numeraire for much of the world's business. In earlier times when, say, sterling meant London, the financial centre associated with the leading currency had certain functions to perform: the distribution of additions to world reserves, the accumulation and allocation of short- and long-term capital and, in time of crisis, serving as a lender of last resort.

Today, key currencies and financial centres cannot be matched so readily, and the capital-accumulation process can take place, for the most part, worldwide in a leading currency. The financial centre responsible for that currency – New York in the case of the dollar – cannot, however, escape its lender-of-last-resort function.

Change in key currencies and leading financial centres seems to follow a law of growth. It may take place slowly, in a long drawn-out process, or suddenly because of the aggressive rise of a new centre, or the collapse of the old in war. One is unable to say much based on either theory or history about what happens with no financial centre in charge, or with two. I have argued that the slow transfer and especially the slow acceptance of responsibility from London to New York in the inter-war period were responsible for the width, depth and length of the world depression of the 1930s, but the case is not proven. London was supported on occasion in the nineteenth century by Paris, but it can hardly be said that the two centres operated a duumvirate: Paris reigned supreme in a narrow area that changed, but London was clearly the dominant centre, and sterling the dominant currency.

This leaves us unable to say whether the dollar and the German mark and New York and Frankfurt can operate as dual key currencies and dual financial centres, sharing responsibility for world financial crises – although I have doubts; or whether the dollar and the world Euro-dollar market, centred perhaps in London, are *en route* to being replaced by the German mark and Frankfurt. Gresham's law, which states that a system with two monies is unstable, is easily extended to the proposition that a world with two key currencies of equal worth, or two key financial centres on a par, is equally unstable. The ageing of the American economy is clear, but the German economy in 1980 has lost some of the energy and drive it had two years earlier (see 'Bonn's World Role', 1980, p. 2). One responsible centre or the other would be satisfactory, possibly, but probably not both would be, or perhaps a third country that emerges (maybe soon) as a dark horse and takes over. What strikes this observer as dangerous is a long period with no one in charge.

Notes

1   The index for this edition has almost four inches of citations under the headings 'key countries' and 'key currencies'.
2   On Antwerp, see Ehrenberg (1896/1928), p. 243; for two others, see Burke (1974), p. 104; Wilson (1941), Pt II, ch. 3. Wilson deals here with the transition of Amsterdam from trade to finance.
3   Bouvier (1973, p. 238) calls Paris the international clearing house in 1820–40, citing Lévy-Leboyer (1964, pp. 437–44). Most writers date the challenge as occurring in the 1850s; see for example Rosenberg (1934, p. 38). Morgenstern (1959, p. 128) states that Paris emerges as the *strongest* (his italics) financial centre in the world before 1914 if the fact that its short-term interest rate is the lowest is an indication of strength. Bonelli simply asserts that Paris was the real centre for regulating world liquidity at the beginning of the second half of 1907, but this may reflect a particular Italian view since Italian finances were tied to Paris (1971, p. 42).
4   The principle of the lender of last resort was asserted at the beginning of the nineteenth century by Henry Thornton (1802/1962, pp. 187–8).
5   Chevalier (1859) calls the exchange of gold for silver in France a 'parachute' that retarded the fall in the price of gold.

References

Bagehot, Walter (1873/1978), *Lombard Street*, in N. St John-Stevas (ed.), *The Collected Works of Walter Bagehot*, vol. IX (London: *The Economist*).

Bagehot, Walter (1978), *The Collected Works of Walter Bagehot*, edited by N. St John-Stevas (London: *The Economist*, 11 vols).

Barbour, Violet (1966), *Capitalism in Amsterdam in the Seventeenth Century* (Ann Arbor, Mich.: University of Michigan Press).

Bergier, Jean-François (1979), 'From the Fifteenth Century in Italy to the Sixteenth in Germany: A New Banking Concept', in Center for Medieval and Renaissance Studies, UCLA (ed.), *The Dawn of Modern Banking* (New Haven, Conn.: Yale University Press).

Bonelli, Franco (1971), *La crisi del 1907: una tappa dello sviluppo industriale in Italia* (Turin: Fondazione Luigi Einaudi).

'Bonn's World Role: Recession is Limiting Leverage' (1980), *New York Times*, 7 November.

Bouvier, Jean (1973), *Un siècle de banque française* (Paris: Hachette Littérature).

Boxer, Charles R. (1970), 'The Dutch Economic Decline', in Carlo M. Cipolla (ed.), *The Economic Decline of Empires* (London: Methuen).

Braudel, Fernand (1973), *The Mediterranean and the Mediterranean World in the Age of Philip II*, Vol. I (New York: Harper).

Braudel, Fernand (1977), *Afterthoughts on Material Civilization and Capitalism*, translated by Patricia M. Ranum (Baltimore, Md: Johns Hopkins University Press).

Burke, Peter (1974), *Venice and Amsterdam: A Study in Seventeenth Century Elites* (London: Temple Smith).

Chevalier, Michel (1859), *On the Probable Fall in the Value of Gold*, translated by Richard Cobden, 3rd edn (Manchester: Alexander Ireland).

Clapham, Sir John (1958), *The Bank of England: a History* (Cambridge: Cambridge University Press, 2 vols).

Coombs, Charles A. (1976), *The Arena of International Finance* (New York: Wiley).

Curzon, Gerard and Curzon, Victoria (1969), 'Options after the Kennedy Round', in Harry G. Johnson (ed.), *New Trade Strategy for the World Economy* (London: Allen & Unwin, for the Trade Policy Research Centre).

de Jong-Keesing, Elizabeth E. (1939), *De economische Crisis van 1763 te Amsterdam* (Amsterdam: Intern. Uitgevers en H. Mij).

Dollinger, Philippe (1970), *The German Hansa*, translated and edited by D. S. Ault and S. H. Steinberg (Stanford, Calif.: Stanford University Press).

Ehrenberg, Richard (1896/1928), *Capital and Finance in the Age of the Renaissance: a Study of the Fuggers and their Connections*, translated from the 1928 German text by H. M. Lucas (New York: Harcourt Brace).

Foreign Relations of the United States, 1947 (1972), vol. III (Washington, DC: US Government Printing Office).

Gilbert, Milton (1980), *Quest for World Monetary Order, the Gold–Dollar System and its Aftermath*, a Twentieth Century Fund Study (New York: Wiley).

Girault, René (1977), 'Investissements et placements français en Russie, 1880–1914', in Maurice Lévy-Leboyer (ed.), *La Position internationale de la France. Aspects économiques et financiers. XIXe–XXe siècles* (Paris: Editions de l'Ecole des Hautes Etudes en Sciences Sociales), pp. 251–62.

Helfferich, Karl (1956), *Georg von Siemens, Ein Lebensbild aus Deutschlands grosser Zeit*, revised and shortened edn (Krefeld: Serpe).

Hughes, Jonathan R. T. (1960), *Fluctuations in Trade, Industry and Finance: a Study of British Economic Development, 1850–1860* (Oxford: Clarendon Press).

Kindleberger, Charles P. (1973), *The World in Depression, 1929–1939* (Berkeley, Calif.: University of California Press).

Kindleberger, Charles P. (1974/1978), *The Formation of Financial Centers: a Study in Comparative Economic History*, Princeton Studies in International Finance, No. 36; reprinted in *Economic Response, Comparative Studies in Trade, Finance and Growth* (Cambridge, Mass.: Harvard University Press).

Kindleberger, Charles P. (1978), *Manias, Panics and Crashes* (New York: Basic Books).

Lévy-Leboyer, Maurice (1964), *Les Banques européennes et l'industrialisation internationale dans la première moitié du XIXe siècle* (Paris: Presses universitaires de France).

Lévy-Leboyer, Maurice (1977), 'La Balance des paiements et l'exportation des capitaux français', in Lévy-Leboyer (ed.), *La Position internationale de la France, Aspects économiques et financiers, XIXe–XXe siècles* (Paris: Editions de l'Ecole des Hautes Etudes en Sciences Sociales), pp. 75–142.

Morgenstern, Oskar (1959), *International Financial Transactions and Business Cycles* (Princeton, NJ: Princeton University Press, for the National Bureau of Economic Research).

Rosenberg, Hans (1934), *Die Weltwirtschaftskrisis von 1857–1859* (Stuttgart and Berlin: W. Kohlhammer).

Silva, José-Gentil da (1969), *Banque et crédit en Italie au XVIIe siècle* (Paris: Editions Klincksieck).

Spooner, Frank C. (1972), *The International Economy and Monetary Movements in France, 1493–1725* Cambridge, Mass.: Harvard University Press).

Stigum, Marcia (1978), *The Money Market: Myth, Reality and Practice* (Homewood, Ill.: Dow-Jones–Irwin).

Strange, Susan (1971), *Sterling and British Policy: a Political Study of an International Currency in Decline* (London: Oxford University Press).

Thornton, Henry (1802/1962), *An Enquiry into the Nature and Effect of Paper Credit of Great Britain*; edited with an introduction by Friedrich A. von Hayek (London: Frank Cass; reprint of 1939 edn, London: Allen & Unwin).

Vilar, Pierre (1976), *A History of Gold and Money, 1450–1920*, translated from the 1969 Spanish original by Judith White (London: New Left Books).

Viner, Jacob (1937), *Studies in the Theory of International Trade* (New York: Harper).

Williams, E. Neville (1970), *The Ancien Regime in Europe, Government and Society in the Major States, 1648–1789* (New York: Harper & Row).

Williams, John H. (1947), *Postwar Monetary Plans and Other Essays*, 3rd revised and expanded edn (New York: Knopf).

Wilson, Charles (1941), *Anglo-Dutch Commerce and Finance in the Eighteenth Century* (Cambridge: Cambridge University Press).

11

The Financial Aftermath of War

I

War imposes great strain on the financial system of a country. How great the strain it imposes is of course a function of the size and duration of the war, on the one hand, and the way it is financed, on the other. The strains are internal and external. As one interested in using comparative economic history to explore the general validity of economic models and policies, I find that the aftermath of war in Europe provides an interesting range of measures and outcomes.

A few preliminary observations may be in order. In the first place, the *Annales* school of history, which is trying to get away from the study of dynasties and wars to observe such topics as family formation, children, disease, cemeteries and death, may not approve, although one can observe a counter-current in the Shelby Cullom Davis Center for Historical Studies program for the study of 'War and Society' in the next two years. But financial history is tied to dynasties and the wars they generate in indissoluble fashion. Note, for example, Goldsmith's financial intermediation ratio – the relation between liquid assets in an economy and national income. In economic development it typically grows from levels of about 0.22 until it reaches roughly 1.75 where it levels off – *'except for war'* (my italics) (1969, p. 40). Secondly, a study of financial history prior to 1914 runs up against W. W. Rostow's generalization that money and finance did little to shape historical processes prior to World War I, in contrast to real factors, being adaptive and permissive (1978, p. xliii). This is a concrete example of a more general view that institutions do not count in economic outcomes, responding easily and readily to changes in endowments, technology and tastes (Coase, 1937; North and Thomas, 1973). Institutionalists take a diametrically opposed position – that institutions shape outcomes. Between the two there is room for an eclectic position suggesting that institutions, ideology and collective memory usually adapt to real factors but occasionally play an independent role of their own. There may even be evidence to support a position contrary to the Chicago School view that economic analysis illuminates social situations, to the effect that, on occasion at least, economic outcomes are determined by sociological conditions.

Published in Italian in Rivista di Storia Economica. *new ser., vol. 1, no 1 (1984), pp. 95–123; to be published in English in 1985.*

II

In his tract of 1940, Keynes wrote that in war the British government gives its citizens tax receipts, the French give theirs *rentes*, and the Germans hand out money. The point was preliminary to a proposal to pay British citizens partly in blocked deposits that would be unfrozen after the war when the decline in national income resulting from the shrinkage in government spending would leave unemployed resources. In the event, the device was a failure since the British public pressed for and obtained unblocking long before unemployment became a significant reality in Britain. As a generalization in war finance, moreover, the point was incomplete because it omitted the possibility of financing war with external resources. On the domestic side, it was something of an exaggeration, though not much, since the British financed 50 percent of World War I expenditure with taxation, as contrasted with the French 14 percent and the Germans 13 percent.

External finance is available for war through drawing down international reserves of gold and foreign exchange, disposal of other assets abroad, and borrowing. In addition, some belligerents feed on indemnities, such as those exacted by Napoleon from successive defeated enemies, and even from allies, and through what lies between indemnities and borrowing – running up large debit balances in bilateral clearing, such as Germany undertook in Belgium in World War I and with western occupied countries in World War II. The financial contribution of external finance can be negative: the British typically fought their wars by buying mercenaries and subsidizing allies. Lend-lease made available by the United States to its allies in World War II could also be said to have been a subsidy, although it was defended at the time, as were British subsidies, as an efficient 'purchase' of self-defense.

Pecunia nervus belli (money is the sinew of war): the quotation from Tacitus is followed by Ehrenberg with a discussion of the importance of money to war (1896/1928, p. 22). Money was used in the Middle Ages to buy mercenaries, largely produced in overpopulated Swiss valleys and those of the Palatinate. Prince William of Hanau, Elector of Hesse-Cassel, grew rich buying his soldiers at one price and selling them to belligerents at a higher one (and Mayer Amschell Rothschild, founder of the great house in Frankfurt with son Nathan, grew equally or more rich transferring from country to country and investing the Elector's gains – Corti, 1928, pp. 11, 25). Money was vital for mercenaries not only when an army was raised, but also when it was in the field. If soldiers were not paid, they tended to become restless and to pillage the surroundings, which their lessor may have owned or wanted to capture intact. Napoleon's army was exceptional in fighting for long stretches of time on *assignats* and victory (Thiers, 1894, I, p. 6); the new Model Army of Cromwell was insufficiently buoyed by political and religious fervor to sustain itself happily, given long arrears of pay, occasionally reduced through issue of dubious debentures (Brailsford, 1961, pp. 167, 297, 506, etc.). On occasion an army might switch sides in response to a better cash offer (Ehrenberg, 1896/1928, p. 79). Machiavelli noted that it was possible with soldiers to get money (*ibid.*, pp. 342–3); mostly it ran the other way. Ehrenberg recounts the story of Louis XII of France who asked the Condottiere Giacomo de Trivulzio in 1499 what was needed to reduce the stronghold of Milan. The answer was 'Three things, Sire: Money, money and money' (*ibid.*, p. 24).

Obtaining money for war meant borrowing for the most part, as explained by Adam Smith in the *Wealth of Nations*:

> The want of parsimony in time of peace imposes the necessity of contracting debt in time of war. When war comes, there is no money in the treasury but what is necessary for carrying on the ordinary expenses of the peace establishment. In war, an establishment three or four times that expense becomes necessary for the defense of the state, and consequently a revenue three or four times greater than the peace revenue. Supposing the sovereign should have, what he scarce ever has, the immediate means of augmenting his revenue in proportion to his expense, yet the produce of taxes from which this increase in revenue must be drawn, will not begin to come into the treasury till perhaps ten or twelve months after which they are imposed. But the moment in which the war . . . appears likely to begin, the army must be augmented, the fleet must be fitted out, the garrison towns must be furnished with arms, ammunition and provisions. An immediate and great expense must be incurred in that moment of immediate danger, which will not wait for the gradual and slow return of the taxes. In this exigency government can have no other recourse than in borrowing. (1776/1937, pp. 861–2)

Other less eloquent writers add further elements of war finance to taxation and borrowing:

> The Governments waging war were permanently short of money, which they tried to obtain by loans, by the levying of tributes and contributions and by inflation. The moneys in question were not collected directly by the places and bodies concerned but advanced by bankers. (de Jong-Keesing, 1939, p. 215)

This introduces three additional ideas: tributes, inflation and bank intermediation.

> It has been said that war is a 'sensible thing' – which means we suppose that it likes hard cash. According to Louis XIV, the last guinea always wins. (Bagehot, 1856/1978, IX, p. 297)

Here is the idea that the quality of money counts, and especially the convertibility of paper money into specie.

So fundamental is money to war that in discussing French and Spanish involvement in the American War of Independence, Vergennes said to Montmorin in Madrid: 'This war has dragged out too long; it is truly a war between treasuries [*une guerre d'écus*]' (Harris, 1979, p. 209).

deJong-Keesing's mention of bankers raises a diversionary thought: whether bankers could stop a given war if they chose not to finance it.

> Does anyone seriously suppose that a great war could be undertaken by any European State, or a great State loan subscribed, if the house of Rothschild and its connections set their face against it? (Hobson, 1938, p. 57)

The same view had been expressed by Kaufmann, who said it was impossible to make war without calling on the Rothschilds for support (Kaufmann, 1914, p. 9). The Rothschilds themselves held a contrary view. Writing to Gerson Bleichröder in Germany in 1865, Baron James de Rothschild of the Paris house said:

> It is a principle of our houses not to advance money for war, and even if it is not in our power to prevent war, then our minds are easy that we have not contributed to it. (Stern, 1977, p. 73)

The date is ironic, for in the following year Bismarck readied himself for war against Austria by still another method not yet mentioned. The Landestag had refused to advance funds; but there were national assets to be sold off – and to bankers, including that admirer of Baron de Rothschild, Bleichröder. Two types of assets were involved: the Cologne–Minden railroad, which belonged to the Prussian state, and indemnities exacted by Bismarck from Saxony and from Frankfurt-am-Main. The former was underwritten as a public issue by Bleichröder and his private bank, with the help of David Hansemann and the Diskontogesellschaft. The indemnities, calling for a stream of payments for a limited period of time, were capitalized by Bismarck and sold to Bleichröder and Hansemann. Later, when the war against Austria had been highly successful, the Landestag was readier to countenance a normal loan, which was easily raised (*ibid.*, pp. 60–90, esp. 85).

There are, of course, many other episodes of bank lending to finance war. One of the more piquant is that of Gabriel Ouvrard: he was both the French munitioneer who supplied the Napoleonic armies on contract, and also a banker, whom Napoleon had arrested and stripped of his wealth on five occasions, but to whom he always had to return. Ouvrard financed Napoleon's 100 days after the return from Elba in 1815, and did it alone when all other bankers turned away (Emden, 1938, p. 17).

The success of Bismarck in 1866, blocked in one direction but finding a method of finance in another, suggests that finance in wartime is adaptive, thus supporting the anti-institutionalists. History is not without counter-examples, however. Bleichröder himself said that Austria's financial weakness in 1866 made it impossible for her to fight a war (Stern, 1977, p. 79). The British sued for peace prematurely in the second Anglo-Dutch war of 1672–4 because their financial machinery had broken down (Coleman, 1963, p. 65). The thesis of a splendid book on French finances in the early 1920s (largely unknown to economists because of its title's emphasis on diplomacy) is that financial weakness prevented the French from achieving their political ends in war debts, reparations, reconstruction and the like, and in fact lost them world status (Schuker, 1976, *passim* and esp. pp. 32–5, 385). On the other hand, financial limitations may prove to be a blessing in disguise: Britain, says Ralph Davis, had the good luck to be governed by a Parliament, with the resulting financial checks holding back the crown from the costly expenditures of war that ruined Louis XIV of France and Philip II of Spain (1973, p. 210).

Whether bankers can stop wars more certainly than financial weakness is beside the point. Europe has fought many wars, financed in various ways. Whatever the effect of finance on the outcome of a war, if any, war surely has a financial aftermath. In wartime, the German General Staff believed *Geld spielt keine Rolle*, which can be translated either literally as 'Money plays no role' or more freely as 'Hang the cost' (Williamson, 1971, p. 126). The same money that may or may not play a role in wartime, however, has an aftermath when the firing dies down.

III

To divide postwar effects of wartime finance into internal and external is somewhat heroic. The two are interrelated. The balance-of-payments school on inflation in Germany after World War I believed that purchases of foreign exchange for restocking the economy and paying reparations produced the depreciation of the exchange rate that led to internal inflation. The monetary school, contrariwise, argued that monetary expansion at home ran ahead of and produced the exchange depreciation. The same debate raged in Britain toward the close of the Napoleonic wars, and afterwards, between the Currency (monetarist) School and the Banking School, the latter primarily committed to exonerating the money supply of responsibility for the agio on gold (depreciation of sterling), but also holding the alternative explanation of blaming depreciation on the foreign balance, especially as affected by subsidies paid to Continental allies, by good and bad harvests – deepening and increasing grain imports, respectively – and by the ebb and flow of the Continental system or Napoleonic blockade (Tooke and Newmarch, 1838/1928, vols I and II; Gayer, Rostow and Schwartz, 1953, I). Many other connections exist, of course; for example: the budget aspect of reparations, and the impact of higher domestic interest rates on international capital flows. None the less, as a first approximation, I shall separate internal and external aspects of war finance and of policies to tidy it up, and start with the internal.

The Chamber of Justice was a peculiar French institution, used particularly to strip profiteers of ill-gotten gains in war. It was applied in 1517, 1559, 1607, 1644, 1648, and especially in 1661, 1713 and 1720. The Chamber of Justice of 1661 directed by Colbert was an attempt at fiscal reform as well as punishment for fraud of financial officials. Nicholas Fouquet, the *surintendant des finances*, was imprisoned for life and deprived of his fortune. Six other *financiers* were jailed, and the remainder had fines levied upon them of 156 million livres (the livre being the equivalent of the later franc), a sum which can be judged by comparing it with the revenues of the French crown in 1661 of 84 million livres (Dent, 1973, pp. 9, 105–8).

The secret Chamber of Justice of 1715 – called Visa I to distinguish it from Visa II, which took place after the collapse of the Mississippi bubble – followed the War of the Spanish Succession in 1713 and the death of Louis XIV in September 1715. Louis XIV was the profligate monarch who said to the Dauphin on his deathbed what has been foreshortened to 'Too many palaces, too many wars' (Faure, 1977, p. 63). The debt of the kingdom amounted to 3½ billion livres, of which ½ billion was floating. The Paris brothers ran the Visa, examining 8,000 accounts and fining 4,000 individuals. The Paris brothers themselves paid 1.2 million livres, and Samuel Bernard, the Lyons banker who had gone bankrupt in 1709 but made a new fortune in the war, made a voluntary contribution of 6 million livres. Although 220 million livres in fines were levied, the state actually collected only 95 million, mostly in depreciated state paper. Thes rest of the debt was converted forcibly into *billets d'état* (state notes) bearing 4 percent interest. These quickly went to a discount of 37½ percent, reducing the value of the total debt from 3½ to 2½ billion livres (Lüthy, 1959, pp. 281–6).

John Law's successive banks, the Banque Générale and the Banque Royale, on the one hand, and the South Sea Company in Britain on the other, can both be regarded as devices to fund debts left over from war. They were more, to be sure, with a gloss of trading and settlement rights in Mississippi for Law and the right (*asiento*) to sell slaves for the silver mines of Peru via Buenos Aires for the South Sea Company. In neither case did the trading rights amount to much, and the attempt to intermediate and fund the chaotic national debts by means of stock issues led to speculative euphoria and to 'overtrading, revulsion and discredit' as classical economists described a bubble followed by collapse. In both cases a post-mortem was held to strip the miscreants of their inordinate profits to the extent possible. In France the operation was again conducted by the Paris brothers, strong opponents of Law, employing 1,500–2,000 clerks in 54 offices. The operation involved a currency conversion. Even on a 1:1 basis, this device after war shrinks currency in circulation, as many with large holdings choose to destroy them rather than risk interrogation on the source of large amounts turned in for conversion. There were 4½ billion livres in government debt and banknotes or shares of the Banque Royale. Only 2½ billion were turned in (Marion, 1926, p. 39). Visa II reduced this amount by 500 million in fines. The remaining state debt of 1.7 billion was forcibly converted into 31 million of perpetual *rentes* annually, plus 16 million of lifetime *rentes*, for a total debt service of 50 million annually with a present discounted value of 1 billion livres (Lüthy, 1959, pp. 414–22).

During the course of his financial manipulations, John Law took over the tobacco monopoly, the General Farm on indirect taxes and the rights to farm the mints, and, in January 1720, became Minister of Finance. His interest in banking and financial reform added up to a 'system'. Hamilton claims that Law's reform of French taxes was one of his most durable achievements (1968, p. 81). This is as forcefully denied by Lüthy (1959, p. 423) and by Levasseur (1854/1970, p. 185), who observe that the reforms went unfinished and that, after Law's collapse, royal finances returned to their inefficient and fraudulent ways. In either case, there was still room for attempted reforms later in the century by Turgot, Necker, and Calonne. The system of running national finances through private contractors working for profit was not overturned until 28 *financiers*, including Lavoisier, were guillotined in the Reign of Terror (Bosher, 1970).

The South Sea bubble does not exactly fit our category of the financial aftermath of war, but represented part of an extended effort to reduce the chaos of government debt to some kind of order after the Stop of the Exchequer by Charles II in January 1672 (which ruined a number of goldsmiths holding government obligations) and the Glorious Revolution of 1688. It also followed the Nine Years' War (1688–97; called on the Continent the War of the League of Augsburg), and the War of the Spanish Succession, 1701–13 (Queen Anne's War). The process of seeking to improve the financial position of government and the quality of the money supply was continuous in this period. An important feature was the establishment of the Bank of England in 1694 to fund £1.2 million of government stock in exchange for the right of note issue. A second was the recoinage of 1696 (Li, 1963). The total effort has been characterized by Dickson as a financial revolution (1967).

In the South Sea operation, holders of various forms of government annuities were persuaded to exchange them for stock in the South Sea Company, which was also available for cash subscription, with the Company intermediating (like the Bank of England) between the debt holder and the government (Carswell, 1960; Dickson, 1967, chs 5, 6).

There is no need to dwell on the explosive rise and collapse of the South Sea Company shares in the spring and summer of 1720, and the parallel Mississippi bubble in France, except to note that attempts at tidying up debt after a war, and to fund it through financial intermediaries, can get thoroughly out of hand. For those with an antiquarian interest, attention may be drawn to the Grand Parti, a major refunding of French royal debt during the six wars between France and Spain–Austria in the first half of the sixteenth century. This consolidated the floating debt issued by Francis I, and by his successor Henry, and sought an additional one-third in new money, providing compound interest on past defaulted borrowings and a sinking fund for the future. The design proved superior to the reality: three months after the Spanish king defaulted on his loans on the enemy side, Henry followed suit in November 1557, ceasing to pay either sinking fund or interest (Ehrenberg, 1896/1928, pp. 302–6).

In all this, we do not dwell on the thoroughly disreputable devices for handling debt after a war: repudiation, which brought down the Ricciardi in 1310, the Bardi and Peruzzi in 1348, the Fuggers in 1596, and many more; new forced loans; or the French monarchy's device of requiring holders of offices to buy them for a second or third time (Dent, 1973, p. 60).

One way to reduce the burden of debt contracted in wartime and to ease the redistribution of income from taxpayers to creditors is to convert bonds issued in wartime to a lower rate of interest afterwards. Like intemediation through specially created banks and companies, the technique occasionally had unexpected side-effects. There were two debt conversions in Britain in the eighteenth century, one incomplete in 1717 after the War of the Spanish Succession, which may have helped stimulate the speculation that led to the South Sea bubble, and one under Henry Pelham, from 4 to 3½ percent in 1749–50, after the War of the Austrian Succession. The Dutch, who held one-third of British government stock, objected to the second (Dickson, 1967, pp. 31, 83–5).

McCulloch's first economic article, written shortly after the end of the Napoleonic War, recommended that interest on the British national debt be reduced on the ground that the creditors had loaned the government depreciated money (Smart, 1911/1964, I, p. 510). The point finds echo in one of Keynes' arguments against revaluation of sterling after World War I – that most of Britain's debt had been contracted after the pound had been depreciated so that to restore the pound to par would be to pay the owners of the debt higher-valued money and would be unjust (1923/1932, pp. 192–3). If the real value of the capital sum were enhanced by revaluation, its present discounted value could be lowered by conversion to a reduced coupon rate.

In 1822 the British government converted £50 million of Navy 5 percents to 4 percent, and in 1824 £75 million of 4 percent stock to 3½ percent. While the bulk of the wartime debt at 3 percent was not converted (Acworth, 1925, p. 128), the conversion of the high-interest portion of it was sufficient to touch off a speculative flurry. Target investors with lowered income turned to more speculative and higher-return securities. The boom and crash of 1825 must be laid partly at the door of the liberation of Spanish colonies in America in 1822 and of the awakened interest in foreign lending following the success of the Baring loans to finance the French indemnity after 1817. Debt conversion shared responsibility.

Across the channel in France, there was little debt after the war because of Napoleon's strong aversion both to debt and to the issuance of banknotes: in 1816 there were only 63 million of *rentes* in France, all owned in Paris (Redlich, 1948, p. 141). Financing of the indemnity and postwar reconstruction requirements changed the position. The Baring loan tranches issued in Paris bore a 5 percent coupon and were originally issued at 55. When this had risen to 98, Jacques Laffitte urged a reduction of one percentage point in the interest paid on the debt of 2.8 billion francs. He wanted to use the saving of 28 million in interest to circulate money in the provinces through public works (such as canals), in Saint-Simonian fashion. The Paris establishment had rather in mind the use of the funds to indemnify emigrés. In the end, the conversion was carried through not by Laffitte but by the rival Rothschild syndicate of 120–150 banking houses, and, as in Britain, gave a stimulus to speculation, though in Paris building sites rather than in foreign bonds (Liesse, 1909, pp. 278–85).

There were many nineteenth-century debt conversions in peacetime in France and Britain that played a role in stimulating speculation but were unconnected with war. In France, there was the Bineau conversion of 1852 (Gille, 1967, II, p. 96), that of Fould in 1862 (Bigo, 1947, p. 112), and refunding of Paris mortgages of the Crédit Foncier in 1878 (Jousseau, 1884, pp. lxvi, lxxx). The large Gambetta conversion of 6 billion in 1882 was war-connected inasmuch as it dealt with the Thiers *rentes* issued to finance the indemnity paid to Prussia after the Franco-Prussian war, but it took place when the crash of the Union Générale was well advanced and had played no role in the earlier speculation (Bouvier, 1960, pp. 158–61). In Britain, the Goschen conversion of consols, begun in 1888 and 'one of the notable milestones in the history of the national debt' (Emden, 1938, p. 304), also gave rise to a stock-market boom that culminated in the Baring crisis. It does not easily fit our scheme.

Sinking funds have been mentioned twice – that of the Grand Parti of 1557 and the 1717 fund in Britain. Neither lasted any length of time. A further series of attempts was made before and after the Napoleonic wars, again with undistinguished results. Distressed by the size of the debt at the conclusion of the American War of Independence, Pitt considered (1) repudiation (and rejected it); (2) a capital levy; (3) reducing the debt burden through conversion, as already described; and (4) gradual reduction through taxation and sinking-fund purchases. The sinking fund was introduced in 1786 and originally consisted of £1 million a year – compared with a national debt of almost £250 million – bought in four equal installments. The stock bought was not cancelled, earned interest in the fund, and was available for re-issue (Binney, 1958, p. 114). On occasion, the government would borrow from the Bank of England to make good its commitment to the sinking fund, thereby in effect monetizing the debt. Funded debt declined, but the unfunded debt often rose in its place. In due course the system was attacked as illogical and pernicious; it was finally abandoned in 1828 (Acworth, 1925, ch. 4).

Another sinking fund was instituted in Great Britain after World War I. Keynes commented that the return to gold increased the real burden of the national debt by £750 million, 'thus wiping out the benefit of all the laborious contributions to the sinking fund since the war' (1923/1932, p. 250). At the end of July 1931, when the pound was under pressure, the sinking fund became a political issue. The May report on financial management insisted that the British budget be balanced, and not only current expenditure against current receipts, but sinking-fund commitments as well, even if it meant cutting the dole for the unemployed. On post-Keynesian notions, such a balance would be regarded as a surplus, and insistence on it in 1931 seems, with hindsight, absurd.

Somewhat related to the sinking-fund idea was the German World War I theory of finance: debt service, including interest and amortization, was carried in the ordinary budget, to be balanced by taxation, whereas all direct war expenditure, amounting to 80 percent of the entire budget, was placed in the category of extraordinary expenditure, and treated as a capital asset. The concept was an old one. In 1778, at the height of the American War of Independence, which proved ruinous for French finances, Necker insisted that he had a balanced budget when taxes and expenditure reductions covered civil expenditure and interest on (perpetual) borrowing to finance the war. The most recent biography of Necker attempts to justify this belief (Harris, 1979, pp. 124,207).

In World War I, Helfferich's first ordinary budget included 69 million marks for amortization of debt as he 'avoided the slippery slope of borrowing to pay interest on the debt' (Williamson, 1971, p. 124). The theory also postulated that the war would be brief and victorious, and that the defeated enemy would be required to pay down its cost again, as in 1871–2. However, the French were operating on the same theory, and the fallacy of composition prevented both governments from being right. The intellectually arrogant Karl Helfferich, a monetary and banking expert, was properly called a financial Ludendorff by Matthias Erzberger (*ibid.*, p. 123).

Some part of the difficulty rested in the structure of German financial powers. As in Canada today, major financial power resided in the states, whether under the Zollverein, the North German Federation or the Reich. The Reich central authority had customs duties, some excise taxes and matricular contributions from the states; after 1880, the central government had given the states a share in certain excise taxes that practically cancelled the matricular contributions. New sources of income were the net profit from Post, Telephone and Telegraph, and, after 1871, the income from the Alsace-Lorraine railroad. In 1906 the Reich received a share in inheritance taxes, and in 1913 and 1914 a small capital levy – the *Wehrbeitrag* (defense contribution) – was added, but amounted to only 1 billion marks a year.

The issue is whether institutions adapt to necessity or shape outcomes. For institutions to adapt to necessity, it is perhaps critical to have strong, dedicated leadership. Helfferich was strong, but not sufficiently dedicated to financial conservatism in war to reorganize the tax structure, or to overcome his ideological opposition to the Socialist's persistent call for taxes on the wartime profits that industry had reaped in abundance.

Inflation is one usual outcome of war or postwar financial difficulties. In the usual view it leaves to market chance the assignment of burdens of wartime expenditure, as contrasted with judicial processes, taxation for sinking funds, interest-rate conversion, and capital levies. Perhaps the outstanding example is that of World War I.

It is hardly necessary to summarize the events of the inflations from 1914 to 1925. The literature is enormous, and is being added to at a rapid rate. In particular, the monetarist school is reinterpreting especially the German and French inflations as a means of testing its theories, finding them – not unnaturally – confirmed (Cagan, 1956; Frenkel, 1977). In addition, there is a school of revisionist historians that has undertaken to re-examine the social consequences of World

War I inflations, and finds them less traumatic than had previously been held (Maier, 1975; Feldman, 1977).

Earlier mention was made of the scholarly dispute between the monetarist and the balance-of-payments schools of thought in the German inflation. However, there is no necessity to choose one over the other as universally superior. One can be true at one time, the other equally so at a different time under different circumstances. Ragnar Nurkse's (1945) insight into the Continental inflations after World War I, recently confirmed for Germany by Holtfrerich (1980) is that in the early stages of the inflation, say in Germany, the monetarist school was right, and the balance-of-payments school wrong; the internal rate of inflation led the external. In fact, bull speculation in the mark, as foreigners clung to expectations that the depreciation of the currency would be overcome in due course and the mark rise in value, meant that the exchange rate was overvalued, the balance of payments on current account showed an import surplus, and foreign factors dampened rather than exacerbated the inflationary pressure. Holtfrerich has shown that in this early stage after World War I Germany received as much real capital from abroad as it did after World War II under the Marshall plan (1980, p. 293). After speculators' expectations had been falsified by continuing inflation, and following a series of events that shattered their hopes – the announcement in May 1921 that the final reparation bill would be 132 billion marks, the failure of the Cannes and Genoa conferences, the report of the committee of international bankers under the chairmanship of J. P. Morgan in June 1922 that long-term loans to Germany could not be recommended under the existing reparation schedule, especially the assassination of Walther Rathenau on 24 June 1922, and the occupation of the Ruhr by France and Belgium in January 1923 – speculators reversed directions. Instead of buying marks, they sold existing holdings of currency, deposits and securities. The forward market shifted from a premium on the mark to a sharp discount, enabling arbitrageurs to buy dollars spot and sell them forward against marks. Depreciation in the exchange market galloped faster than internal price rises, and the balance of payments, instead of dampening internal inflation, accelerated it. At this stage, the monetarists were wrong – relatively at least, if not absolutely – and the balance-of-payments school correct. The money supply in fact shrank in real terms as printing presses failed to keep pace with the rise of prices. Many price quotations were derived directly from the exchange rate, and some exporters of capital short-cut the foreign-exchange market by buying goods in Germany, shipping them abroad for sale, and retaining the foreign exchange.

There had been Socialist proposals in 1922 for forced loans, for a mortgage on all real property, for shares in major firms being turned over to the state, for selling the railroads back to the public in exchange for Reich debt (Williamson, 1971, pp. 300, 356, 360). Bourgeois parties in the Reichstag and industrial interest groups opposed them all, although there were differences in nuance, between heavy industry, which preferred inflation, and the chemical–electrical complex, which looked favorably on paying reparations as a means of flooding Europe with cheap goods and driving the competition out of business (Rupieper, 1979, pp. 32, 359). Among the clashing groups, the weak Socialist government of the Weimar regime and even the compromise businessman with Anglo-British connections, Wilhelm Cuno, could do nothing. Suggestions for recycling German reparations to France through an American loan to Germany were abundant from the French side, not altogether absent in Germany, and finally realized in a modest, pump-priming way with the Dawes loan of 1924, after the explosion of hyper-inflation. The early idea of recycling the total reparations bill – such as had occurred in the Baring indemnity loans of 1817–19 and the Thiers *rentes* of 1871–2 – appealed little to the Germans and not at all to the American bankers who would have been called upon for the money.

The contrast, of course, is with German monetary reform in 1948. The Colm–Dodge–Goldsmith report of 1946 was based on a study of some thirty or so German proposals (Wandel, 1979, p. 324). Its essence lay in two measures, one a conversion of all debt in Reichsmarks into a new currency at a rate (above certain minima) of 1 unit of the new for 10 of the old. Debt included not only banknotes and Reichs obligations, but all deposits, bank loans, mortgages, insurance policies, promissory notes, etc. The second element was a *Lastenausgleich* (equalization of burdens) or capital levy in the form of a mortgage on all real property (and equity ownership) of 50 percent. This was more heroic than the normal postwar capital levies of, say, Belgian monetary reform after World War II at 5 percent (Dupriez, 1947, p. 36), which was regarded merely as a tax on current income. The shortfall between 50 percent on real assets and 90 percent on debt is explicable in terms of the uncertainty of capital valuations and the possibility that a much higher rate might have left some real assets with negative value. The mortgage was granted to a Fund for the Equalization of War Losses, which disbursed the proceeds of its receipts for interest and amortization to those who had suffered during the war in an order based on priority of need – with widows, wounded, displaced persons and the like coming ahead of those with property losses.

Some explanation of why Germany was able to undertake a capital levy to pay for war in 1948 but not in 1922 is offered later. Here I note that the American Secretary of War, Kenneth Royall, opposed the capital levy and refused to allow it to be imposed by the occupation forces, although the Currency Reform Law of 21 June 1948 designated it as an urgent task of the new German government to take office, to be completed within a year. This veto rested on an ideological view held personally and did not represent governmental positions as Maier hints (1981, pp. 343 n. 39; 364). Capital levies have been proposed to reduce government debt (though not to correct inequities between creditors and owners of real assets) as early as 1714, after the Peace of Utrecht, and by many important figures, including David Ricardo in 1815 (Acworth, 1925, ch. 5). For the most part, the proposals dealt with measures at the 5–10 percent level, and until World War II were largely ignored.

Failure to take steps to reform the monetary position after war in, say,

France in the 1920s is ascribed as a rule to illusions: *Le Boche paiera* (the Germans will pay – through reparations). France had two separate budgets, the ordinary and the extraordinary, the latter with reconstruction expenditure 'balanced' by reparation receipts entered on the books though not yet received (Jeanneney, 1977, pp. 31, 61). In addition to illusion, however, there was a deep political rift between the Socialist and Radical center parties on the one hand (the Cartel des Gauches), which wanted a capital levy, progressive income taxes, and even forced conversion of the enormous floating debt in *rentes*, and the Right, which saw inflation in any breaching of the ceilings in Treasury borrowing from the Bank of France and the Bank of France's note circulation, and refused either to buy long-term bonds or to vote new taxes. Monetary reform was impossible after World War I and World War II largely for political as opposed to technical economic reasons. The most that was done was the sleight of hand of allowing depreciation to cumulate to 100 percent and then moving to a position of strength by substituting one 'new' strong franc for 100 old ones.

The inability of France to refund its floating debt and lock in its capitalists so that they could not quickly monetize their assets (and move the money abroad) when they did not like the government's policies is not a technical financial question but a socio-political one. Equally so was the confrontation of the United States Treasury and the Federal Reserve System that gave rise to the accord of 1951. At one level this was a bureaucratic struggle between the Treasury, which wanted to stabilize interest on its debt, and the Federal Reserve, which sought to hold down increases in the money supply that would arise from stabilizing the interest rate through an elastic demand for government bonds. At a more profound level, however, it was a political issue between interest groups over the return to capital on the one hand, and the rate of inflation on the other.

IV

Time and space permit only the most succinct treatment of inter-national issues. On reparations, it deserves mention that economists studying the transfer mechanism since the 1920s seem to have missed an essential point, left to be discovered after the Organization of Petroleum Exporting Countries (OPEC) price rise of 1973, that most successful reparation transfers – in 1817–19, 1871–2, and to a limited extent under the Dawes and Young loans of 1924 and 1930 – were effected in the first instance by recycling. The Baring loans of the post-Napoleonic period allowed the modest 700 million francs of reparations to be paid off in cash, with real payment taking place later when France paid back the loan. Foreign subscriptions to the Thiers *rentes* of 1871 and 1872 and domestic subscriptions for which the funds were provided by liquidating holdings of foreign securities enabled France to pay off the Franco-Prussian indemnity of 5 billion francs in two years. Real transfer occurred when the French reconstituted their portfolios of foreign bonds, and foreign subscribers to the *rentes* took their profits and returned to their normal financial 'habitats', as Angell (1926, Appendix B, pp. 520–1) and Machlup (1964, p. 381) recognized, though they did not call it recycling or regard the process as part of the usual mechanism. The Dawes and Young loans were intended not to recycle much reparation payment but to prime the pump. In this capacity the Dawes loan was a success, the Young loan not.

All three loans had the side-effect of unleashing a new wave of foreign investment: first to Europe and then to Latin America in Britain in the 1820s; somewhat belatedly principally to Russia from France in the 1880s – actually taking over German loans to Russia coming due, so that real capital was transferred from France to Germany; and from New York to German municipalities and states, as well as Latin America and the rest of the world after the Dawes loan. A sharp decline occurred in the quality of United States foreign loans after 1924, because success of the US tranche of the Dawes loan, oversubscribed eleven times, touched off a mania for foreign bonds.

A real, not a financial aftermath of World War II was the United States in effect paying German reparations to the Soviet Union, despite efforts to avoid that outcome based on recognition that German reparations to France had been paid by the United States bond market's purchases of German bonds. The Potsdam declaration of August 1945 laid down among other principles, and on United States insistence, that the four occupation zones of Germany would be treated as a single economic unit, and that a first charge on all exports of current production was to be the cost of imports into (any zone of) Germany. In the event, the Soviet Union, disappointed in the efficacy of a program of reparations based on removal of capital assets excess to a peacetime German economy, violated the agreement and turned to reparations out of current production from its eastern agricultural zone of occupation, at a time when Britain and the United States – and, after December 1947 and the adjustment in the bizonal agreement, mostly the United States – had to furnish food and raw materials to the western zones.

The financial shambles left by war debts, though familiar, has been re-emphasized by two new studies on French war debts to the United States (Artaud, 1978; Schrecker, 1978). Straightforward cancellation was recommended, of course, by the debtors, but also early and frequently by the eastern financial community in the United States, which, however, was unable to prevail over the rest of the country until the Hoover moratorium of 1931, when events had gone precipitously downhill.

In the Napoleonic wars, there was only one such episode of which I am aware – the Austrian imperial loans from Britain in 1795 and 1797, regarded as a subsidy by Austria and as a commercial loan by the British. These were ultimately settled after years of bickering for £2.5 million cash in 1823, covering an original principal of £6.2 billion and accumulated arrears of interest of almost £16.3 million.

Lend-lease would seem to have ended most discussion about whether advances took the form of loan or subsidy, and this was almost true.

Some residual differences of opinion exist, on national grounds, especially over the precipitous halt of Lend-lease to Britain in August 1945 and over the final settlement. To Gardner, an American, the generosity of the settlement 'surpassed expectation', although he recognized that the requirement of payment for surplus property and 'pipeline' goods was a violation of the principle that had been agreed as to the postwar transition (1980, p. 209). To Milward, a Britisher, on the other hand, 'the methods of Lend-lease accounting were not very convincing economically'. One could argue that American tanks could have hired British crews as readily as British crews hired American tanks (1977, p. 351). But the Lend-lease settlement was quickly followed by the Anglo-American Financial Agreement – a loan of $3.75 billion based on the key-currency view of J. H. Williams, in contrast with the Bretton Woods more general provisions for reconstruction, development, and balance-of-payments financing. All this left war debts some distance behind.

The Lend-lease agreements and settlements committed the participants to join in constructing an open world economy. While more successful, this too was not a new idea. After the Napoleonic wars, the British government sought to obtain assurances from Austria, Portugal, Prussia, Russia and Spain, which it subsidized, that they would lower their tariffs on British goods. In this it had no success, except for a limited number of concessions from Prussia, and a promise from Portugal to end the slave trade north of the equator in return for an additional gift of £300,000 and a promise to pay off £900,000 borrowed privately by Portugal in London (Sherwig, 1969, pp. 311, 330). After the war, Brougham asked in Parliament how it was that, after a war of unexampled suffering, the glorious peace it purchased came without restoring British foreign markets and France, Prussia and Russia continued to keep out British products (Acworth, 1925, p. 121).

With a new currency, such as the Reichsmark for the mark (ignoring the Rentenmark), the exchange rate and the price level adjust to each other simultaneously in a tatonnement process. Where the currency continues to exist and has been depreciated in wartime, or after wartime pegging is released, there is a policy decision to be made: whether to adjust the currency to the price level in the purchasing-power-parity mode, or the price level to the historic value of the currency.

> During the nineteenth century, ... inflation was exclusively a wartime and postwar phenomenon. Moreover responsible governments tried to offset wartime inflation with peacetime deflation, and eventually to restore gold convertibility of their currency at the prewar parity. (Bladen, 1980, p. 2)

The teachings of modern history were also in favor of the assumption that the war would not cause any fundamental change in financial policy. The Crimean War left the currencies of Britain and France unaffected. After the Franco-Prussian War, in spite of the complete defeat of France, the internal upheaval and the heavy reparation payment, the depreciation of the franc never exceeded $3\frac{1}{2}$ percent. The South African War left the pound unimpaired, and the currencies of the Balkan States were hardly affected by the War of 1912. It would appear reasonable to assume, therefore, that the World War would produce no abnormal effects upon the monetary situation. (Einzig, 1935, pp. 29–30)

The Einzig quotation ignores the size and duration of the war, matters that were not irrelevant to the issue, as comments of Henry Thornton and David Ricardo emphasize. In a speech on the Bullion Report on 7 May 1811, Thornton stated that, after a long depreciation, he would favor changing the standard rather than going back to the old one. Justice required it in such a circumstance. If depreciation lasted two or three years, it was one thing, but if it were to last 15 or 20 years, that would be something else (Thornton, 1811/1962, p. 345). Ricardo in 1809 thought devaluation a 'shocking injustice' and he probably contributed to the Bullion Committee's conclusion that devaluation would be 'a breach of public faith and dereliction of a primary duty of Government' (Bullion Report, quoted by Viner, 1937, p. 203). After resumption of specie payments at the old parity in 1819, he stated in speeches and letters that he had supported resumption at par because the agio on gold had fallen to a small amount (*ibid.*, pp. 204n. and 205n.). To Wheatley he said that he would never have advised a government to restore a currency to par that was depreciated 30 percent (Foxwell, 1909, p. xx), and in 1822 he stated that, if the currency had stood at 14s. in 1819, as in 1813, he would have thought upon a balance of all the advantages and disadvantages of the case that it would have been well to fix the currency at the then value, *'according to which most of the existing contracts had been made* (Viner, 1937, p. 205 n., Viner's italics).

These views ignore how the depreciation became so little – a discount called 'trifling' by Tooke and Newmarch (1838/1962, II, pp. 65, 76) and, referring to 1925, by Hawtrey (1927, p. 351). When resumption is forecast by the market, destabilizing speculation bids the rate up to a level within shooting distance of par. The exchange rate is then over-valued, as adjustment of the price level downward to the new rate remains to be achieved.

British resumption at par in 1925 is widely recognized to have been a mistake. The issue is not so clear about 1819. The Banking and Currency Schools agreed on little else, but both believed that resumption in 1819 was justified. Some agricultural and exporting interests – the latter centered particularly in Birmingham (Checkland, 1948) – took exception. Sidney Buxton called the first seven years of peace after 1815 the darkest in modern British history (quoted in Acworth, 1925, p. 115). Cobbett's prediction of a million people dying of hunger as a result of resumption was perhaps influenced by his £13,000 mortgage on a £30,000 farm bought in 1813 at the height of the wartime inflation (Smart, 1911, I, p. 739) and exaggerates out of all proportion (Doubleday, 1847, p. 249).

After the disasters of 1923–6 in France, with the defeat of the Cartel des Gauches by Poincaré and his Bloc National, French capital began to return to France. For a considerable time people like Poincaré and de Wendel, steel magnate and regent of the Bank of France, clung to the idea that a return to par was possible (Jeanneney, 1976, Pt 5, ch. 1). When the automobile interests and Leon Jouhaux of the Confédération Générale de Travail expressed concern about the fate of exports and the level of employment as the franc appreciated in 1926, par – more than a trifling distance away – was abandoned in favor of tangible interests.

V

Several conclusions emerge from this wide-ranging survey:

(1) War is an important test of financial strength and adaptability. It widens the returns to financial innovation, and produces a lot of it. It may not produce all that is necessary, however, despite the Coase theorem, because the supply of innovation may be inelastic. Society may be rigid and incapable of adapting, as in the case of France in the eighteenth century, which needed a bloody revolution to remove the *financiers'* opposition to change; or such an intelligent (if disagreeable) man as Helfferich may be too committed to narrow interests and ideology to work to overall national aims. To achieve adaptation, there must be a mobile society, highly effective leadership, or preferably both.

(2) Cleaning up the financial aftermath of war is less a matter of clean-cut technical solutions to problems of money, foreign exchange, banking, fiscal and capital market reform than of the social and political strength of group interests. Wilhelm Cuno may not have been a powerful political leader – Moritz Bonn thought him a charming man who would have made an excellent reception clerk in a luxury hotel (Rupieper, 1979, p. 18) – but he was supported by intelligent men such as Melchior and Rathenau. His failure was due less to his deficiencies than to the bourgeois parties in the Reichstag and the industrial interest groups (*ibid.*, p. 259).

Mancur Olson, Jr (1979) has suggested that the economic effectiveness of Germany and Japan after World War II was related to the destruction of powerful class and occupational interests. In my judgement, the differences between German monetary performances after World War I and World War II had their origin in the fact that powerful interests – the Junkers, iron and steel, and heavy industry generally – survived World War I more or less intact in political cohesion, whereas World War II discredited and dissolved all groups, permitting a technically effective solution that balanced major interests. It is true that there was a mass demonstration against the monetary reform of 1948, demanding retention of goods rationing and arguing that monetary reform favored the moneyed classes (Domes and Wolffsohn, 1979, p. 341).

It was on the whole *pro forma* and not deeply felt. The skill of the Allied and German officials that went into monetary reform should not be downplayed, but no amount of skill in presenting proposals would have succeeded in 1922–3.

(3)   A number of financial devices and events have unanticipated side-effects. Debt conversions and unexpected success in floating a recycling loan can lead in positive feedback fashion to dynamic outcomes impossible to predict.

(4)   As Thornton and Ricardo observed, monetary and fiscal policies are affected by the size of disturbances, their duration and the width of the gap between existing conditions and desired outcomes. The British were unlucky in 1925 at finding their currency so near to par – perhaps an ironic and perverse punishment for having financed the war in such exemplary fashion. In France, the notion of a return to par, nostalgically entertained, was seen by realists to be hopeless. Thornton and Ricardo may have been merely rationalizing their financial class interests in dismissing devaluation on the ground that depreciation had been limited in size and time. There is none the less something to their point.

(5)   History affects the future, but not always in ways that can be taken into account unambiguously. Einzig's rationalization of the return to par in 1925, on the ground that it was easily effected after Crimea, the Franco-Prussian war, Boer war and the war in the Balkans, failed to take into account the difficulties of 1819. Collective memory is an important force in shaping policy: witness both German fear of depreciation, which the country identified with inflation in 1931, and still does today, and continuous British preoccupation with unemployment originating in the 1920s. Collective memory works over 50 years, but not, on this showing, over a century. A handful of economists and financial journalists in 1925 were conscious of the 1819 parallel, but not always with the same conclusion. For Acworth, Gregory and Keynes, the analogy raised a question about the wisdom of the return to par (Acworth. 1925; Gregory, 1928; Keynes, 1925, quoted in Perrot, 1955, p. 35); for Hawtrey, the distance between the market and par was 'trifling' in the two cases (1927, p. 351). Perhaps it is just as well that most economic policy-makers are not at the same time economic historians. The contrast of Lend-lease of World War II with war debts after World War I is on the whole hopeful, but one must always bear in mind the Maginot Line.

References

Acworth, A. W. (1925), *Financial Reconstruction in England, 1815–1822* (London: P. S. King).

Angell, James W. (1926), *The Theory of International Prices: History, Criticism and Restatement* (Cambridge, Mass.: Harvard University Press).

Artaud, Denise (1978), *La Question des dettes interalliées et la reconstruction de l'Europe (1917–1929)* (Paris: Librairie Honoré Champion, 2 vols).

Bagehot, Walter (1856/1978), 'Money', *Saturday Review*; reprinted in *The Collected Works of Walter Bagehot*, edited by N. St John-Stevas (London: The Economist, 11 vols), vol. IX.

Bigo, Robert (1947), *Les Banques françaises au cours du XIXᵉ siècle* (Paris: Sirey).

Binney, J. E. D. (1958), *British Public Finance and Administration, 1774–92* (Oxford: Clarendon Press).

Bladen, Ashby (1980), 'How Life Insurance Companies Can Cope with the Developing Financial Crisis', address to the Society of Actuaries, 20 October 1980, Montreal, Canada, mimeo.

Bosher, J. F. (1970), *French Finances, 1770–1795: From Business to Bureaucracy* (Cambridge: Cambridge University Press).

Bouvier, Jean (1960), *Le Krach de l'Union Générale, 1878–1885* (Paris: Presses universitaires de France).

Brailsford, H. N. (1961), *The Levellers and the English Revolution*, edited and prepared for publication by Christopher Hill (Stanford, Calif.: Stanford University Press).

Cagan, Philip (1956), 'The Monetary Dynamics of Hyperinflation', in M. Friedman (ed.), *Studies in the Quantity Theory of Money* (Chicago, Ill.: University of Chicago Press), pp. 25–117.

Carswell, John (1960), *The South Sea Bubble* (London: Cresset Press).

Checkland, S. G. (1948), 'The Birmingham Economists, 1815–1850', *Economic History Review*, 2nd ser., vol. 1, no. 1, pp. 1–19.

Coase, Ronald H. (1937), 'The Nature of the Firm', *Economica*, new ser., vol. 4, pp. 386–405.

Coleman, D. C. (1963), *Sir John Banks, Baronet and Businessman, A Study of Business, Politics and Society in Later Stuart England* (Oxford: Clarendon Press).

Corti, Count Ego Caesar (1928), *The Rise of the House of Rothschild* (New York: Blue Ribbon Books).

Davis, Ralph (1973), *The Rise of the Atlantic Economies* (Ithaca, NY: Cornell University Press).

deJong-Keesing, Elizabeth E. (1939), *De economische Crisis van 1763 te Amsterdam* (Amsterdam: N.V. Intern).

Dent, Julian (1973), *Crisis in Finance: Crown, Financiers and Society in Seventeenth Century France* (New York: St Martin's Press).

Dickson, P. G. M. (1967), *The Financial Revolution in England: A Study in the Development of Public Credit, 1688–1756* (New York: St Martin's Press).

Domes, Jürgen and Wolffsohn, Michael (1979), 'Setting the Course for the Federal Republic of Germany: Major Policy Decisions in the Bizonal Economic Council and Party Images, 1947–49', *Zeitschrift für die gesamte Staatswissenschaft*, vol. 135, no. 3 (September), pp. 332–51.

Doubleday, Thomas (1847), *A Financial, Monetary and Statistical History of England from the Revolution of 1688 to the Present Time* (London: Effingham, Wilson).

Dupriez, Léon H. (1947), *Monetary Reconstruction in Belgium* (New York: King's Crown Press).

Ehrenberg, Richard (1896/1928), *Capital and Finance in the Age of the Renaissance, A Study of the Fuggers*, translated from the German by H. M. Lucas (New York: Harcourt Brace).

Einzig, Paul (1935), *World Finance, 1914–1935* (New York: Macmillan).

Emden, Paul H. (1938), *Money Powers of Europe in the Nineteenth and Twentieth Centuries* (New York: Appleton-Century).

Faure, Edgar (1977), *La Banqueroute de Law, 17 juillet 1720* (Paris: Gallimard).
Feldman, Gerald D. (1977), *Iron and Steel in the German Inflation, 1916–23* (Princeton, NJ: Princeton University Press).
Foxwell, H. S. (1909), Preface to A. Andréadès, *History of the Bank of England* (London: P. S. King, 2 vols in one).
Frenkel, J. A. (1977), 'The Forward Exchange Rate, Expectations and the Demand for Money: the German Hyperinflation', *American Economic Review*, vol. 67, no. 4, pp. 653–70.
Gardner, Richard N. (1980), *Sterling–Dollar Diplomacy in Current Perspective: the Origins and Prospects of our International Economic Order* (New York: Columbia University Press).
Gayer, Arthur D., Rostow, W. W. and Schwartz, Anna Jacobson (1953), *The Growth and Fluctuation of the British Economy, 1790–1850. An Historical, Statistical and Theoretical Study of Britain's Economic Development* (Oxford: Clarendon Press, 2 vols).
Gille, Bertrand (1965, 1967), *Histoire de la Maison Rothschild* (Geneva: Droz, 2 vols).
Goldsmith, Raymond W. (1969), *Financial Structure and Development* (New Haven, Conn.: Yale University Press).
Gregory, T. E. (1928), 'Introduction' to Thomas Tooke and William Newmarch, *A History of Prices and of the State of Circulation from 1792 to 1856*, reproduced from the original (New York: Adelphi, 6 vols; first 2 vols originally 1838).
Hamilton, Earl J. (1968), 'John Law', *International Encyclopedia of the Social Sciences* (Chicago, Ill.: Macmillan and Free Press), vol. IX, pp. 78–81.
Harris, Robert D. (1979), *Necker, Reform Statesman of the Ancien Régime* (Berkeley, Calif.: University of California Press).
Hawtrey, Ralph G. (1927), *Currency and Credit*, 3rd edn (London: Longmans, Green).
Helleiner, K. F. (1965), *The Imperial Loans: A Study in Financial and Diplomatic History* (Oxford: Clarendon Press).
Hobson, John A. (1938), *Imperialism: A Study*, 3rd edn (London: Oxford University Press).
Holtfrerich, Carl-Ludwig (1980), *Die deutsche Inflation, 1914–1923* (Berlin and New York: Walter de Gruyter).
Jeanneney, Jean-Noël (1976), *François de Wendel en république: l'argent et le pouvoir, 1914–1940* (Paris: Seuil).
Jeanneney, Jean-Noël (1977), *Leçon d'histoire pour une gauche au pouvoir: la faillite du Cartel (1924–26)* (Paris: Seuil).
Jousseau, J. B. (1884), *Traité du Crédit Foncier*, 3rd edn (Paris: Marchal, Billiard).
Kaufmann, Eugèn (1914), *La Banque en France*, translated from the German by A. S. Becker (Paris: Girard et Brière).
Keynes, John Maynard (1923/1932), 'Alternative Aims to Monetary Policy'; reprinted in *Essays in Persuasion* (New York: Harcourt Brace).
Keynes, John Maynard (1940), *How to Pay for the War: a Radical Plan for the Chancellor of the Exchequer* (New York: Harcourt Brace).
Levasseur, E. (1854/1970), *Recherches historiques sur le système de Law*, reprint edn (New York: Burt Franklin).
Li, Ming-Hsun (1963), *The Great Recoinage of 1696–1699* (London: Weidenfeld & Nicolson).
Liesse, André (1909), *Evolution of Credit and Banks in France* (Washington,

DC: US Government Printing Office, for the National Monetary Commission).

Lüthy, Herbert (1959), *La Banque protestante en France de la révocation de l'édit de Nantes à la révolution.* Vol. I: *Dispersion et regroupement (1685–1730)* (Paris: SEVPEN).

Machlup, Fritz (1964), *International Payments, Debts and Gold* (New York: Charles Scribners).

Maier, Charles S. (1975), *Recasting Bourgeois Europe: Stabilization in France, Germany and Italy in the Decade after World War I* (Princeton, NJ: Princeton University Press).

Maier, Charles S. (1981), 'The Two Postwar Eras and the Conditions for Stability in Twentieth-Century Western Europe', *American Historical Review*, vol. 86, no. 2 (April), pp. 327–52.

Marion, Marcel (1926), *Ce qu'il faut connaître des crises financières de notre histoire* (Paris: Boivin).

Milward, Alan S. (1977), *War, Economy and Society, 1935–1945* (Berkeley, Calif.: University of California Press).

Mintz, Ilse (1951), *Deterioration in the Quality of Foreign Bonds Issued in the United States, 1920–1930* (New York: National Bureau of Economic Research).

North, Douglass C. and Thomas, Robert Paul (1973), *The Rise of the Western World: A New Economic History* (Cambridge: Cambridge University Press).

Nurkse, R. (1946), *The Course and Control of Inflation: A Review of Monetary Experience in Europe after World War I* (Princeton, NJ: League of Nations).

Olson, Mancur, Jr (1979), 'The Political Economy of Comparative Growth Rates', in James Gapinski and Charles Rockwood (eds), *Essays in Post-Keynesian Inflation* (Cambridge, Mass.: Harvard University Press), pp. 137–59.

Perrot, Marguerite (1955), *La Monnaie et l'opinion publique en France et en Angleterre, 1924–36* (Paris: Colin).

Redlich, Fritz (1948), 'Jacques Laffitte and the Beginnings of Investment Banking in France', *Bulletin of the Business Historical Society*, vol. 22 (December), pp. 137–60.

Rostow, W. W. (1978), *The World Economy: History and Prospect* (Austin, Tex.: University of Texas Press).

Rupieper, Hermann J. (1979), *The Cuno Government and Reparations, 1922–23. Politics and Economics* (The Hague: Martinus Nijhoff).

Schrecker, Ellen (1978), *The Hired Money: The French Debt to the United States* (New York: Arno Press).

Schuker, Stephen A. (1976), *The End of French Predominance in Europe, The Financial Crisis of 1924 and the Adoption of the Dawes Plan* (Chapel Hill, NC: University of North Carolina Press).

Sherwig, John M. (1969), *Guineas and Gunpowder, British Foreign Aid in the Wars with France, 1793–1815* Cambridge, Mass.: Harvard University Press).

Smart, William (1911/1964), *Economic Annals of the Nineteenth Century*, reprint edn (New York: Kelley, 2 vols).

Smith, Adam (1776/1937), *An Inquiry into the Nature and Causes of the Wealth of Nations*, Cannan edn (New York: Modern Library).

Stern, Fritz (1977), *Gold and Iron: Bismarck, Bleichröder and the Building of the German Empire* (London: Allen & Unwin).

Thiers, Louis Adolphe (1894), *History of the Consulate and the Empire in France under Napoleon* (Philadelphia, Pa.: J. B. Lippencott, 12 vols).

Thornton, Henry (1802/1962), *An Enquiry into the Nature and the Effect of the Paper Credit of Great Britain, together with the Evidence*, edited with an introduction by F. A. Hayek (London: Frank Cass; reprint of 1939 edn, London: Allen & Unwin); includes 1811 speech.

Tooke, Thomas and Newmarch, William (1838/1928), *A History of Prices and of the State of Circulation from 1792 to 1856*, reproduced from the original with an introduction by T. E. Gregory (New York: Adelphi, n.d.; introduction dated 1928; 6 vols, first 2 vols originally 1838).

Viner, Jacob (1937), *Studies in the Theory of International Trade* (New York: Harper).

Wandel, Eckhard (1979), 'Historical Developments prior to the German Currency Reform of 1948', *Zeitschrift für die gesamte Staatswissenschaft*, vol. 135, no. 3, pp. 320–31.

Williamson, John (1971), *Karl Helfferich, 1872–1924, Economist, Financier, Politician* (Princeton, NJ: Princeton University Press).

12

Historical Perspective on Today's Third-World Debt Problem

Extensive international capital flows from leading financial centers to less developed areas, leading first to boom and then, in frequent cases, to financial crisis have occurred in economic history with remarkable frequency and regularity. The morphology of these episodes, moreover, bears a strong family resemblance – up to a point at least – to the problem that seems to be posed today by syndicated bank loans to Third World countries. The historical numbers are of course smaller, the institutions different, the objects of investment or speculation on the whole otherwise in the past than those today. There is none the less something to be learned for today from a study of yesterday, at least as far back as a century and a half.

In *Manias, Panics and Crashes: A History of Financial Crises* (1978), I produced a model of the phases of expansion and crisis, and a stylized outline of national and international financial crises from 1720 to 1975. In addition, the study contains some discussion of policies to contend with financial crises, as investors seek to get out of feared assets into limited cash, especially the function of a lender of last resort in calming panic by making the sought-for liquidity available. The model involves phases of a 'displacement' or autonomous shock that alters profitability in various lines of investment; speculation leading to euphoria or what Adam Smith called 'overtrading'; 'distress', a period in which the exuberant optimism of the euphoric period gradually or quickly erodes and is threatened with excessive pessimism in which investors strive to get liquid; and sometimes a panic or crash. Whether or not the panic is alleviated by a lender of last resort that furnishes or promises to furnish the system with adequate liquidity is an open question. If a panic does occur and is alleviated, it often happens that the crisis passes, liquidation is forgotten, postponed or undertaken in leisurely fashion. For the last year and a half, I have been asserting that the world's financial system is in distress, largely but not wholly as a consequence of Third-World debt, having lost the buoyant expectations and verve that led to the rapid build-up of syndicated bank loans, without, as yet, succumbing to the despair that would lead to panic.

To throw historical light on the processes involved, let me discuss the

Paper written for the World Bank (November 1983).

stages of displacement, speculation, distress and panic as they occurred between major lending centers and the Third World in the 1820s, 1830s, 1850s, 1860s, 1870s, 1885–90, 1907, 1920–1 and 1929–33. The discussion will be analytical rather than chronological, calling attention in each stage to features that may shed light on the present position.

Displacement

The autonomous shock to the system that may give rise to speculative investment that goes to excess can be of almost any kind: political, economic and financial. Within the political have been the outbreak of war, the ending of war, internal revolution, revolt of colonies against a mother country. A major factor giving rise to the surge in British lending to Latin American governments and investment in mining in the area in 1823–5 was the series of wars of liberation of colonies from Spain and Portugal that took place in 1820 and 1821 (Smart, 1911/1964, ch. 18, pp. 187–8, ch. 26). Greece's contemporaneous struggle to free itself from the bonds of the Ottoman empire produced a wave of British investment in the obligations of the rebelling government (Wynne, 1951/1983; Jenks, 1938, pp. 50–1). In the 1850s, there had been first the Continental revolutions of 1848 that caused British investors to turn away especially from French railroads, after one or two British workmen engaged on them had been killed in rioting, followed by the Crimean war (Jenks, 1938, pp. 153–7). The cotton famine produced by the American Civil War and the Northern blockade of Southern ports led to high hopes for economic expansion in Sicily, Egypt and India growing cotton, only to be frustrated by the end of the war, which let loose a flood of Southern cotton on Europe and drove down prices (Landes, 1958; Marlowe, 1974). The boom of 1872–3 was fed by Prussia's victory over France in 1871 and the formation of the German Reich. The end of World War I in 1918 held out the prospect for Britain of taking over German markets in coal, shipping and cotton textiles (Youngson, 1960, ch. 2, esp. pp. 35–46).

Economic displacements have tended to take the form of discoveries, innovations, the diffusion of innovations from one country to another, a sudden rise in price, owing to an abrupt change in supply or demand. The discoveries included diamonds and gold in South Africa in 1881 and 1886, respectively (Frankel, 1938/1969, pp. 53–75), the new silver-lead mine at Broken Hill in Australia in 1883 (Boehm, 1971, p. 242), oil finds in Canada and Mexico in the 1970s. Among booms brought on by innovations, the best known perhaps are the canal mania in 1791–3 (Bagwell, 1974, pp. 17–18), and the railway mania in 1846–8 (Evans, 1849/1969; Lewis, 1968), both in Britain and both shocks leading to domestic rather than international booms. The extension of the railroad to the United States in the 1860s and 1870s, and to Argentina, Brazil and Australia in the late 1880s, all coupled with international migration and inflows of capital, produced an international boom ending first in the United States in 1873 and then in the Regions of Recent Settlement named in 1890–3 (see Chapter 14 below). Price changes leading to boom and bust include those in cotton in the 1830s, responding to the expansion of textile manufacturing in Britain and leading to a movement of the center of cotton cultivation from the sea islands off Georgia and South Carolina to the Mississippi delta, with speculation in bonds of Southern states and public lands (Lévy-Leboyer, 1982; Jenks, 1938, ch. 3). This occurred close to one end of our period; at the other end were the sharp increases in the price of petroleum engineered by the Organization of Petroleum Exporting Countries (OPEC) in 1973 and 1979. The OPEC actions had two effects: one on oil producers like the United States, Canada, Mexico, Nigeria, etc., which overexpanded production; the other on oil-importing countries, which were drained of exchange reserves and forced to resort to major borrowing to sustain consumption and existing investment projects.

Financial shocks, operating mainly on the side of push, rather than pull, take a number of forms: the unexpected success of a financial operation that leads to a wave of imitations and in some cases to overshooting. Particularly striking examples are three operations designed to recycle indemnities levied on the loser of war in the subsequent peace treaty: the Baring loan of 1817 to finance the French indemnity of 700 million francs due to the Allies under the 1815 Treaty of Vienna (Jenks, 1938, pp. 31–44); the Thiers *rentes* of 1871 and 1872, which recycled the Franco-Prussian indemnity of 5 billion marks as French investors sold off foreign securities to buy the French bonds, and investors in Germany, Austria, Sweden and throughout Europe bought francs to acquire *rentes*, especially the second, after the first, issued at 84.50, had gone to par in a few months (Kindleberger, 1984, ch. 13); and the Dawes loan of 1924 in the amount of $200 millions, of which $111 millions consisting of the New York tranche was oversubscribed 11 times and led to a rush of New York financial houses to underwrite new issues of bonds for foreign borrowers (Kindleberger, 1973, pp. 37–9; Mintz, 1951/1978). An orderly conversion of maturing or callable debt with a high coupon rate may have the unexpected side-effect of inducing investors faced with a reduction in income to cast about for higher-yield, higher-risk outlets for the funds repaid them or their new savings. This effect contributed to the wave of foreign lending in 1824–5 when the British Treasury undertook in 1822 to lower the coupon rate on the war debts piled up during the struggle against Napoleon (Smart, 1911/1964, pp. 66, 82–3). In similar fashion, the Goschen conversion of British 3 percent debt to first $2\frac{3}{4}$ percent and then $2\frac{1}{2}$ (thought about by Gladstone as early as the 1850s, undertaken abortively in 1884, and finally successful in 1888) helped propel the wave of foreign lending that culminated in the Baring crisis of 1890 (Spinner, 1973, pp. 140 ff). The effect is based on something akin to a backward-bending supply curve for capital, as investors seek to maintain a target level of living. A familiar remark in the nineteenth century in Britain, repeated three times by Walter Bagehot in his *Collected Works* is that 'John Bull can stand many things, but he can't stand 2 percent' (1978, pp. 118, 273, 300).

Further displacements from the field of finance are mistakes in

monetary policy that produce unexpected effects in one direction or
another. In 1765 Prussia undertook to recoin its silver after debasement
in a war, but borrowed in Amsterdam to acquire the metal, taking it off
the market well in advance of issuing new coins (Wirth 1890/1968,
p. 92). This produced sharp deflation and a panic. A century later, the
newly unified German Empire established the Reichsbank and went
over to the gold standard, new gold coins (from metal obtained in the
French indemnity) being issued before the old silver coins were retired,
setting off an expansionary shock wave (*ibid.*, p. 458). The relevance of
the latter episode for today is strong. Expansion of syndicated bank
loans to the Third World antedates by almost two years the OPEC price
rise of 1973, and rests, in my judgement, on a mistake in monetary
policy made jointly by the United States and Germany in 1970 and
1971. The United States political administration was anxious to have a
full-bodied expansion under way at the time of the 1972 presidential
elections. To this end, the Federal Reserve Board, under the leadership
of Arthur F. Burns, undertook a policy of cheap money at the end of
1970 and early in 1971, at a time when the Federal Republic of
Germany, in the institution of the Bundesbank, was engaged on a policy
of dear money to help curb inflation. The result was a massive outflow of
funds from the United States to the Euro-currency market, and
extensive refinancing – first by multinational corporations in Germany,
later by German corporations – in the Euro-currency market. Euro-
dollars borrowed by German firms to refund their D-mark debts were
sold to the Bundesbank, which deposited them in the Euro-currency
market. The deficit in the balance of payments of the United States on
the (unsatisfactory) liquidity definition rose from roughly $4 billion in
1970 to $20 billion in 1971 and $30 billion in 1972. Euro-currency
banks, flooded with dollars, looked about for opportunities to relend the
monies. Before long, bankers were camping on doorsteps of Latin
American finance ministers as they had done in the 1820s, the 1850s,
from 1885 to 1889, and from 1925 to 1928.

Speculation

In the *a priori* world of rational expectations, an autonomous shock to
an economic equilibrium gives rise to a smooth transition to another
stable equilibrium that reflects all old and new information in its array
of output, goods prices, factor prices, incomes, asset prices and wealth.
Economic and financial history, however, reveals that the process is not
so direct or simple. Just as there may be cobwebs in commodity prices,
and overshooting in exchange-rate fluctuations, so commodity and asset
prices may rise (or fall) beyond the levels implicit in a new and stable
equilibrium. Bubbles may occur, with rising prices inducing
speculation, which gives rise to still further price increases.
    A bubble following an autonomous shock to the system may subside
in due course without having any effect on the economy as a whole: a
cogent example is furnished by the Florida land boom in 1925, and by

the more recent successive waves of excited investment in supertankers, 747 aircraft and Real Estate Investment Trusts (REITS), all in the United States. Bubbles in single commodities that collapsed and might have spread had their effects not been mitigated are the highly similar corner in copper by Denfert-Rochereau in Paris in 1888 (Wirth, 1893, p. 222), and that in silver in 1980 by Bunker Hunt (Fay, 1982). When speculation in several commodities or assets in more than one country has expanded through the spread of speculative excitement, the micro-economic aberration may lead to macro-economic disturbance.

The mechanism is the feeding of speculation by the rapid expansion of credit in any one of a number of forms. Adam Smith described the eighteenth-century practice of chains of accommodation bills of exchange, in which A drew on B and B on A, both discounting the bills simultaneously, or B or C, C on D and so on, piling a mountain of debt on a small capital base (1776/1937, pp. 294–7). The technique was widely practised in Holland (Bloom, 1937, p. 193) and in Germany (Wirth, 1890/1968, p. 94). Or in the nineteenth century new securities were issued for a small down-payment of 5 or 10 percent, with the rest subject to future calls; many buyers lacked the capital for full payment of the total price but counted on selling out at a profit after one or two payments. Speculation, as well as hedging, could take place in futures contracts – in commodities, foreign exchange, and, in more modern times, all sorts of financial assets. The practice goes back to Holland in the seventeenth century and was called *windhandel* or trade in wind (Barbour, 1950/1966, ch. 4). In the Third World today, borrowers with long-term investment projects have borrowed at relatively short term, counting on renewing the credit and borrowing the interest due as they wait for production to start up and product to be sold. In all these cases, credit expansion leads to further credit expansion.

Monetary economists tend on the whole to think that such credit expansion is readily contained or prevented by holding the money supply either constant or growing at some suitable rate. This under-estimates the ingenuity of the market, which, when it has got the bit in its teeth, has usually been able to create new forms of money – banknotes to supplement coin, or bills of exchange, bank deposits, certificates of deposit, NOW accounts, credit cards, and most recently in 1982 in Kuwait the most easily produced money-substitute, post-dated checks. The point was recognized by Thornton in 1802:

> If bills and bank notes were both extinguished, other substitutes for gold would be found . . . Credit would still exist, credit in books, credit depending upon the testimony of witnesses, or on merely verbal promises.

In 1825 it was the English country banks that expanded rapidly from 1823 before collapsing in 1825 (Pressnell, 1956, p. 11; Smart, 1911/1964, pp. 298–9). In the 1860s, a series of English imitations of the French Crédit Mobilier went bankrupt along with Overend, Gurney & Co; all had been lending profligately. 1871 and 1872 saw the formation in Germany and Austria of *Baubanken* (construction banks) and *Maklerbanken* (brokers' banks) to finance the building boom (Wirth, 1890/1968, pp. 472–9), plus, in the United States, the expansion of Jay Cooke and company in railroading (McCartney, 1935, ch. 6). The most prominent failure a decade before the turn of the century was Baring Brothers of London (Ferns, 1960, ch. 14), but a long series of other banks expanded rapidly and in numerous cases failed in France, Italy, and in the Third World, Argentina, Brazil, Chile and Australia (see Chapter 14 below). The 1919–20 boom in Britain was financed by the banks, which underwrote loans in steel, shipbuilding and textiles that they had to carry through the decade (Youngson, 1960). The banks that got into trouble through overexpansion in the boom of the 1920s, as revealed by bankruptcies in the 1930s, were found especially in the United States, Italy, Germany and Austria (Kindleberger, 1973, ch. 7; Chapter 20 below). It is notable that, unlike the 1970s and 1980s, Latin American banks did not collapse in the 1930s. Many were state and provincial banks with governmental support. In Argentina, for example, the state bank had 30 percent of the system's loans and 40 percent of the deposits (see Chapter 18 below). The contrast is sharp with the 1890s when Latin American banks were loaded with mortgage loans (but not British banks in Latin America, which had confined their lending to commercial credits) (Joslin, 1963, chs 6, 7, esp. pp. 121–9; Jones, 1977, esp. pp. 27–41), as well as with the recent years when Argentine and Chilean banks failed in large numbers after expansions brought on by deregulation based on the theories about financial deepening and financial repression of Edward Shaw (1973) and Roland McKinnon (1973).[1]

The propagation of boom (and collapse) lies through prices of real and financial assets on the one hand, and through capital movements on the other. The real assets have been largely commodities, land and buildings; the financial assets primarily stocks and bonds, plus, in present circumstances, syndicated bank loans. The assets transmit boom through being joined by the law of one price in international markets. Even where commodities are not traded internationally, or securities not quoted in more than one market, there may be strong psychological connections. The French attempt to corner the world copper market in 1887 was said to have been influenced by the example of the diamond syndicate formed by Cecil Rhodes after the shakeout of diamond companies in 1882 (Wirth, 1893, p.222). An Australian boom in urban land was inspired to a considerable extent by the Argentine boom in grazing land after the Indians had been cleared from Patagonia, as well as the fact that both countries were expanding railroad networks and were financed through the London capital market (Hobson, 1914, p. 148).

Foreign and domestic security issues in major financial centers are sometimes positively, sometimes negatively, correlated. The outcome in a particular instance depends partly on the length of time a country may have been lending, partly on the strengths of business expansion and contraction at home and abroad (see Chapter 9 above). On the whole, British investors in the period 1850–1914 switched the flow of savings from domestic to foreign outlets, and back again, as home and foreign relative demands dictated. There were, however, periods when domestic and foreign investment went up and down together, as in 1885–96; and an enormous upsurge in foreign lending in 1910–13 was accompanied by rising domestic investment. The boom in foreign investment in 1913 when half of British savings were invested abroad (Cairncross, 1953, pp. 3–4) might well have ended in bust had not the surge been throttled by the outbreak of war.

There is a certain 'madness of crowds' in these waves of investment excitement and pessimism when they get beyond a certain size. Nothing seems so to upset investor judgement as to see someone nearby suddenly and unexpectedly become rich. One investor follows another: regional investors, stock exchanges and banks follow their metropolitan leaders. There is often the equivalent to a chain letter, with each investor rationally judging that it will get into the market, make a profit, and get out again before others realize that prices have overshot. Few actually succeed in so doing, and of course it is impossible for all to do so. It is remarkable in the annals of foreign investment that German investors sold off their Argentine securities in advance of the Baring collapse of November 1890, whether because of worry over the depreciating Argentine peso (Morgenstern, 1959, p. 523), because of a general disinterest in foreign securities (Ferns, 1960, p. 433), or because of the pull of the domestic boom that diverted attention from foreign bonds (Lauck, 1907, p. 60). If the last explanation is the valid one, it is one of the few times that a country with so little experience in foreign lending has adopted the model of lending at home and abroad on a counterpoised basis.

In its psychological aspects, foreign lending is a lot like migration. Both flow in channels. Information is scarce and costly, and no investor or potential migrant scans the entire world for opportunities for placing capital or moving bodily. Some displacement, perhaps a random event, produces a change in the horizon of opportunities scanned, and some early investors and/or migrants take advantage of the new opportunities thereby created. Success of the first investors or migrants leads others to follow in their footsteps. The channels become more deeply dug, and the flow of men or people builds up in a positive feedback process until something occurs, or some obstacle is encountered that serves to break it.

Brinley Thomas's model (1954) of transatlantic migration, moreover, emphasizes that capital and migrants, at least part of the time, head for the same receiving areas, if not always from the same sending ones. The decline in the worldwide price of wheat in the early 1880s dislodged a significant number of southern Italians, who migrated to the United States and to Argentina, to be followed by British and Continental capital. A wave of German emigration in the 1840s, and another in the late 1870s, took place primarily to the United States and later to Brazil (Walker, 1964). Like the outflow of capital at the end of the 1880s from Germany, they were cut off by domestic expansion. British migrants were attracted during the nineteenth century to the United States and to the dominions, while British capital was invested in those places and in Latin America as well. It is noteworthy, however, that British capital and migrants did not favor New Zealand or Canada in the boom of 1885–90. New Zealand had already experienced an earlier wave of migration and capital inflow in the 1860s, and remained uninfected by the Australian excitement of the 1880s (Simkin, 1951, p. 104). Why Canada did not participate in the boom of the late 1880s, waiting instead for 1904–13 (Viner, 1924), is not altogether apparent. One explanation is that prior to the building of the railroads, Canadian expansion was handicapped by the fact that the St Lawrence was blocked by ice for half the year (Hall, 1963, p. 162).

Distress

Financial distress is difficult to define precisely. The term has been borrowed from corporate finance, where a corporation is said to be in distress, as it surveys the probable course of future cash flows, in and out, when it can see a possibility that it may not be able to meet the demands on it for liquid payment (Gordon, 1971). Distress by no means implies the certainty of financial crisis, or, in the case of a corporation, bankruptcy. The cash flows involved have probability distributions that tend to be relatively flat, so that the actual outcome can vary within a wide range. Unlike chess, where in a game between strong players when one gets significantly ahead the other resigns because the outcome is foreordained, financial distress of a general sort may or may not lead to crisis. It is often described in meteorological terms as 'tension', a 'thundery' or 'oppressive' atmosphere, 'ominous conditions' and the like (see Kindleberger, 1978, pp. 100–1). Whether the storm breaks or not, however, tends to be highly uncertain.

The essence of distress is that the expectations that led to the euphoric expectations and overtrading have begun to erode. The realization may occur to different people at different times and with different force. If all participants in a financial market abandon their old expectations at the same time, and possibly reverse them, financial crisis occurs immediately without much in the way of preliminary distress, as in the sharp declines in the New York and London stock markets in 1921, 1929 and, for New York, September 1937. Rational expectations tends to regard markets as unanimous in formulating anticipated outcomes, rather like the thought processes of a single individual. In the historical world, periods of distress have been stretched out for years. In 1845, two years before the financial crisis of 1847, Lord Overstone wrote in a letter 'We have no crash at present but only a slight premonitory movement under our feet' (O'Brien, 1971, I, p. 368). The banking crisis of April–May 1893 in Australia was said to have been long overdue: some observers thought it had been inevitable for ten years; others from 1889 when the troubles began in Argentina (see Boehm, 1971, pp. 255, 277; Baster, 1929, p. 148; Hall, 1963, p. 171; Butlin, 1961, p. 279).

Since distress has strong psychological components, its duration can be affected by irrational considerations. The boom in 1871 and 1872 in Berlin that spread to Vienna was seen in the latter city as early as January 1873 to have been wildly overdone. Investors in Austria looked forward, however, to the Universal Exhibition, scheduled to open on 1 May 1873, and thought that somehow that event would affect the economic and financial outlook favorably. The stock market held up through the first four months of the year, but when the opening of the Exhibition was seen to have changed nothing it collapsed on 5 May (Wirth, 1890/1968, p. 508).

The point to underline is that the world today continues in financial distress as the bright expectations entertained by banks (as reflected in their syndicated loans to the Third World and the Socialist bloc) have proven to be overblown since well before the Mexican refinancing of August 1982. A series of mini-crises has been encountered and thus far successfully overcome. Whether the present distress subsides slowly and ultimately gives way to confident stability or ends in a more serious financial crisis, with or without significant economic effects on world stability, remains an open question.

Financial crisis

Financial crisis occurs when a sizeable body of investors tries, all at the same time, to get out of the objects of speculation or investment into more liquid assets. The initial precipitant can be almost anything from a bankruptcy, bank run, revelation of a swindle, sharp decline in commodity or financial-asset prices, halt or reversal in international capital flows, or any combination of the foregoing. Domestic crisis may also ensue when a highly leveraged investment stops rising in price and the investors, unwilling or unable to borrow further to make the necessary payments, start to liquidate the asset. This is akin to a multiplier-accelerator model in macro-economic analysis, in which a halt in the rise of investment spending culminates in its decline.

The spread of liquidation and crisis from one market to another within a country, and from one country to another, takes place in the same fashion as the spread of investment and speculation on the upswing. The connections can be through the prices of real or financial assets traded in more than one country, the halt or reversal of capital flows, or the psychological spread of pessimism. Commodity and stock-market prices fell drastically in all the major countries of the world from September to December 1929. The collapse of the stock market in the United States spread to commodities through its impact on interest rates and bank willingness to finance the purchase of commodities sent to New York for sale. Simultaneously, commodity prices fell worldwide through the law of one price (Schwartz, 1981, Table 5, p. 24; Kindleberger, 1973, Table 9, p. 143), whereas stock-market prices fell worldwide without much in the way of arbitrage among the major markets (Kindleberger, 1973, Fig. 6 and following table, pp. 121–3).

The diffusion of bankruptcies takes place through falling asset prices and strains on banks. The outcome of the process can be seen in a table showing numbers of bankruptcies by cities by months. (Unhappily, the data show bankruptcies only by number, not the amount of liabilities, and fail to distinguish between banks, with wider external effects, and non-banks.) Bankruptcies started in the crisis of 1847–8 in London in August, spread to Liverpool on a larger scale in October, to Italian cities in November, reached Calcutta in January 1848, Paris and Amsterdam in March, Marseilles, Belgium and Germany in April, New York and elsewhere in the United States in the last quarter of that year (Kindleberger, 1978, table p. 127). The 1848 revolution on the European continent is generally regarded as unconnected with the railway mania panic in London, although there is a roundabout connection with the sharp rise and fall in wheat prices arising from the potato famine and the short crop in wheat followed by the bumper harvest. The bubble and collapse in wheat prices in London exacerbated the boom and bust in railroad shares and the parallel movement on the Continent played a strong role in the revolutionary disturbances. Similar connections ran across the Atlantic and around Europe in 1836–9, 1857, 1866, 1873, 1890, 1907, 1920–1, and of course 1929–33. Such writers as Clapham maintain that the Overend, Gurney crisis of 1866 in London was a purely British affair (1945, II, p. 268), but the timing makes this conclusion most unlikely. The cotton famine produced by the American Civil War had led to sidespread speculation and extension of debt in Egypt, the Mediterranean generally and in shipping, in which Overend, Gurney participated. The changeover of the banking house from a partnership to a limited liability company following the laws favoring general incorporation in 1856 and 1862 had changed the character of the firm's personnel (King, 1936, pp. 246–55). A first European crisis occurred in Berlin on 1 May 1866 when the Prussian army mobilized against Austria. This led to a sudden tightness of money in Paris, and to a reversal of earlier capital movements to Italy. The Italian monetary authorities abandoned convertibility of the lira into silver on 2 May. Tight money through Europe precipitated the bankruptcy of the 'Corner House' (Overend, Gurney) on 11 May.

Among the more interesting financial crises for comparison with the present day is that of 1888–93. The boom, as mentioned earlier, had been based partly on psychological connections from South Africa to Latin America and Australia, and from Argentina to Australia, and on the flow of capital from London and other European financial centers to these areas and to the United States. The Goschen conversion had contributed to lower interest rates and the search for riskier securities to maintain investor income. In addition, a prospective change in the company law in Britain led to a wave of public flotations of private companies before the process became more difficult. The enormous success of an issue for the Guinness brewery set off a succession of similar issues for English, American, and even Canadian beers (Cottrell, 1980, pp. 169–71; Simon, 1978, p. 459; Lauck, 1907, p. 41). A parallel series of share issues for Chilean nitrate companies took place, and refunding and new bond issues for Brazilian account. New banks came into being in South Africa, Argentina, Brazil and Australia. British investors bought not only the securities of the governments of Argentina and the provinces, plus railroads, all denominated in sterling, but also peso *cedulas*, or land mortgage bonds issued by Argentine banks. Why the peso depreciated, whether because of the overissue of banknotes in Argentina, or because of the sudden halt in new foreign lending, is still debated in the literature (Williams, 1920, ch. 6, esp. 95–6). Similar questions arose in the case of Brazil.[2] The issue is a hardy perennial that has cropped up many times in economic history, perhaps most notably in Britain in the debate between the Currency and the Banking Schools over the depreciation of the pound, or the agio on gold, from 1797 to 1819 (Viner, 1937, ch. 5), and in that between the monetarists and the balance-of-payments school in Germany in the analysis of the inflation of 1919–23 (see, for example, Holtfrerich, 1980, esp. pp. 154–62). What was clear, however, was that, once Baring Brothers found itself unable to sell to the public more of the issue of a Buenos Aires Water Supply bond that it had underwritten in 1888, and found itself, even after selling off good American securities in New York, unable to make the third payment due to the borrower, lending slowed down drastically or stopped altogether for all overseas borrowers. New British foreign issues fell from £138.5 million in 1889 to £30 million in 1892 and £31.5 million in 1893 (Simon, 1968, p. 38).

The crisis was communicated in some small part to London by German selling of Argentine securities. London then dumped American securities on the markets of Paris and New York. Paris had its own problems with the collapse of the copper corner and the Panama scandal (Castronovo, 1969, Pt II, ch. 2, esp. pp. 121–9), but the sharp pullback of funds from Italy (also affected by the tariff war between France and Italy) led to bank failures in that country (see Chapter 14 below).

Financial crises in Britain, France, Italy, Argentina, Brazil, Australia, South Africa and the United States between 1888 and 1893 had a number of local contributing factors, but the dominating force was the sharp decline in new lending to the developing countries, and the reversal of capital flows to European financial centers through the dumping of existing securities. The contagion of crisis would have been mitigated if London, Paris, Berlin, etc., had kept on lending to the periphery, and not reversed earlier capital flows by selling existing securities. There is a significant difference today from the position then, since there was no possibility of sustaining lending at that time. The individual investor felt no responsibility for continuing to lend, and it would have been impossible to mobilize him in an effort to this end if an attempt had been made to do so. Syndicated bank loans have the advantage, as compared with bonds sold to individual investors, that financial leadership may be able through persuasion and arm-twisting to sustain the capital flow. The other major difference between bonds and syndicated bank loans favors the former as against the latter. Default on a bond has wealth effects for the individual investor but as a rule does not threaten the safety of the banking system as a whole. the difficulty with major defaults on syndicated bank loans.

Default

The nineteenth century is filled with accounts of default on foreign debt. Such default can take many forms, generally involving extensive negotiations between representatives of bondholders and borrowing entities, sometimes backed on one or the other side by governments. Today's analogue is the Paris Club. Winkler lists various distinct types of default affecting either interest, sinking fund or both: repudiation, reduction, postponement, suspension, payment in depreciated currency, payment in blocked currency, payment in scrip, forced conversion of debt. and taxation of interest (Winkler, 1933, p. 16). He cites a 'typical case' of Guatemala, which borrowed in 1825, defaulted in 1828, settled in 1856, borrowed again in 1863, 1864 and 1869, defaulted in 1876, settled in 1887, borrowed in 1888, defaulted in 1894, made a new arrangement in 1895. When this was violated, a new settlement was reached in each of 1901-2, 1903 and 1904, all involving pledging of the proceeds of the coffee tax. In 1913 there was a return to the 1895 agreement. New loans were contracted in 1924, and default took place again in 1932 (Winkler, 1933, pp. 41-4). The literature is replete with accounts of wasteful borrowing, exorbitant terms imposed by lenders on borrowers, and subsequent repudiation (see Wynne, 1951/1983; Jenks, 1938, esp. ch. 10; Winkler, 1933; Feis, 1930, Pt III). Among the more colorful accounts of the process are those dealing with the experience of Egypt from the middle of the nineteenth century to default in 1878 and ultimate occupation by British troops (Marlowe, 1974, esp. chs 11 and 12).

Where borrowing is excessive and suddenly cut off, or the terms of the loan extortionate, the spending practices of the borrower wasteful, or the conditions under which the borrowing was undertaken have drastically changed, as in a turn from world prosperity to world depression, default on past borrowing may be inescapable. A point of possible relevance to the 1980s beyond these reasons is that in a number of cases – Argentina and Brazil in 1890 and Colombia in 1932 after two years of striving to maintain debt service (Thorp and Londoño, 1984) – default was precipitated by depreciation of the currency, which suddenly and drastically raised the local-currency counterpart of the fixed foreign obligation for interest and amortization.

Major borrowing countries today may be anxious to avoid default because of the sanctity they attach to their pledged word, or for concern for the stability of the world economy, which might be endangered if the banking system were forced to mark down their sizeable holdings of Third-World loans. The historical record, however, reveals another cogent reason: default in most cases delayed for about thirty years a country's access to borrowing from abroad. The measure is rough, but Third-World borrowing rose and fell in the middle 1820s, the 1850s. the late 1880s, and, with interruptions for world wars, in the 1920s and 1970s.

The Lender of Last Resort

Whether a financial crisis is superficial, so that the economy can bounce back, or leads to prolonged deflation and depression depends in large part on whether there is a lender of last resort. The crises of 1847, 1857 and 1866 left little lasting impression either in Britain or in Europe as a whole because the Bank of England stood ready in that country, after the suspension of the Bank Act of 1844, to make liquidity freely available, and because in 1847 and 1860 the Bank of England and the Bank of France cooperated. When cash was seen to be available, the demand for it subsided. The swap arrangements put into effect among the leading financial centers in March 1961 and used in a number of exchange crises of Britain, Canada, Italy and the United States achieved the same purpose of staving off sharp deflation in the country under pressure that might spread more widely.

In *The World in Depression, 1929–39* (1973) and *Manias, Panics and Crashes* (1978) I claimed to have found that the financial crises of 1873, 1921 and 1929 were followed by extended depression because there was no international lender of last resort. I would now add the world depression of 1890–6 to that list. It is remarkable that discoveries of gold in California in 1849 and Australia in 1851 quickly fueled a world boom, despite an offsetting drain of silver to the East, whereas the much more substantial discoveries in the Witwatersrand in 1886 produced stimulation of the world economy only after a decade. Deflation in Britain was partly staunched by the guarantee of the liabilities of the Baring bank, led by the Bank of England, but recovery worldwide was slow compared to recovery in the crises of 1847, 1857 and 1866.

D. E. Moggridge (1982) takes exception to these views, especially for the crises of 1921 and 1929. He maintains that much more fundamental therapy was required, more nearly on the order of the Marshall Plan that prevented deflationary collapse after World War II. He may well be right. The opposite view rests on the hypothesis that, if prolonged deflation can be avoided, the world economic system based on markets has the capacity to make the necessary structural adjustments through the normal response of entrepreneurship and resources to goods and asset prices. The view goes on that, if deflation is prolonged, adjustment is much more difficult and extended. I see no way objectively to determine the dividing line between structural maladjustments that can and those that cannot be corrected, given some considerable degree of macro-economic stability. Gottfried Haberler (1948), Friederich Lutz (1948), Sir Roy Harrod (1947) and others maintained after World War II that the Marshall Plan was unnecessary, and that the disequilibria in the world economy could be corrected provided that the inflation was halted and exchange rates adjusted. While I did not share this view (Kindleberger, 1950), I am disposed to believe that structural adjust-

ment after World War I was possible, provided that the financial crisis of
1929 had not been allowed to deepen.

The same issue is posed today by some observers who maintain that
the Third World needs less liquidity maintenance than a Marshall Plan
('Venezuelan asks Marshall Plan . . .', 1983). This ignores the point that
the Marshall Plan in Europe in 1948–52 was largely the restoration of an
economic *status quo ante*, whereas the Third World needs economic
development – which appears to be a much more difficult process – and
would not benefit from hysteresis.

The national lender of last resort is the central bank or Treasury. The
provision of an international lender of last resort historically was done
by the leading central bank (the Bank of England), through cooperation
among leading central banks lending gold or swapping gold for silver, or
it was not undertaken at all. Swap arrangements among leading
financial centers were not undertaken until March 1961 in the Basle
Agreement of the Bank for International Settlements, although Michel
Chevalier mentioned the possibility in 1867 (Ministère des Finances *et
al.*, 1865–7, III, p. 105), and Jørgen Pedersen expressed surprise in
1933 that they had not been used in 1931 (League of Nations, 1934,
pp. 132–3).

But swaps are probably not available for stemming financial crises
involving the Third World. Leading financial centers trust each other to
undo swaps or fund any part of them that cannot be readily reversed at
the end of a period such as six months. The same could not be counted
on for swaps between developed financial centers and Third World
central banks. The financial centers, and the cash-rich countries among
the OPEC 'low-absorbers' want the intermediation of the International
Monetary Fund.

At Bretton Woods, the World Bank was thought of as an organization
to lend counter-cyclically. This would have gone a long way, if the scale
had been adequate, to offset the tendency of private loans to surge and
ebb. At the time of Bretton Woods, private long-term lending had fallen
to such a low that the World Bank was thought of as a major replacement
for it, rather than a stabilizer. In the event, the World Bank early
renounced the role of an anti-cyclical lender, stating that the best it
could hope for was lending that was stable and growing (submission to
the UN Economic and Employment Commission; IBRD, 1949).

The International Monetary Fund was initially thought of as help for
balance-of-payments disequilibria, not financial crises. Foreign-
exchange crises, it was thought, would be contained by foreign-
exchange control. Funds available to help the balance of payments were
spaced out widely, with no more than one tranche (a fourth) of a given
quota per year. Later, under Ivar Rooth, provision was made to provide
two tranches back-to-back on successive days, with a new year starting
on the evening of the first, and to provide assured access to future credit
for a small fee. There remains, however, a long distance between the
capacity of a central bank in a domestic crisis, or major central banks in
combination in an international one, and that of the IMF.

In the first place, the decision-making procedure of the IMF takes weeks or even months instead of days or hours. In a crisis, time counts. In 1931, the French had not been consulted beforehand about the Hoover moratorium, and their response to the proposal – based on the solid legal ground that the Young Plan of 1930 called for some conditional payments but some unconditional – led to three weeks of negotiation, during which Germany experienced renewal of massive foreign withdrawals and domestic capital flight and was obliged to suspend convertibility. As the swap arrangements under the Basle Agreement show, it is sometimes vital to activate lender-of-last-resort arrangements overnight. This the Fund cannot do. The device of bridging loans, either from the Bank for International Settlements (BIS) or the Federal Reserve Bank of New York, has worked effectively in 1982 and 1983. The resources of the BIS are limited, however, and growing uncertainty that the IMF will be able to take over bridging loans in all cases after time makes bridging by the New York Fed perilously close to swap arrangements between a financial-center central bank and one on the periphery, a device either unthought-of or tacitly rejected.

Secondly, the IMF cannot in crisis create money as central banks do, but must rely for its resources on decisions of its member countries, which are virtually unanimous. Whether funds are provided through increases in quotas, enlargement of the General Arrangements to Borrow (GAB) among leading financial powers, or through new issues of Special Drawing Rights, the process in many countries requires legislation, which puts the lender-of-last-resort function into a political rather than a technical area. The impasse in current legislation in the United States to provide $8.4 billion as the US share of expanded GAB quotas illustrates the difficulty. Politicizing rescue operations took place in 1931 when the French wanted to attach conditions to BIS salvage operations for the Creditanstalt. It brought down the Austrian government. If the IMF were equipped to issue SDRs on its own responsibility it could serve much better as a lender of last resort. The readiness politically to delegate such emergency powers to the IMF in advance is lacking in the world today.

One further point of IMF capacity to serve as a lender of last resort in crisis concerns the decision – pushed through by US Secretary of the Treasury Donald Regan on the eve of the IMF meeting at the end of September 1983 – to limit the amount the Fund would be able to make available to a country to 102 percent of its quota, or for a time for countries in trouble, 125 percent, reduced from the existing standard of 150 percent. The purpose, of course, was to conserve the resources of the Fund, and stretch them, on the one hand, and to impress on potential claimants their need to take strong action in their own behalf, on the other. But limits on the part of a lender of last resort are often dysfunctional, and exacerbate rather than alleviate panic. In the eighteenth century, the Bank of England in 1772 and 1797 (and perhaps again in 1809) tried to limit discounting for banks in trouble to a uniform proportion of the amounts sought, and found that such devices increased the panic (Clapham, 1945, I, pp. 245, 269; Foxwell, 1909, p. xvii). In introducing the bill to indemnify the Bank of England for any harm that came to it for violating the Bank Act of 1844, Sir G. S. Lewis, the Chancellor of the Exchequer, observed in 1857 that: '. . . whereever you impose a limit, there is no question that the existence of that limit, provided it makes itself felt in a moment of crisis, must increase the alarm' (quoted in Evans, 1859/1969, p. 203). Walter Bagehot's prescription for a panic is to lend at a penalty rate, but to lend freely.

Conclusions

This summary historical examination suggests conclusions that are widely understood and perhaps on that account a little banal:

(1) The financial world is in 'distress' as a consequence of a positive feed-back process of syndicated bank loans to Third World countries, which started with the deliberate reduction in interest rates in the United States in 1970 and 1971 and was sharply exacerbated by the OPEC price rise;

(2) Distress may or may not lead to default by individual Third World countries. Such default might be precipitated by any one of a number of untoward events, but a particular contingency to guard against is a sharp decline or reversal in the capital flows to these countries. The experience of crises under the National Bank Act in the United States makes clear that the danger lies not in the money-center banks, which operate responsibly in distress (if not always in the boom that produces it), but in the regional banks, which feel no responsibility and are inclined to 'free ride'. (Sprague, 1910/1968, pp. 88 ff and esp. p. 103).

(3) The distress of 1982 and after has the advantage that the money-market banks have accepted responsibility for continued lending and have exerted pressure on the regional banks to the same end, but the disadvantage that, if default occurs on a scale involving more than one major debtor within a limited period, the threat to the world banking system is considerable. The smaller debtors can be cared for, provided their difficulties are spaced in time, by the Paris Club. But the historical record shows that a number of the countries that are smaller in a financial sense, acting simultaneously, can wreak the havoc equivalent to that of major financial countries.

(4) The International Monetary Fund as international lender of last resort between developed (plus OPEC 'low absorbers') and Third World countries needs faster mechanisms, more resources, and probably, in some cases, an absence of limits.

Notes

1 McKinnon later recognized the need for careful removal of repression. See McKinnon and Mathieson (1981).
2 I am told this is the conclusion of a thesis by Franco (1982).

References

Bagehot, Walter (1978), *The Collected Works of Walter Bagehot*, edited by N. St John-Stevas (London: *The Economist*, 11 vols).

Bagwell, Philip S. (1974), *The Transport Revolution from 1770* (London: Batsford).

Barbour, Violet (1950/1966), *Capitalism in Amsterdam in the Seventeenth Century* (Ann Arbor, Mich.: University of Michigan Press, paperback).

Baster, A. S. J. (1929), *The Imperial Banks* (London: P. S. King).

Bloom, Herbert I. (1937), *The Economic Activities of the Jews of Amsterdam in the 17th and 18th Centuries* (Williamsport, Pa.: Bayard).

Boehm, E. A. (1971), *Prosperity and Depression in Australia, 1887–1897* (Oxford: Clarendon Press).

Butlin, S. J. (1961), *Australia and New Zealand Bank, The Bank of Australasia, and the Union Bank of Australia, Ltd* (Croydon, Australia: Longmans, Green).

Cairncross, A. K. (1953), *Home and Foreign Investment, 1870–1913: Studies in Capital Accumulation* (Cambridge: Cambridge University Press).

Castronovo, Valerio (1969), *Economia e societa in Piemonte dell'unita al 1914* (Milan: Banca Commerciale Italiana).

Clapham, Sir John (1945), *The Bank of England, A History* (Cambridge: Cambridge University Press, 2 vols).

Cottrell, P. L. (1980), *Industrial Finance, 1830–1914. The Finance and Organization of English Manufacturing Industry* (London: Methuen).

Evans, D. Morier (1849/1969), *The Commercial Crisis, 1847–48*, 2nd edn (New York: Kelley, Reprints of Economic Classics).

Evans, D. Morier (1859/1969), *The History of the Commercial Crisis, 1857–1858* (New York: Kelley, Reprints of Economic Classics).

Fay, Stephen (1982), *Beyond Greed* (New York: Viking).

Feis, Herbert (1930), *Europe, The World's Banker, 1870–1914* (New Haven, Conn.: Yale University Press).

Ferns, H. S. (1960), *Britain and Argentina in the Nineteenth Century* (Oxford: Clarendon Press).

Foxwell, H. S. (1909), Preface to A. Andréadès, *History of the Bank of England* (London: P. S. King).

Franco, G. H. B. (1982), 'Reforma monetaria e instabilidade durante a transico republicana', unpublished thesis, Department of Economics, Catholic University of Rio de Janeiro, July.

Frankel, S. Herbert (1938/1969), *Capital Investment in Africa: its Course and Effects* (London: Oxford University Press); reprint edn (New York: Howard Fertig).

Gordon, M. J. (1971), 'Toward a Theory of Financial Distress', *Journal of Finance*, vol. 26 (May), pp. 347–56.

Haberler, Gottfried (1948), 'Dollar Shortage', in S. E. Harris (ed.), *Foreign Economic Policy for the United States* (Cambridge, Mass.: Harvard University Press).

Hall, A. R. (1963), *The London Capital Market and Australia, 1870–1914* (Canberra: ANU Social Science Monograph No. 21).

Harrod, Roy F. (1947), *Are These Hardships Necessary?* (London: Hart-Davis).

Hobson, C. K. (1914), *The Export of Capital* (London: Constable).

Holtfrerich, Carl-Ludwig (1980), *Die deutsche Inflation, 1914–23* (Berlin: de Gruyter).

International Bank for Reconstruction and Development (IBRD) (1949), Press Release No. 134 (11 May).

Jenks, Leland H. (1938, *The Migration of British Capital to 1875* (New York: Knopf).
Jones, Charles (1977), 'Commercial Banks and Mortgage Companies', in D. C. M. Platt (ed.), *Business Imperialism, 1840–1930. An Inquiry Based on British Experience in Latin America* (Oxford: Clarendon Press).
Joslin, David (1963), *A Century of Banking in Latin America* (London: Oxford University Press).
Kindleberger, Charles P. (1950), *The Dollar Shortage* (Cambridge and New York: The Technology Press and Wiley).
Kindleberger, Charles P. (1973), *The World in Depression, 1929–1939* (Berkeley, Calif.: University of California Press).
Kindleberger, Charles P. (1978), *Manias, Panics and Crashes: A History of Financial Crises* (New York: Basic Books).
Kindleberger, Charles P. (1982), 'The Cyclical Pattern of Long-Term Lending', in Mark Gersovitz *et al.* (eds), *The Theory and Experience of Economic Development. Essays in Honor of Sir W. Arthur Lewis* (London: Allen & Unwin). pp. 300–12.
Kindleberger, Charles P. (1984), *A Financial History of Western Europe* (London: Allen & Unwin).
King, W. C. T. (1936), *History of the London Discount Market* (London: P. S. King).
Landes, David S. (1958), *Bankers and Pashas* (Cambridge, Mass.: Harvard University Press).
Lauck, W. Jett (1907), *The Causes of the Panic of 1893* (Boston, Mass.: Houghton Mifflin).
League of Nations (1934), Sixth International Studies Conference, A Record of a Second Study Conference on The *State and Economic Life*, London, 29 May to 2 June 1933 (Paris: International Institute of Intellectual Cooperation).
Lévy-Leboyer, Maurice (1982), 'Central Banking and Foreign Trade', in C. P. Kindleberger and J.-P. Laffargue (eds), *Financial Crises: Theory, History and Policy* (Cambridge: Cambridge University Press) pp. 66–110.
Lewis, Henry Grotw (1968), *The Railway Mania and its Aftermath, 1845–1852* (New York: Kelley, Reprints of Economic Classics).
Lutz, Friederich A. (1948), 'The Marshall Plan and European Economic Policy', *Princeton Essays in International Finance* (spring).
McCartney, E. Ray (1935), *The Crisis of 1873* (Minneapolis, Minn.: Burgess).
McKinnon, Ronald I. (1973), *Money and Capital in Economic Development* (Washington, DC: Brookings).
McKinnon, Ronald I. and Mathieson, Donald J. (1981), 'How to Manage a Repressed Economy', *Princeton Essays in International Finance*, No. 145 (December).
Marlowe, John (pseudonym) (1974), *Spoiling the Egyptians* (London: Andre Deutsch).
Ministère des Finances et Ministère de l'Agriculture, du Commerce et des Travaux Publics (1865–7), *Enquête sur les principes et les faits généraux qui régissent la circulation monétaire et fiduciaire* (Paris: Imprimerie impériale, 6 vols).
Mintz, Ilse (1951/1978), *Deterioration in the Quality of Foreign Bonds Issued in the United States, 1920–1930* (New York: National Bureau of Economic Research); reprint edn (New York: Arno).
Moggridge, D. E. (1982), 'Policy in the Crises of 1920 and 1929', in C. P. Kindleberger and J.-P. Laffargue (eds), *Financial Crises: Theory, History and Policy* (Cambridge: Cambridge University Press), pp. 171–87.
Morgenstern, Oscar (1959), *International Financial Transactions and Business*

Cycles (Princeton, NJ: Princeton University Press, for the National Bureau of Economic Research).

O'Brien, D. P. (ed.) (1971), *The Correspondence of Lord Overstone* (Cambridge: Cambridge University Press, 3 vols).

Pressnell, L. S. (1956), *Country Banking in the Industrial Revolution* (Oxford: Clarendon Press).

Schwartz, Anna J. (1981), 'Understanding 1929–1933', in Karl Brunner (ed.), *The Great Depression Revisited* (Boston, Mass.: Martinus Nijhoff).

Shaw, Edward S. (1973), *Financial Deepening in Economic Development* (New York: Oxford University Press).

Simkin, C. G. F. (1951), *The Instability of a Dependent Economy. Economic Fluctuations in New Zealand, 1840–1914* (Oxford: Oxford University Press).

Simon, Maron J. (1971), *The Panama Affair* (New York: Scribners).

Simon, Matthew (1968), 'The Pattern of New British Portfolio Foreign Investment, 1865–1914', in A. R. Hall (ed.), *The Export of Capital from Britain, 1870–1914* (London: Methuen).

Simon, Matthew (1978), *Cyclical Fluctuations and the International Capital Movements of the United States, 1865–1897* (New York: Arno Press).

Smart, William (1911/1964), *Economic Annals of the Nineteenth Century*. Vol. II: *1821–1830*, reprint edn (New York: Kelley, Reprints of Economic Classics).

Smith, Adam (1776/1937), *An Inquiry into the Nature and Causes of the Wealth of Nations*, Cannan edn (New York: Modern Library).

Spinner, T. J., Jr (1973), *George Joachim Goschen, The Transformation of a Victorian Liberal* (Cambridge: Cambridge University Press).

Sprague, O. M. W. (1910/1968), *History of Crises under the National Banking System*, for the National Monetary Commission; reprint edn (New York: Kelley).

Thomas, Brinley (1954), *Migration and Economic Growth: A Study of Great Britain and the Atlantic Economy* (Cambridge: Cambridge University Press).

Thornton, Henry (1802/1962), *An Enquiry into the Nature and Effect of the Paper Credit of Great Britain*, edited with an introduction by F. A. Hayek (London: Frank Cass; reprint of 1939 edn, London: Allen & Unwin).

Thorp, Rosemary and Londoño, Carlos (1984), 'The Effect of the Great Depression on the Economies of Peru and Colombia', in Rosemary Thorp (ed.), *Latin America in the 1930s: The Role of the Periphery in World Crisis* (London: Macmillan, in association with St Anthony's College, Oxford).

'Venezuelan asks Marshall Plan to save heavily indebted Latin America' (1983), *The Boston Globe*, 20 September.

Viner, Jacob (1924), *Canada's Balance of International Indebtedness, 1900–1913, An Inductive Study in the Theory of International Trade* (Cambridge, Mass.: Harvard University Press).

Viner, Jacob (1937), *Studies in the Theory of International Trade* (New York: Harper).

Walker, Mack (1964), *Germany and the Emigration, 1816–1885* (Cambridge, Mass.: Harvard University Press).

Williams, John H. (1920), *Argentine International Trade under Inconvertible Paper Money, 1880–1900* (Cambridge, Mass.: Harvard University Press).

Winkler, Max (1933), *Foreign Bonds: An Autopsy. A Study of Defaults and Repudiations of Government Obligations* (Philadelphia, Pa.: Swain).

Wirth, Max (1890/1968), *Geschichte der Handelskrisen*, 3rd edn (Frankfurt am Main: Sauerländer); reprint edn (New York: Burt Franklin).

Wirth, Max (1893), 'The Crisis of 1890', *Journal of Political Economy*, vol. 1, no. 2 (March), pp. 214–356.

Wynne, William H. (1951/1983), *State Solvency and Foreign Bondholders*. Vol. II: *Selected Case Histories of Governmental Bond Defaults and Debt Adjustments* (New Haven, Conn.: Yale University Press); reprint edn (New York: Garland).

Youngson, A. J. (1960), *The British Economy, 1920–1957* (London: Allen & Unwin).

Part IV

The Nineteenth Century

13

International Monetary Reform in the Nineteenth Century

Next to Keynes, Robert Triffin is surely the most noted advocate of international monetary reform in the twentieth century. In honoring him by calling attention to proposals for international monetary reform in the nineteenth century, I am guilty of the venial sin of what Jonathan Hughes calls 'colligation' – urging that the roots of a particular event or idea extend further back in time than is ordinarily thought. The practice is of course a form of antiquarianism, and, if this be an impeachment, I plead guilty. If one were trying to compete, one could go further back – for example, to the monetary union of the Wendish towns of Lübeck, Hamburg, Wismark, and Luneberg, formed in 1379 – and later joined by Rostock and Pomeranian towns, with the Wendish standard later spreading to virtually all of Scandinavia (Dollinger, 1970, pp. 207–8) – but it would be a mistake; Robert Mundell would find an example from the pre-Christian era. The nineteenth century is interesting enough.

Three related examples will be offered – all unsuccessful. These are decimalization of the pound sterling, the Latin Monetary Union, and 'universal money' – that is, the production of uniform coinage in Europe and the United States. A case may be made that decimalization in Britain is not international but a national monetary reform. It should be remembered, however, that, by the mid-nineteenth century, France, Lombardy, Sardinia, Rome, Tuscany, Naples, Holland, Switzerland, Russia, Greece, Portugal, the United States, Mexico, China, Egypt, and Persia had adopted the decimal system for money (O'Brien, 1971, III, p. 1384). According to a representative to the International Monetary Conference in Paris in 1867, the government of Sweden had sought to introduce the metric system of weights and measures into the kingdom between 1847 and 1854, but had not been entirely successful because of the resistance of the clergy and of agriculture. The metric system had been introduced, but the old units had been retained (US Senate, 1879/1978, p. 827). Had Britain followed, however, the calculation of most exchange rates through the pound would have been greatly eased. The Commission on Decimal Coinage reached its negative decision largely on domestic grounds, but pressure for decimalization came to a great extent from merchants with international purposes.

Reprinted with permission from Richard N. Cooper, Peter B. Kenen, Jorge Braga de Macedo, Jacques van Ypersele (eds), The International Monetary System under Flexible Exchange Rates, Global, Regional, and National. Essays in Honor of Robert Triffin *(Cambridge, Mass.: Ballinger, 1982), pp. 203–16.*

Decimalization of the pound

The decimal system goes back to the fourteenth century, but interest in converting British currency from the traditional European system of pounds, solidus, and denier – in English, pounds, shillings, and pence – arose shortly after the French adoption of the metric system for weights and measures at the time of the French Revolution. The *franc germinal* replaced the *livre tournois* in 1803 and was divided into centimes rather than sous and deniers. Immediately after 1815 voices began to be raised in the British Parliament. John Wilson Croker suggested decimalization of British money in the debate on Lord Liverpool's coinage act of 1816 (Fetter, 1965, p. 66). He received no support. A similar suggestion was put forward by Lord Stanhope in the House of Lords (Smart, 1911/1964, I, p. 508). A memorandum prepared for the Decimal Coinage Commissioners by Lord Monteagle, who strongly favored decimalization and was a member of the commission, picks up the history of the movement with the proposal for an inquiry into the applicability of the decimal scale to coins made by Sir John Wrottesley in the House of Commons in 1824 (O'Brien, 1971, III, p. 1381). This was opposed by the master of the mint on the ground that the government planned to assimilate the currencies of Great Britain and Ireland. The question arose again in 1838 when the standard weights and measures of Britain had been destroyed in the fire at the Houses of Parliament and restoration of the standards was considered. Various inquiries followed, largely in the first instance by scientists, such as astronomers.

In 1847, Dr John Bowring, an economist, moved the adoption of the coinage and issue of silver pieces equal to one-tenth and one-hundredth of the value of the pound. He withdrew the motion when the government proceeded with the initial step of issuing the florin, a two-shilling piece, equal to one-tenth of a pound, as the first experimental step in a process of decimalization.

The commissioners of 1843 reported again in 1853, urging the adoption of the decimal system not only for money but for the linear foot and the pound avoirdupois. This was followed by the appointment of a Select Committee of the House of Commons, which sat for fourteen days, examined twenty-eight witnesses, and recommended decimalization of the pound sterling. No legislation was introduced on the subject in 1854, but many declarations, petitions, and memorials favoring it were presented to the government and the Parliament in 1854 and 1855 by merchants, bankers, municipal governments, chambers of commerce, and so forth. A considerable pamphlet literature on decimalization of coinage developed with works by Bowring and Rathbone (O'Brien, 1971, II, p. 579) and by T. Wilson and Laurie (US Senate, 1879/1978, p. 760). In June 1855 further resolutions were introduced to accept the success of the florin and extend decimalization by the production of a silver coin equal to one one-hundredth of a pound and a copper coin of one one-thousandth. The government replied by appointing a new board of commissioners, consisting of J. G. Hubbard (later Lord Addington), Lord Monteagle (previously T. Spring-Rice), and Lord Overstone (previously Samuel Jones Loyd). The most readily accessible source on the work of the commission is found in *The Correspondence of Lord Overstone* (O'Brien, 1971), which included, along with a discussion of the work of the commission in Lord Overstone's letters, a summary analysis by the editor in Volume I and a number of papers – seven by Overstone, two by Monteagle (from the first of which the summary history in the preceding paragraph was drawn), and two by Hubbard – in an appendix in Volume III.

Lord Overstone opposed decimalization and defeated it so thoroughly in the commission that it was a dead issue for another fifty years (O'Brien, 1971, I, p. 52). The Commission was supposed to be a rubber stamp endorsing decimalization, but Overstone was a man of strong views – even prejudices – and of effective tactics. He started out by admitting that the decimal system was superior for 'abstract calculations' like insurance and convenient for banking, affecting the rich, but argued that it did not fit the needs of everyday practicality. Tactics consisted of delaying action by the commission through various devices until the public lost interest and the movement lost momentum (O'Brien, 1971, II, p. 886).

It seems hardly necessary to set forth the arguments in favor of decimalization. Against it was one quandary: how best to go about it – whether to keep the pound sterling as a unit of account and the florin and then adjust the shilling and the penny or to start with the penny and introduce a whole new set of coins at the upper end, such as the 'dollar' of 100 pennies. While one or two pundits favored the shilling or the penny as the basic unit, virtually everyone came out in favor of retention of the pound. This meant, first, 'crying down' the shilling from twelve to ten pence and the sixpence to fivepence and, second, not stopping at the 'cent' or one one-hundredth of a pound but going on to the mil, one-tenth of the cent. The cent would have been almost $2\frac{1}{2}$d and too large a unit. One-tenth of it was less than a farthing or quarter of a penny, but most proposals called for it.

Overstone's negation was first expressed as a series of questions, to which he finally gave his own answers. In essence, however, he objected to change and couched his opposition in the form of the adverse impact on the transactions of the poor. There were more abstract arguments:

1 A pound under the old system was divided into 240 pennies or 960 farthings, whereas a decimal pound would consist of 1000 mils. Nine-hundred and sixty is divisible by twenty-seven numbers without a remainder, 1000 only by fifteen.

2 The binary system is 'natural', as opposed to the decimal system, which is contrived. Weights and measures used by the British conform to binary reckoning, especially for quarts, pints, gills, or the pound avoirdupois, which is divided into 16 ounces. Hence it is natural to have a pound, crown, and half-crown and then, with a shift, the shilling, sixpence, and threepence, before another shift to the penny.

3   As an extension of the binary character of nature, he observed frequently that the United States had retained in circulation the 12½ cent and 6¼ cent Spanish coins – the bit and the half-bit.
4   To change the monetary system without changing the system of weights and measures would be confusing, as, for example, to charge 10 pennies for a dozen eggs.
5   The penny would be too large a coin in copper and too small in silver.
6   The poor would have great difficulty in adjusting to new values for the shilling and the penny and to the new coin, the mil.

It is not the position of the historian to seek to counter these arguments, although the binary nature of British weights and measures is somewhat dubious. The system is partly duodecimal and partly binary. It should be recalled that at one time British money had the 'angel', a gold coin equal to one-third of a pound sterling, or 6s 8d. When the price of gold was raised in 1526, this coin was 'called up' to 7s 6d, which was not a useful denomination, so it was replaced by the 'noble' a lighter coin again at 6s 8d (De Roover, 1949, p. 74). One could make an argument for having world money on the duodecimal system, embracing first the arguments of Lord Overstone and covering also the linear measures of foot and inch and the avoirdupois measure of the troy pound, not to mention the temporal measures of months, hours, minutes, and seconds. It is clearly wrong to claim that the British system was consistent or binary throughout. It is also worth noting that the United States demonetized the 12½ cent and 6¼ cent foreign coins in 1857, at the same time that Lord Overstone was arguing from their existence.

Lord Overstone was clearly correct that any change in money is disturbing to the poor. Overstone, leader of the Currency School, and Thomas Tooke, leader of the Banking School, were at loggerheads on most things. Tooke did write Overstone, however, to assert that he had started his career as a merchant in the Russian trade in St Petersburg and had found no difficulty in shifting to the combined binary, decimal, duodecimal system when he returned. He thought the experiment in changing standards imprudent (O'Brien, 1971, II, pp. 738–40). But changing systems for less-educated and experienced calculators clearly was likely to pose difficulties, especially if a number of coins were changed at one time. The various commissions were aware of the problem and examined school officials as witnesses to discuss the education of children in the new money, were it to be adopted.

It is evident to most of us that the French people had difficulty in changing from the old to the new franc in the 1950s, with children and tourists calculating in new franc long before French adults had accomplished the task of converting from 10,000 old francs to 100 new francs, dividing by 100. A similar problem is posed for the United States today in the slow progress made in moving to the metric system – in temperature, liquid measures, and distance – with what we suppose to be a highly literate and educated populace. For the nineteenth century the difficulties were more formidable in light of limited education and circulation. Eugen Weber's brilliant *Peasants into Frenchmen* (1976), with the thesis that peasants remained stuck in the *ancien régime* until 1860–1880, when railroads, compulsory education, military conscription, and the press began to force them to become contemporary Frenchmen, has an early chapter entitled 'The King's Foot' that describes the difficulties. In places like Limousin, the peasant counted by *pistola, louis,* and *escu* as late as 1895; in 1917 in Brittany, peasant vocabulary clung to fourteenth century *blancs, écus,* and a Spanish survival, the *real* (Weber 1976:32–33). the same cultural lag obtained in dry, liquid, linear, and ounce weight measures: fathom and foot; ell and bushel; quart, pound, and ounce; *poids de marc* and *poids de table* persisted into the twentieth century.

Changing standards is traumatic, even when the improvement is substantial. Adjustments have to be made all at once, everywhere, whereas the costs of the inadequate standard are regarded as sunk. It is not by accident that the French adopted the metric system for weights and measures, plus money, as a result of a revolution or that the United States and Britain adopted a common standard for the pitch of the screwthread during a war. A high national rate of interest puts the cost of nearby trouble above the benefits of far-off gains from the public good of an improved standard, unless there is trouble in abundance already, so that the addition from changing standards is not striking. It is not without relevance that Sweden made an extended study of the costs of shifting from driving on the left to driving on the right and decided, the first time, against change on cost–benefit grounds. In Austria. the switch was made abruptly by German order one day after Anschluss, with the problems posed by the passenger doors of buses and trolleys facing the street rather than the sidewalk to be worked out pragmatically over time. The Swiss change to the franc and the centime in 1852 and the metric system of weights and measures in 1857, characterized by O'Brien as much superior to the old chaos although causing some inconvenience to lower income groups (O'Brien, 1971, II, p. 731), resulted from the close ties of Switzerland to the French economy.

It is curious that Lord Overstone should have been so opposed to change. As a banker, he could see the benefits from the gain in abstract reckoning – in insurance, foreign exchange, calculation of interest. Despite a strong Christian interest in the poor and the Poor Laws of 1834, he lacked contact with the ordinary poor and can hardly have been dominated by their concerns. While O'Brien withholds any attempt to calculate his motives, it seems evident from reading the 1500 pages of O'Brien's Introduction and Overstone's Correspondence that primarily he was a conservative. What existed, and worked more or less, should be left alone. Even when it did not work as well as he had anticipated – as, for example, the Bank Act of 1844 – keep it and do not try to improve it. It is hard for a modern academic economist to understand the adulation that, say, McCulloch and Torrens rendered Overstone. In Torrens' case, he 'ventured on what may perhaps be regarded as heresy; inasmuch as I have placed in the category of Money,

Deposits not actually represented by Bullion' (O'Brien, 1971, II, p. 707).
Overstone came back at him like a Dutch uncle: 'If you publish this you
let loose upon us the Floodgates of Confusion – It will be the Deluge of
Monetary science, Tooke will be in third Heaven . . .' (*ibid.*, p. 713). To
which Torrens abjectly replied: 'I have no confidence unless you
approve. I throw Deposits to the dogs' (*ibid.*, p. 717). 'Confusion'
provides the key. Overstone had certainty and wanted to keep it. His
support of the Bank Act of 1844 was directed to his Bullionist certainty.
An evident reform to decimalize the pound sterling and help business
and banking reckoning introduced uncertainty. There was no merit in
it.

Decimalization was rejected by a second royal commission in 1918
and finally came in 1971 after the favorable *Report of the Committee of
Inquiry on Decimal Currency* in 1963. The move came after a number
of countries of the Commonwealth had adopted decimalization or
recommended it and despite one suggestion that Britain adopt
duodecimalization. The parliamentary committee had been asked not
to recommend for or against decimalization but to suggest how it be
done – particularly how to rationalize the system of coinage.

Overstone was suspicious that decimalization of money was the thin
end of the wedge to introduce the metric system of weights and measures
more generally. We shall see below in the discussion of the universal
money how he – or rather his alter ego, G. W. Norman – regarded the
trivial adjustment in seigniorage required as an 'Appendage to an
International Coinage and Decimalization – the Metric System &c, &c.'
(O'Brien, 1971, III, pp. 1183–4).

The story comes to an end in the nineteenth century with the passage
of an act in 1862 that permitted the use of the metric system in contracts
and dealings by declaring that any contracts or dealings containing
metric measures shall not by that fact be deemed invalid or open to
objection. Leone Levi, who hailed the memorial of the Lords
Commissioners of the Great Exhibition of 1851, urging decimalization
of money and metrication of weights and measures as a reflection of the
growing intelligence and education of the British and a sweeping away of
antipathy in international relations, regarded a permissive measure as
doubtless insufficient. 'Sooner or later', he continued 'we may
anticipate the entire substitution of the metric system for the present
practice. Considerable progress has also been made regarding international coinage' (Levi, 1872, pp. 469–70). Later, not sooner.

Latin monetary union

A series of monetary steps were taken to unify currencies among the
principalities and states of the Zollverein, including Austria, in the
Coinage Treaty of Vienna of January 1857 and in Scandinavia in
December 1872. The major step at the international level, however, was
the Latin Monetary Union of December 1865, ratified by the four
signatories – France, Belgium, Switzerland, and Italy – to take effect by

August 1, 1866; acceded to by the Papal States that same year and by Greece and Rumania in 1867; and renewed in November 1878 after the collapse of the International Monetary Conference (US Senate, 1879/1978, pp. 779–80). The immediate stimulus to the arrangement is of interest as it evokes echoes of the 'optimal currency area' of Mundell and McKinnon. As the French economy grew in the 1850s and 1860s, the practice of settling large sums in sacks of silver 5-franc pieces became cumbersome, so that gold coins were introduced. Silver having been overvalued in the process, silver coins were melted down or exported, so that adjustment of the fineness of the 5-franc piece had to be undertaken. France, Switzerland, and Italy all moved to reduce the fineness of their coins from 9/10. When France and Italy chose 835/1000 for the grade of silver, Switzerland's choice of 800/1000 threatened to lead to replacement of French and Italian by Swiss coins. The French in 1864 prohibited the use of Swiss coins. Then Belgium saw the virtue of making its change in fineness conform to that of the neighboring states and proposed an agreement among the countries using the franc, but including also Italy, whose lira was equal to a franc.

Small countries have difficulty managing a national currency and preventing the intrusion and use domestically of the moneys of larger states. The fact was observed by Adam Smith at a time when Belgium was a large, not a small, state:

> The currency of a great state, such as France or Belgium, generally consists almost entirely of its own coin. . . . But the currency of a small state, such as Genoa or Hamburgh, can seldom consist altogether of its own coin, but must be made up, in a great measure, of the coins of all the neighboring states with which its inhabitants have a continual intercourse. (Smith, 1776/1937, Book IV, ch. III, pt. I, Digression)

Forty years later, the same phenomenon was observed in the Rhineland, where, in 1816, at least seventy coins from Holland, France, Belgium, and various German states were reportedly in local circulation, and Prussian coin was rarely seen (Tilly, 1966, p. 20). Some areas are too small to be optimum currency areas and must use moneys of other countries.

In 1865, the Swiss, Belgians, and Italians all favored going over from bimetallism to the gold standard, but French loyalty to the 'double standard' carried the day. The French had been debating bimetallism with some fervor since the great flood of gold let loose by the discoveries of 1849 in California and 1851 in Australia. The question was settled regularly, but as regularly arose again. One commission met on the issue in 1857, a second in 1861, a third in 1867, and a fourth in 1869 (Wolowski, 1869, pp. 183–98). Most of the members of the various commissions continued to vote in favor of bimetallism. Only Michael Chevalier and Esquirou de Parieu opposed it, Chevalier favoring silver in the light of the gold discoveries and de Parieu gold, presumably on the basis of the British *de jure* adoption of gold in 1816, following *de facto* adoption in 1717. De Parieu was a member of the French delegation to the 1867 International Monetary Conference and its vice-president, presiding in the frequent absence of the Prince Jerome Napoleon and of the foreign minister. He was also an indefatigable writer on international money between 1859 and at least 1878 (US Senate, 1879/1978, pp. 761–72).

The articles of the 'Treaty Constituting the Latin Union' cover barely three pages and regulate the weight, title, form, and circulation of their gold and silver coins. Five-franc (lira) silver coins were held to 0.9 fineness; silver coins of 2 francs, 1 franc, 50 centimes, and 20 centimes were limited to a fineness of 0.835. Since the seigniorage on these coins was positive, it was agreed that each country would hold down the number of such coins issued to no more than 6 francs per inhabitant, lest one country would gain at the expense of its neighbors.

The Latin Monetary Union met some strain when Italy proved unable to sustain convertibility of the lira in May 1866 and adopted forced circulation of its banknotes (*corso forzoso*). The export of silver from that country prior to inconvertibility is sometimes held to have contributed to the decline in silver. This source of pressure was small, however, compared with the discovery of the Comstock load in Nevada in 1859, the electrolytic process for refining silver, and the more serious sales of silver by the German Reichsbank after the adoption of the gold standard in 1875. From 1865 to 1877 the Latin Monetary Union maintained bimetallism, restricting the coinage of silver in the latter year. In 1867 the success of the union was so widely recognized that it was thought useful to proceed from it to the adoption of a universal money.

Universal money

The term 'universal' money was used as early as 1588 by Davanzati in his 'Discourse on Coin' to the Florence Academy. He explained that, while the prince could make money out of iron, leather, wood, cork, lead, paper, salt, or the like, as sometimes had happened, this money could not circulate outside of his realm and thus could not be universal money (Vilar, 1976, p. 190). François Nicholas Mollien, Napoleon's minister of finance, approaches the idea, if not the term, in writing in his *Mémoires* that it was desirable that all people adopt a uniform system of measures and that, of these measures, the uniformity that brings most to the convenience of nations is uncontestably that of money (Mollien, 1845, III, p. 498). The pressure for a universal money in the second half of the nineteenth century came largely from France and especially from Esquirou de Parieu, an economist and vice-president of the Conseil d'Etat, who wrote prodigiously but whose reputation has not stood the test of time. De Parieu was intimately connected with the Latin Monetary Union. He was also a leading spirit in calling the International Monetary Conference of 1867 in Paris to explore the possibilities of extending the achievement of the union to more countries. The conference was held in connection with the Universal

Exposition of 1867, also held in Paris, and the US representative to the monetary conference was not a member of government or the director of the mint, as in the case of other countries, but the US commissioner to the Universal Exposition.

The idea behind 'universal money' was partly to assist travelers by having coins interchangeable, but primarily for the sake of commerce (US Senate, 1879/1978, p. 817). There is an echo of Lord Overstone in the remark of a Norwegian delegate that it would be desirable to have international understanding with respect to subsidiary coinage, with equivalent subdivisions, for the sake of the laboring classes – but the point of view was international and long-run rather than domestic and focusing on maintaining the status quo.

De Parieu opened the conference by propounding a series of questions, again with echoes of Lord Overstone's technique. Again here, however, the purpose was different – to elicit agreement, rather than to prevent change. The first question is as relevant today as it was more than a century ago:

1   By what means is it most easy to realize monetary unification; whether by the creation of a system altogether new, independent of existing systems – and in such what should be the basis of such system – or, by the mutual co-ordination of existing systems, taking into account the scientific advantages of certain types, and the number of the populations which have already adopted them? In this case, what monetary system should be principally taken into consideration, reserving the changes of which might be susceptible for making it perfect? (US Senate, 1879/1978, p. 811)

On this I fear that I disagree with Robert Triffin, who along with Keynes, the IMF, the European Monetary System, and the like would favor the creation of a new international money. In fact, the conference of June 1867 worked on how to create a universal money out of existing currencies. The negotiating problem strongly resembled the question of the decimalization of the pound – what denominations of existing coins to keep and what to cry up or call down.

Most of the discussion revolved around the French franc. One scheme, favored by the British, was to start with a new 25-franc piece, equal to the pound sterling after adjustment of the sovereign to change its fineness from 11/12 to 0.9 through a mintage charge of approximately (in French reckoning) 20 centimes (out of 2500). The mintage charge was discussed in 1869 by Lord Overstone and G. W. Norman of the Bank of England, who saw it as a new attempt by the routed proponents of decimal currency to institute international coinage and 'ultimately Decimalization and the Metric System' (O'Brien, 1971, III, p. 1184). Norman thought mintage the small end of the wedge: 'At any rate I can not believe that a sovereign with a portion of gold abstracted from it will be worth as much as the present coin in foreign countries' (*ibid.*). A third memorandum by Lord Overstone on gold coinage concludes 'that the sovereign can not be tampered with as regards weight and fineness of the gold upon any plea. It is fraud in disguise' (*ibid.*, p. 1187).

The minting of a 25-franc piece and the adjustment of the sovereign through mintage called next for adjustment of the dollar from $4.8665 to the pound sterling to $5.00, a small devaluation that the American delegate to the 1867 conference, and later John Sherman as a US senator (prior to becoming Secretary of the Treasury), thought entirely feasible. The former, one Samuel B. Ruggles, US commissioner to the Paris Exposition of 1867, thought that the dollar could not be eliminated, but that its value might be altered 3.5 percent. The Portuguese representative then expressed the key currency notion: if agreement could be worked out among France, England, and the United States, other countries would sooner or later rally round (O'Brien, 1971, III, p. 813).

Twenty-five francs was not very satisfactory to the French. They would have preferred the Napoleon of 20 francs or the 10-franc piece, once called the ducat, with its neater fit into the metric system. The British representative noted that the British might have preferred 20 francs as the standard as well, since they were used to dividing by twenty. There was thus a possibility, that having adjusted the pound to 25 francs from 25 francs, 20 centimes, they would have to undertake a second recoinage. In addition, half of 25 francs is 12.5 francs, an awkward designation.

In a remark anticipating the distinction between national and international public goods, the French prince, who presided at the conference in the final days, said:

> Certainly, if France consulted only its own convenience, she [*sic*] would see no necessity for issuing this new [25-franc] coin; but to facilitate the work of unification, the object of the labors of the conference, it would make the concession requested by the United States. It also appeared that the 25-franc piece would equally accommodate both England and Austria. (US Senate, 1879/1978, p. 858)

Other countries were not content to let the issue be settled among France, Britain, and the United States. The Swedish delegate kept coming back to 10 francs as the standard and thought that the United States could issue a $2 gold coin, more convenient than the silver dollar. The Prussian representative suggested a 2.5-franc coin. Supported by South Germany and Wurtemberg, the Dutch insisted on a 15-franc standard, which Austria opposed. Prussia abstained from voting on either the 25-franc or the 15-franc coin because its delegate had no instructions beyond voting for the gold standard, even though Prussia was on the silver standard.

Bimetallism was one issue. Although off the gold standard in 1867, the United States did not insist on bimetallism as it later did in calling the unsuccessful International Monetary Conference of 1878. The other issue was that to which so much attention has thus far been given –

which national currency unit to follow. All agreed that it would occasion too much artificiality to start afresh with a brand new currency. Britain's leadership was not so clearly established, either in the calling of the conference, which had been done by the French, or in taking a lead in the discussion, to induce the Continent to follow.

The conference ended on July 6, 1867. It concluded in favor of the gold standard, with a gradual transition from bimetallism and the common denominator of the franc, especially the 5-franc gold piece (dollar), 0.9 fine, but with recommendation for the coinage of a 25-franc piece to equal the pound sterling, the half-eagle of $5, and a piece adopted by the Vienna conference of 1857 to represent 10 florins. No conclusion was reached on the gold piece of 15 francs. The recommendations were given to governments 'with the hope that some decision may be reached by the middle of February 1868, or at least some instructive steps taken by governments' (US Senate, 1879/1978, p. 877). In the event, nothing happened. The outcome is reminiscent of the International Economic Conference of 1927, when all countries agreed to lower tariffs, but none did.

Discussion of monetary reform continued into the next years. Walter Bagehot wrote a series of articles in *The Economist* between October and December 1868, which were then assembled in a pamphlet entitled *Universal Money* and reproduced in his *Collected Works* (Bagehot, 1978, XI, pp. 55–104).

Universal Money focuses less on the technical details of how to reach monetary unification and more on the purposes of reform. The author states:

A remarkable movement is going on in the world towards a uniformity of coinage between different nations. And it was begun in what seems the way of the nineteenth century; the way Germany was created, and the unity of Italy too; that is, not by a great number of states, of set design and in combination, chalking out something new, but on the contrary, by some great state acting first for its own convenience, and then other lesser and contiguous nations imitating its plan and falling in with its example. . . .

The advantages of a single coinage, which are explained in the following papers, seem to me fully equivalent. But I fear, when looked at strictly, it will be found that the difficulties of such a step are simply insurmountable. And if this is so, and we do nothing, what then? Why, we shall, to use a vulgar expression, be left out in the cold. . . .

Every person must see that the demand for uniformity in currency is only one case of the growing demand for uniformity in matters between nations really similar. . . . Commerce is everywhere identical; buying and selling, lending and borrowing, are alike all the world over, and all matters concerning them ought universally to be alike too. . . . Ultimately the world will see one *code de commerce*, and one money as the symbol of it. (*ibid.*, pp. 64–6)

In one chapter Bagehot shoots down a series of alleged advantages of a universal money – convenience of travelers, simplification of international remittances, and ease of statistical calculation internationally. Since foreign transactions are small in relation to internal ones, he concludes that the slight advantages do not outweigh the inconvenience to domestic trade. Moreover, he is not impressed by the arguments of Michael Chevalier in favor of the naturalness of the metric system. The advantage of a universal money lies in the unit of account function, in enabling foreigners to understand English '*price language*' (his italics – *ibid.*, p. 71) and in enabling British bankers to know how much bullion there is in the Bank of France: 'Of course all English bankers can *turn* francs into pounds, and some think they *will*; but few ever do' (*ibid.*, p. 73).

But the exercise shatters on the same rock as the 1867 conference, to which he refers. Should the basic international coin be the sovereign equal to 25 francs (after adjustment) or the 10-franc piece equal to 8 shillings (after adjustment), which could be coined into a 'gold florin' or 'metrical pound' of 100 (originally 96) pence? The French, he is sure, would be unwilling to take the pound (25 francs). He is persuaded that a new 8-shilling gold piece in circulation with the old 10-shilling gold piece would create insuperable difficulties for bank cashiers and the public and discredit the plan. In the end he comes down to two systems – a great Anglo-Saxon system based on the sovereign and the half-eagle ($5) on the one hand and the Latin unit on the other. Germany, in his view, would choose to align itself with the former to constitute a Teutonic coinage league to go with the Latin coinage league.

One may wonder about the political feasibility of the scheme. On the economic technical level, two world moneys suffer the disability of being subject to Gresham's law, the warning implicit in Triffin's criticism of the gold exchange standard.

The International Monetary Conference of 1878

A footnote to the above cautionary tale of monetary reform in the nineteenth century should indicate that the 1878 conference, larger and more encompassing than that of 1867, was called by the United States to explore the possibility of restoring bimetallism. Political pressures from mining senators were intense. John Sherman, now Secretary of the Treasury, was now a political bimetallist, whereas he had been for gold as a senator. It proved impossible to get Humpty-Dumpty back together again. The Latin Monetary Union had left bimetallism. The new German Reichsbank had adopted the gold standard in 1875, selling off more silver to add to that pouring from Nevada mines. This was perhaps the significant monetary reform of the nineteenth century, taken long after 1774, when Britain demonetized silver; resisted by the United States; and defensive rather than positive.

Bagehot follows his introduction to *Universal Money* with a postscript to the long quotation given above, ending 'One *code de commerce*, and one money as the symbol of it'. 'We are, as yet,' he says, 'very distant from so perfect an age' (Bagehot, 1978, XI, p. 66). Despite the talent and the drive of Robert Triffin, we still are.

References

Bagehot, Walter (1978), *The Collected Works of Walter Bagehot*, edited by Norman St John-Stevas, Vols IX–XI: *The Economic Essays* (London: *The Economist*, 11 vols).

De Roover, Raymond (1949), *Gresham on Foreign Exchange* (Cambridge, Mass.: Harvard University Press).

Dollinger, Philippe (1970), *The German Hansa*, translated and edited by D. S. Ault and S. H. Steinberg (Stanford, Calif.: Stanford University Press).

Fetter, Frank Whitson (1965), *Development of British Monetary Orthodoxy, 1797–1875* (Cambridge, Mass.: Harvard University Press).

Levi, Leone (1872), *History of British Commerce, and of the Economic Progress of British Nation, 1763–1870* (London: John Murray).

Mollien, François Nicholas (1845), *Mémoires d'un ministre du Trésor Public, 1780–1815* (Paris: Fournier, 4 vols).

O'Brien, D. P. (ed.) (1971), *The Correspondence of Lord Overstone* (Cambridge: Cambridge University Press, 3 vols).

Report of the Committee of Inquiry on Decimal Currency (1963), Cmnd 2145 (London: HMSO, September).

Smart, William (1911/1964), *Economic Annals of the Nineteenth Century*, reprint edn (New York: Augustus M. Kelley, 2 vols).

Smith, Adam (1776/1937), *An Inquiry into the Nature and Causes of the Wealth of Nations*, Cannan edn (New York: Modern Library).

Tilly, Richard H. (1966), *Financial Institutions and Industrialization in the Rhineland, 1815–1870* (Madison, Wis.: University of Wisconsin Press).

US Senate (1879/1978), *International Monetary Conference* (Washington, DC: US Government Printing Office); reprint edn (New York: Arno Press).

Vilar, Pierre (1976), *A History of Gold and Money, 1450–1920*, translated from the 1969 Spanish original by Judith White (London: New Left Books).

Weber, Eugen (1976), *Peasants into Frenchmen, The Modernization of Rural France, 1870–1914* (Stanford, Calif.: Stanford University Press).

Wolowski, Louis (1869), *La Question monétaire*. 2nd edn (Paris: Guillaumin).

14

International Propagation of Financial Crises: The Experience of 1888–93

I

I first met Wilfried Guth, if my memory serves, in 1939. A student interested in international capital movements, he had written to me because I had just finished and published my thesis on the subject. We met when I was at the Bank for International Settlements, on a visit from Basle to Frankfort. Since that time I have continued as a student of international capital movements and he has gone on to produce them – in government at the Kreditanstalt für Wiederaufbau, and at the Deutsche Bank. It may be appropriate then for me to honor him in recurring to capital movements in which we share a long-lived and keen, if perhaps diverging, interest.

There is another reason to study the crisis of 1890–93. Of all the crises in the last hundred years or so, it most closely resembles the difficulties the world is passing through in 1983. 1929 is the analogy that comes to the people's minds when they contemplate the present taut state of world credit. The comparison with 1888–93 seems to me, thus far, to run more closely parallel.

Some crises are clearly international; others, such as 1866 and 1907, appear to be national in extent, when they are in my judgement linked through an international propagation mechanism. It was no accident in 1866 that the collapse of the stock market in Berlin, the push of Italy off the gold standard, and the Overend, Gurney crisis in London all occurred within the first 11 days of May; this despite the assured statement of Clapham that the last was strictly British (1945, II, p. 267). In 1907, crises in New York and Turin were connected, not directly but through Paris and London, which kept largely unaffected. The timing need not be so tight-knit as in 1866. The wobbly backgrounds of crises in one country and another may develop independently or have a common origin in speculative euphoria. The contention, however, is that monetary tightness in one market is readily communicated to others and, when the credit system is stretched, may well propagate financial crisis from one market to another.

In what follows I hope to demonstrate a strong presumptive case – it is

Reprinted with permission from Wolfram Engels, Armin Gutowski and Henry C. Wallich (eds), International Capital Movements. Debt and Monetary System *(Mainz: v. Hase & Koehler Verlag, 1984), pp. 217–34. I acknowledge with thanks references kindly furnished by Knut Borchardt.*

virtually impossible to offer proof – that the series of financial crises from 1888 to 1893 were intimately connected. These crises include:

The Baring crisis running between London and Buenos Aires with repercussions in New York, Rio de Janeiro, and Santiago;

The Parisian Panama crisis starting in 1888 and ending in scandal in 1893, plus the copper corner and the collapse of the Comptoir d'Escompte in 1889;

The collapse of the market for diamond shares in 1881 and for gold shares in South Africa in 1889;

The collapse of a series of Italian banks running from 1887 to 1893;

The wave of bank suspensions in Australia in March and April 1893;

The gold panic in New York from July to October 1893 (following the lesser crisis of 1890 noted above);

Less certainly, the failure of two banks in Berlin in November 1891.

Most of these episodes are treated in economic history as separate. Both Lauck and Morgenstern, who pay some attention to international connections, emphasize the European connections, aside from Italy which they ignore, and tend to leave out the so-called periphery – Latin America, South Africa, and Australia (1907, ch. iv; 1959, esp. Chart 72, p. 548).

The mechanism of propagation of boom and crisis is largely capital movements and prices, including prices both of commodities and of financial assets. Morgenstern quotes Schumpeter to the effect that the chief channel through which influences are transmitted internationally is the interaction of stock markets (1959, p. 508, quoting Schumpeter, 1939, II, pp. 66–7). The connection can be direct as investors in one market buy or sell securities in another, or it can be psychological as two markets mark commodity or asset prices up or down in parallel, without transactions between them taking place. Psychological influences may in fact cross from one commodity to another. The attempted corner in copper was inspired, according to Wirth (1893, p. 222), by the success of the diamond syndicate in South Africa after the 1882 debacle in diamond shares, and by that of the Rothschild syndicate in mercury in Spain. There is no significant connection through national income, though not for the reason given by Morgenstern that there are no reliable data (1959, p. 566), but because the mechanism of exports, foreign-trade multiplier, national income and imports is too strung out with lags to explain the near simultaneity of upswings and crises.

The nature of capital movements differs rather widely between those among the financial centers of Europe, and those between Europe and the periphery, especially South Africa, Latin America, and Australia. Relations between the European financial centers and New York reflect both patterns. Within Europe, capital movements largely took the form of purchases and sales of existing securities, whereas with overseas areas the majority of capital flows went through newly issued securities. Like New York, the Russian connection with financial centers involved both new issues and existing securities, plus what lay between them,

maturing bonds that needed to be refunded. It is a curious phenomenon
that a major problem in international capital movements of the 1880s
and '90s was the shift of the Russian source of loans from Berlin to Paris,
a shift that took place relatively smoothly without involving Russia in
the financial crises that seized the major financial centers.

II

The vortex of the world crisis was London. It financed the boom.
Cutting down on capital exports brought about the crisis. There were
whirlpools such as Paris and Berlin with their separate causes and
effects, related to the main source of tumult in London, but not central.
Part of the boom and bust was domestic in origin, part foreign. The
foreign crises were connected to London especially through the creation
of companies in London for investment in diamonds and gold in South
Africa, banks that operated especially in South Africa, Australia, and
Latin America, railroads in those continents and in the United States,
mortgage companies in Argentina and Australia, nitrates companies in
Chile, and the like.

The boom was incited by two domestic factors: the Goschen
conversion of 1888, which made investors search for higher-earning
assets, and the anticipation of a tightening of the company law of 1862,
which stimulated a number of private companies to go public before it
was too late to do so easily. The conversion under Viscount Goschen,
Chancellor of the Exchequer, occurred in March 1888 when three issues
of outstanding 3 percent government debt were changed for a single
issue bearing 2¾ percent coupon for 15 years and 2½ percent for 20 years
thereafter (Spinner, 1973, p. 140). An attempt had been made at
conversion in 1884 and abandoned. By the time it took place in 1888 it
had long been anticipated. Some of the gains from lower interest rates
accrued to foreigners. In October 1888 the Brazilian government under
the Empire converted its sterling loans of 1865, 1871, 1875 and 1876, all
issued through the house of N. M. Rothschild and bearing 5 percent
interest, to 4 percent plus a ½ percent amortization charge (Calogeras,
1910, p. 199). For the most part, the reduction in investor income in
Britain pushed private investors and trustees into foreign bonds to
prevent a decline in income.

The boom in private companies tended, like many manias, to run in
channels. The private brewing company, Guinness, sold a nominal £3½
million in October 1886, and the success of the issue acted like a starting
pistol, according to Cottrell. By November 1890, 86 other breweries had
gone public or increased their capital (1980, p. 169).

A contribution to the enthusiasm for beer in Britain was the
phylloxera which attacked French vineyards and reduced the
prospective supply of wine (Wirth, 1893, p. 220). Mathias claims
additionally that the size of brewing firms increased rapidly with
economies of scale in distribution (1969, pp. 369 ff, quoted in Edelstein,
1982, p. 60). The contagion soon crossed the Atlantic. Within the year

ended August 1, 1889, 14 American breweries had registered securities in England (M. Simon, 1955/1979, p. 450). The boom even extended to Canadian breweries, although as noted below Canada was left largely aside in the boom of the 1880s (Lauck, 1907, p. 41). In all, 12,068 companies with a nominal share capital of £1 billion went public between 1886 and 1890 (*ibid.*).

Table 1   *New Portfolio Investment, 1885–1893 (in millions of pounds sterling)*

	World Capital markets RR, Ind. (creations)	British foreign issues	British new issues by area					
			Europe	NA	SA	Africa	Asia	Austr
1885	124.7	52.7	3.4	14.1	7.1	4.7	11.0	14.9
1886	251.7	74.4	5.0	14.0	19.3	2.5	9.6	19.4
1887	190.0	83.7	12.9	23.9	18.9	1.5	10.5	16.5
1888	295.9	133.3	10.1	37.2	40.3	4.2	10.7	15.7
1889	501.9	138.5	11.2	37.2	40.2	8.9	11.2	14.2
1890	223.9	110.7	12.3	52.8	23.3	4.6	10.8	12.8
1891	225.5	51.8	5.0	18.7	9.4	6.6	5.7	12.3
1892	93.5	40.1	2.7	14.9	5.4	3.3	4.1	9.2
1893	134.7	31.5	1.7	13.1	5.4	2.6	2.5	6.7

Source: M. Simon (1967/1978), pp. 38, 40.

Table 2   *Balance of Payments on Current Account, 1885–1893 (in millions of specified units)*

	United Kingdom (pounds sterling)	France (French francs)	Germany (marks)
1885	39.5	420	507
1886	60.9	505	486
1887	67.8	700	431
1888	74.6	805	686
1889	72.5	685	590
1890	94.4	590	430
1891	52.3	390	334
1892	37.4	490	185
1893	42.1	695	361

Sources: UK: Cairncross (1953), p. 180.
France: White (1933), p. 122.
Germany: Mitchell (1978), p. 437.

In addition there were foreign stimuli to the boom: the discoveries of diamonds in South Africa, of gold in South Africa and Australia, and of nitrates in Chile. Likewise, the clearing of Patagonia of Indians by Argentina during the early 1880s and the shift from grain to meat in both Argentina and Australia with the development of the refrigerator ship about 1875 both led to land booms in those countries, paralleled by similar booms in the Southern United States and in South Africa. Whether the push was stronger than the pull is probably unanswerable and in any event an idle subject for speculation as both were necessary.

Whatever the case, a substantial outflow of capital took place from London and from European capitals (see Table 1).

The World Capital Market new issues, taken from the Belgian publication, *Le Moniteur des intérêts matériels*, is incomparable with the British figure for the par value of issues. It is limited to railroads and industrial securities on the one hand, and includes domestic issues along with foreign on the other. British new issues by areas, moreover, differs from total capital flows since it excludes trade in existing securities, both listed on stock exchanges and unlisted. *Cedulas*, for example, the special sort of Argentine mortgage bond in which there was much speculation in the 1880s, were never listed (Ferns, 1960, p. 423). But there is some indication that the swing in British lending was wider than that of Germany on the upswing and of France on the downswing if one compares the 'outflow of capital' as measured by the balance of payments on current account (Table 2).

The booms in diamonds and gold in South Africa did not perhaps involve enormous amounts of capital, as Table 1 shows, but the psychological stimuli were great. The impact of the diamond cartel on the copper corner has been mentioned. Hobson observes that the boom in South African mines was the 'signal for unhealthy inflation in other countries, notably Australia and South America' (1914, p. 148) and goes on to remark that Continental investors 'went wild' over South African mining shares, even when they were not registered on local bourses. Most of the South African mining companies were headquartered and registered in London. Three hundred and ninety-six South African companies in mining, finance, exploration and landowning in 1880 had risen to 642 in 1889, and those having offices in London increased from 145 in 1888 with a paid-in capital of £5.8 million to 315 in 1890 with a paid-in capital of £44 million, although there was much duplication (Frankel, 1938/1969, p. 81).

British lending to Latin America peaked in 1888 and 1889 and started down in 1890. German investors seem to have taken alarm earlier. Hobson states that German investors participated in the Panama mania only to a slight extent, and became involved in Latin America when their enthusiasm for Russian securities had been curbed, as 'many of the most risky issues were wisely sold in Belgium when prices were still at a high level' (1914, p. 148). The caution of German investors and the hostility of the German government are noted by Ferns (1960, pp. xx, 433). One source claims that the Germans had been trained to regard Argentine securities as first-class but became uneasy in 1888 (Lauck, 1907, pp. 59–60) and sold all but 100 million marks worth by the end of 1890. Another view is that the German investor was troubled by the depreciation of the Argentine peso (Morgenstern, 1959, p. 523). Whatever the reason, here is one of the few cases where the enthusiasm of one class of investor for a security failed to communicate itself for long to another.

British investments in Argentina took the form of *cedulas*, that is mortgage bonds denominated in pesos, in railway securities and in bonds issued by the Argentine government and the provinces. The crisis came in stages, first when a series of new issues failed and were left on the underwriters' hands, and secondly when Baring Brothers was unable to make the payment due in 1890 on the Buenos Aires Water Supply bonds, which they had underwritten in 1888 and still held in considerable measure. Baring Brothers' reputation was so high from its successes in Anglo-American trade finance in the first half of the nineteenth century that the market in London was reassured by its continued involvement in Argentine securities. One analyst argues that the loans were sound in the long run, but the lending stopped before the investment projects could be completed, leaving high debt service without the exports to meet them (Ford, 1962, pp. 28, 142 n).

A general problem is how much to blame events in the overseas country for the crisis, and how much the cut-off of the capital flow from the center. A monetarist position tends to ascribe the crisis almost entirely to events in the periphery, especially new bank laws passed in Argentina in 1887 (and Brazil in 1888), plus political events such as revolutions or coups d'état. Williams' classic study of the depreciation of the Argentine peso insists that the cut-off of the capital flow produced the depreciation, rather than the expansion of the note issue. He goes further and suggests that the expansion was required by the depreciation, rather than being the cause of it (1920, pp. 103, 107). A recent study of the Brazilian crisis, I am told, makes the same point about Brazilian experience in 1889–91 (Franco, 1982). The issue is an old one, of course, in the debate between the Banking and the Currency School in England over the Bullion Report, and the similar controversy between monetarists and the balance-of-payments school over responsibility for the German hyperinflation of 1923. It is perhaps relevant that Williams adhered to the balance-of-payments school in the 1923 German debate (1922), as well as in his analysis of the Baring crisis in Argentina.

Brazilian borrowing overall was relatively modest, roughly $66 per capita, excluding the floating debt, compared to such numbers as $400 for Argentina and $412 for Australia (Wileman, 1896, p. 45, based on data of the French *Annuaire Statistique* for 1888). Most borrowing was for government account, but some was to expand coffee production and railroads. The borrowing helped bid up the milreis (which had fallen to 17½d in 1885 from par of 27d in 1875) back to par in 1889, when the lending stopped. How much the halt was owing to the Baring crisis, and how much to particular developments in Brazil – the fall in the price of coffee worldwide, the end of the Empire and its replacement by an unstable republic, a new banking law which provided for the issue of banknotes on the security of national government bonds (patterned after the US National Bank Act of 1863) – is a matter of some contention. Students of British banking in Latin America incline to believe that the crisis was communicated from one country to another through British banks (Joslin, 1963, pp. 123, 133; Jones, 1977, p. 24). Most current observers blamed the separate banking changes and the issue of more banknotes. A modern student raises the question whether the halt in lending might not have given rise to the need for new issues of banknotes

(Franco, 1982). Whether reason or excuse, when the Republic's finance minister appealed to Brazil's financial agents in London, N. M. Rothschild & Sons, for a loan after the 1891 coup d'état, stating that there was neither a political nor an economic crisis, he received a reply accepting his affirmation as to the political crisis, but differing on the financial: 'the decline on the exchange and the depression of Brazilian securities [in London] reveal a very grave crisis, caused principally by the fears of new issues of paper money' (Calogeras, 1910, p. 177).

The historiography of the Chilean crises of 1888 to 1893 focuses on monetary and political events local to the country, especially the war with Peru and the Civil War (Fetter, 1931). The depreciation of the peso in 1892 was precipitated by a withdrawal of capital, but loss of European investor confidence was the result of the landed classes insisting on inflation as a means of reducing the load of debt (*ibid.*, pp. 76, 85). There should, however, be some room for the preceding boom engineered by Colonel John Thomas North who created nitrate companies in 1883, 1885, and 1886. In all, 17 nitrate companies were organized between 1883 and 1889, of which four were created in 1888 and nine in 1889, including four in the single month of January 1889 (O'Brien, 1982, p. 115). Established companies sold out to the newcomers for high profits, and bought back in later in much the same way as shipping companies in London after World War I (Macrosty, 1927, quoted in Youngson, 1960, p. 45). Just as the brewery companies that had gone public in London could not meet their promised dividends (Wirth, 1893, p. 221), so six of nine nitrate companies reporting in June 1890 paid no dividends, and by December 1890 nitrate shares were quoted at one-quarter to one-eighth of the prices they had reached in 1889 (O'Brien, 1982, p. 122).

The Australian wave of bank and mortgage company failures occurred primarily in the spring of 1893. The data from which Table 1 is drawn show that Australia borrowed more in the first half of the 1880s than in the second. The boom went on into 1891, after the Baring crisis, but its ending was said to be 'inevitable' (Baster, 1929, p. 148); that is, merely the 'final explosion' of the banking crisis from 1891, the break in the boom of 1888 (Butlin, 1961, p. 279) and the 'eventuality which financial writers had prophesied for a decade or so' (Hall, 1963, p. 171). Most of these writers insist that the Australian boom had purely local causes in the land and mortgage company boom (e.g. Butlin, 1961, p. 280; Hall, 1963, p. 148; Boehm, 1971, chs 9, 10; Pressnell, 1982, p. 160), but all mention the leveling out of the capital inflow into Australia. Hall ascribes the slowdown in British lending partly to misgivings in London over the Argentine inflation, the Brazilian revolution and the Kaffir circus (1963, p. 159). But he blames it primarily on a 'breakdown in the marketing mechanism' for Australian securities in London, rather than a loss of investor interest in Australian issues (*ibid.*, pp. 101, 136, 171). The distinction seems overdrawn. Problems were found with the tendering system that awarded an entire issue to a particular syndicate, which might have much of the issue left on its hands, and a quarrel took place between the Bank of England and the Queensland government over a failure of an issue for the latter in 1891. The fact was, however, that the failure of syndicates to tender for Australian government bonds was not solely a technical question. Three provincial issues failed along with an Australian one, and the Queensland sum was ultimately raised only by a sharp reduction in the issue price. British investors could not but have been aware that the Australian and Argentine booms in land speculation were similar and that the failure of mortgage companies in Argentina might be paralleled in Australia. It is true that some lenders to Australia, such as the Scottish depositors in British offices of Australian banks, were slow to withdraw their deposits until after March 1893 (Hall, 1963, Table 20, p. 115). But these were time deposits for periods ranging from one to three years, and after 1893 they were drawn down as fast as they matured. I conclude that the Australian boom was part of the worldwide upswing of the 1880s fed by the flow of capital from London, and the crisis, while delayed, was part of the movement precipitated by the halt in that flow.

III

France was connected with the boom and crisis centered in London in 1889–93 in two plus respects, and disconnected in two others. The attempted copper corner, as noted, derived its inspiration partly from the diamond syndicate of 1882. Its analogue today is the attempted corner in silver by Bunker Hunt that collapsed in 1980 (Fay, 1982). The Société des Métaux, supported by the Comptoir d'Escompte, one of the leading deposit banks of the country, tried to buy copper worldwide at a price up to £70 a ton and hoped to sell it for more than £80. New mines opened up as the price rose, and old copper was reclaimed and sold to the syndicate. By March 1889 the syndicate's holdings amounted to 160,000 tons, its financial resources were exhausted, and the price was declining, reaching £38 in 1889 before recovering to £60 in 1890. Isaac Denfert-Rocherau, who was also connected with financing the Panama canal and with an unsuccessful attempt to lend to Russia (Kennan, 1979, p. 386), committed suicide. The Bank of France organized a syndicate to underwrite the liabilities of the Comptoir, providing a precedent, according to Pressnell, for the guarantees of liabilities organized by the Bank of England and Rothschild to rescue Baring Brothers the following year (1968, p. 205). It was widely noted that this behavior contrasted with that of the banking establishment of Paris when in 1882 they allowed the Union Générale, an outsider upstart bank, to fail (Bouvier, 1960, pp. 151–3).

One relatively independent source of crisis in France was the financing of the Panama canal project of De Lesseps. The Universal Panama Interoceanic Company was floated in December 1880 with a three-day stampede for shares. In a short time, 5,000 franc shares were selling for 380,000 francs. Success in digging a sea-level canal, however, proved elusive as costs kept rising, and the Company borrowed four times in the first six years. The first two issues were enormously successful, the second two found public interest drooping. The Company tried to revive investor interest with exotic issues. A straight lottery loan was refused authorization in 1886, and a substitute failed. A lottery loan was finally approved by a close vote in 1888, but that issue failed, and the company was forced to abandon the project. It was later revealed that enormous sums had been spent for publicity and bribing deputies. When the scandal was revealed in 1892, there was more financial turmoil in Paris markets. But the company had collapsed in 1889 (M. J. Simon, 1971).

The two other substantial French operations, one associated with the general financial crisis of the late 1880s and early 1890s and the other not, are surprisingly similar. Both involve Germany, and both involve recycling outstanding debt from one creditor to another. Both were also highly political. The first occurred when Bismarck sought to use financial weapons along with tariffs in cold war against Czarist Russia. In July 1887 Orphans Courts were forbidden to invest in Russian bonds; and in November a *Lombardverbot* instructed the Reichsbank to make no loans against the security of Russian bonds. But the prices of Russian bonds in Berlin did not fall substantially (Mai, 1970, p. 131). French investors were ready for economic and political reasons to buy Russian bonds in Berlin, to refund German issues of Russian bonds as they came due and to make new loans. In effect, German loans to Russia were recycled quietly, to the side of the financial crisis or crises, without major impact on other financial markets (Girault, 1973, 1977).

If one were to judge on the basis of lack of connection in the literature, the same would seem to have been the case in Italy. Here France backed away as the main lender, partly as a reaction to the Franco-Italian 'silent' tariff war of 1887, and Germany took over. There is no record of an explicit *Lombardverbot* as there had been in a similar episode in 1866 when the Bank of France refused to discount Italian loans for the Crédit Lyonnais and for a Paris banker, Erlanger (Gille, 1968, p. 190). But the German response was belated and intermittent, sometimes lead by Bleichröder, a private banker and Bismarck's confidant (Stern, 1977, pp. 432–4), and sometimes by Georg von Siemens of the Deutsche Bank (Helfferich, 1921–3/1956, pp. 125–8). A number of Turin banks had been speculating heavily in Roman real estate, and were squeezed when French borrowing stopped in 1887. The Banca Romana was then caught having violated its ceiling on note issues. French dumping of Italian foreign bonds in Paris in July 1889 led to the creation in September of that year of a German syndicate which provided 50 million lire in support of those bonds. The syndicate was organized by the Berliner Handelsgesellschaft and the Deutsche Bank, and in April 1890 by a group headed by Bleichröder (Luzzato, 1963, I, pp. 143–4). But support for Italian bonds in Paris helped France more than it did Italy, as recycling Russian debt from Germany to France helped Germany. In 1893 the Credito Mobiliaro and the Banca Generale collapsed under the weight of industrial loans, largely to the steel industry at Terni. New banks were started in 1894 with German help. The assistance was again limited as the German investors quickly sold out to French and Italian investors, but the initial stimulus this time was sufficient to lift Italian economic growth and activity until the new crisis in 1907.

I conclude that on balance Russian capital imports continued during the switch from German to French investing, but the Italian borrowing lapsed, as France turned away from lending to that country and Germany picked up the load only sporadically. While Italy is located in Europe, it was in financial terms, as Bonelli asserts with respect to 1907, a 'colonial country' at a time when 'colonial countries found themselves suddenly deprived of capital' (1971, p. 43).

Finally, it should be noted that France participated in the London–New York–Berlin–Paris group of connected financial markets in which a country in trouble could get help by selling securities abroad. This was especially the case with outstanding American securities, which were sold in New York by French during the copper-corner crisis in the summer of 1889, by British during the Baring crisis, and by German investors in November 1891 (M. Simon, 1955/1978, pp. 454, 473, 501). The 1890 financial crisis in the United States was entitled 'derivative' for such reasons (Sprague, 1910, p. 127). As the British dumped securities 7 to 9 percent below pre-panic levels, French sources reported that the British also sold huge quantities of US rails, both stocks and bonds, to Paris during the Baring crisis, with the Bank of England powerless to prevent the English investor from flooding the Paris market (Théry, 1908, quoted in Morgenstern, 1959, p. 526). This sort of distress selling is of course different from the anticipatory selling of Argentine bonds in the London market undertaken by Germans, as already mentioned.

I find little or no connection between the failure of two German banks in Berlin in November 1891, Bankhaus Hirschfeld u. Wolff and Friedlander und Sonnenfeld. These firms were not engaged in world trade, had only small depositors, and were totally different than the major D banks that operated worldwide. Their troubles doubtless came from the stock-market decline, which was worldwide. The stock-market index for domestic companies had dropped sharply from its high in December 1889 – the annual averages went from 126 in 1876 to 178 in 1889 and down to 149 in 1891 (Deutsche Bundesbank, 1976, p. 294). One banker was arrested after '60 years of Lucullan profligacy', and two brothers committed suicide (Kuczynski, 1961, ch. 3). Morgenstern's chart notes influences running from this Berlin panic to Paris and to Vienna (1959, Chart 72, p. 548).

The United States participated in international financial markets both as a major borrower for new issues and as a developed market in which other financial centers bought and sold existing securities. The crisis of 1890, as noted, derived from the second relationship and was an echo of European markets (mainly London) dumping good US securities in New York in order to be able to hold longer on to their speculative Latin American, South African, and Australian issues. The panic of 1893 was more like those of the periphery. In the first place, there had been a land boom akin to those in Argentina and Australia, largely concentrated in the Southern states (Sprague, 1910, p. 161). Excessive expansion had been undertaken by railroads, especially the Philadelphia and Reading and the Erie, and by the National Cordage Company, which paid a 100 percent stock dividend in January, but went into receivership in May. The Sherman Silver Purchase Act of 1890 led to fears that the country would be drained of gold and led to short-term capital withdrawals. Overall, the banking system of the country was fragile, with frequent panics occurring in the fall when credit was taut in order to move the crops, and when neither the Treasury (Taus, 1943) nor the money market banks had developed adequate monetary techniques to cope with the shortage. In 1873, 1884, and 1890, the Treasury had given aid to the money market by issuing more notes. In 1893, its position was endangered by the acquisition of silver and loss of gold, so that it added to rather than lessened the pressure. It is perhaps going too far to claim that the 1893 crisis in the United States was an integral part of the broad world financial crisis of 1888–93, but it would probably have been mitigated if credit conditions had been easier in Europe and the decline in new issues floated in Britain for North America had not been so sharp (see Table 1).

Having connected up so much of the world in a single financial crisis, a puzzle is provided by two countries, Canada and New Zealand, which, in spite of their similarities with South Africa, Argentina, Brazil, Chile, and Australia, were not connected with the 1893 crisis. Both were members of the Empire and both were regions of recent settlement. Both, moreover, participated in financial booms and crises on a large scale at other times, New Zealand in the period 1860–80 and Canada later, from 1904 to 1913 when it borrowed on the order of £300 million from London (Viner, 1924). New Zealand was a 'dependent economy' *par excellence*, the term having been applied to it relatively early (Simkin, 1951). New Zealand suffered from the Baring crisis, but did not enjoy the boom that preceded it, borrowing not even enough to pay the service on its earlier contracted debt. Its land boom had collapsed earlier, about 1880, and its credit position in London was poor, with no contagion coming from mining, railroads, or land in South Africa, Latin America and Australia. On the contrary, in the late 1880s, the Australian banks in New Zealand utilized funds there to feed the Australian boom (*ibid.*, ch. x).

The Canadian delay is more puzzling. One explanation is that the country was ice-bound half the year before the railroad connections with the United States, and direct access to Montreal was still blocked in 1904 when the investment boom of the sort earlier enjoyed by Argentina and Australia took place (Hall, 1963, p. 162). A further hypothesis, perhaps worth mention, is that the boom in international lending by London running from 1904 to 1913 would have resulted in another crisis, comparable to the Baring episode of 1890, had not the outbreak of war supervened to produce a crisis of a different sort. The crisis from 1888 to 1893 produced a depression that lasted to 1895 or 1896. It helps explain why the gold discoveries of California and Australia produced an immediate boom in the 1850s, whereas the 1886 discovery of the

Rand did not result in world monetary expansion for a decade. There are two critical counterfactual questions: whether a conscious effort on the part of London to stabilize lending rather than to halt it would have moderated the cycle, and whether a lender of last resort would have helped with or without stabilized British lending.

The fact is, of course, that the Bank of England operated the gold standard on a narrow margin, and shot bank rate up to 6 percent in December 1889 and again after the Baring crisis in December 1890. The lesson Goschen drew from the incident was that the London banks needed more reserves and less dependence on the Bank (Pressnell, 1968).

The Bank of France and the State Bank of Russia did come to the aid of the Bank of England as lenders of last resort for the pivot wheel of the world financial system. The Bank of France advanced £3 million in gold and the State Bank of Russia £1.5 million. In addition the State Bank of Russia agreed not to withdraw its deposit of £2.4 million. But this aid for the Bank of England did nothing to stabilize lending or to provide new loans for the periphery – for Argentina, Brazil, South Africa, the United States (in which J. P. Morgan rescued the US Treasury with gold).

In the USA children play a game called 'snap-the-whip'; a long line of children hold hands and run, and then one end stops. Centrifugal force leads the children at the other end to go faster and faster and then spin off into space. The surge of lending from 1886 to 1889 and its sudden stop in 1890 closely resembled that game.

References

Baster, A. S. J. (1929), *The Imperial Banks* (London: P. S. King).

Bonelli, F. (1971), *La crisi del 1907: una tappa dello sviluppo industriale in Italia* (Turin: Einaudi).

Boehm, E. A. (1971), *Prosperity and Depression in Australia, 1887–1897* (Oxford: Clarendon Press).

Bouvier, J. (1960), *Le Krach de l'Union Générale, 1878–1885* (Paris: Prenes universitaires de France).

Butlin, S. J. (1961), *Australia and New Zealand Bank, the Bank of Australasia and the Union Bank of Australia, Limited* (Croydon, Australia: Longmans, Green).

Cairncross, A. K. (1953), *Home and Foreign Investment, 1870–1913: Studies in Capital Accumulation* (Cambridge: Cambridge University Press).

Calogeras, J. P. (1910), *La Politique monétaire du Brazil* (Rio de Janeiro: Imprimerie National).

Clapham, Sir John (1945), *The Bank of England: A History* (Cambridge: Cambridge University Press, 2 vols).

Cottrell, P. L. (1980), *Industrial Finance, 1830–1914* (London: Methuen).

Deutsche Bundesbank (1976), *Deutsches Geld- und Bankwesen in Zahlen, 1876–1975* (Frankfurt-am-Main: Fritz Knapp).

Edelstein, M. (1982), *Overseas Investment in the Age of High Imperialism: The United Kingdom, 1850–1914* (New York: Columbia University Press).

Fay, S. (1982), *Beyond Greed* (New York: Viking).

Ferns. H. S. (1960), *Britain and Argentina in the Nineteenth Century* (Oxford: Clarendon).

Fetter, F. W. (1931), *Monetary Inflation in Chile* (Princeton, NJ: Princeton University Press).

Ford, A. G. (1962), *The Gold Standard, 1880–1914: Britain and Argentina* (Oxford: Clarendon).

Franco, G. H. B. (1982), 'Reforma monetaria e instabilidade durante a transico republicana', unpublished thesis, Department of Economics, Catholic University of Rio de Janeiro, July.

Frankel, S. H. (1938/1969), *Capital Investment in Africa: its Course and Effects* (London: Oxford University Press); reprint edn (New York: Howard Fertig).

Gille, B. (1968), *Les Investissements français en Italie (1815–1914)* (Turin: ILTE).

Girault, R. (1973), *Emprunts russes et investissements français en Russie, 1887–1914* (Paris: Colin).

Girault, R. (1977), 'Investissements et placements français en Russie, 1880–1914', in M. Lévy-Leboyer (ed.), *La Position internationale de la France* (Paris: Editions de l'Ecole des Hautes Etudes en Sciences Sociales).

Hall, A. R. (1963), *The London Capital Market and Australia, 1870–1914* (Canberra: ANV Social Science Monograph No. 21).

Helfferich, K. (1956), *Georg von Siemens: Ein Lebensbild aus Deutschlands großer Zeit*, revised and shortened edition of the 1921–23 three-volume work (Krefeld: Serpe).

Hobson, C. K. (1914), *The Export of Capital* (London: Constable).

Jones, C. (1977), 'Commercial Bank and Mortgage Companies', in D. C. M. Platt (ed.), *Business Imperialism 1840–1930: An Inquiry Based on British Experience in Latin America* (Oxford: Clarendon Press).

Joslin, D. (1963), *A Century of Banking in Latin America* (London: Oxford University Press).

Kennan, G. F. (1979), *The Decline of Bismarck's European Order: Franco–Russian Relations, 1875–1890* (Princeton, NJ: Princeton University Press).

Kuczynski, J. (1961), *Studien zur Geschichte der zyklischen Überproduktions-krisen in Deutschland, 1873–1914* (Berlin: Akademie Verlag).

Lauck, W. J. (1907), *The Causes of the Panic of 1893* (Boston, Mass.: Houghton Mifflin).

Luzzatto, G. (1963), *L'Economia italiana dal 1861 al 1914*. Vol. I: *1861–1894* (Milan: Banca Commerciale Italiana).

Macrosty, H. W. (1927), article in *Journal of Royal Statistical Society*.

Mai, J. (1970), *Das deutsche Kapital in Rußland, 1850–1894* (Berlin: VEB Deutsche Verlag).

Mathias, P. (1969), *The First Industrial Nation* (London: Methuen).

Mitchell, B. R. (1978), *European Historical Statistics, 1750–1950*, abridged edn (New York: Columbia University Press).

Morgenstern, O. (1959), *International Financial Transactions and Business Cycles* (Princeton, NJ: Princeton University Press, for the National Bureau of Economic Research).

O'Brien, T. F. (1982), *The Nitrate Industry and Chile's Crucial Transition. 1870–1891* (New York: New York University Press).

Pressnell, L. S. (1968), 'Gold Reserves, Banking Reserves and the Baring Crisis of 1890', in C. R. Whittlesey and J. S. G. Wilson (eds), *Essays in Money and Banking in Honour of R. S. Sayers* (Oxford: Clarendon).

Pressnell, L. S. (1982), 'The Sterling System and Financial Crisis before 1914', in C. P. Kindleberger and J. P. Laffargue (eds), *Financial Crises: Theory, History and Policy* (Cambridge and Paris: Cambridge University Press and Editions de la Maison des Sciences de l'Homme), pp. 148–64.

Schumpeter, J. A. (1939), *Business Cycles: A Theoretical. Historical, and*

Statistical Analysis of the Capitalist Process (New York: McGraw Hill).

Simkin, C. G. F. (1951), *The Instability of a Dependent Economy. Economic Fluctuations in New Zealand, 1840–1914* (Oxford: Oxford University Press).

Simon, M. (1955/1978), 'Cyclical Fluctuations and the International Capital Movements of the United States, 1865–1895', doctoral dissertation Columbia University; published (New York: Arno).

Simon, M. (1967/1968), 'The Pattern of New British Portfolio Foreign Investment, 1865–1914', in J. H. Adler (ed.), *Capital Movements and Economic Development* (London: Macmillan); reprinted in A. R. Hall (ed.), *The Export of Capital from Britain, 1870–1914* (London: Methuen).

Simon, M. J. (1971), *The Panama Affair* (New York: Charles Scribners Sons).

Spinner, T. J., Jr (1973), *George Joachim Goschen: The Transformation of a Victorian Liberal* (Cambridge: Cambridge University Press).

Sprague, O. M. W. (1910/1978), *History of Crises under the National Banking System*, reprint edn (New York: Kelley).

Stern, F. (1977), *Gold and Iron: Bismarck, Bleichröder and the Building of the German Empire* (London: Allen & Unwin).

Taus, E. R. (1943), *Central Banking Functions of the United States Treasury, 1789–1941* (New York: Columbia University Press).

Théry, E. (1908), *Les Progrès économiques de la France* (Paris: Economiste européen).

Viner, J. (1924), *Canada's Balance of International Indebtedness, 1900–1913, An Inductive Study in the Theory of International Trade* (Cambridge, Mass.: Harvard University Press).

White, H. D. (1933), *The French International Accounts, 1880–1913* (Cambridge, Mass.: Harvard University Press).

Wileman, J. P. (1896), *Brazilian Exchange: The Study of an Inconvertible Currency* (Buenos Aires: Galli Brothers).

Williams, J. H. (1920), *Argentine International Trade under Inconvertible Paper Money, 1880–1900* (Cambridge, Mass.: Harvard University Press).

Williams, J. H. (1922), 'German Foreign Trade and the Reparation Payments', *Quarterly Journal of Economics*, vol. 36.

Wirth, M. (1893), 'The Crisis of 1890', *Journal of Political Economy*, vol. I, no. 2 (March), pp. 214–356.

Youngson, A. J. (1960), *The British Economy, 1920–1957* (London: Allen & Unwin).

15

Sweden in 1850 as an 'Impoverished Sophisticate': Comment

Lars G. Sandberg has twice in the *Journal of Economic History* described Sweden in the middle of the nineteenth century as an 'impoverished sophisticate', whose institutions and stock of human capital were well in advance of its income per capita as compared with other countries in Continental Europe (1978, 1979). The term 'impoverished sophisticate' may be questioned for the adjective, which suggests a dynamic process of falling income, whereas prior to 1850 Swedish income was not growing rapidly as it was in later decades, but had been sustained by the introduction of the potato. This note is directed, however, to the question of the sophistication of Swedish financial institutions, prior to the rapid development of banking in all countries of Europe in the 1850s and 1860s. I have no question on education or literacy.

Sandberg is sometimes hesitant to be precise as to whether he is characterizing Sweden as sophisticated in 1850 or 1870[1] There can be no dispute about the latter date. Rapid export-led growth in the 1850s and 1860s contributed vigorous stimulation to the founding of credit institutions, beginning with the Stockholms Enskilda Bank in 1856 and continuing with the joint-stock banks of the early 1860s. The issue for 1850 is of moment because of the Coase theorem, which maintains that institutions spring into place as needed (Coase, 1939). There can of course be institutional borrowing in advance of demand, notably in political science where constitution-writing patterned after other countries and bicameral legislatures have sprung up early in newly independent countries, and even in finance where Kemmerers, H. Parker Willises, and Triffins have produced central banks in many countries in advance of the country's capacity for its effective use. The demonstration effect in consumption, first noted perhaps by Ragnar Nurkse (1953), is familiar. But financial innovation in advance of need on a wide front would constitute, along with the lag postulated by the school of institutionalists, a counter example to the Coase theorem.

Designation of Sweden in 1850 as sophisticated raises a question primarily because so many writers on the subject take the view that the Swedish banking and credit system prior to 1850 was antiquated.

Reprinted with permission from The Journal of Economic History, *vol. 42, no. 4 (December 1982), pp. 918–20.*

Heckscher, for example, finds it illuminating that when banks appeared they were likely to seek the assistance of the trading houses, rather than vice versa. He goes on to say that Swedish trading houses were far inferior to the leading houses in the principal countries of Europe (1954, p. 245). Joint-stock companies were not accepted until the late date of 1895 (*ibid.*, p. 247). Banking history in Sweden was essentially that of the Riksbank. Its contribution to commercial credit, moreover, was highly limited. There was no such thing as a capital market (*ibid.*). There was no such thing as a credit market (*ibid.*, p. 249).

Fridlizius, studying the financing of the export trade in grain – largely oats for the horses of Britain – notes that Sweden at mid-century belonged to the underdeveloped areas of Europe with a weak money market (1957, p. 266). Credit from Swedish sources was unimportant because banking was underdeveloped (*ibid.*, pp. 205, 207). Söderlund states that the money market in the middle of the nineteenth century had 'only a very primitive form of organization' (1952, p. 198). Samuelsson asks why it took so long for a modern banking system to reach Sweden (1968). A general historian writing on Scandinavia as a whole calls the national banks of the area 'limited in their functions and obsolete in their techniques', despite the fact that they were the most important banking institutions in Scandinavia until the founding of the large private banks in the 1850s. The policy of self-supply in agriculture explains 'why it was possible for the Scandinavian countries to do without a modern credit system during the first half of the century' (Hovde, 1943/1972, pp. 241–2). An earlier student writes that change in the financial structure of Sweden was first evident in the 1850s and 1860s and made increasing headway in later decades (Montgomery, 1939, p. 126).

Some ambiguous support to the Sandberg position is offered by Gasslander's account of the early years of the Stockholms Enskilda Bank (SEB). He notes first that Sven Brisman attacked Theodor Frölander's account of the founding of the bank, which followed the traditional view outlined in the previous paragraphs, and maintains that Swedish banking had not reached a very advanced state of development by the 1850s when it was entirely changed by the foundation of the SEB (1962, p. 7). The same changes occurred in Sweden that took place throughout Europe in the 1850s, following the example of the Crédit Mobilier, which made it possible to attract long-term deposits for use in dealings in bonds and foreign exchange. Gasslander stresses the continuity of the system through the 1850s. The founding of the SEB combined the solidarity and established practices of the old system with methods derived from the active business life after 1850 (*ibid.*, p. 21).

In support of his position, Sandberg makes a number of points about Swedish financial sophistication that deserve attention. The first is that Sweden is the oldest country in Europe, bar none, to have the continuous circulation of banknotes. This was innovation, not imitation, and had its origin in the very primitive form of Swedish copper money (the state owned the largest copper mine in Europe, Stora Kopparberg, at Falun). The copper standard introduced by Gustavus

Adolphus in 1625 was a serious inconvenience because of the weight of metal needed for ordinary payments. A 10 Rixdaler slab weighed 19.7 kilograms. Any sizeable sum of money needed wagons for transport, and burglars could not steal the money because they could not lift it (Heckscher, 1954, pp. 88–90). It is true, as Sandberg says, that there was no lasting aversion to paper notes as was the case in France after John Law and the *assignats*.

The next innovation was the so-called discount banks. Sandberg states that these go back to the 1770s. My version of Flux, whom Sandberg cites as authority, records that the first such bank was established in Gothenburg in 1802, the second the following year in Malmö. Their purpose was to spread the circulation of credit obtained from the Riksbank. They failed to contribute to the institutional pattern of 1850 because they went in for excessive issues during the Napoleonic War and had all failed by 1817 (Flux, 1910, p. 23).

Then came the *enskilda* (private) banks, formed according to Sandberg on the inspiration of the Scottish joint-stock banks. The law authorizing them was passed in 1824, and the first bank under it was established in 1831. They grew up in the country far from business centers, and, as Gasslander observes, their 'dealings could hardly be said to be termed credit operations, but were more in the nature of a note-issuing monopoly (1962, p. 10). A second bank was established in 1832, a third in 1835, and three more (bringing the total to six) in 1837. There followed a gap of ten years before the seventh and eighth were founded, in 1847 and 1848. Flux asserts that the 'slowness with which the new institutions were created would seem to suggest that the development of the country did not call very urgently for a widespread system of bank offices' (1910, p. 2). Their note issue did grow rapidly, however, and by 1850 accounted for almost one-third of total banknotes in circulation (Sandberg, 1978, Table 2, p. 661).

Neither the discount houses nor the *enskilda* banks played a large role in the rapid expansion of exports of iron, timber, and grain, which formed the backbone of rapid Swedish growth in the 1850s and 1860s after the repeal of the Corn Laws, the Timber duties, and the Navigation Acts in Britain in 1846–1851. These trades were financed by merchant houses, located mainly in Stockholm and Gothenberg, and these depended in turn on foreign credit (see especially, Fridlizius, 1957; Söderlund, 1952).[2] A number of merchant houses were of British origin, one or two were Norwegian or German. The system was loosely organized and flexible (Gasslander, 1962, p. 11). It illustrates the Coase theorem well. But it can hardly be said that it was sophisticated. By the 1860s a new set of institutions was called for and was forthcoming.

Notes

1 'Sweden's relatively very sophisticated system of financial institutions, in 1850 or 1870, meant . . . This stock of knowledge about and general acceptance of modern financial institutions and procedures greatly facilitated their rapid expansion during the period of speedy economic growth after 1850' (Sandberg, 1979, p. 232).

2 The financing of iron exports by Gothenburg dealers lending to ironmasters is discussed in Adamson (1968), esp. pp. 54, 76, 94.

References

Adamson, Rolf (1968), 'Finance and Marketing in the Swedish Iron Industry, 1800–1860', *Scandinavian Economic History Review*, vol. 16, no. 1.

Coase, Ronald H. (1939), 'The Nature of the Firm', *Economica*, n.s., vol. 4, pp. 386–405.

Flux, A. W. (1910), *The Swedish Banking System* (Washington, DC: US Government Printing Office).

Fridlizius, Gunnar (1957), *Swedish Corn Exports in the Free Trade Era. Patterns in the Oats Trade, 1850–1880* (Lund: CWK Gleerup).

Gasslander, Olle (1962), *History of the Stockholms Enskilda Banks to 1914* (Stockholm: privately printed).

Heckscher, Eli K. (1954), *An Economic History of Sweden*, translated from the Swedish original by Goran Ohlin (Cambridge, Mass.: Harvard University Press).

Hovde, B. J. (1943/1972), *The Scandinavian Countries, 1720–1865: The Rise of the Middle Classes*, reprint edn (Port Washington, NY: Kennikat).

Montgomery, Arthur G. (1939), *The Rise of Modern Industry in Sweden* (London: P. S. King).

Nurkse, Ragnar (1953), *Problems of Capital Formation of Underdeveloped Countries* (Oxford: Blackwell).

Samuelsson, Kurt (1968), *From Great Power to Welfare State* (London: Allen & Unwin).

Sandberg, Lars G. (1978), 'Banking and Economic Growth in Sweden before World War I', *Journal of Economic History*, vol. 38 (September), pp. 650–80.

Sandberg, Lars G. (1979), 'The Case of the Impoverished Sophisticate: Human Capital and Swedish Economic Growth before World War I', *Journal of Economic History*, vol. 39 (March), pp. 225–41.

Söderlund, E. F. (1952), *Swedish Timber Exports, 1850–1950. A History of the Swedish Timber Trade Edited for the Swedish Wood Exporters Association* (Uppsala: Almquist & Wicksells).

Part V

The Twentieth Century

16

A Structural View of the German Inflation

German inflation after World War I is rapidly becoming, like the French Revolution, a classic historical conundrum, useful because it allows ample scope for teaching undergraduates and training scholars in the complexity of social events, and furnishes a virtually infinite range for further monographic research and magisterial syntheses. Like British long-term lending to Canada from 1896 to 1913, the historical analysis is rewritten with each succeeding generation. If the German inflation achieves equal status in history, economic history, and economic analysis, it will be largely attributable to the entrepreneurial dynamism of Professors Feldman, Holtfrerich, Ritter, and Witt who have created a new industry around the problem, with workshops and meetings, an outpouring of articles, monographs, and books. On the economic side, the National Bureau of Economic Research and the University of Chicago economics department and *Journal of Political Economy* contribute to the deluge as theories of monetarism, rational expectations, bubbles, efficient markets, rigorous purchasing-power parity and the like are measured against the somewhat spotty data of the episode.

If one were to read the entire literature on the French Revolution, that convulsive event would seem to be overdetermined. There are more independent variables than are necessary to explain the dependent variables, more equations than there are unknowns. Different schools of thought have developed encompassing theories: Marxists on the *sans-culottes*, historians and economic historians on peasant–noble relationships in agriculture, on bourgeois energy, which found it imperative to burst the restraints of the *ancien régime*, the resistance to change of the *financiers* in tax farming and handling government expenditure. The significance of the socio-political matrix to historic outcomes is illustrated in this last connection by the fact that a 'financial revolution' was accomplished peacefully in England after the Glorious Revolution of 1688 (Dickson, 1967), but required the guillotining of 28 *financiers* and *officiers* in France before the handling of governmental finances could be transformed from private enterprise into a bureaucratic governmental function (Bosher, 1970; Chaussinand-Nogaret, 1970, p.

Reprinted with permission from G. D. Feldman, C.-L. Holtfrerich, G. A. Ritter and P.-C. Witt (eds), Die Erfahrung der Inflation im internationalen Zusammenhang und Vergleich *(Berlin: Walter de Gruyter, 1984), pp. 10–33.*

315). Like German inflation, moreover, it is likely that the forces responsible for the convulsion were not necessarily its beneficiaries. In one usual view, the peasants led the way, and the middle class reaped the major gains. What is significant for our purposes, however, is the energy and verve that go into the study of this historical event now almost 200 years old. My historian-daughter tells me that the eighteenth century is the century of choice within French historiography and the French Revolution the central topic in that century.

Another analogy: true believers come to the French Revolution with a strong *a priori* position, seeking support in the uprising for a theory of social forces developed primarily by deduction. I refer of course to the Marxists who ascribe *causa causans* to the lumpen proletariat of the city, the *sans-culottes*, in the face of profound scepticism over the importance of this role on the part of the vast majority of mainstream scholars. So, too, the monetarist school of the University of Chicago, which has now spilled well beyond the confines of that city, comes to German inflation with what Melvin Reder (1982, esp. p. 11) calls 'strong priors' – a belief in the centrality of the quantity theory of money, the efficiency of markets, rational expectations, purchasing-power parity, etc. Reder notes that the analyst with strong priors requires his findings to be consistent with his theory. When an apparent inconsistency is encountered, it is treated as anomalous and as requiring either (1) re-examination of the data to produce new material that will reverse the finding; (2) redefinition or augmentation of the variables of the model; or (3) placing the finding on the research agenda as a researchable anomaly. Only *in extremis*, and as a last resort, will the researcher with strong priors consider an alteration of the theory.

The problem of German inflation from 1914 to 1923 has developed at least three more-or less distinct schools with many combinations and compromises among them. Economists, both at the time and today, generally fall into either the monetarist or the balance-of-payment camp, the former sometimes called the purchasing-power-parity school. Monetarists take money creation and destruction as central to inflation and deflation, and tend to believe in a fairly short-run adherence of economies to the quantity theory of money that says that prices vary positively with the current and expected money supply, and to the purchasing-power-parity doctrine that holds that, with flexible exchange rates, the value of a country's currency will measure with a high degree of accuracy the relative extent of its current and expected internal inflation. The balance-of-payments school, on the other hand, maintains that exchange rates may be determined by independent movements affecting the balance of payments, and changes in rates feed back on the price level and on the money supply. On occasion, the rise in prices will lead to increases in wages which require the issue of more money to avoid unemployment. Monetarists find this anathema. With efficient markets, industrialists cannot raise prices and labor unions cannot raise wages. All inflation rests on excessive expansion of the money supply.

It is of some interest that the controversy between the monetarist and balance-of-payments schools which has been underway over the German episode since immediately after World War I is the exact replica of the argument between the Currency School and the Banking School in England almost a century earlier (Fetter, 1965). Monetarism was represented by the Currency School, led initially by David Ricardo, afterwards by Lord Overstone, which held that the agio on gold during the period of suspension of the gold standard – virtually the same as exchange depreciation of sterling – was the consequence of the excessive issue of banknotes by the Bank of England. The Banking School, which emerged under the intellectual leadership of Thomas Tooke, a 'Russian merchant' and insurance leader, ascribed the depreciation to a series of independent events adversely affecting the British balance of payments, viz. bad harvests requiring inordinately large imports of food, the Continental blockade of Napoleon, which cut off British export markets, and the necessity to provide military subsidies to such Allies as Prussia, Austria, Russia, Portugal and Spain. The expansion of bank-notes took place in response to the requirements of trade – the so-called 'real-bills' doctrine to which the Banking School subscribed – and was thought (erroneously) therefore to have had no effect on prices. In this view the agio (depreciation) was autonomous and led to price increases that increased the value of goods moving in trade and thus justified expansion of the money supply.

In the German case, the monetarist school – notably Bresciani-Turroni (1937) and, in contemporary time, Phillip Cagan (1956) – blame the inflation principally on the budget deficit and its financing by short-term debt sold to banks that enlarged the money supply, whereas the balance-of-payments school – Karl Helfferich (Williamson, 1971, pp. 383–4), Moritz Bonn (1922), Frank D. Graham (1930), and John H. Williams (Malamud, 1983) – placed the emphasis on exchange depreciation of the mark set in motion by the short-term need to restock the German economy with raw materials on the one hand and the long-term necessity to pay reparations on the other. Third and fourth independent sources of early exchange depreciation after the release of exchange control and a fixed rate in September 1919 were the insistence of German iron and steel industry in paying off its debts to Sweden for wartime purchases of iron ore in order to be able to buy more – a factor which could be subsumed under restocking – and an outflow of German capital (Feldman, 1977, pp. 93ff, 140ff; Bresciani-Turroni, 1937, p. 56).

There is an impoitant difference between the British inflation at the end of the Napoleonic Wars and the German inflation after World War I. The latter exploded; the former did not. In 1819 and in 1925, Britain returned to the prewar gold price, at some cost (Kindleberger, 1982). German inflation has to be divided into two phases: the initial substantial inflation to about June 1922 and a hyperinflation which followed. Even confirmed monetarists recognize the necessity for this distinction. In his initial study, Cagan (1956) stopped his statistical investigation at July 1923 when the hyperinflation began to climax. In a recent article, however, Flood and Garber (1980) of the monetarist persuasion seek to demonstrate that the later period was not a 'bubble' in the sense that increases in the price level led to further increases in the price level. I shall return to the question of dividing up the period into segments later. At the moment, I assert that, despite Flood and Garber's inability to reject the hypothesis that the peak of hyperinflation was not the result of money issues, it is not self-evident that a single theory can cover the entire process of inflation.

There is a third possible school not discussed in the classic economic literature, although there are hints of it in Laursen and Pedersen (1964) (and Helfferich) who blame labor for raising real wages when depreciation of the mark started to lower them. Elements of a sort that may be called 'structural' can be incorporated into the balance-of-payments theory as a step between depreciation and the rise in international prices on the one hand, and the increase in the money supply on the other. But the theory may be viewed as more general. Mancur Olson, Jr. has extended his *Logic of Collective Action* (1965) in a new work entitled *The Rise and Decline of Nations: Economic Growth, Stagflation and Social Rigidities* (1982), which, while it does not discuss the case of the German inflation of 1923, can be applied to it. The thesis is that, in a society where various interests – called 'distributional coalitions' – fight for a greater share of national income in order to gain the lion's share on any increase in income, or more usually in order to avoid bearing a significant portion of a loss, inflation is a likely outcome. Olson's new book applies the theory largely to growth and lack of growth, but does spend a considerable amount of time on stagflation in the United States, where his theory produces a model with a strong family resemblance to the sociological theory of Fred Hirsch and John Goldthorpe in *The Political Economy of Inflation* (1978) and the 'core inflation' theory of Otto Eckstein (1981). In the German post-World War I setting, agriculture, industry and labour – and especially subgroups within these broad aggregates – clashed over which group or groups were to bear the burdens of destruction, with its immediate loss of income, and of reparations.

The theory of structural inflation is of course not new with Olson. An early analyst with a model along these lines was Henri Aujac (1950) who ascribed inflation after World War II in France to the fact that agriculture, industry and labor all had market power and all were determined to resist having the burden of reconstruction imposed on them. Agriculture resists by raising prices, which increases the cost of living. This leads to a demand for higher wages, perhaps supported by strikes, which induces industrialists to raise the price of manufactured goods. If government is included in the model it is obliged to raise taxes in order to keep real spending unchanged. The rise in taxes and in industrial prices sets off new increases in farm prices and a new round. In an open economy, higher prices lead to import surpluses, which typically induce exchange depreciation, raising traded-goods prices (the prices of exports and imports), and stimulating agriculture, labor, and non-traded-goods producers to push up their prices and wages. The model has been developed especially for Latin America by Albert Hirschman (1963, esp. pp. 208ff) and David Felix (essays in Hirschman, 1961, pp. 81–94, 95–124).

The structural model is connected with monetarism and with budget deficits in a number of ways. If the government fails to raise taxes but rather runs a deficit, this is inflationary unless it is financed by real savings. If it is financed by short-term debt placed with the banking system, it can be argued that the inflation is monetary. But this assumes that the government or central bank has a free range of choice, and finances the deficit through the banking system only because it made a mistake in economic policy, based perhaps on erroneous theories. The structural school would deny this. Raising taxes calls for an explicit political set of decisions on how to allocate the burden, and each group on which a significant tax may fall may either defeat the tax by the exercise of political power or render its effects nugatory economically by raising prices or wages to make up for it. Or in the case of industry, monetarists would claim that manufacturers would be unable to pay higher wages and raise prices unless the banking system provided them with additional credit, so that here again a rise of prices and wages can occur only if the banking system, including the central bank, makes the mistake of not holding down the supply of high-powered money and letting the increased demand raise interest rates until savings rise or other spending is reduced, or some combination of the two. Again it is assumed that the banking system has free will, in contrast to the structural assumption that central bankers are endogenous and are forced to respond in particular ways by the pressures of the system.

Mistakes are possible, to be sure. Karl Helfferich, as Secretary of the Reich Treasury during the war, clung to a theory of war finance widely held as far back as Jacques Necker, but now recognized as untenable, that if the budget is balanced it is not inflationary, and that it is sufficient to balance ordinary receipts, including in the former, service on the debt incurred to finance the extraordinary budget including military expenditure (Williamson, 1971, pp. 23–5; see also Harris, 1979, pp. 123–4). Monetarists are right in regarding acceptance of such a theory as a serious mistake. But, to the extent that Helfferich refused to balance the overall budget because he did not want to tax company profits or to levy income taxes on the rich as the Socialists desired, the resultant inflation can more properly be regarded as structural, arising from the inability of society to agree on how to bear the burden of the war (Williamson, 1971, pp. 129–41). After the hostilities, the tax reforms of Erzberger were sabotaged by the propertied classes. There were mistakes, to be sure, in the long lags allowed between levying and payment, but compliance was minimal and capital flight to escape taxation took place on an important scale. After the London ultimatum of May 1921 there was a 'violent' debate on taxation (Bresciani-Turroni, 1937, p. 57; Epstein, 1959, ch. 9). This was complicated to be sure by the reluctance of many groups to pay reparations to France (in sharp contrast to the attitude of the French in 1871 and 1872 when national pride united all groups in paying off the Franco-Prussian indemnity well ahead of schedule). But it would be a mistake to call the inflation of the period monetary if this implied that there was a monetary choice to be taken – by experts in a vacuum – that would have avoided the inflation.

Among the other mistakes of the Social Democratic/Center Party Coalition if one focuses narrowly on inflation was the initial reluctance to raise interest rates for fear of unemployment, though historians today are beginning to regard that as a virtue as they contemplate the deflationary troubles of the United States and the United Kingdom in 1920–21 (Feldman, 1983), and the real-bills doctrine of the Reichsbank in June 1922 when it was discounting commercial bills at a sharply increasing rate during the credit squeeze, although recent work by Holtfrerich on Reichsbank sources suggests that the directors knew what they were doing and made their choice deliberately (1980, pp. 71–2, 307–8). One can add the disregard of the quantity theory of money which is valid in the long run, even though it may not be helpful in shaping short-run policy. Wirth, the Center Party prime minister, on the other hand, is regarded as stupid (Williamson, 1971, p. 347).

With mistakes, it is necessary for the accusor to specify the counter-factual, i.e. what would have happened if a different course had been followed. Was an optimal or even better policy possible or were there forces blocking that route so that the choice basically lay between the 5th, 6th, or 7th-best policies, or perhaps between the 4th best and the 7th best. Note that contemporaries are recorded frequently as having been highly critical of the policies followed, but on many occasions with nothing positive to offer as an alternative.[1] Or the Reichsbank and the government would each call on the other to take the appropriate action, as in the case today in the United States between the Treasury and the Federal Reserve System.

If one moves out from Germany alone to Germany and France together, the balance-of-payments theory can also be brought under the structural umbrella. If one aggregates Germany and France, it is clear that no peaceful compromise was possible to the reparations problem. Occupation of the Ruhr in January 1923 by France and Belgium was the violent unsuccessful method to resolve the impasse. The problem was where – in France or in Germany – to assign the burden of recon-structing northwest France. Rathenau and Loucheur had agreed on a form of reparations in kind with German workers building in France, but this was rejected by the French building unions (Sauvy, 1965, p. 140). Loucheur said 'If I told the French the truth, they would kill me' (*ibid.*, p. 148).

Monetarists scorn the idea of structural inflation. Firstly they deny that any group has market power. In Reder's list of tight priors is included 'No capacity to affect prices'. Moreover, monetarists insist that if such an increase in prices were to take place, it could be stopped by central-bank refusal to expand the money supply in the amounts necessary to validate a price increase. Since the velocity of money moves only narrowly, this would mean that an attempt to raise prices or wages would induce unemployment which would halt inflation. Industrialists or labor or agriculture or government cannot raise prices or wages if the money supply is held steady. Money is a handle on the economy. It is exogenous. Mistakes occur but are errors of analysis or of judgement, or result from weaknesses of will or character. The structural-inflation school claims rather that politicians are endogenous and behave in predictable ways, responding to the explicit situation, and virtually certain to be dismissed from office if they try to behave like strict monetarists. There is, on this score, limited scope for monetary choice.

In the structural-inflation model a good deal depends upon the nature of the underlying society, something on which historians dilate, but economists, political scientists and even macro-sociologists, apart from few like Dahrendorf and Crozier, do not. In this view the fact that the British achieved the financial revolution peacefully and the French shed blood a century later to accomplish the same transformation is not a random accident but an outcome shaped by national character – a weak concept and one virtually impossible to incorporate in a mathematical model, but nevertheless one which on occasion is critical.[2]

German democracy was notoriously weak, that country having failed to overcome autocracy in the abortive revolution of 1848. Moreover the economy was strongly prone to cartel formation from at least 1880. Different groups did not trust one another. Worse, there was often hatred, both for individuals such as Erzberger, Helfferich, Rathenau, etc., and for large groups such as the Jews, accused of responsibility for German defeat through the stab in the back. David Felix's (the historian not the economist) book on Rathenau has a chapter on 'The Tendency to Acts of Violence' (1971, ch. 9). The end of one period in the inflation was marked by the Kapp Putsch, followed at the end of the hyper-inflation in November 1923 by Hitler's Beer Hall Putsch. The extreme right wing of the Nationalist party was said not to be *koalitionsfähig*, lacking the ability to make the compromises necessary to work with other parties (Williamson, 1971, p. 368). One aspect of the violence in addition to the Putsches was the series of assassinations – of Rosa Luxemburg, Liebknecht, Eisner, Erzberger, and Rathenau, the last two perhaps partly stimulated by the extravagance of the political attacks on them by Helfferich. The assassination of Rathenau marked a turning point in the rate of inflation as it changed expectations about the exchange rate, the capital flow, and hence changed the rate of exchange depreciation. There seems to be a distinct ideological difference between the American assassinations and attempted assassinations of 1963 to 1981 from those of post-World-War-I Germany – though the writer's competence in the area is minimal. In the American case the attempts seemed to stem from psychological disorders – although there remains a possibility that that of John F. Kennedy had an international political element. Those of Germany in 1919–22 were strongly rooted in national politics and based on group hatred, hatred being a word that permeates the historiography of the period but has little place in econometric models.[3]

The monetarist school, as already discussed, emphasizes economic mistakes. The balance-of-payments school emphasizes '*forces des choses*' as opposed to '*forces des hommes*'. With reparations, war debts, the need to restock and to pay off debts, inflation was inevitable regardless of the policies chosen. But this view must contend with the fact that the French paid the indemnity in 1871–72, well ahead of

schedule, by means of an united effort. The Germans were united only
in opposing any payment to France. Apposite is Sir Edward Peacock's
remark of May 1922: 'The French have been technical and unyielding
... unhelpful, almost destructive, but in the main they have been
technically correct. The Germans on the other hand are not only
technically but to a large extent morally wrong. The French ask
impossible things, but the Germans have not yet begun to do the
possible' (Sayers, 1976, p. 174). The structural school starts from a
burden imposed on society – restocking, reconstruction, reparations, in
today's world a sharp increase in the price of oil – which burden must be
allocated. The problem is how to allocate it in an acceptable way, that is,
a way acceptable to those with political and economic clout. As already
noted, this was particularly difficult to do in German society, which
possessed strong groupings such as cartels, weak democracy, weak
capacity to compromise, a tendency to hatred and violence. The
Communist revolution of 1919 was violently suppressed, Karl
Liebknecht and Rosa Luxemburg assassinated, the Kapp Putsch
attempted and failed. The right wing was unwilling to pay taxes on
profits or submit to a capital levy, the Social Democratic/Center Party
governments chose expansion over deflation as a means to ensure social
peace. The Junkers according to Gerschenkron (1943) were a group
with dominance that managed to land on its feet after victory, defeat,
inflation, deflation. Recent research has rejected Gerschenkron's view
that the peasants followed the leadership of the Junkers blindly, but
makes clear that the peasants were sharply opposed to labor and the
Socialists over *Zwangswirtschaft* (compulsory planting of particular
crops) and price controls (Feldman, 1981, pp. 30–2; Moeller, 1982,
p. 225). Within industry, there were different interests of protectionist,
labor-intensive, cartelized heavy industry – iron and steel, and coal –
and the export-oriented capital-intensive dynamic industrial sectors –
machine-building, electro-technical, and chemical (Abraham, 1981).
Both were anxious to break the eight-hour day, increase productivity,
return to piece work. Civil servants whose salaries lagged behind wages
and profits were the worst hit, along with the rentier who had faithfully
accumulated war loan. While these interests occasionally cooperated
with one or another against the rest, for the most part they dug in. After a
time it became impossible for the Social Democratic/Center Party
coalition to govern. Cuno, with connections to the Allies and to all
business groups, presumably had a better chance to reconcile the
groups. One can debate how much his personal qualities handicapped
him in trying to effect compromise (Rupieper, 1979). The structural
inflationist would maintain that only an unusually charismatic leader –
which Cuno was not – would have had a chance to pull it off. Inflation –
of the vigorous sort short of hyperinflation – was a means of turning the
task of distributing income over to outside depersonalized forces.

There is one strong argument for this view of structural inflation,
based on incapacity to resolve the clashes among distributional
coalitions, and one or two against. Favoring the structural explanation is
the contrast between the means adopted for burden-sharing after World

Wars I and II. After World War I, all groups survived intact and even strengthened by the 'organizational mania' of 1918–19 (Feldman, 1977, p. 102). During the Nazi period, trade unions and a number of farm organizations were weakened. After World War II all groups were effectively dissolved. The Junkers lost their economic base in Eastern Germany. Heavy industry was handicapped both by destruction and by its record of having helped the Nazis. There were in fact no interests to stand in the way of a sensible socially engineered solution. The Colm–Dodge–Goldsmith report of 1946, based on suggestions drawn from more than thirty memoranda by German economists, could be devised in an atmosphere that was politically free of pressures.

There are several misunderstandings about the German monetary reform of 1948. Gordon Craig (1982, pp. 104–25) has suggested that the measure was delayed for a long time because the American occupation forces were content to tolerate the black market and the cigarette economy. If this meant to imply that Morgenthauism of the sort implicit in the Joint Chiefs of Staff Directive No. 1067 lasted until 1948 it is misleading. Already by the end of 1945, the US Department of State had turned its back on the Morgenthau plan (Byrnes, 1950; US Department of State, 1946). The Colm–Dodge–Goldsmith committee, for example, was appointed in March 1946 after some months of preparation. Charles Maier writes that both the West Germans and the occupation forces hesitated to write off the losses of the war years and avoided imposing deflationary reforms (1981, pp. 343, 364). This is not my recollection and ignores the difficulties faced by the Allied Control Council in printing a new currency for a four-party monetary reform, given the suspicion in a number of quarters, especially Congressional, that the United States had been in error during the war in furnishing the Russians with plates for printing the occupation currency. The issues involved in the currency-printing question are replete with misunderstandings and errors, but that this was the cause of delay, and not any hesitation in proceeding with monetary reform, is clear to the participants, if not to the scholars of later decades.

A second error of historical understanding has to do with the Friedman view that the occupation forces had muddled monetary reform and were saved from ruining it by the wisdom and force of Ludwig Erhard. This is a thoroughly misguided view, based on strong priors, although it is part of legend (Tenenbaum, 1980; Sauermann, 1979, p. 316).

German monetary reform in 1948 was a model of social engineering. In addition to writing down monetary claims – currency, deposits, debts of all kinds, including bonds, insurance policies and the like – it imposed a mortgage of 50 percent on real property with the interest paid into a *Lastenausgleich Fonds* (Fund for the Equalization of War Losses), the proceeds of which were disbursed to sufferers in the war on the basis of need. It should be noted that labor unions demonstrated against the monetary reform on the ground that it unduly favored the propertied classes, but this demonstration appears to have been passionless and largely pro forma (Domes and Wolffsohn, 1979, p. 341).

This comparison between the financial aftermaths of World Wars I and II in Germany neglects the roles of GARIOA and the Marshall Plan. Holtfrerich has made the point, however, that Germany after World War I received a capital inflow from abroad which was larger than the Marshall Plan aid (1980, p. 293; see also Holtfrerich, 1977). The comparison is of course far from exact, since the Marshall Plan funds were invested positively whereas the capital inflow, apart from some portion which went into buying businesses, was largely held in short-term debt and land. A similar contrast is made for Austria between the League Loans of 1923 which served purely financial ends and Marshall Plan assistance which produced real investment (März, 1982, p. 190). It is of course possible for the recipients of financial assistance to transmute it into real investment – stocks of materials and components, machines, bricks, and mortar. As a matter of some historical interest, Helfferich worried in the early 1920s about *Überfremdung* – the over-foreignization (to coin an unattractive word) of the German economy (Williamson, 1971, p. 358).

A second difference lies in reparations. But monetary payments from the acceptance of the London ultimatum in May 1921 until cash payments were stopped in July 1922 were 1.7 billion marks out of the 8.1 billion paid by Germany up to August 31, 1924 when the Dawes plan took over, roughly a quarter of the 7–8 billion gold marks received by Germany from the capital inflow (Holtfrerich, 1980, p. 145).

It should be emphasized further that Germany went well beyond Belgium, Italy and especially France in reforming the monetary system and imposing a capital levy to equalize war losses – a move discussed in Britain after the Napoleonic wars, and by the major countries in Europe after World Wars I and II, but undertaken on a significant scale only in West Germany where vested interests which might have opposed it did not exist. The French holding back from monetary reform is something of a puzzle. Certainly the view of the Resistance economic leader, René Courtin, that amputating part of the stock of currency and reducing bank deposits would have been 'unpopular, unfair, arbitrary, and ineffective' (Kuisel, 1981, p. 183), is difficult to comprehend unless perhaps, as seems unlikely, it refers to a monetary reform without a capital levy to equalize the burden between creditors and owners of real property.

Another interesting contrast of the aftermath of war is with the position in Prussia in 1806 after the defeat at Jena and the treaty of Tilsit. New energy surged in the economy and the state, together with reforms. Moellendorff was mindful of them more than a century later (Feldman, 1977, p. 101). But in the absence of any semblance of democracy, the reforms were imposed from above by von Stein and Hardenberg. The agricultural reforms moreover were later undermined.

The arguments against an explanation of the difference between the inflation of World War I and the monetary reform after World War II based on the survival of vested interests in the first and their dissolution on the second occasion include first that the difference may be due simply to learning. The United States learned over the quarter-century and was careful not to repeat the errors of war debts and reparations, substituting in their place lend-lease settlements and various forms of aid for reconstruction. The external burden on Germany, and some part of the internal were drastically reduced. That learning affects the operation of economic models is strikingly shown in a comparison of the speed of hyperinflation in Hungary after World War I and World War II (Nogaro, 1948). Hyperinflation was reached in 4½ years after the former, in thirteen months after the latter, because of a distinct difference in the anticipations of economic actors at home and abroad.

A second and more compelling argument against the structuralist view of the inflation is that while the Olson analysis applies strikingly to Germany of 1921–23 (and the opposite case to 1945–48), it is far from self-evident that it fits the other countries that experienced hyper-inflation after World War I: Poland, Hungary, Austria, and Russia. Feldman (1983, pp. 4–5) has provided a useful categorization of three grades of inflation in the period: hyper, substantial, and reversible. If the structural view is both necessary and sufficient, it should fit the entire class. In the hyperinflation category, however, the problems of the sepa-rate countries seem to be somewhat different, Russia with a revolution, Austria, a capital severed from its hinterland, Poland fashioned from a collection of remnants of countries – Germany, Russia, and the Austrian-Hungarian empire from which an attempt was made to forge a unit. I am not sufficiently versed in the histories of Eastern Europe to know whether there are any similarities with the German case – antithetical groups finding it difficult to agree on burden-sharing, and postponing resolution of distributional conflicts by a consensus for inflation in the early stages, followed by hyperinflation at a later stage when matters get out of hand.

There are then three schools. But there is no need for mono-causality except perhaps the academic predilection for parsimony in theorizing. It is possible that all three schools have a part of the truth, and especially that one school may be right at one time, another at another. The first suggestion along these lines was an attempt to reconcile the balance-of-payments and the monetary schools, made by Nurkse (1946). In the first stage the monetarist explanation was valid, with domestic expenditure financed by government deficits and central-bank expansion leading to rising prices followed by exchange depreciation. Foreign speculators, plus German, believed that the currency would ultimately be restored to par and supported the currency. The inflow of capital enabled the exchange rate to be overvalued. This meant that despite depreciation of the exchange rate the internal inflation was greater than the external. Germany developed an import surplus – as least relatively to other periods – though the data are poor as the *Statistisches Reichsamt* didn't publish trade statistics from the beginning of World War I until May 1921 and there was substantial smuggling in the Rhineland ('the Hole in the West'). Exports from May to December 1921 covered only 60 percent of exports, according to the League of Nations, and 64 percent in 1922, as contrasted with 70 percent in 1921 and 99 percent in 1923 (*ibid.*, p. 50n). When the inelastic expectations of a return of the exchange rate to its old level were reversed and followed by elastic expectations of continued depreciation, the monetarist model was superseded by the balance-of-payments model – a large outflow of capital, sharp depreciation of the exchange rate, external inflation leading internal inflation as the exchange rate became undervalued and pushed up prices. Exports rose and led to an export surplus. Inflation accelerated from June 1922, the time when expectations changed according to Holtfrerich. In the final stages, capital exports bypassed the foreign-exchange market altogether as foreigners and Germans bought goods in Germany and shipped them for sale abroad, retaining the proceeds in foreign exchange.

In contrast to this pattern of monetarism, overvaluation and import surpluses which dampened the domestic inflation, followed by the balance-of-payments explanation of outflows, depreciation, rising prices, and money supplies trying to catch up, Bernholz has undertaken to establish an opposite sequence, of undervaluation followed by overvaluation, that is, the balance-of-payments school right in the first period, and the monetarists in the second (1982, pp. 26–9). There is great difficulty with the data because he uses the short-period tables of Bresciani-Turroni (1937) with their different base periods, no one of which bases can be said to be an equilibrium position. Thus his first period of undervaluation is measured on the basis of October 1918 (Table II in Bresciani-Turroni, p. 28) at a time when the exchange rate was pegged and controlled, and the wholesale price level was held down by price and wages controls. Holtfrerich's Table 1 (1980, p. 15) gives October 1918 as 1.57 for the exchange rate, taking 1913 as 1, and 2.34 for wholesale prices. For the second period, when the exchange rate was overvalued and the monetarist theory valid, Bernholz uses Bresciani-Turroni's Table VII (pp. 35–6) with July 31, 1923 as a base. According to the previous table (VI, p. 35) however, the previous year had seen the exchange rate falling at three times the rate of the note circulation and almost twice that of the inflation in food prices. Bernholz' paper was focused not solely on German inflation, but on the dynamic behavior of flexible exchange rates generally. He was trying to show that with the adoption of flexible exchange rates an initial period of undervaluation – because of the J-curve in imports and capital outflows – is generally followed by subsequent overvaluation when the balance of payments has had time to adjust. In this case it is not persuasive.

Other periodization includes the detailed breakdowns in diagrams of Bresciani-Turroni (1937, pp. 25–38) as follows, with an indication whether the lead is taken by the money supply (floating debt) or the exchange rate:

1913–1918	money in circulation
October 1918 to February 1920	dollar exchange rate
February 1920 to May 1921	floating debt
May 1921 to July 1922	dollar exchange
July 1922 to June 1923	dollar exchange
July 31, 1923 to November 20, 1923	all together

Feldman's analysis provides a similar breakdown with emphasis on the difference in the rate of inflation between May 1921–June 1922, and June 1922–November 1923, even though both were led by the exchange rate (1983, pp. 7–8).

In addition to these differences in periodicity, there is considerable (mild) disagreement on the turning point from inflation to hyper-inflation. Knut Borchardt maintains (in a private discussion) that this occurred in May 1921 at the time of the London Ultimatum. Raymond Goldsmith informally pinned the inflection on the Franco-Belgian occupation of the Ruhr in January 1923. Holtfrerich's candidate is June 1922 with the piling up of the French rejection of any change in the reparation agreement, the J. P. Morgan committee insistance that reparations had to be changed to make possible an American loan, and finally, and most critical, the assassination of Walther Rathenau (Holtfrerich, 1980, pp. 287–91). The mark went from 272 to the dollar on June 1 to 318 on the 12th when the Morgan report came out, and from 332 to 355 on the day of the assassination (June 24). On June 30 it hit 374, and the next day 401. By July 31 it was 670 and by the end of August 1,725. Speculation in favor of the mark by foreigners (and some Germans) had been completely reversed.

This analysis suggests that the path of German inflation after World War I involved changing balance-of-payments and domestic monetary and fiscal forces, against the background of a struggle of vested interests that can be regarded as the fundamental pattern of structural inflation that can be succinctly summarized as follows:

1. Versailles to the Kapp Putsch of March 1920, marked by revolution, counter-revolution, assassinations of Leibknecht and Luxemburg. Exchange control was abandoned in September 1919, and the exchange rate depreciated under the influence of payments of raw materials, repayment of Swedish debts by iron and steel manufacturers, and some capital outflow. At the same time, there were internal causes of inflation from the center-left programs of work creation, support for unemployment, a relaxed attitude toward price and wage increases, the eight-hour day. The first attempt at fiscal reform was unsuccessful. It is possible to make a case for either the balance-of-payments or the monetarist school, against the background of structural inflation. Any monetarist explanation, however, has a strong admixture of the Laursen and Pedersen view, with inflation emanating from cost-push on the side of labor struggling to cut hours and raise wages.

2. From March 1920 to May 1921, relative stability, brought about by the inflow of capital. The exchange rate had plunged from 2¼ in March 1919, on the basis of 1913 as 1, to 23.6 in February 1920 before recovering to a range of 9 to 18. In May 1921 it was 14.8. This stability was based entirely on the inflow of capital from abroad. Wholesale prices were held down by the fall in import prices and the import of goods. Because of the limitations in Erzberger's financial reforms, domestic debt almost doubled from 92 to 162 billion marks, and the volume of high-powered (Reichsbank) money rose from 67 billion marks at the end of February 1920 to 102 billion marks at the end of

April 1921 (Holtfrerich, 1980, pp. 51–2). Allowing for the world depression abroad, German exports were relatively strong because of the depreciation of the mark of the previous period and despite the relative import surplus. Feldman (1983, p. 5) makes the point that booming exports and somewhat expansionary policy based on the capital inflow spared Germany the deflation and unemployment of other countries. The period fits into none of the three inflationary models, being characterized by overvaluation of the currency, expansion of the money supply, and a fall in prices from 17 (1913 = 1) in March 1920 to 13 in May 1921.

3. The third period runs from the acceptance of the London Ultimatum in May 1921 – characterized in Germany as the second stab in the back – to the traumatic events of June 1922. The dollar exchange rate and the prices of imported goods rose together, closely followed by the prices of domestic commodities and the cost of food. Expansion of the floating debt and the volume of circulation lagged behind. There was a 'violent' struggle over new taxes to pay the agreed reparations, the assassination of Erzberger in August 1921, and inability of the Wirth government to find a satisfactory basis for meeting the obligations it had accepted. Labor pushed hard to keep pace with rising prices, to furnish support to the Laursen–Pedersen model. In general it may be characterized as a period of distress – to use a word borrowed from financial crises (Kindleberger, 1978, pp. 100 ff) – with rising tension but before an absolute break. Foreign capital stopped coming in, and perhaps began slowly to ebb away. But the panic rush to withdraw was yet to occur.

4. The break came, as already noted, in June 1922, with the French rejection of a change in reparations, the J. P. Morgan refusal to lend in these circumstances, and the Rathenau assassination. Foreign capital, which had been favoring the mark from March 1920 to May 1921, and wavering and uncertain to June, now took the bit in its teeth and headed out of Germany, closely followed by German speculation. The exchange rate led the expansion of money in circulation and the floating debt, to conform to the balance-of-payments model, but the Reichsbank undertook to expand its portfolio of commercial bills, at low or negative real rates of interest. In part, however, it was a deliberate decision to try to maintain the liquidity of the banking system in the face of pell-mell foreign (and domestic) dumping of German money for foreign exchange. To this extent the Reichsbank was acting as a lender of last resort to prevent a breakdown in the banking system.

This fourth period could be further disaggregated to mark a shift in the fall of 1922 to direct valuations in foreign prices instead of calculating through to foreign prices from domestic prices and the exchange rate; and again, with the occupation of the Ruhr in January 1923, when the Reichsbank turned on the presses full speed to assist the government in subsidizing the strikers. At the end, as already noted, internal and external inflation exploded together.

The explosion and the possibility of disintegration of the country as the Rhineland contemplated separation, including a separate currency and Bank of the Rhineland, substituted the stabilization consensus for the inflation consensus (Born, 1977, p. 116; Sayers, 1976, p. 177). How the Rentenmark and the Reichsmark, plus the German acceptance of the Dawes loan, fit into the structural model is a topic worth pursuit, but not in an already overlong paper.

In normal historiography and economic history, and especially in a discussion of the structural model of inflation, it is useful to sort out which groups won and which groups lost. Again, I have little time or space to review this extensive literature, but I should like to record my objection to the implicit conclusion of a number of historian revisionists that the inflation after World War 1 in Germany was on the whole relatively inconsequential, with no group losing particularly, in fact, not much worse than a bad cold. It is true that the inflation may have been superior to violent revolution and internecine warfare, on the model of the Spanish revolution. The consensus for inflation was a comparative one, not absolute. I admire the work of Gerschenkron, Moeller, Webb, Feldman, Holtfrerich *et al.* in sorting out the winners and groups that held their own, but it seems to me clear that the inflation was fateful for the German middle class, including large parts of the peasantry, and that its memory shaped and distorted policy choices of the country for the next half century or more (see Chapter 8 above). It may be that the emergence of the Nazis in government in the 1930s is overdetermined, like the French Revolution and the German inflation, finding its origins in German national character, the depth of the depression in Germany after foreign borrowing stopped, the deflationary policies of Brüning, etc. It would be hard, however, to deny a significant role to the trauma of the German middle class in the years from 1914 to 1924.

A corollary of the point of view presented in this paper – that the German inflation rested at basis on the incapacity of organized and powerful groups to agree on how to share among them the burdens of reconstruction and reparations (and of France and Germany to agree on how much reparation should be paid to make good the destruction of the great war) overlain by policy decisions, including mistakes, in which monetary, fiscal and exchange policy in Germany and speculation for and against the mark abroad and at home form a confusing pattern – is that much of the technical economic literature on the German inflation is beside the point because it fails to specify the socio-political matrix in which the economic events take place. Especially is this true of testing of theories involving tight priors, such as:

(1) Inflation is purely monetary, or purely the result of depreciation of the exchange rate based on balance-of-payments events of an autonomous sort.
(2) The rate of exchange is always at the purchasing-power-parity level or is almost never there.
(3) The forward exchange rate is an unbiassed estimator of the future exchange rate (Frenkel, 1976).
(4) Speculation is always stabilizing (Frenkel, 1967; Salemi, 1980; Frenkel, 1980).

(5) Demand functions for money can be written as if domestic holders and foreign holders respond in the same way to the same economic events and stimuli (see Debeir, 1982; Frenkel, 1982).
(6) Because of rational expectations and efficient markets, there cannot be price bubbles (Flood and Garber, 1980).

Economists seem frequently to take up the German inflation to prove some point in monetary or foreign-exchange theory and study little more than statistical series with no flesh and blood, no political parties, interest groups, politics, revolutions, violence, assassinations, etc. When they bring out their conclusions that the German inflation supports the theory they brought to its study, I am led to react with the Duke of Wellington when someone approached him and said 'Mr. Smith, I believe'; 'If you believe that you can believe anything'.

Summary

The impressive literature on the German inflation of 1914 to 1923 is for the most part divided in economic, as distinct from political history, into the monetarist and balance-of-payment schools. The monetarists blame the issue of money to finance government deficits: the balance-of-payments school tends to regard the causation coming from international payments, largely for reparations, which led to depreciation of the mark, higher import prices and only finally to an expansion of money. One variant of the balance-of-payments version attaches importance to the role of labor insisting on higher wages as the cost of living is raised by import and export prices. The clash between monetary and balance-of-payments explanations is by no means confined to the German inflation, but is present in the Banking vs the Currency School debate in England after the Napoleonic war, and in other debates.

This paper makes two main points: first, that there is a third 'structural' explanation at a more profound level which emphasizes the burden that German society had to bear and the difficulty of distributing it in a society where various competing interests were antagonistic and unwilling to compromise. Emphasis on labor's drive for higher wages touches only one aspect of this. Other interest groups – large-scale business in iron and steel, chemicals, electricity and the like, the Junkers in agriculture, the peasants of western Germany, civil servants, etc. – all resisted. Temporizing solution was found by giving various groups the nominal income they sought, with real burden being allocated by rising prices. Economic policy is thus powerless.

In the second place, there is no need to subscribe to any one explanation, good for the entire period. At one time and another, monetary expansion, the balance of payments, and interest demands take the lead. Such a theory is less parsimonious, but far richer.

Notes

1 See Felix (1971), p. 172; Moeller (1982), p. 226; Williamson (1971), p. 362; and Feldman (1983), apropos of the Hirsch plan, rejected by all sides without offers of an alternative.
2 Cf. 'If we wish to understand why one country yielded to inflation and another stood by its old standard, we must take into account many elements which are not primarily of an economic character' (Lopez, 1951, p. 222).
3 On the hatred of Helfferich by the left see Williamson (1971), p. 342; that Erzberger was the object of 'monumental and vicious hatred', and 'His enemies could enjoy hating Rathenau', see Felix (1971), p. 126; and Epstein (1959), p. 397. The prevalence of hatred and violence indicates how far postwar Germany was from the condition in which Adam Smith's 'obvious and simple system of natural liberty' could establish itself. This system required the sovereign to discharge but three duties: (1) to protect society from the violence and invasion of other independent societies; (2) to protect, as far as possible, every member from the injustice and oppression of every other member; (3) public works (1776/1937, p. 651).

References

Abraham, David (1981), *The Collapse of the Weimar Republic: Political Economy and Crisis* (Princeton, NJ: Princeton University Press).
Aujac, Henri (1950), 'Inflation as a Monetary Consequence of the Behavior of Social Groups: A Working Hypothesis', *International Economic Papers*, No. 4; reprinted from *Economie Appliquée*, vol. 3, no. 2 (April–June), pp. 280–300.
Bernholz, Peter (1982), *Flexible Exchange Rates in Historical Perspective*, Princeton Studies in International Finance, No. 49 (July).
Bonn, Moritz J. (1922), *Stabilization of the Mark* (Chicago, Ill.: First National Bank of Chicago, April).
Born, Karl Erich (1977), 'The German Inflation after the First World War', *Journal of European Economic History*, vol. 6, no. 1 (Spring).
Bosher, J. F. (1970), *French Finances, 1770–1795: From Business to Bureaucracy* (Cambridge: Cambridge University Press).
Bresciani-Turroni, Costantino (1937), *The Economics of Inflation. A Study of Currency Depreciation in Post-War Germany, 1914–1923* (London: Allen & Unwin).
Byrnes, J. E. (1950), 'Restatement of U.S. Policy on Germany: Address by Secretary James E. Byrnes, Stuttgart, September 6, 1946', in US Department of State, *Germany, 1947–1949: The Story in Documents* (Washington, DC: US Government Printing Office), pp. 3–8.
Cagan, Philip (1956), 'The Monetary Dynamics of Hyperinflation', in Milton Friedman (ed.), *Studies in the Quantity Theory of Money* (Chicago, Ill.: University of Chicago Press), pp. 25–117.
Chaussinand-Nogaret, Guy (1970), *Les Financiers de Languedoc au XVIIIᵉ siècle* (Paris: SEVPEN).
Craig, Gordon A. (1982), *The Germans* (New York: Putnam).
Debeir, Jean-Claude (1982), 'Comment' on Carl-L. Holtfrerich, *Domestic and Foreign Expectations and the Demand for Money during the German Inflation, 1920–1923*, in C. P. Kindleberger and J. P. Laffargue (eds), *Financial Crises: Theory, History and Policy* (Cambridge: Cambridge University Press), pp. 132–6.
Dickson, P. G. M. (1967), *The Financial Revolution in England: A Study in the Development of Public Credit, 1688–1756* (New York: St Martin's Press).

Domes, Jürgen and Wolffsohn, Michael (1979), 'Setting the Course for the Federal Republic of Germany: Major Policy Decisions in the Bizonal Economic Council and Party Images, 1947–1949', in Rudolph Richter (ed.), 'Currency and Economic Reform: West Germany after World War II', *Zeitschrift für die gesamte Staatswissenschaft*, vol. 135, no. 35 (September), pp. 332–51.

Eckstein, Otto (1981), *Core Inflation* (Englewood Cliffs, NJ: Prentice-Hall).

Epstein, Klaus (1959), *Matthias Erzberger and the Dilemma of German Democracy* (Princeton, NJ: Princeton University Press).

Feldman, Gerald D. (1977), *Iron and Steel in the German Inflation 1916–1923* (Princeton, NJ: Princeton University Press).

Feldman, Gerald D. (1981), 'The Political Economy of Germany's Relative Stabilization during the 1920–21 World Depression', preliminary paper presented to a Lehrman Institute Study Group, 2 December.

Feldman, Gerald D. (1983), 'The Historian and the German Inflation', in Nathan Schmukler and Edward Marcus (eds), *Inflation through the Ages. Economic, Social, Psychological and Historical Aspects* (New York: Columbia University Press), pp. 386–99.

Felix, David (1971), *Walter Rathenau and the Weimar Republic: The Politics of Reparations* (Baltimore, Md: Johns Hopkins University Press).

Fetter, Frank Whitson (1965), *Development of British Monetary Orthodoxy, 1797–1875* (Cambridge, Mass.: Harvard University Press).

Flood, Robert P. and Garber, Peter M. (1980), 'Market Fundamentals versus Price Bubbles: The First Tests', *Journal of Political Economy*, vol. 88, no. 4 (August), pp. 745–70.

Frenkel, J. A. (1976), 'A Monetary Approach to the Exchange Rate: Doctrinal Aspects and Empirical Evidence', *Scandinavian Journal of Economics*, vol. 78, no. 2, pp. 200–24.

Frenkel, J. A. (1977), 'The Forward Exchange Rate, Expectations and the Demand for Money: The German Hyperinflation', *American Economic Review*, vol. 67, no. 4 (September), pp. 653–70.

Frenkel, J. A. (1980), 'Reply' to M. K. Salemi's 'Comment', *American Economic Review*, vol. 70, no. 4 (September), pp. 771–5.

Frenkel, J. A. (1982), 'Comment' on Carl-L. Holtfrerich, *Domestic and Foreign Expectations and the Demand for Money during the German Inflation, 1920–1923*, in C. P. Kindleberger and J. P. Laffargue (eds), *Financial Crises, Theory, History and Policy* (Cambridge: Cambridge University Press), pp. 136–43.

Gerschenkron, Alexander (1943), *Bread and Democracy in Germany* (Berkeley, Calif.: University of California Press).

Graham, Frank D. (1930), *Exchange, Prices and Production in Hyperinflation, Germany, 1920–1923* (Princeton, NJ: Princeton University Press).

Harris, Robert D. (1979), *Necker, Reform Statesman of the Ancien Régime* (Berkeley, Calif.: University of California Press).

Hirsch, Fred and Goldthorpe, John (eds) (1978), *The Political Economy of Inflation* (Cambridge, Mass.: Harvard University Press).

Hirschman, Albert O. (1961), *Latin American Issues* (New York: Twentieth Century Fund).

Hirschman, Albert (1963), 'Inflation in Chile', ch. 3 in *Journeys toward Progress: Studies of Economic Policymaking in Latin America* (New York: Twentieth Century Fund).

Holtfrerich, Carl-Ludwig (1977), 'Amerikanischer Kapitalexport und Wiederaufbau der deutschen Wirtschaft 1919–1923 im Vergleich zu 1924–1929', *Vierteljahresschrift für Sozial- und Wirtschaftgeschichte*, vol.

64, pp. 497–529; reprinted in Michael Stürmer (ed.), *Die Weimarer Republik. Belagerte Civitas* (Berlin: Verlagsgruppe Athenaum, 1980), pp. 131–57.

Holtfrerich, Carl-Ludwig (1980), *Die deutsche Inflation, 1914–1923. Ursachen und Folgen in internationaler Perspektive* (Berlin: Walter de Gruyter).

Kindleberger, C. P. (1978), *Manias, Panics and Crashes* (New York: Basic Books).

Kindleberger, C. P. (1982), 'British Financial Reconstruction, 1815–22 and 1918–25' in C. P. Kindleberger and G. di Tella (eds), *Economics in the Long View* (London: Macmillan), vol. III, pp. 105–20.

Kuisel, Richard F. (1981), *Capitalism and the State in Modern France: Renovation and Economic Management in the Twentieth Century* (Cambridge: Cambridge University Press).

Laursen, Karsten and Pedersen, Jørgen (1964), *The German Inflation, 1918–1923* (Amsterdam: North Holland).

Lopez, Robert S. (1951), 'The Dollar of the Middle Ages', *Journal of Economic History*, vol. 21.

Maier, Charles S. (1981), 'The Two Postwar Eras and the Conditions for Stability in Twentieth-Century Western Europe' and 'Reply', *American Historical Review*, vol. 86, no. 2 (April), pp. 327–52.

Malamud, Bernard (1983), 'John H. Williams on the German Inflation: The International Amplification of Monetary Disturbances', in Nathan Schmukler and Edward Marcus (eds), *Inflation through the Ages. Economic, Social, Psychological and Historical Aspects* (New York: Columbia University Press), pp. 417–34.

März, E. (1982), 'Comment' on D. E. Moggridge, *Policy in the Crises of 1920 and 1929*, in C. P. Kindleberger and J. P. Laffargue (eds), *Financial Crises: Theory, History and Policy* (Cambridge: Cambridge University Press).

Moeller, Robert G. (1982), 'Peasants, Politics, and Pressure Groups in War and Inflation: A Study of the Rhineland and Westphalia, 1914–1924', *Journal of Economic History*, vol. 42, no. 1 (March).

Nogaro, Bertrand (1948), 'Hungary's Recent Monetary Crisis and its Theoretical Meaning', *American Economic Review*, vol. 38, no. 4, pp. 526–42.

Nurkse, Ragnar (1946), *The Course and Control of Inflation: A Review of Monetary Experience in Europe after World War I* (Princeton, NJ: League of Nations).

Olson, Mancur, Jr (1965), *The Logic of Collective Action* (Cambridge, Mass.: Harvard University Press).

Olson, Mancur, Jr (1982), *The Rise and Decline of Nations: Economic Growth, Stagflation and Social Rigidities* (New Haven, Conn.: Yale University Press).

Reder, Melvin W. (1982), 'Chicago Economics: Permanence and Change', *The Journal of Economic Literature*, vol. 20, no. 1 (March), pp. 1–38.

Rupieper, Hermann J. (1979), *The Cuno Government and Reparations, 1922–23: Politics and Economics* (The Hague: Martinus Nijhoff).

Salemi, M. K. (1980), 'Comment' [on Frenkel, 1977], *American Economic Review*, vol. 70, no. 4 (September), pp. 663–70.

Sauermann, Heinz (1979), 'On the Economic and Financial Rehabilitation of Western Germany (1945–1949)', in Rudolph Richter (ed.), 'Currency and Economic Reform: West Germany after World War II', *Zeitschrift für die gesamte Staatswissenschaft*, vol. 135, no. 35 (September).

Sauvy, Alfred (1965), *Histoire économique de la France entre les deux guerres. Vol. I: 1918–1931* (Paris: Fayard).

Sayers, Richard S. (1976), *The Bank of England, 1891–1944* (Cambridge: Cambridge University Press), vol. I.

Smith, Adam (1776/1937), *An Inquiry into the Nature and Causes of the Wealth of Nations*, Cannan edn (New York: Modern Library).

Tenenbaum, J. Kipp (1980), 'Free to Choose', letter to the *New York Review of Books*, 20 November.

US Department of State (1946), *United States Policy towards Germany* (Washington, DC: US Government Printing Office), Publication No. 2630 (Fall).

Williamson, John G. (1971), *Karl Helfferich, 1872–1924, Economist, Financier, Politician* (Princeton, NJ: Princeton University Press).

17

The International Causes and Consequences of the Great Crash

The stock market both contributed to the international financial crisis and shared in its agonies

History is a fable agreed upon, and the fable that is getting the play these days is the Friedman and Schwartz view that the Great Depression was caused by monetary policy in the United States, and nothing else (1965, ch. 7). The stock market crash of 1929 had nothing to do with it. Other voices are heard faintly. Some monetarists, as Cleveland and Brittain (1975), extend the blame for monetary policy from the United States to include France, Britain, and Germany, without, however, explaining how errors of monetary policy are bunched in this fashion instead of being distributed in time normally. In the rising interest in the Great Depression, nonmonetarists appear here and there: Rostow (1978a) blaming the played out leading sector, automobiles; Barber (1978), population growth and housing (to echo the stagnation thesis of the late Alvin Hansen); and Temin (1976) attacking monetarism directly by insisting that spending changed first, with monetary changes being induced rather than autonomous. A student of Temin, Frederic Miskin (1978, pp. 918–37 and n. 36), asserts that the reduction in spending was brought about by the decline in nominal wealth, due to the stock market crash, and regards the depression abroad as derivative, rather than integral to the picture.

This fablist takes exception to the findings of these blind men, handling pieces of the elephant, insists that the origins of the Great Depression were international, and finds the 1929 crash's role not in the effect of the decline in wealth on consumption, but in its impact on credit and through credit on prices. The collapse of the stock market was precipitated by short-term capital outflows, as its rise after June 1928 had sown the seeds of depression in Germany and at the world periphery by cutting off the inflow of US long-term capital. And the freezing up of New York credit – as New York banks got ready to take over brokers' loans withdrawn by out-of-town banks and 'others' – was responsible for

Reprinted with permission from The Journal of Portfolio Management, *vol. 6, no. 1 (Fall 1979), pp. 11–14.*

the plunge of commodity prices (and of automobile sales) that ricocheted back on bank failures and led finally – after March 1931 – to a serious decline in the money stock (Kindleberger, 1973).

The effects of suddenly halting capital outflows in June 1928, as the plungers turned from foreign bonds to domestic stocks, are relevant today. A serious depression in 1974–75 was averted by the courage(?) or insensitivity(?) of the world capital market in continuing lending (especially interest due but also new money) on REITs, 747s, tankers on the mud, and to importunate LDCs. In riding a tiger, or holding a bear by the tail, it is often optimal to hang on.

Background

President Hoover thought the world depression was entirely the fault of the Europeans (1952, pp. 61–2). Friedman and Schwartz blame it exclusively on American monetary authorities (1965, pp. 339-60). This observer sides with the view of Robin Matthews (1954, p. 69) on the financial crisis of 1836, as between Andrew Jackson and London and Liverpool, that it is useless to try to fix geographical responsibilities in these matters. The same would hold for the transatlantic financial crises of 1857, 1873, and 1907, in all of which the precipitant was the halting of lending, or capital withdrawals.

The European background of the world depression was the Versailles treaty, reparations, war debts (compounded by US unwillingness to associate war debts with reparations), overvaluation of the pound, undervaluation of the French franc, and the accumulation of large-scale sterling balances by France. On the US side, there was the burst of foreign lending after the surprising success of the Dawes loan of 1924, its abrupt halt in June 1928, followed by short-term lending to Germany that borrowed time but dug the hole deeper.

Worldwide, there were the slowdown of the spurt of postwar building and the comeback of European commodity production without a compensating shrinkage of enlarged output outside Europe. Business in the United States was slipping as firms joined with banks in lending money to finance broker's loans. Commodity prices were also slipping. Security prices were high, but finding it difficult to advance. Credit was tight. The system was taut. Markets were in what has been called 'distress'.

The spark

A French historian, J. Néré (1968, p. 78), has identified the Mother Leary's cow of the crash in a piquant episode that occurred in The Hague in August 1929. Wrangling over reparations in discussions that ultimately led to the Young Plan of 1930, Philip Snowden, British Chancellor of the Exchequer, lost his temper and characterized some proposal by French Finance Minister Cheron as 'ridiculous and grotesque', which the interpreter rendered into French as '*ridicule et grotesque*'. It is now widely agreed that this was a very poor translation because the English expression is acceptable in the House of Commons, while the French is unparliamentary and insulting in the Chamber of Deputies.[1]

According to the story, the French withdrew sterling balances from London, tighter interest rates in the city precipitated the collapse of the Hatry empire, revealing a swindle, English short-term funds were drawn back from brokers' loans in New York, and the stock market peaked out in September to collapse October 24 and 29, Black Thursday and Black Tuesday respectively. The collapse was caused by the withdrawal of brokers' loans as prices fell, many non-banks and perhaps out-of-town banks withdrawing their money as they recalled the closing of the stock exchange in September 1873, which converted highly liquid day-to-day or call loans into frozen assets. New York banks had been reducing their call loans earlier in the year to prepare for the possible necessity of replacing withdrawn funds. This they did to a degree; in the panic, they clamped down on loans in all other directions.

Liquidity crisis

The precipitous decline in liquidity in the New York money market communicated the price decline from securities to commodities. Internationally traded goods at that time were largely sold on consignment, that is, shipped to New York to be sold in commodity markets on arrival rather than bought abroad by the American importer and then shipped. Buyers needed financing; when they could not get it they were unable to buy, or bought only at lower prices. Coffee fell from an average of 22½c a pound in September 1929 to 15½c in December; rubber from 20.10c per pound to 16.06c, tin from 45.38c per pound to 39.79c.

There is no way in which these price declines can be connected with a mechanism that goes through either the quantity theory of money, since money aggregates barely changed at all, or through Keynesian effects on spending by consumers, with or without wealth in consumption functions.

Industrial production fell from 110 in October to 100 in December, the sharpest decline in the Federal Reserve index since 1920; within the total, automobile production dropped from 440,000 units in August to 319,000 in October, 169,500 in November, and 92,500 in December, a decline of almost 80 percent. (Model change was partly involved but the usual low was November, not December.) Driven by the price decline in commodities, US imports dropped from $396 million in October to $283 million in February 1930, nearly 30 percent. The decline in M1 between August 1929 and September 1930, when the world depression was off and running, amounted to slightly more than 5 percent.

The Federal Reserve Bank of New York responded positively to the stock market crash, but not the Federal Reserve system as a whole. Governor Harrison, President of the New York Bank, bought $160 million of securities for the Open Market portfolio in the week ended October 30, and another $210 million in November, in violation of his standing limit of $25 million a week, incurring the wrath of the Board of Governors in Washington. If monetary policy is to be faulted before March 1931, this failure to carry through better as a lender of last resort in a crisis should draw the blame.

A crucial point must be made about long-term capital flows from the United States. Experienced capital markets direct the flow of capital to domestic lenders or abroad, depending upon relative profit opportunities. Thus, Britain demonstrated a counter-cyclical outflow of capital in the period from 1870 to 1914. In domestic boom, the movement slowed down. When domestic business slipped, foreign lending picked up. A given flow of savings could be said to be distributed between domestic and foreign uses through a 'demand' model. In the United States in the 1920s, foreign bonds were a new experience for many lenders, and there were thought to be many unrealized opportunities, especially in Germany and Latin America. The success of the Dawes loan encouraged a positive feedback process in which, until June 1928 when the stock market took over, both foreign and domestic investment picked up with income and savings, in a supply model. And when the stock market crashed, collapse of imports followed cutting-off of foreign lending, to deal a one–two set of blows to the outside world.

1930 recovery?

The money market had recovered by the spring of 1930. Interest rates were down, foreign lending picked up. A distinct possibility of recovery was detected, but not realized. By September 1930, when the Nazis made big gains in the German elections, short-term capital started to unravel. The failure of an upturn in the second quarter of 1930 remains something of a mystery, although it has nothing whatsoever to do with the quantity of money. Here, perhaps, is where Rostow's emphasis on automobiles or Barber's on housing comes in. This writer, however, believes the decline of commodity and goods prices provides the key.

Modern monetary theory dismisses the idea of significance to prices on the grounds of 'money illusion'. If producers lose through price declines, consumers or other purchasers have corresponding and off-setting gains. Changes in prices redistribute a given income but do not change the level, so the theory goes. But this *a priori* and ahistorical view not only flies in the face of 1930s opinion, which was eager to restore the price level; it ignores lags and dynamic reactions.

On lags, producers whose prices fall know immediately they have lost income, and so do their banks; consumers take somewhat more time to realize that the cost of living has fallen, and that their real income has increased. Producers default on bank loans, cut payrolls, and start a cumulative process of bank failure and spreading unemployment that gets out of hand before it can be overtaken by increased spending from increased real income on the part of households that have not been hurt by unemployment, pay cuts, or bank failures. And the price declines produced bank failures on both sides of the Atlantic, not only the Bank of the United States in New York, and smaller banks throughout the agricultural states induced by the collapse in prices of wheat, cotton, corn, and lard, but also the Austrian Creditanstalt in May 1931, and the German Danat bank two months later.

This was the stage at which the depression turned into a monetary phenomenon of international rather than United States dimensions, that ricocheted from Austria, to Germany, to Britain, to Japan, to the United States and by 1935 back to the gold bloc. Monetary policy was shortsighted, especially the failure of Britain, France, and the United States to bolster Austria and Germany in May and June 1931, and the 'every-man-for-himself' attitude of France and the gold bloc in converting $750 million in dollars into gold in the fall of 1931 after Britain went off sterling. There was no international lender of last resort. But the Great Depression had been underway for two years.

Relevance today

In the 50 years that have supervened since 1929, a number of changes have taken place that would seem to render the chances of repetition small.

Cleveland and Brittain (1975) look to changes on the monetary side; there cannot now be the 18 percent decline in money supply that took place in Britain, France, Germany, and the United States between 1930 and 1932 (close to 26 percent in the United States alone, when a 10 percent increase was needed). Barber is working on the question whether demographic trends foreshadow another major depression. Rostow's preoccupation with the Kondratieff 50-year cycle enables him to forecast an upswing based on energy investment (1978b, ch. 2), when other Kondratieff enthusiasts such as Jay W. Forrester (1978) divine, instead, a downswing from declining general investment (see also Forrester, 1976). One or the other may be right.

There *are* major financial differences between 1929 and 1979. Commodities are no longer shipped on consignment, but sold before shipment, so that suppliers can more readily hold back when credit is tight. Margin trading is regulated, reducing the role of brokers' loans. The FDIC lessens the danger of spreading bank collapse. The tinder of war debts and reparations was tidied up by the Lend-Lease, the Marshall plan, etc., but may have found a substitute in the giddy structure of Eurocurrency debts of developing countries and Eastern Europe.

Prices are more rigid downward and the highly competitive agricultural sector both is smaller in importance in national income and elicits government support faster, so that sharp price declines are unlikely, and, should they occur, their impact would be lessened. In the financial area, the experienced Eurocurrency market and the World Bank keep lending in recession, rather than cutting off foreign borrowers, with the result that the one–two knockout punch is less of a threat. The need for a domestic lender of last resort is firmly established. The 'distress' to the international capital market occasioned by the failures of the Herstatt and Franklin National Banks in 1974 was efficiently handled in Germany by the banking system at large and in the United States by the Federal Reserve System, acting as lender of last resort.

The major similarity between 1979 and 1929, however, is the absence of certainty as to who will fill the role of international lender of last resort, should the occasion arise. In the period to 1914, the function was discharged by the Bank of England, which, however, was occasionally helped by the Bank of France, and in separate incidents by the Bank of Hamburg and the State Bank of Russia as well. After 1945, the United States acted as the system stabilizer, helped from 1961 on by the system of swaps in the forefront and the International Monetary Fund to follow along and consolidate crisis loans. Between 1919 and, say, 1936, Britain couldn't act as lender of last resort, and the United States wouldn't. Central bank cooperation carried the system only so far, but broke down in emergency. In this observer's judgement, the 1929 depression was so wide, so long, and so deep because there was no place for the buck to stop, no one minding the store, no country accepting the responsibility of acting as stabilizer with the task of halting downward liquidity spirals.

In the last ten years, the system has limped along again without any designated lender of last resort. Central bank cooperation through swaps and the IMF has stumbled from time to time, with echoes of the competitive currency depreciation of 1931–32, but has not fallen. What is worrying, however, is the apparent withdrawal of the United States from its economic leadership role in trade, exchange rate stability, macroeconomic coordination, and especially as a lender of last resort. And Germany and Japan, the candidates as world successor, act in ways reminiscent of the United States in the 1920s – cooperative, helpful, but unwilling to assert responsibility.

Do we face the dangerous position where the economically aging United States can't, and vigorous Germany and Japan won't?

Note

1   René David, French professor of international law, to whom I told this story, extended it. He had been staying in London at the time, and said that the French interpreter, realizing his mistake, apologized and offered a correction, 'Ridiculous', he said, meant 'laughable', or 'funny', or 'amusing', while 'grotesque' meant 'bizarre', or 'curious', or 'original'. He should, therefore, properly have translated 'ridiculous and grotesque' as *'amusant et originale'*.

References

Barber, Clarence L. (1978), 'On the Origins of the Great Depression', *Southern Economic Journal*. vol. 44, no. 3 (January), pp. 432–56.

Cleveland, Harold van B. and Brittain, W. H. Bruce (1975), 'A World Depression?', *Foreign Affairs*, vol. 53, no. 2 (January), pp. 223–5.

Forrester, Jay W. (1976), 'A New View of Business Dynamics', *The Journal of Portfolio Management*, vol. 3, no. 1 (Fall).

Forrester, Jay W. (1978), 'Changing Economic Patterns', *Technology Review*, August–September, pp. 43–53.

Friedman, Milton and Schwartz, Anna J. (1965), *A Monetary History of the United States, 1867–1960* (Princeton, NJ: Princeton University Press).

Hoover, Herbert (1952), *The Memoirs of Herbert Hoover. Vol III: The Great Depression, 1929–1941* (New York: Macmillan).

Kindleberger, Charles P. (1973), *The World in Depression, 1929–1939* (Berkeley, Calif.: University of California Press).

Matthews, R. C. O. (1954), *A Study of Trade-Cycle History: Economic Fluctuations in Great Britain, 1832–1842* (Cambridge: Cambridge University Press).

Miskin, Frederic S. (1978), 'The Household Balance Sheet and the Great Depression', *Journal of Economic History*, vol. 38, no. 4 (December), pp. 918–37.

Néré, J. (1968), *La Crise de 1929* (Paris: A. Colin).

Rostow, W. W. (1978a), *The World Economy. History and Prospect* (Austin, Tex.: University of Texas Press).

Rostow, W. W. (1978b), *Getting from Here to There. A Policy for the Post Keynesian Age* (New York: Norton).

Temin, Peter (1976), *Did Monetary Forces Cause the Great Depression?* (New York: W. W. Norton).

18

The 1929 World Depression in Latin America – from the Outside

I am an impostor at a meeting of Latin American experts. I know little of the area, read neither Portuguese nor Spanish, and, apart from a few yards into Mexico at various points in Texas and California, have not even been to the area except to Panama and Cuban territorial waters in 1929 and 1930, rather before the events under discussion, and when I had no knowledge of or interest in economic history. I am here to learn. But perhaps I can stimulate your thought by reading the papers, listening to the discussion, commenting on them from the vantage point of what I may know, and comparing one account with another.

Let me start by commenting on Latin America's contribution to the start and continuation of the depression, and then deal with the papers under several headings:

- uniformity vs. diversity, especially
  (a) by commodities
  (b) in policy response
- the role of prices
- foreign borrowing and its halting
- foreign direct investment
- capacity to transform
- dependence vs. self-reliance.

For complete coverage of the papers, one should address the question of the political consequences of the depression, but my ignorance at this level is so abysmal that I leave it to others.

Latin America's contribution to the start and continuation of the depression

The usual positions on the start of the 1929 world depression are that it started exclusively in the United States, as Friedman and Schwartz

A paper presented at the 44th International Congress of Americanists, Manchester, England, September 1982, and published in Rosemary Thorp (ed.), Latin America in the 1930s: the Periphery in World Crisis (London: Macmillan, in association with St Anthony's College, Oxford, 1984), pp. 315–29.

(1963) assert, or that it was the consequence of European mistakes, as President Hoover of the United States insisted (1952). As between these two positions it seems to be sensible to give the answer of R. C. O. Matthews (1954) on the issue of whether the 1836–7 depression was caused by Britain or the United States: so intricate is the chain of causation linking the two areas that the question cannot be answered. Few have found causes of the 1929 depression outside the United States and Europe, apart from A. J. H. Latham (1981), who ascribes a portion of its origin to Asian overproduction of rice (added, to be sure, to world surpluses of wheat).

I come to the role of commodity prices later, but at this stage consider the difference between the price collapses of 1921 on the one hand, and of 1929 on the other: 1921 was traumatic for producers of many commodities, but recovery proceeded relatively quickly thereafter (except in Britain, burdened by heavy debt structures piled on the 1920 boom); in 1929, prices fell sharply, but failed to recover – in fact continuing to decline worldwide. The difference between the two periods has been ascribed to a change in the downward flexibility of wages – union contracts after 1921 no longer providing for two-way adjustment to the cost of living (Temin, 1971, p. 67) – and to the earlier absence of bank failures. The essential difference seems to me to lie in the difference in world commodity production and stocks. In 1921, correction of the boomlet left production barely recovering in Europe and stocks worldwide low. In 1929, on the other hand, the sellers' market of the early 1920s had turned into a buyers' market. Prices of agricultural products and minerals had been slipping since 1925 as European production after the war was added to expanded wartime supplies outside Europe. Cobwebs in some products, especially sugar and coffee, led to excessive responses to postwar price increases, and production in minerals – petroleum, copper, lead, zinc and, in Asia, tin – had expanded dangerously. Attempts to hold up prices in coffee and linseed accumulated stocks over the market. Latin America contributed to much of this oversupply, which accounted for the failure of prices and production to recover quickly after the sharp drop in commodity prices communicated from the stock market to commodity markets.

Secondly, Latin America was hit hard – especially Argentina, Brazil, Colombia – by the abrupt halt in foreign lending in June 1928 when the New York stock market started its meteoric rise and interest rates tightened on the call-money market. On this score, a number of Latin American countries date the start of the depression from the second half of 1928. Argentina lost $111 million in gold in 1929. In addition, its exchange rate started to slip from 97 cents to the US dollar in the first half of 1928 to 95 cents at the end of 1928, a rate held through November 1929 when exchange depreciation went further.

Thirdly, Latin America (and Australia–New Zealand) contributed to the world depression by early depreciation of their exchange rates in the face of falling commodity prices, exhausted reserves, and inability to borrow. Few other choices existed, but in a world poised on the edge of deflation, depreciation leaves domestic prices unchanged and the corresponding appreciation reduces them abroad. The area cannot be blamed for looking after its own interests at a cost to the rest of the world, since it had no responsibility for world economic stability. It may be observed further that, in a world of shortages, poised on the edge of inflation, depreciation raises domestic prices and appreciation abroad leaves them unchanged there. The ratchet works for world inflation under the conditions of the 1970s, for structural deflation under those of the 1930s.

Uniformity and diversity

The standard paradigm on the 1929 depression in Latin America referred to by many of the papers is that prior to 1929 Latin America was a dependent area, tightly attached to the world economy and led by changes in spending and lending by Europe and the United States. With the world depression, export-led growth and fluctuations gave way to import substitution in the form of manufacturing industry because of adverse balances of payments, and to more active stabilization policies, requiring in some instances the development of appropriate institutions. Most papers at the conference found this generalized description oversimplified, failing in one or more respects to fit the particular country under consideration: the break was less sharp, or went back to 1920–1 or to World War I; import substitution as a process had long been underway, as had the construction of central banks, the imposition of tariffs, exchange depreciation, and the like; O'Connell (1984) insists that Argentine troubles began much earlier than 1928 or 1929, and Palma (1984) traced industrialization in Chile back to the collapse of nitrates exports in 1919 following the development of synthetic ammonia during the war; Cuba's troubles went back to 1925, whereas those of Honduras did not start until 1932; in the case of Brazil, industrialization of the 1930s rested on excess capacity in textiles built in the 1920s, and the positive policy seen by Furtado (1963) in coffee valorization financed by central bank credit was an extension of policies on coffee prices that originated as early as 1900.

While separate scholars quite properly emphasize the distinctive features of the national experience they study, divergences from the paradigm take off in different directions, so that the generalization holds up as an average description. The question remains perhaps whether the central tendency is sufficiently peaked to warrant its use as a description of the experience of the area as a whole.

Commodities

The various papers explicitly and implicitly insist that one export commodity differs from another. Bulmer-Thomas (1984) points to the wide differences in Central America between coffee and bananas, the former produced on the whole by small producers, the latter foreign-owned, marketed by foreigners, subject to disease. Thorp and Londoño

(1984) ring the changes on the differences between Colombia coffee, benefiting from Brazil's attempt at sustaining prices and the American preference for soft coffee but requiring social overhead capital to bring it cheaply to market, and Peruvian metals, foreign-owned, needing little public construction. Fitzgerald (1984) observes similar differences within Mexico between metals and agricultural exports, and O'Connell (1984) notes the different demand and supply conditions in wheat and beef, although both are marketed by a handful of oligopolistic sellers. Implicit in these distinctions is the need for a staple theory relevant to depression and recovery comparable to that developed by Harold Innis for Canadian commodities with respect to growth. In a paper given in another symposium at the Congress John Fogarty explored the relevance of Innis' staple theory for Argentina, Australia and Canada, and found it limited. The econometric work of Michael Twomey (1981) found that Latin American exports were generally in highly inelastic supply (at least for price decreases). My reading of the papers, however, emphasizes diversity, and Diaz Alejandro's (1984) expression 'the commodity lottery' emphasizes that cyclical outcomes depended to a considerable extent on the nature of the commodity – its ownership, production function, linkages, demand conditions and marketing – that a country happened to produce for export.

Policy responses

Diaz Alejandro (1984) divided the countries of Latin America into two categories, the 'reactive' and the 'passive'. He insisted that this is not the same distinction as between the large and the small. Among medium-sized countries, for example, Chile and Uruguay were active, and Cuba, without a central bank until 1935 and with the US dollar circulating side by side with the peso, was passive. Argentina was far less active than Brazil, and Colombia was passive until late in 1931, maintaining its exchange rate and debt service through 1932, but then becoming very active.

An interesting generalization emerged during the discussion to the effect that policy in a number of countries was held within highly orthodox lines by the memory of disasters consequent on financial unorthodoxy of the past. Argentina's financial woes of 1890–3, the Colombian inflation from the Thousand Days War of the same epoch, Mexico's experience with wildcat issuance of banknotes after the 1914 revolution and continuing through to the early 1920s, and Central American inflationary experience in the 1920–1 commodity bubble all inhibited policy for a time, until the need to take some kind of governmental action became overwhelming. The examples echo a series of extra-Latin American episodes – John Law's Mississippi bubble and the *assignats* in France, the revaluation of the pound sterling in 1925 followed by a decade of high unemployment, and German hyper-inflation of 1923 – where 'collective memories' appear to have inhibited the adoption of rational policies for periods as long as 50 years or even (in the case of John Law) more than a century (Kindleberger, 1982).

Some considerable difference of opinion surfaced over the question whether active policies required the antecedent construction of appropriate institutions, or whether such institutions could be hastily built when the need became acute (as the Coase theorem, 1937, implies). There was plenty of antecedent experience with tariffs and exchange depreciation, and foreign-exchange controls were put into action with some alacrity once the need was clear. In Central America, however, fiscal policy implied monetary policy, since there was no money or capital market on which domestic debt could be issued, whereas the Andean countries had benefited from the visit by Edwin Kemmerer in the late 1920s, setting up central banks to operate the gold standard, even though, in the case of Peru, the gold standard was adopted in a single day (information communicated by Paul Drake) so that the roots of the institution could be said not to penetrate deeply.

There was something of a temptation to say that the monetarism of the 1920s was followed by Keynesianism in the 1930s, but in discussion the symposium decided that this was overstating it. Neither the gold standard of the 1920s nor the combination of government deficits with tariffs, depreciation and, in most cases, foreign exchange control represented coherent and thought-out conscious policies so much as spontaneous reactions to the exigencies of foreign financial advisers capable of blessing foreign loans (in the case of the gold standard) and to declines in exports and consequently government revenues in the later period. In fact, government deficits in a number of Central American countries represented primarily unpaid civil servant salaries.

Considerable discussion turned on whether conscious policy choices were made in the general interest or on behalf of a particular dominant elite. Where the dominant economic interest was foreign, as in Cuba, policy might be undertaken deliberately on behalf of small native planters. Surprise was implied in Versiani's (1984) statement that the interests of the coffee elite were not always consistently pursued, and in some important instances were opposed. Debate took place over whether the Roca–Runciman treaty between Argentina and Britain in 1933 strongly favored the cattle interests, as O'Connell (1984) and Abreu (1984) thought, or could be interpreted as providing the country as a whole with important financial gains, permitting the raising of wheat prices and conversion of the internal debt to a lower rate of interest and the government to balance its budget, as Ahladeff insisted (unpublished paper). In Central America, passivity seems to have favored the working classes, as wages were depressed less than profits, but there was dispute whether the end of peonage and the passage of a vagrancy law in Guatemala were beneficial in enabling the proletariat to plant food crops in land rented beneath the coffee trees, or constituted a device to force it to work on behalf of landowners to the latter's benefit.

The useful suggestion was made that import substitution and deficit financing were induced prior to about 1932 in most countries and undertaken more actively as chosen policy thereafter. This would make the dividing line between orthodox and Keynesian policies not 1929 but later, at a time when governments found themselves forced to do something – perhaps anything. But there was considerable variation from country to country.

Prices and the terms of trade

A number of the papers emphasize that Latin America suffered but little in real terms, as measured by gross domestic product (GDP), and recovered 1929 levels of output early in the subsequent decade. Suffering, however, should be measured by gross national income, not GDP, taking into account the relative fall in export and import prices. On this score, Chile and Cuba were the worst-hit countries of Latin America, and Chile the worst hit in the world. There were some buffers, notably the decline in profits that made the fall in the terms of trade on returned value (foreign sales less profits, or, more positively, primarily wages and taxes) considerably less than that in exports and imports as wholes. Other buffers were default, and blocking of profits. The fact that GDP was sustained may help relieve unemployment but, if the terms of trade turn sharply adverse, does little to maintain consumption and investment.

A number of points on the fall of export prices are worth noting. Most of us are so bemused by Keynesian analysis that we tend to think of a decline in prices as affecting national income through its impact on the value of exports. This is by no means the only connection. Where a country consumes a substantial portion of the goods it exports, the price decline on the retained amount may have significant macro-economic consequences. Modern monetary theorists tend to dismiss changes in prices within a country as unimportant, suggesting that the loss of a producer whose price has fallen is made up for by the gain of a consumer or purchaser who gets it more cheaply. To think otherwise, in their view, is 'money illusion', i.e. to confuse nominal quantities with real quantities. I am unable to accept this view as it applies to 1929.

As Fitzgerald (1984) rightly says, depression can be transmitted through prices without impinging on the balance of payments. There are lags between the losses of the producer and the recognition of gains by the domestic consumer. In addition, the producers' bank may fail, and the consumer is unlikely to start new banks. The dynamic consequences of price changes are ignored at the analyst's peril, and Ragnar Nurkse (1947), for example, made a serious mistake when he said that the fact of an export surplus in the balance of payments of the United States in 1932 meant that it was wrong for the United States to devalue because the balance of payments was expansionary. In reality, the deflation communicated through falling world prices was driving down imports faster than exports were being reduced, and the impact of the outside world on the United States was highly deflationary. The point, while worth noting, is not extensively relevant to Latin America, which for the most part exports 'colonial products' (defining that category as goods not extensively consumed in the exporting country or produced in the importing country).

It is worth mention in this connection that Latin American banks on the whole did not fail in the 1929 depression. The reason, brought out in the discussion rather than treated in the papers, was that many were state and provincial banks with governmental support. In Argentina, for example, the state bank had 30 percent of the system's loans and 40 percent of deposits. The contrast with the 1970s and 1980s is striking, since in the later period there have been banking crises in Argentina, Chile, Colombia and Mexico, and the end of such crises is not in sight.

It has already been noted that currency depreciation in depression by Latin American countries with heavy stocks of commodities tended to push world prices down further. O'Connell (1984) observes that devaluation in Argentina failed to raise domestic prices. It follows that it lowered them abroad. This was especially true in wheat, where lack of storage space in Argentina (and Australia) made export supply unresponsive to price. Canada and the United States tried through their Wheat Pool and Farm Board to hold the price up, but failed as early as May 1929. The unremitting availability of Argentine and Australian wheat hurt, especially after France imposed quantitative restrictions in 1930 as it struggled to raise the price paid to its farmers.

One further item on prices, in part to correct a mistake I made in *The World in Depression, 1929–1939* (1973). In that work, I emphasized how the liquidity crisis in the New York stock market had been communicated to the commodity markets through a squeeze on New York banks. Typically in those days, commodities were shipped to New York to be sold on consignment, rather than bought in the producing region and imported for the owner's account. A financial seizure caused by withdrawal of call-money from the stock market spread to commodities when the New York banks stopped other lending in order to be ready to replace out-of-town banks and 'others' withdrawing call funds. Merchandise shipped to New York for sale on consignment could not find buyers for lack of credit, and prices fell drastically between September and December 1929. Commodities financed in the interior of the United States, such as wheat, corn, sugar, did not fall to the same degree as rubber (26 percent), hides (18 percent), zinc (17 percent). I originally included in this list coffee, which fell from 22½ cents to 15 cents, or by one-third, but I learn from Ocampo's (1984) neat discussion of coffee prices that this was due in part, perhaps large part, to the collapse in October 1929 of Brazilian efforts to stabilize prices, as well as to lack of credit on the part of New York commission merchants.

Foreign borrowing and its halting

Like 'commodity lottery', the expression 'Dance of the Millions' is new to me. I find it in the Thorp and Londoño paper (1984) and in Pollitt's oral presentation on Cuba, and it is graphic. Thorp and Londoño are particularly eloquent on the speculation, corruption, greed and waste that accompanied the frenzied borrowing, largely from the United States and after 1925. These seem to be endemic in booms, called 'manias' on occasion (Kindleberger, 1978). The question is how to think today about this borrowing.

Diaz Alejandro (1984) blames the lenders for pushing loans on the borrowers, and is disposed to explain away Latin American default on the ground that everybody defaulted: the British on war debts, the Germans on short-term balances under the Standstill Agreements, the United States in repudiating the gold clause in its bonds. There are other ways to view it. Borrowing helped stimulate the boom and default cushioned the depression for Latin America. An important difference from the borrowing of the 1920s and that of half a century later is that the earlier debts were mostly owed to private individuals whose losses had little effect in spreading depression, apart from a wealth effect that may have reduced consumpion. Default on the debts of the 1970s contracted to banks, if it takes place, would have a much greater spread effect by threatening the stability of individual banks, and possibly of the financial system as a whole if two or more large defaults occurred close to one another and impaired the capital of several important banks. Unlike the 1920s, the public good of world monetary stability is involved in the contract along with what might be regarded as a private national interest.

Whatever the merits of US bankers in pushing foreign lending from 1925 to 1928, they were surely at fault in cutting it off abruptly in June of the latter year. Deflation is imposed by the center on the periphery whenever the former suddenly stops lending, as in 1825, 1857, 1866, 1873, 1890 and 1907. First halting lending and then cutting way down on imports are a recipe for disaster. It is worth noting that, in the 1980s, world bankers, who can do nothing about the decline in developed-country imports from the developing world, are acutely conscious of the need to avoid a sudden cut-off in lending that would precipitate serious deflation at the periphery, which would be certain to reflect back on the developed world and on their institutions.

The national interest of separate countries contemplating default, then and now involves one argument scarcely mentioned in the papers: the need or desire of the borrowing country to maintain access to the international capital market. History suggests that there has been typically a thirty-year lag between default and a country's being welcomed back into good standing as a borrower. Latin American defaults in the nineteenth century took place in 1825, 1857, 1890. A lending boom underway in the period 1910–13 would probably have become excessive and ended in repudiation of debt had not World War I supervened. This stretched the new borrowing to the second half of the 1920s and default to the 1930s. The Mexican revolution of 1914 involved an earlier default, which was about to be repaired in the Pani–Lamont agreement until its operation was rendered impossible by the depression.

An interesting point to me is the connection running between devaluation and default, stressed by Thorp and Londoño (1984).

Colombia hung on to the gold standard and paying its debts on the nail as long as it could. Devaluation, says Ocampo (1984), was then undertaken in the interest of the coffee elite, but brought about a drastic increase in the local-currency cost of servicing foreign debt, leading thus to default.

Foreign direct investment

Direct investment is mentioned at many points in the various papers but I find it hard to draw much in the way of generalizations. Foreign owners of mines suffered major losses in profits in Peru, Mexico and Chile. In addition, such positive profits as remained in Chile were blocked. In Mexico, prospects were so discouraging that a process of withdrawal was begun. The banana-exporting countries had little control over the price, quantity or growth of exports, which were entirely in the hands of the big fruit companies, and in Cuba the large American growers with extensive plantations, plus the American and Canadian banks that lent to them, left the Cuban government with little control over events in its jurisdiction. The British government bargained strongly on behalf of its nationals owning the Argentine railroads in the Roca–Runciman agreement, taking advantage of Argentina's dependence on the British market and responding to Dominion demands put forward at Ottawa in 1932. Argentine utilities increasingly were owned by American investors, rather than British, the financial switch occurring also in borrowing through bonds and compounding over the long run the problem of selling to Britain and buying from the United States when sterling was not convertible.

The role of foreign direct investment in import-substitution was little stressed. The 1920s saw the beginnings of foreign investment in automobiles, tires, cement, electrical appliances, some of it protected by new tariffs, which the foreign entrepreneurs 'jumped', to use Diaz Alejandro's phrase. Presumably local entrepreneurship was too little developed that tariffs combined with restrictions on foreign direct investment, such as are widespread today, would have produced locally led industry. Versiani (1984) observed the development of some repair shops, required in World War I by shortages to manufacture parts, into factories, but they seem not to have been many. There was also some infusion of entrepreneurship from European immigration. I judge that at this early stage of industrialization, however, direct investment from abroad in industry but not in mines and plantations was welcomed as a contributor to industrialization, and that most governments were willing to provide it with tariffs and other inducements. O'Connell emphasized in discussion that the 1930 road-building program of Argentina ran not from farms to railheads to assist the agriculturalists, but parallel to trunk line rails, presumably to stimulate the birth of the automobile age.

Capacity to transform

In his contribution to the Triffin *Festschrift*, Diaz Alejandro calls Latin American capacity to transform resources into new sectors impressive (1982, p. 179). Leading sectors were textiles, building materials (especially cement), oil refining, tires, toiletries and food processing. The role of foreign enterprise has already been noted, along with the expansion of cotton growing in Brazil and Nicaragua under the umbrella of American efforts to raise prices. Much of the transformation was in import-substituting agriculture, and some of that was at the expense of other Latin American countries. O'Connell (1984) cites a shift from cattle breeding to cattle fattening, with its induced demand for feed grains, but also observes the transformation of Argentine agriculture from its traditional beef, wheat, maize and linseed to new products such as sunflower seeds, cotton and peanuts for the domestic market. There was intensive competition within the region in export products – coffee, bananas and petroleum – and a movement to substitute domestic production for such imports as sugar.

This transformation occurred largely in the reactive countries. Others such as Peru, Cuba and Central America waited for recovery of the world market. Diaz Alejandro (1984) hypothesized that active policies of import-substitution in world depression produced a less satisfactory outcome than would the absence of the depression and continued reliance on export-led growth. It is not clear whether this judgement assumes that import-substitution would have continued as a natural process, resulting from the spillover of demand from export staples into market-oriented products, giving rise to the growth of local industry, or not.

A significant point was made by Bulmer-Thomas (1984) about Central America: that export-led growth led to the neglect of financial institutions. Coffee exports were financed by foreign merchants, bananas by the fruit companies, and little savings were available for other productive activities. Perhaps this was so in Central America in this period. It may be observed, however, that export-led growth of Sweden in feed grains, timber and iron in the 1850s and 1860s, originally financed by foreign merchants, did not inhibit the rapid development of strong financial institutions capable of intermediating between foreign capital and local borrowers, and in fact doubtless accelerated it. Bulmer-Thomas' point may have more to do with Central America than with export-led growth in general.

Dependence vs Self-reliance

Diaz Alejandro's paper ends with the statement that the time has come for Latin America to achieve self-reliance. The Cocoyoc declaration of 1976 made a similar demand. I have not seen the paper by Johan Galtung entitled 'Self-reliance: An Overriding Strategy for Transition' (1982), but the experience of Latin America in the depression raises a number of issues related to self-reliance by developing countries in a large world.

In the first place, there is a strong contrast between the experience of Argentina on the one hand and Brazil on the other. Both were potentially dependent on triangular trade, selling to one trading partner and buying from another, but Argentina suffered from the fact that its trade partner, Britain, was prepared to take advantage of its position, whereas Brazil, selling mainly to the United States, found the latter unwilling to exploit its bilateral advantage. The United States, unlike Great Britain, did not use its import market to collect debts owed to its investors, force trade into bilateral channels, or object when Brazil slipped into advantageous bilateral trading relations with Germany, displacing the United States from the German cotton market. Abreu (1984) may even approve of the emerging hegemony of United States in the 1930s as he notes the absence of a hegemonic country in the world economy today.

While Brazil benefited from the indifference of the United States to exploitation of its position, that indifference came close to being harmful for Mexico, whose interests in silver were, to say the least, totally ignored. Cárdenas (1984) describes how, when Mexico ran out of gold, it got a benefit from coining silver, then low in price, through gaining substantial seigniorage. This failed to last, as the US Treasury, under pressure from western silver senators, started bidding up the price of silver. The seigniorage was lost, but Mexican silver mines got a better price. With great good luck, and possibly some management, the Bank of Mexico found its peso notes gradually gain acceptance in place of coins. Thus Mexico gained a high price for its silver as bullion, and 100 percent seigniorage on currency issues, instead of the earlier 60 percent. Had it had to depend solely on silver for money creation, however, it might have found itself drained of its money supply, as proved to be the fate of China.

Secondly, it is not clear in this context whether self-reliance means reliance on self by country, region, continent, hemisphere or by developing countries on some world basis. Thorp and Londoño (1984) note how Colombia prospered under Brazilian efforts to raise the price of coffee; Colombia's gain was at Brazil's expense. The same was true of a certain amount of agricultural import-substitution, especially in sugar.

Price-raising activities, moreover, have to extend beyond Latin American boundaries, as was then evident in copper, tin, petroleum, lead, silver and zinc, and is now true of coffee as well, in that Latin American producers of basic commodities share the world market with other countries outside the hemisphere.

Since World War II, attempts at integration involving groups such as the Central American republics, the Andean countries and Latin America as a whole have fallen short of widely held hopes for self-reliance by regional blocs.

It may be argued, as some of the participants do for separate countries, that machinery is needed before policy can be formulated and implemented – machinery going beyond trade policy for the region perhaps into monetary and fiscal policy, public works, even commodity-price stabilization. Efforts in these directions in Europe and in the wider Atlantic community, including that honorary Atlantic power, Japan, do not offer strong hope. Self-reliance, it would seem, must take hold at the national level, and may thus contain substantial elements of beggar-thy-good-neighbor about it. If the United States were not losing in power and concern, it might well be that dependence of the separate members of the periphery on the American public role of stabilizer would be preferable. It is widely agreed among political scientists that the best form of government is benevolent despotism, so long as one can rest completely assured that the despot remains benevolent. That hope, alas, seems generally vain.

Perhaps a better long-run guide to policy would be to strengthen the responses of economic elements to the market on trend, and to reserve strong government policy – on an international basis to the extent possible – to the (it is hoped) rare lapses from trend into crisis in commodity markets (either dearth or glut), in capital flows, or in finance.

References

Abreu, Marcelo de Paiva (1984), 'Argentina and Brazil during the 1930s: The Impact of British and American International Economic Policies', in Thorp (ed.), pp. 144–62.

Bulmer-Thomas, Victor (1984), 'Central America in the Interwar Period', in Thorp (ed.), pp. 279–314.

Cárdenas, Enrique (1984), 'The Great Depression and Industrialization: The Case of Mexico', in Thorp (ed.), pp. 222–41.

Coase, Ronald H. (1937), 'The Nature of the Firm', *Economica*, new ser., vol. 4, pp. 386–405.

Diaz Alejandro, Carlos F. (1982), 'Some Historical Vicissitudes of Open Economies in Latin America', in Richard N. Cooper *et al.* (eds), *The International Monetary System under Flexible Exchange Rates* (Cambridge, Mass.: Ballinger).

Diaz Alejandro, Carlos F. (1984), 'Latin America in the 1930s', in Thorp (ed.), pp. 17–49.

Fitzgerald, E. V. K. (1984), 'Restructuring through the Depression: the State and Capital Accumulation in Mexico, 1925–1940', in Thorp (ed.), pp. 242–65.

Friedman, Milton and Schwartz, Anna J. (1963), *A Monetary History of the United States, 1867–1960* (Princeton, NJ: Princeton University Press).

Furtado, Celso (1963), *The Economic Growth of Brazil* (Berkeley, Calif.: University of California Press).

Galtung, Johan (1982), 'Self-reliance: An Overriding Strategy for Transition', in Richard Falk *et al.* (eds), *Toward a Just World Order* (New York: Praeger International).

Hoover, Herbert (1952), *The Memoirs of Herbert Hoover*. Vol. III: *The Great Depression, 1929–1941* (New York: Macmillan).

Kindleberger, Charles P. (1973), *The World in Depression, 1929–1939* (Berkeley, Calif.: The University of California Press).

Kindleberger, Charles P. (1978), *Manias, Panics and Crashes: A History of Financial Crises* (New York: Basic Books).

Kindleberger, Charles P. (1982), 'Collective Memory vs. Rational Expectations: Some Historical Puzzles in Economic Behavior', *National okonomisk Tidsskrift*, pp. 860–71.

Latham, A. J. H. (1981), *The Depression and the Developing World, 1914–39* (London: Croom Helm).

Matthews, R. C. O. (1954), *A Study of Trade-Cycle History: Economic Fluctuations in Great Britain, 1832–1842* (Cambridge: Cambridge University Press).

Nurkse, Ragnar (1947), 'Equilibrium in Foreign Exchange', in American Economic Association, *Readings in the Theory of International Trade* (Philadelphia, Pa: Blakiston Co.), pp. 1–25.

Ocampo, José Antonio (1984), 'The Colombia Economy in the 1930s', in Thorp (ed.), pp. 117–43.

O'Connell, Arturo (1984), 'Argentina into the Depression: Problems of an Open Economy', in Thorp (ed.), pp. 188–221.

Palma, Gabriel (1984, 'From an Export-led to an Import-substituting Economy: Chile 1914–39', in Thorp (ed.), pp. 50–80.

Temin, Peter (1971), 'Three Problems in Economic History', *Journal of Economic History*, vol. 31, no. 1 (March), pp. 58–75.

Thorp, Rosemary (ed.) (1984), *Latin America in the 1930s: The Role of the Periphery in World Crisis* (London: Macmillan, in association with St Antony's College, Oxford).

Thorp, Rosemary and Londoño, Carlos (1984), 'The Effect of the Great Depression on the Economies of Peru and Colombia', in Thorp (ed.), pp. 81–116.

Twomey, M. (1981), 'Aggregate Supply and Demand during the Great Depression', University of Michigan, mimeo.

Versiani, Flavia Rabelo (1984), 'Before the Depression: Brazilian Industry in the 1920s', in Thorp (ed.), pp. 163–87.

19

Keynesianism vs. Monetarism in the 1930s Depression and Recovery

Debate over macro-economic events and policy is often forced into a narrow confrontation between two seemingly polar analytical positions. In Britain, debate over banking in the first half of the nineteenth century ran between the Banking School and the Currency School; that over the causes of the German hyperinflation of 1923 between the monetary school and the balance-of-payments position. In my own way, I have been guilty of such oversimplification in writing on 'Keynesianism vs Monetarism in Eighteenth- and Nineteenth-Century France' (Kindleberger, 1980 – Chapter 3 above). It is well to remember the law enunciated by a colleague in physics at the Massachusetts Institute of Technology; Evans' law (after Robley Evans) states that 'Everything is more complicated than most people think'.

The clash between monetarism and Keynesianism is particularly exasperating when one addresses the 1929 depression. Friedman and Schwartz (1966, ch. 7) insist that the depression was caused by a decline in the money supply. Peter Temin (1976) takes the contrary view that the decline in spending produced both the depression and the fall in the money stock. He does not elaborate why spending declined, but other authors point to their favorite candidates: Rostow (1978) to automobiles, and Barber (1978) to a slump in housing resulting from a fall-off in population growth. All these writers ignore international aspects of the 1929 depression, as if the depression were concentrated in the United States, which happened to be a closed economy.

Recently there has been a grudging and limited admission of one international factor in the depression, the Smoot–Hawley tariff act of June 1930. Jude Wanniski (1977, p. 130) finds that an early, and he thinks critical, test of tariff strengths in October 1929 produced the crash of the New York stock market on 24 and 29 October. The theory of rational expectations requires that all movements in prices reflect real economic factors and there is no other candidate to explain the crash, unlikely as it is that the stock market anticipated accurately the course of the legislation over the following eight-plus months, President Hoover's attitude toward it, and the retaliation of the thirty to forty countries that expressed displeasure by raising tariffs on US goods.

A paper written for the Colloquium on Récession et Relance *held 5 and 6 November 1982 in the halls of the National Assembly, Paris, but not delivered because of absence.*

Allan Meltzer, Anna Schwartz, Robert Gordon and James Wilcox also leave some room – but not much – for the single international factor, this tariff (see their essays in Brunner, 1981). These American analysts ignore a host of other international factors: the recovery of European production after 1925, which led to surpluses in many lines in which regions outside Europe had expanded to make up for the shortfalls during World War I (notably in sugar and wheat), overvaluation of the pound, undervaluation of the French franc, war debts, reparations, the boom in foreign lending following the success of the Dawes loan, cut off by New York in June 1928 when the stock market started its meteoric rise, and followed by short-term loans especially to Central Europe. No one other than me makes much of the transmission of the squeeze in liquidity because of bank worry over loans to the stock market from securities to commodities, which fell 10–15 percent worldwide from September to December 1929, or to the pressure on commodity prices applied by exchange depreciation, first in a series of countries such as Argentina, Uruguay, Australia and New Zealand, pushing down particularly farm prices, and then the most critically when Britain left the gold standard in 1931 and the dollar appreciated from $4.86 to the pound in September to $3.25 in December, or almost 40 percent. Nor are people who concern themselves with the onslaught of the depression interested in the role of the lender of last resort, which Britain could not fulfill and neither the United States nor France was willing to. (In the 1980s, to be sure, there is much more acknowledgement of the need for a lender of last resort if the banking system should become unstuck.)

As for the fall into depression, so for the long climb out, the analysis runs almost entirely in terms of Keynesianism vs monetarism. The monetarists on the whole have a difficult task. They had earlier had difficulty explaining how industrial production in the United States could fall by 30 percent from December 1928 to December 1930, and prices over the same period by 19 percent, when the money supply fell on various measures by only 5 or 6 percent. They solved this on the whole by taking the entire period from 1929 to 1933 as one, without acknowledging that in the first period the money supply fell a little and output and prices a lot, whereas from 1931 to the spring of 1933 output and prices continued to fall but money supply fell a great deal as banks went into liquidation. In the period after 1933, on the other hand, the money supply rose sharply, and output moved up more slowly. The Keynesians explained this by liquidity preference: as interest rates fell to very low levels, asset holders preferred money to bonds because of the risk that interest rates would rise and inflict capital losses on the holders of bonds. Money was sought not for transactions or for precautionary motives, but as a capital asset. Income velocity, which had been as high as 3.42 (for currency and demand deposits) per annum in 1929, fell to 2.16 in 1932 and by 1936 had risen only to 2.35 (Friedman and Schwartz, 1966, p. 774).

The major mistake alleged against the Federal Reserve system in the downswing was raising the discount rate and refusing to undertake expansionary open-market operations in the fall of 1931, after the appreciation of the dollar (depreciation of sterling) and the withdrawal of $750 million of gold by the gold bloc, led by Belgium but closely followed by France (Kindleberger, 1973, pp. 167–70). Friedman and Schwartz reject the Federal Reserve's excuse or explanation – that it was required to, by law, since it was out of 'free gold'. Under the law setting up the system in 1913, the note and deposit liabilities of the Federal Reserve had to be backed by a minimum of 40 percent gold and the rest discounted eligible paper (largely bankers' acceptances generated in foreign trade). The decline in trade had reduced the volume of eligible paper in the market to very low amounts. Most Federal Reserve credit consisted of government bonds, which were not eligible as backing for notes and deposits – at least until the passage of the first Glass–Steagall act in February 1932. Friedman and Schwartz presumably take the view that the Federal Reserve could have been expected to go to the Congress and explain the necessity to violate the act, to hold government bonds against that portion of its liabilities up to 60 percent that lacked eligible paper, and thus to free gold in excess of the 40 percent minimally required that had been held instead of eligible paper. There is something to be said on each side. The claim has been made that the Bank of France should have violated the *plafonde* in the crisis of 1924, Herriot going to the Chamber of Deputies and saying that the crisis demanded it, rather than disguising the violation and making matters much worse when the transgression was ultimately revealed (Schuker, 1976; Jeanneney, 1977). German finances during World War I were conducted in an inflationary manner without raising income taxes partly because of the class bias of the financiers such as Karl Helfferich, but partly because the constitution of the Reich in 1871 assigned all but a few limited taxes to the states and municipalities. Mathias Erzberger called Helfferich 'a financial Ludendorff' for not getting the rules changed in the war emergency (Williamson, 1971), but the case can be made that rules are rules, and that the government is committed to stick to them or change them in an orderly fashion. Such a writer as Elmus Wicker takes the excuse seriously that the Federal Reserve could not increase the money supply until the Glass–Steagall act was passed. Friedman and Schwartz regard the explanation as unacceptable.

Whatever the position down to February 1932, after that time the Federal Reserve did try to expand the money supply, failing to do so for another year as the harvest of bankrupt banks continued to multiply. With the turnaround in April 1933, however, the money supply grew and, as noted, failed to produce the recovery that the monetarists expected because of low interest rates and high liquidity preference. Investors and banks gave up their bonds to the system and took cash, which they held rather than spent.

This failure to conform to the monetarist doctrine does not pass unnoticed today in monetarist circles. They have erected a defense of sorts in claiming that other policies of the Roosevelt administration in the field of industrial organization – notably the National Recovery Act, which until it was declared unconstitutional was a measure promoting cartelization, and such labor legislation as the Wagner Act encouraging

unionization – stifled the normal course of recovery that would have
been brought about by the expansion of money (Weinstein in Brunner,
1981). There is reason to be skeptical. The important point was that the
money merely substituted for securities in investor portfolios, rather
than having been created by banks in response to a demand for money
for investment or other spending.

It cannot be contended that Keynesian analysis explains the 1930s
any better than monetarism. In the first place, *The General Theory of
Employment, Interest and Money* did not appear until 1936, even
though the multiplier had been developed as early as 1931 (Kahn,
1931), and hints of the new doctrines had been seeping out of Cambridge
in the year or two before 1936. In the United States, there had been no
acceptance of Keynesian doctrine in the highest levels of government
until after the recession starting in September 1937, not, that is, until the
spring of 1938. Even then, the move to substitute government spending
for private spending was undertaken timidly and in highly limited
fashion (Brown, 1956). Government spending on a substantial scale did
not take place until the armament programs of 1939, 1940 and 1941.

There were Keynesian and monetary effects. Some theorists attribute
the boomlet of 1936 and the first nine months of 1937 to the Veterans'
bonus payment of $1.7 billion in fiscal 1936. How much of the money
was saved, how much used to pay down debt, and how much actually
spent is not known. $1.4 billion was cashed. But the usual view is that
the boomlet to 1937 had different origins than either monetarism or
Keynesianism. It was a speculative flurry in inventory investment,
brought on by the Wagner Act, the merger of the American Federation
of Labor (AFL) with the Congress of Industrial Organizations (CIO) and
the anticipation of a period of strikes and demands for higher wages.
Long-term investment did not pick up in any striking way. Inventories
by September 1937 were estimated to have risen 50 percent above the
1929 high figure. When it was seen that the price rise was leveling off,
the process of adding to inventories came to an end and some
disinvestment and a sharp drop in production took place. Anticipations
had been falsified, the bulge of spending undertaken earlier could not be
sustained, and recession ensued.

There has been some attempt to connect the 1937 recession to United
States monetary policy. The rise in the price of gold from $20.67 an
ounce in the years since 1879 to $35.00 in February 1934 had led to
widespread dishoarding in Europe and especially in India. For the most
part the dishoarded gold, plus enhanced new production, moved to the
United States. US gold stocks rose from $6.8 billion in January 1934 to
$11 billion in October 1936. Reserve requirements of the member banks
of the Federal Reserve system were raised in August 1936 to mop up
some of the excess reserves generated by the inflow. This failed to halt,
and indeed intensified, the inflow, as gold holders, including even a few
central banks, became worried that the United States might reduce the
gold price from $35. In December 1936 the US Treasury undertook a
policy of sterilizing gold inflows by borrowing the money from the
market to buy them. In January 1937 a new increase in reserve require-

ments was announced, to take place one-half in March and one-half in May. The height of the so-called 'gold scare' was reached in April 1937, but the dishoarding continued at a heavy pace through June 1937 when the weakening of raw-material prices made the possibility of a policy reduction in the price of gold much less pressing. The suggestion that the increases in reserve requirements of August 1936 and March and May 1937 were responsible for the short sharp recession in the prices of securities, commodities and in output has been made. The fact that excess reserves were plentiful throughout the period, however, makes it one that is difficult to entertain seriously.

Can one blame the 1937 recession on perverse Keynesian policies? It has been done (Roose, 1954). The Treasury deficit was $4.6 billion in fiscal 1936 ending 30 June of that year and $3.1 billion in fiscal 1937. For the calendar years, the decline in the deficit was $2.2 billion. Most of both declines was the result of the payment of the bonus in 1936 and no such payment the following year. Whatever the responsibility of fiscal policy as opposed to the overshooting in inventory accumulation, the recession of 1937–8 led to adoption of Keynesian measures, but on a modest scale. Proposed were $2 billion of spending and $1 billion of loans to spending bodies. These commitments made in April 1938 were late and limited, and are said to belie the widespread impression that the New Deal was a spending spree of the Keynesian type (Brown, 1956).

The recovery program in April 1938 contained an element of monetarism. Reserve requirements of the member banks were reduced by $750 million and the Treasury's inactive gold account of almost $1.2 billion of gold was closed out. One would have a hard time, however, judging either monetarism or Keynesianism as effective policies in this period.

In the following three years, an armament program quickly brought about full employment and spending financed by monetary expansion as the Treasury sold bonds to the public and the Federal Reserve system bought bonds from the public (both bodies disdaining the inflationary path where the Treasury sells bonds directly to the central bank). Monetarism or Keynesianism? The answer is, rather, Keynesianism *and* monetarism. To restrict the analysis to either–or of these limited policies is once again *simpliste* and insufficiently *nuancé*.

I do not know if the remark appears in print, but there is an oral tradition that Friedman has said that it would have been possible for the United States to finance the war with an equilibrium amount of money, a balanced budget, and a constant price level. This would have required, after full employment was reached, not only heavy taxation, but also contraction in some sectors of the economy with declines in prices, wages and output to match expanding sectors of the war economy with rising prices and wages necessary to attract resources from the rest of the economy to increase output. For all its heuristic value, the suggestion, which Friedman may in fact not have made, embodies a touch of masochism. Increases in investment needed to expand military output would have had to come from voluntary rather than forced savings. Government would have had to pay higher interest rates on these borrowed savings. While perhaps agreeable from the technical point of view – though I would worry about the frictions – this would have imposed a social strain by making the rich richer (perhaps only before taxes) at a time when all classes were called upon for sacrifice. It was surely easier, more efficient and more equitable to bring about the vast reallocation of resources with some (limited) inflation in expanding sectors, not fully matched by deflation in those sectors slated to contract.

Let me return to my theme. To pose the question of policy choices in the 1930s – whether those policies actually followed or those that would have been desirable – in terms of the choice between Keynesianism and monetarism is, in my judgement, mistaken. A judicious mixture of both policies and of elements of many other sorts of policies regarding taxation, exchange rates, occasional government direct intervention and the like is called for in depression, in prosperity, and in war and in peace.

References

Barber, Clarence L. (1978), 'On the Origins of the Great Depression', *Southern Economic Journal*, vol. 44, no. 3 (January), pp. 432–56.

Brown, E. Cary (1956), 'Fiscal Policy in the 'Thirties, A Reappraisal', *American Economic Review*, vol. 46, no. 5 (December), pp. 857/79.

Brunner, Karl (ed.) (1981), *The Great Depression Revisited* (The Hague: Martinus Nijhoff).

Friedman, Milton and Schwartz, Anna J. (1963), *A Monetary History of the United States, 1867–1960* (Princeton University Press).

Jeanneney, Jean-Noël (1977), *Leçon d'histoire pour une gauche au pouvoir: La Faillite du Cartel (1924–26)* (Paris: Seuil).

Kahn, R. F. (1931), 'The Relation of Home Investment to Unemployment', *Economic Journal*, vol. 41, no. 2 (June), pp. 193–8.

Keynes, John Maynard (1936), *The General Theory of Employment, Interest and Money* (New York: Harcourt Brace).

Kindleberger, C. P. (1973), *The World in Depression, 1929–1939* (London: Allen Lane).

Kindleberger, C. P. (1980), 'Keynesianism vs Monetarism in Eighteenth- and Nineteenth-Century France', *History of Political Economy*, vol. 12, no. 4 (Winter), pp. 499–523.

Roose, Kenneth D. (1954), *The Economics of Recession and Revival. An Interpretation of 1937–38* (New Haven, Conn.: Yale University Press).

Rostow, W. W. (1978), *The World Economy: History, and Prospect* (London: Macmillan).

Schuker, Stephen A. (1976), *The End of French Predominance in Europe: The Financial Crisis of 1924 and the Adoption of the Dawes Plan* (Chapel Hill, NC: University of North Carolina Press).

Temin, Peter (1976), *Did Monetary Forces Cause the Great Depression?* (New York: W. W. Norton).

Wanniski, Jude (1977), *The Way the World Works* (New York: Basic Books).

Williamson, John (1971), *Karl Helfferich, 1872–1924. Economist, Financier, Politician* (Princeton, NJ: Princeton University Press).

20

Banking and Industry between the Two Wars: An International Comparison

Introduction

The topic chosen for its centennial celebration by the Banca di Roma could hardly be more timely. Action is taking place on several fronts. In the United States, the Reagan administration appears to be earnestly considering plans to undo much of the regulatory legislation of the 1930s. In France, on the contrary, the new Socialist administration of President Mitterand is engaged on a program of carrying through the nationalization of important segments of the credit market, begun feebly in 1936, and carried out with great restraint in 1945 with the nationalization of the *banques d'affaires*. These had been spared from nationalization in 1946 by President de Gaulle in a sort of Passover (Kuisel, 1981, p. 207).

Before I get to the interwar period, however, I propose to start with a bit of historical background, and then a smattering of economic theory.

Background

A series of eminent economic historians (Hoselitz, 1956; Cameron, 1961; and Gerschenkron, 1962) has held that the major innovation in industrial financing in the nineteenth century was the Crédit Mobilier, founded in 1852 by Emile and Isaac Pereire. Gerschenkron's theory was elaborated into a model of backwardness, in which first banks, then government, depending on how backward a country was, substituted for the entrepreneurship that had been the driving force in the United Kingdom, which Peter Mathias calls 'The first industrial nation'. Cameron explained in detail how the Crédit Mobilier and its imitators were responsible for the economic development not only of France, but of continental Europe as a whole. The imitators included the Bank of Darmstadt in Germany, the Creditanstalt in Austria, a series of banks established in Italy and Spain by the Crédit Mobilier itself and by its

A paper prepared for a seminar on 'Banking and Industry in the Inter-War Period', sponsored by the Banca di Roma in cooperation with the Alfred P. Sloan School of Management, Massachusetts Institute of Technology, 23–24 October 1981. Published in a special issue of Journal of European Economic History, *vol. 13, no. 2 (Fall 1984), pp. 7–28.*

French rivals, with strong influences apparent in such countries as Sweden and Belgium. Cameron also traces the origin of these industrial or mixed banks of the Crédit Mobilier to the Société Générale de Belgique of the 1820s.

Evolution proceeded rather differently in different countries. Britain had a flurry of imitations of the Crédit Mobilier in the 1860s, but all expired in the Overend, Gurney panic of 1866. Thereafter, British banks appeared to provide only short-term credit to industry, leaving long-term capital either to the informal local market, or to the more structured London stock exchange. These appearances are somewhat deceiving, as Jeffrys (1938) points out for the nineteenth century, especially in the north. In addition, the major banks, by this time consolidated into a network of large branched banks with headquarters in London, lent heavily to industry in the securities boom after World War I, and took on a load of frozen debt that weighed them down all during the 1920s.

In France, as Bouvier has explained elsewhere (1965/1970) the new banks were founded in the 1860s after the Crédit Mobilier turned away from industry. There were some tragi-comic episodes, such as the case of La Fuschine in which the Crédit Lyonnais cut off credit to the pioneer dye firm of France and drove it to Switzerland (Bouvier, 1955, I, pp. 374–81). In 1903, Henri Germain (or perhaps it was another banker, the source is unclear) was quoted in reply to a stockholder asking about loans to industry – sarcastically I believe – as saying 'There are advantages and more security in lending abroad since the credit of a state represents the best guarantee' (Charpenay, 1939, p. 28). The large profits made in the Thiers *rente* in the early 1870s induced both deposit banks and *banques d'affaires* that survived the decade to speculate in foreign bonds. Only slowly at the end of the century did the *banques d'affaires* lend to industry, as did the regional banks of Lorraine and the Dauphiné (Grenoble). The Bank of France began direct discounting to industry at this time, partly perhaps to maintain its profits but largely, I believe, because the governor, Georges Pallain, was a 'neo-Keynesian' who thought that more credit was needed in the system. Its initiative was resented by the deposit banks. As Bouvier's present paper (1984) shows, to be sure, most large companies financed their fixed-capital needs with plowed-back profits. After 1919, the banks employed their funds mainly in lending to government and financing speculation in foreign exchange.

German development took the example of the Crédit Mobilier and developed it to the utmost. Apart from Hamburg and Frankfurt, which clung longer to commercial banking, the German banks went in for close relations with industrial and mining firms. Even the Deutsche Bank, created in 1872 for the express purpose of financing foreign trade (and freeing Germany from London's domination of the European foreign exchange market), quickly turned in the euphoria of the *Gründungszeit* to financing industrial enterprise. Close relationships build up between particular companies and particular banks, between Siemens and the Deutsche Bank, for example, AEG and the Berliner

Handelsgesellschaft, between the Gelsenkirchen Bergwerkgesellschaft and the Diskontogesellschaft. Riesser's classic study notes that Thyssen and Stinnes pursued policies of friendly relations with a number of banks, without wedding themselves to any one, and that for years the chemical industry made large profits that it plowed back so that banks had little influence with those companies (1911, pp. 721, 741). In chemicals, to be sure, Germany was a pioneer, as was Britain in textiles, iron and steel, coal, etc., so that the backwardness thesis did not apply.

There was French capital, as well as a French idea, in German banking, especially in the Bank of Darmstadt. Borchardt's classic article (1961) on the capital shortage so complained about in German economic history makes clear that the problem lay not in the supply of savings – despite an underdeveloped mercantile sector – but in the initial lack of demand. Gerschenkron (1962) and Cohen (1966) have demonstrated to their satisfaction that the Italian economic spurt of the two decades prior to World War I was the consequence of German founding of the Banca Commerciale Italiano (Comit) and the Credito Italiano in the 1880s, without, however, fully explaining why the surge of French banking into Italy in the 1860s did not produce a similar result, and without noting that the German investors of the 1890s quickly sold off their holdings to French and Italian investors (Confalonieri, 1976, III, p. 3–17).

Bouvier's paper (1984) mentions banking crises in France in 1848, 1867, 1882 and 1891. The first two were international, the second two local. Italian crises occurred in 1866, 1893 and 1907, each precipitated by withdrawals of foreign capital. In 1893 the Banca Tiberina and the French-inspired Credito Mobiliare collapsed; and in 1907 the Società Bancaria Italiana. The 1907 crisis has been studied in depth by Franco Bonelli, who found it connected with the 1907 stock-market panic in New York. That event tightened interest rates in New York, London and Paris, and pulled funds from Milan and Turin to Paris. Bonelli comments that colonial countries, among them Italy, suddenly found themselves deprived of capital (1971, p. 43). The adjective 'colonial' is evocative as it suggests Italian inability to provide for its own capital needs and dependence on a flow of funds from abroad.

I shall not pursue this sketch of historical background to Austria, Hungary, Spain or the United States, largely because of ignorance, but also, in the case of the United States, to spare many of you a recital of the familiar. The federal United States had long had free banking, sometimes called 'wildcat banking', with prohibitions against branching, chaining, and even spilling out beyond the confines of the county in many states. Various ways around these restrictions, through trust companies and the like, took place before World War I. With the surge of industrial growth stimulated by that war, a new spurt of innovation occurred in the 1920s, as Minsky's paper (1984) indicates. I want at this stage only to call your attention to the fact that both Italy and the United States found it necessary at the outbreak of war to create new institutions for financing wartime expansion of industry – in Italy, the Consortium for the Support of Industrial Securities, created in

December 1914, the father of the Autonomous Section of March 1922, grandfather of the Liquidation Institute of 1926, and great-grandfather of the Instituto per la Ricostruzione Industriale (IRI) of January 1933; and in the United States, the War Finance Corporation, father of the Reconstruction Finance Corporation (RFC) of 1931, and grandfather of the Defense Plant Corporation of 1941. The point to be borne in mind is that Italy kept IRI going, whereas the United States wound down the RFC, only to have to rev it up again at the outbreak of World War II as the Defense Plant Corporation to help finance major industrial expansion of military equipment. It functioned brilliantly but was liquidated at the end of the war, selling off its assets without a breath of scandal. Some economists would have liked to have had it in existence in 1974 after the OPEC price rise to help finance major energy projects, too large, expensive, or uncertain for the private market, as a public good, i.e. as part of expenditure for national defense.

In my analysis of monetary policy, I make a distinction between trend and crisis – trend when a monetarist policy of a growing supply of money at some appropriate rate is desirable, and crisis when a lender of last resort is required to make money freely available. A similar distinction may not be amiss in the capital field, where the market should be left to its own devices on trend, but where in crisis, as in a world war, a deep depression, or drastic sudden demand for investment, governmental steps of the last-resort type may need to be taken. In the field of money, the problem is often how to get back on trend by mopping up the large amounts of money produced in crisis. In capital, the question is whether to wind down emergency measures, as in the cases of the United States and, as we shall see, Germany, or to elevate an expedient into a principle, as in Austria and Italy.

Theory

In my paper for the Banca di Roma meeting last December, I suggested that IRI, IMI and the like were a second-best solution to the problem of providing external finance for industry. Gianni Toniolo took exception to this designation, on the ground that there were no 'missed opportunities' (1981, p. 135). I am sorry to have been misunderstood. I was using the term in the technical sense developed by international-trade economists, in which a normally desirable policy step, such as a move to freer trade, may not be appropriate if the conditions for a Pareto-optimal solution are not met, such as, for example, if there are distortions between private and social marginal cost, or if lowering a tariff in a customs union results in more trade diversion than trade creation. In these circumstances, the optimal solution may consist in moving away from the normally recommended direction, e.g. to impose a tariff instead of taking one off. For general audiences, the theory of the second best can be summarized concisely as: if the market doesn't work, don't use it.

Partisans of rational expectations and efficient markets tend to believe that markets always work. The Coase theorem, for example, suggests that institutions don't matter, or at least that they adapt themselves readily to changing conditions – in the absence of a minor exception where transactions costs are high – so that they can be disregarded. Institutionalists, of course, take the opposite view – that institutions determine historical outcomes. Between the two positions there is room for an eclectic (or wishy-washy) view – that markets mostly work but occasionally breakdown, and that sometimes institutions adapt to underlying changes in demand and supply conditions and sometimes do not. Even in Britain, where external finance for industry was provided initially for small firms at the local level, and for the few big firms in the London capital market, a gap has been detected for middle-sized firms – the so-called Macmillan gap – too big for the local market and too small to cover the overhead costs of finance in the City. While this gap was discovered only in the Macmillan report of 1931, and said by it not to have existed before World War I, its existence has now been established for the nineteenth century (Committee on Finance and Industry, 1931, para. 377; Jeffrys, 1938, p. 370). A similar gap existed in the 1930s in medium-term credits to finance the foreign sale of capital equipment, too long-lived to be financed by three–nine months acceptances, and too short to warrant the expense of floating long-term bonds. This gap was filled by governments with the Export Credit Guarantee Department in Britain, the Export–Import Bank in the United States, COFACE in France, the Kreditanstalt für Wiederaufbau in Germany (after World War II), etc.

In a perfect capital market, private external finance would be available for every conceivable financial need, at least for hedge finance (to use Minsky's term), whether from a continuum of different specialized institutions or from large department-store-like credit institutions which maintained a full line of financial devices. The establishment of the Crédit Mobilier and its spread throughout Europe can be regarded as a demonstration of the Coase theorem at work – an innovation adapting to a felt need – although in my view of the matter the Crédit Mobilier was more interested in public works than in industry. When *government* moves in to fill a gap, however, it must be scored as a point against the Coase theorem, since it implies market failure at the private level. There may be adequate explanation; in the case of war, insufficient time may be available for the private market to devise the appropriate institutions. But government intervention is 'second best' in the sense that the private market has failed to provide the necessary production or finance or management that is called for by efficient markets and the Coase theorem.

Other theories of government exist, of course. It is a provider of the public goods of national defense; it may be a monster in which egoistic politicians maximize their importance by undertaking unnecessary and even harmful tasks. The theory implied here is a vacuum theory of government in which government is called upon from time to time to repair gaps left by market failure. Such failures may be structural, as in an anemic capital market, or ephemeral, as in the lender-of-last-resort task in financial crises, where markets normally function effectively on trend, but occasionally break down in crisis. Trend and crisis may get mixed up, as when an evanescent crisis leads to undertaking structural repairs not actually necessary.

A few words may be useful on the view of government as a monster, intervening in ways that are so pervasive, inconsistent and misguided that the private market becomes incapable of responding to underlying conditions of demand and supply as they evolve. The move in the United States today to deregulate industry and banking rests on the assumption that years of government intervention in one direction and another have produced so distorted a set of incentives and restraints that it is urgent to sweep them away and start afresh. Joseph Pechman (1983, pp. 125–8) regards the income tax in the United States in this light and wants to make a bonfire of all deductions, shelters, loopholes and exceptions and start afresh, taxing all income at a lower set of rates. It is a counsel of perfection, but note that European governments have taken steps of this character on at least two occasions historically, once when the Navigation Acts were swept off the books of the United Kingdom in 1846 after having become so complicated with regulations, exceptions, special discriminatory treaties and the like that only three men in England understood them (Clapham, 1910/1961, p. 161); and in Baden, where *Gewerbefönderung* – the system of encouraging industry through patents, monopolies, subsidies, prohibitions and other governmental guidance became so complex that it proved useful to make a dash for *Gewerbefreiheit* – freedom of entry into any and all industries (Fischer, 1962, p. 82). A modern example from the United States is the action of Secretary of the Treasury, George P. Shultz, under President Nixon, wiping the books clean of the I.E.T., Gore amendment, Voluntary Credit Restraint Program and Mandatory Credit Restraint Program, which tried successively to restrain capital exports from the United States through one and another channel.

On the other hand, there may be occasions when the underlying conditions for a successful market solution may be missing. In such cases, the second-best expedient must be adopted as a principle. The presumption emerging from Italian financial history of the interwar period is that the 'colonial' experience of the Italian capital market, plus low company profits partly resulting from negative rates of protection for a number of industries, made savers wary of equity investments and disposed to favor liquid claims on banks and government bonds. In these circumstances, risk capital was provided initially by banks and, when this proved unstable, by governmental institutions. But it is time to focus on the interwar period.

The 1920s

The experience of the countries under observation in the 1920s was sharply disparate. All experienced in varying degrees the boom and bust of 1919–20. Thereafter, some like the United States enjoyed prosperous growth for the rest of the decade. Others like Austria remained depressed. Between were cases of a turbulent first half of economic and financial reconstruction followed by entry into the smoother waters of 1925–1929 before encountering new storms.

The impact of the speculative boom of 1919–1920 on traditional British industry and the banks that financed it has already been mentioned. Peace and the prospect of reduced competition from Germany in coal, steel, shipping and cotton textiles led to a wave of takeovers, mergers and formation of new companies, financed by bank lending, that left a heavy burden of debt on traditional industry, and a lump of frozen loans in banks when the collapse of prices in 1920 and 1921 altered the rosy prospect. Restoration of the pound to par in 1925 and the coal and general strikes of 1925 and 1926 compounded the difficulties of the industries on which the British economy had rested in the nineteenth century. The record was not uniformly stagnant, as new industries grew in the South, especially west of London, as opposed to the depressed areas of northern England, Wales and Scotland. Over-valuation of the pound and subsequent undervaluation of the French franc piled up foreign complications that would yield trouble in the 1930s, but bank lending to industry after 1921 was limited to short-term advances, and the long-term capital needs of the new growing industries were supplied by the private market and by direct foreign investment from abroad.

Austria, defeated in war and cut off from its empire, was a basket case. Some assistance was rendered by League of Nations loans in the early 1920s, but the amounts in retrospect proved far short of the structural needs. The banking system was weakened by participating in the 1924 speculative attack on the French franc, and, one by one, weak banks began to fail in that year, to be taken over by larger and putatively stronger banks. At the beginning of 1927 the Unionbank and the Verkehrbank were taken over *in extremis* by the Bodenkreditanstalt, and in early 1929 the Bodenkreditanstalt was merged overnight into the Creditanstalt, leaving it the only sizeable bank in Austria, loaded with industrial loans and equities, and with many more liabilities than assets from its enforced merger. It was in no position to weather a decline in the Viennese stock market.

France and Germany spent the first years of the decade preoccupied with problems of reconstruction, reparations, war debts, hyperinflation in the case of Germany and exchange depreciation for France. A new beginning occurred in 1924 for Germany with the Dawes loan and the start of US lending. Governments borrowed abroad and a few industries. For the most part, industry went back into its cosy relationship with large banks. In France, the breathing room acquired by the successful squeeze against bear speculators in the franc in March 1924 was frittered away. *De facto* stabilization of the franc in 1926, however, touched off a five-year recovery period, but one in which a heavy reflow of capital enlarged the money supply, rendered the Bank of France liquid, and, with substantial profits, left the banks concerned with government bonds and foreign exchange but with little activity in lending to industry.

The United States recovered rapidly from 1921 and started a boom based on wartime innovations and heavy capital accumulation. There were new holding companies in utilities, speculation in shares of rapidly growing companies, notably in electrical equipment, radio and auto-mobiles. A highly leveraged securities market provided opportunities for risky and highly risky investment with borrowed funds – called 'speculative' and 'Ponzi' finance by Minsky, though the designations come in for criticism – as compared with financing fully covered by anticipated receipts – which he calls 'hedge' finance. The success of the Dawes loan led to a boom in foreign securities, which was positively correlated with the business cycle, in contrast with contra-cyclical British lending for most of the period before the war. Financial innovation was widespread, and some banks broke away from the unit atomistic pattern to form, in certain permissive states, branching and chains.

By way of digression it should be noted that branch and chain banking are not unambiguously helpful to bank stability. If the trouble – that is, the poor assets – are in the home unit, it is helpful for it to be part of a system, helped by assistance from other parts of the system. But if the trouble occurs elsewhere, in another part of an integrated whole, integration transmits it to the home unit. The first major collapse in the United States was not that of the unit Bank of the United States in December 1930, but the bankruptcy of the Caldwell chain a month earlier. Here the poor investments of the Nashville head office pulled down the other members of the group and spread the loss of banking and the decline in deposits from Tennessee to three other states (Wicker, 1980).

The first 4 million share days on the New York stock exchange were recorded in March 1928 and the boom in shares became so pronounced by June that attention began to turn from foreign and domestic bonds to stocks on the one hand, and call loans to finance stock-market speculation on the other. The flow of capital turned inward from Europe. Germany had to shift from borrowing through bonds to attracting short-term capital on deposit. The same was true of the under-developed periphery – especially Australia, Argentina, Chile, Brazil. By June of 1929, business peaked in the United States with rising interest rates, pulled along by the tightening call-money market, cutting down long-term investment and consumer borrowing.

Spain remained for the most part on the edge of the boom of the second half of the 1920s, cut off from the ebb and flow of international funds. The relations of banks to industrial borrowers were not central to the macro-economic picture. Some banks increased their industrial stakes; others shrank theirs.

The 1920s saw further developments in the Italian progress to govern-mental domination of the provision of long-term capital to industry. After the deflationary squeeze of 1921, in which the Banca Italiana di Sconto went down along with the Perrone brothers, though their industrial interests in Ilva and Ansaldo were saved, there was a brilliant if brief period of recovery. From a low of 80 in 1921 (1922 = 100) the stock-exchange index rose to 183 by February 1925. At this stage Mussolini called for appreciation of the lira from 150 to the pound to 90 (the infamous *quota novanta*). The action was taken against the advice of economists, and in foolish imitation of the British action appreciating the pound. It harmed the balance of payments, knocked down prices of raw materials and manufactured goods in Italy, and particularly dealt a savage blow to the stock market. In March 1926, Volpi for the Treasury and Stringher for the Bank of Italy asked the leading four banks to borrow 500 million lire and to support security prices with it. When these banks had lost 200 million lire in operations of 600 million (through an instrument called the Società Finanziamento Titoli), they petitioned the Bank of Italy to be allowed to suspend interest on the loan. In November of 1926, beyond this, the Bank of Italy decided to convert the Special Section of the Consortium for the Support of Industrial Securities – the Consortium formed in 1914, the Special Section at the time of the liquidation of the Banca Italiana di Sconto – into a Liquidation Institute to mop up some of the excess liquidity generated by these salvage operations. From 1926 to 1930, this effort to withdraw from industrial finance, and to limit money creation, went forward successfully, with the debt of the Liquidation Institute to the Bank of Italy declining from 1,900 million in November 1926 to less than 1,300 million by 1930.

1929 – the turning point

Friedman and most monetarists think that the collapse of the New York stock market in 1929 was an exogenous event, with no particular explanation, and of no particular importance in the great depression that followed. Jude Wanniski, with his rational expectations/efficient markets theories of security markets, has found an explanation for the declines of Black Thursday (24 October 1929) and Black Tuesday (29 October 1929) in the defeat in the US Senate of a group of liberal free traders who sought to prevent a rise in the tariff on carbide (1977, pp. 133–6). This victory for higher tariffs is seen as an indication that the Hawley–Smoot tariff act of almost nine months later would raise tariffs substantially, lead to massive retaliation and plunge the world into depression. Some elements of this explanation have recently been subscribed to by Allan Meltzer (1981) and Anna Schwartz (1981), who admit the Hawley–Smoot tariff into an otherwise exclusively monetarist explanation of the depression, in the face of the normal international-trade model in which tariffs are expansionary rather than lead to contraction. With retaliation on a vast scale, a tariff can of course be contractive, but it is difficult to see how the market in October 1929 can instantly form a judgement on how much tariff retaliation will be undertaken, when and if the bill will be passed and signed.

Minsky's model (1984) of the impact of the credit system on the prices of financial assets, and their repercussions back on banking, credit and income, is much richer than the simple monetary model. It is none the less limited, as Minsky indicates: it is limited to the United States; there are no capital movements, no exchange rates, no international commodity prices, nor even any impact of price changes on bank liquidity for domestic commodities; all assets are financial. In combination, these limitations mean that Minsky is not interested in the communication of the collapse of stock-market prices to commodity markets between September and December 1929, or in the further pressure on United States, German and gold-bloc prices from the depreciation of sterling (appreciation of the dollar, Reichsmark, French franc, etc.) in September 1931. On an unweighted basis, this was a 30 percent appreciation and was strongly deflationary in its effects on prices, and through commodity prices on bank liquidity. It is of great interest that a lively literature has sprung up in Germany in the last one or two years over whether Germany made a mistake in 1931 in not depreciating the Reichsmark along with the pound sterling (Schliemann, 1980; Borchardt, 1980).

There is not much interest for us in choosing *causa proxima, causa remota* or *causa causans* on the start of the 1929 depression. Candidates for *causa remota* include the cut-off of United States lending to Germany in 1928; those for *causa proxima* include French pressure on the London money market in August 1929 that led to the Hatry crisis of September, that tightened interest rates and pulled 'all other' funds out of the stock market to precipitate liquidation. Friedman and Schwartz (1966) of course ascribe *causa causans* to monetary policy in the United States, although the money stock declined only minimally to December 1930 or March 1931, whereas Herbert Hoover (1952) insisted that the origin of the depression was squarely in Europe. The exercise is futile, and wisdom lies in R. C. O. Matthew's statement, about the depression of almost one hundred years earlier in 1836, that it is futile to draw any hard-and-fast line assigning to either country causal supremacy in the cycle as a whole or its individual phases (1954, p. 69).

Note the parallel collapse of stock-market prices on other national exchanges (evocative of the Granville collapse of stock-market prices in Paris, London and Tokyo on 28 September 1981) with only psychological connections between them. The 32 percent fall in the New York stock market between the September average and that of December 1929 (after a recovery from the November low) was exceeded in Canada with a decline of 33 percent, almost matched in Belgium with 30 percent, and echoed in declines in other markets running from 16 percent in Britain, 15 percent in the Netherlands, 14 percent in Germany, 12.5 percent in Italy (from February 1929 to January 1930), 11 percent in France, 10 percent in Switzerland and 8 percent in Sweden. The fall in Germany came on top of an earlier decline between 28 June and September 1929 of 15 percent. That in Italy followed a collapse due to *quota novanta* of 32 percent between February 1925 and December 1927, with some subsequent recovery (23 percent) to February 1929.

A point on which I insist, but one neglected by virtually all other observers, is that the decline in stock prices was communicated to commodity prices through the banking system. Non-bank lenders to the call-money market were mordantly afraid that the authorities would close the stock market, as had been done in 1873, converting their one-day loans to frozen assets. They therefore pulled out. Out-of-town banks followed suit in somewhat less panic, leaving New York banks to bear the brunt of refinancing loans with adequate margin. To manage this, they cut down drastically on all other credit outlets, including financing commodity brokers and traders. In consequence, foreign commodities, then normally sold in New York on consignment, plunged in price between September and December 1929 in a range from 25.7 percent for rubber to 10 percent for silk. Export commodities, such as cotton and wheat, and commodities normally financed in the United States, such as sugar, declined much less. Moreover, the fall in prices was worldwide: 22 percent in Japan, 16 percent in Canada, 15 percent in the United Kingdom, 14 percent in Italy and 12 percent in the United States and Germany. No monetarist or Keynesian model can account for such precipitous declines. It is true that monetarists wave away declines of commodity prices on the ground that losses are matched by gains, unless there is money illusion. I regard this as an absurdity as it ignores lags on the one hand, and dynamic effects of price declines on creditworthiness and liquidity of loans on the other.

The course of the depression should be divided between 1929–30 on the one hand, and 1931–33 on the other. This distinction is usefully made by Robert Gordon and James Wilcox (1981), but by few others and certainly not by Friedman and Schwartz, who measure the change in money supply always from 1929 at the top to 1932 or 1933 at the bottom, or by Temin (1976), or, in the extant case, by Minsky (1984). The empty debate between Friedman and Schwartz (now Schwartz alone – 1981) on the one hand, and Temin on the other, as to whether the *IS* curve moved first or the *LM*, focuses on a model with no international capital movements, no commodity prices, no prices of financial assets. Minsky's paper has the merit of explaining bank failures through changes in asset prices, rather than dragging the failures in exogenously. Mishkin's (1976) attempt to link consumption to wealth through asset prices extends the analysis slightly but falls well short of connecting asset prices with bank failures and the money supply. Here Wicker's (1980) paper on the collapse of the Caldwell chain in Tennessee, Kentucky, North Carolina and Arkansas in November 1930 is particularly helpful. This is connected with speculation in insurance and mortgages, not the farm products that later wrought devastation to banks in the Middle West and South. One should add, to be sure, that the Keynesians either do not attempt to find a cause for the decline in income that preceded the decline in money, as in the case of Temin, or produce emphases on automobiles – Rostow (1978) and Aaron Gordon (1952) – or housing – Barber (1978), who ties it to population change, and Robert Gordon and Wilcox (1981) – none of which can explain the precipitous character of the 75 percent drop in automobile sales in the United States from March 1929 to December of the same year, a decline unrelated to the Keynesian consumption function but easily explicable in terms of a sudden drastic credit squeeze.

Contraction

The research of the Italian team set to work by the Banca di Roma has produced a most striking result in emphasizing the troubles of Italian banks well ahead of those of the Caldwell chain and the Bank of the United States, not to mention the Austrian Creditanstalt. We have not learned about these troubles until fifty years after the events because trouble was taken to keep the information secret. Provincial banks were failing and being rescued in the summer of 1930, and the troubles of the Credito Italiano and the Banca Commerciale Italiana had occupied them from the spring of 1930. Toniolo notes that they followed two lines of action: one to segregate low-quality securities and industrial credits so as to buoy depositor confidence; a second, to assert more effective control over industrial enterprises to increase their profitability and capacity to yield a return (Toniolo, 1980, pp. 207–9). These efforts, such as the creation by Comit of the Società Finanziaria Industriale Italiana (Sofindit), were publicized. The state intervention discussed from the end of 1930 to the February convention between state officials and the Credito Italiano in February 1931, to 'demobilize' its industrial investments, was secret. Participations were transferred to a new institution (Società Finanziaria Italiana, or Sfi) and losses were absorbed by the Institute of Liquidation.

The secrecy with which these operations were surrounded is of course a double-edged sword. On the one hand, the public is not alarmed. On the other, it is possible in secret dealings of this sort to play favorites, taking care of insiders, and freezing out others. There is no hint of such favoritism in the Italian salvage operations of 1930, but it is strongly suggested that the Bank of the United States was done in in December 1930 by the New York clearing house because it was not loved by its competitors. On the first issue, that publicity breeds panic, there is ample evidence. The difficulties of the Creditanstalt in Austria went public in May 1931, those of the Danatbank in Germany two months later, and each started a chain reaction that ended in national bankruptcy. The Reconstruction Finance Corporation (RFC) started in December 1931 by President Hoover, on the suggestion of bankers put to him in October, had its effectiveness ruined by a subsequent requirement that bankers receiving loans should have their names made public. This was a partisan Democratic requirement forced through the Congress because of the fact becoming public that Charles G. Dawes' bank had received an RFC loan. Dawes was the Republican vice-president of the country, and aid to his bank was sardonically known as the 'second Dawes' loan'. The requirement proved to be a disaster because thereafter bankers were unwilling to use the RFC as it would advertize the weakness of their institutions. It should also be noted that Hans Luther, the president of the Reichsbank, tried to keep secret in June 1931 the small amount of the loan – $100 million, when he sought to borrow $1 billion – on the ground that it would disclose how limited his defensive ammunition was. Oskar Wasserman of the Deutsche Bank felt obliged to respond to the news published in Switzerland that a German bank was in trouble by pinpointing the Danatbank of Jacob Goldschmidt, to prevent the public thinking the 'bank in trouble was his' (Born, 1967, p. 89). But Goldschmidt was also an outsider, thoroughly disliked, whose bank was later allowed to fail. Heinrich Irmler has lately commented that, from today's standpoint, it is not understandable that the Reichsbank could let it fail (1976, p. 287).

Recovery

After a crisis, as noted earlier, the question is whether to undo the emergency measures and return to trend, to limp along, or to accept the new position brought on by crisis measures and to proceed from there. The choices are neatly illustrated in the recoveries of the 1930s by the histories of Austria, Germany, France and Italy.

The failure of the Creditanstalt in May 1931 set in motion a series of international rescue operations, first through the Rothschild network, and then at the official level through the Bank for International Settlements, which proved to be too little and too late. The government ended up owning the Creditanstalt, and the Creditanstalt in turn owned 64 companies and 65 per cent of the nominal capital of Austrian business enterprise. Despite Socialist governments, however, there was no change in the relationships between banks and industry, and government stood aside.

In Germany, the runs of 1931 ended up with the Standstill agreement to freeze foreign deposits in process of withdrawal, the establishment of the Akzept- und Garantiebank in July to provide a third signature for rediscounting at the Reichsbank, and a guarantee of deposit liabilities organized by the Golddiskontobank established at the time of the Dawes loan. Bank capital had been weakened by the maintenance of dividends in the face of losses, and by the device used in both Austria and Germany of banks using reserves to support their own stock in the capital market. The government then came to the rescue with subsidies, advances and purchases of bank shares, as Hardach (1984) explains, the last at artificially high prices, and ended up owning percentages of the capital of the major banks ranging from 67 percent for the Norddeutsche Kreditbank to 91 percent for the Dresdener, which absorbed the Darmstädter und Nationalbank. Bit by bit, however, the banks were reprivatized. First public works, and then rearmament plus the four-year plans, provided a quiet time for the banks. Rearmaments were financed outside the banking system. Profits were high, bank deposits piled up, and the government was able to sell off its holding of bank shares.

In Italy in 1914 and in the United States in 1914 and 1941, government created special institutions for war finance. In Germany in the 1930s, small firms delivering *matériel* to the armed forces used the so-called Mefo-wechsel – bills drawn on the Metallische Forschungsgesellschaft m.b.H., a special corporation set up by Siemens, Gutehoffnungshütte, Krupp and Rheinstahl, which in turn rediscounted the paper with the Reichsbank. The paper was guaranteed by the Reich, ran three months, and was usually prolonged to five. At the height, the amount of Mefo-wechsel outstanding was 12 billion RM. It was placed with the private market not as Mefo-wechsel, but as blocked exchange or Solawechsel of the Golddiskontobank, for the sake of secrecy. When the demand for these bills dried up, financing switched to Lieferschatzanweisungen (deliverer's certificates) in April 1938. These amounted to 4 billion by the outbreak of the war (Hansmeyer and Caesar, 1976, p. 392 note). This system of defense finance allowed the banks to work their way clear of the government and return to the traditional system of close relations between large banks and large firms.

As Bouvier's paper (1984) emphasizes, France was under no pressure to innovate in finance during the 1930s for economic, as opposed to ideological and political reasons. The liquidity piled up by the return flow of capital after 1926 was enormous. There were some salvage operations in the depression, that of the Compagnie Générale Transatlantique for one, and Kuisel refers somewhat vaguely to rescue operations for major banks (1981, p. 96), though Bouvier specifies only the Banque Nationale de Crédit, which was allowed to fail in 1931 despite massive infusions from the Bank of France and the Caisse des Dépots et Consignations, the fund that gathered the deposits of the savings banks and typically invested them in the government bond market. (The Segré report – EEC Commission, 1966 – and the capital market study of the OECD – 1967 – after the war would both claim that European capital markets suffered from the structural weakness that governments reserved a large fraction of private savings for their own use).

It was only after the war, with the development of the Monnet plan, that the French developed their own second-best system of financing industry – the coordination of counterpart funds developed by Marshall-plan aid, and savings gathered by the Caisse des Dépots et Consignations – as a supplement to private savings needed by firms expanding in conformity with the plans. It is not clear to me how closely the nationalized banks were required to conform in their lending to the plans, although most observers agree with Bouvier that the reform involved in nationalization was more apparent than real.

It was in Italy above all that the expedient of salvage operations was gradually developed into a new system. IMI was formed in 1931 when business profits were low and the mixed banks were unable to undertake further industrial lending, although the demand for more credit was low and IMI was not very active until after World War II. IRI, formed in 1933, took over the assets of the Liquidation Institute and of Sofindit and Sfi, provided the banks more capital, and settled down to a program of liquidating the government's holdings and getting back to a private system. The need of the companies it acquired for direction, management and more capital, however, meant that the hope of liquidation was gradually given up, and, about 1935, IRI settled down to become a new sort of institution.

The view is widely held, especially in England, that state intervention through IMI as a financing institution and IRI as an administrative one, as developed between the wars, now constitutes the best of all possible worlds. The state is entrepreneur and financier, but indirectly, avoiding state socialism with its overweaning bureaucracies, and using intermediaries as a device to obtain industrial policies conforming to social objectives (Holland, 1972). There can be no doubt that IRI has been useful in the postwar period in making good the deficiencies in the Italian capital market, in buying up, for example, major Italian firms in temporary illiquid condition that would otherwise have been sold to foreign investors, taking advantage of the illiquidity on the one hand, and the imperfection of the market that prevented adequate financing at home. On the other hand, the government has frequently pressed IRI into projects – coal mining in Sardinia, or establishing an automobile plan for Alfa Romeo in Naples – that are generally agreed as uneconomic but socially desirable to sustain employment. To the purist, business organizations should seek to maximize profit so as to achieve Pareto-optimality in resource allocation, while social objectives should be handled through the government's budget, rather than through the market.

Banking reform

There was little if any reform of the relationships between banks and industry in Austria, England or Spain, while that in France and Germany was minimal or superficial. In Germany, as Hardach (1984) explains, there was an investigation in 1933, a reform law in December 1934. This provided for the appointment of a governmental supervisory body, and rules regarding reserve ratios and restraints on speculation and illiquid assets. But there was no fundamental change in the relations between banks and industry. Hans Luther was attracted to the idea of separating investment banking from the deposit banks, but the banks resisted and nothing came of it. When the government had sold off its holdings of bank shares, the system was more or less restored to the position it had been.

French reform had a strongly ideological basis, and went back to the 1924–1926 clash between the Cartel des Gauches – a series of mildly left-wing governments – and the regents of the Bank of France, who refused cooperation on occasion, especially when it came to pledging the gold of the Bank as collateral for a second Morgan loan. When the Popular Front came to power under the Socialist Léon Blum in 1936, it seemed inevitable that the banking system would be reformed as the left wing took its revenge on the *mur d'argent* which had frustrated it a decade earlier. Little of importance was accomplished. The statutes of the Bank of France were revised to eliminate private interests as regents, but that was all. After the war, the nationalization of the Bank of France, that of the four largest banks and of major insurance companies was again a fairly empty gesture – called by Bouvier (1984) 'nationalization without reform' – with the more important structural changes involving the Caisse and counterpart funds coming later. It remains to be seen whether the new Socialist government under President Mitterand will produce an important change. Nationalization of industrial firms of national prominence adds a dimension to the possibilities. In private control, these firms could escape the regulation of national government by borrowing abroad, as Hardach (1984) points out for the larger German firms in the interwar period, but as is particularly the case in the 1970s and 1980s with the rise to eminence of the Eurocurrency money and capital markets.

Minsky (1984) has compiled a long list of reforms in the United States: the Federal Deposit Insurance Act, the Security and Exchange Act, the Holding Company Act, new forms of mortgages, the Glass–Steagall Act of 1933, which separated investment and deposit banking, etc. May I call your attention to a new interpretation of the origin of the Glass-Steagall Act of 1933 by Thomas Ferguson (1981)? He asserts that in considerable part it originated not in a groundswell of Populist resentment against the Chase Bank and the National City Bank of New York, whose leaders Albert Wiggins and Charles Mitchell had been guilty of highly questionable practices, such as continuing to peddle bonds to their customers after they had learned that default was imminent. The proximate origin of the act, at least in his view, was an attack of Winthrop Aldrich of the Chase Bank (Wiggins' successor) against J. P. Morgan and Co., an attack born of Aldrich's desire to push Morgans out of banking, and to take revenge on the house for its hesitancy in helping to finance the newly building Rockefeller Center (Ferguson, 1981, pp. 707–8, 720–9). Lamont defended the Morgan bank by insisting that J. P. Morgan never solicited deposits, but that its customers found it convenient to keep monies there. Aldrich's public statement of 9 March 1933 advocating a separation of deposit and investment banking was a bombshell, very pleasing to the financial houses that specialized only in security underwriting. Thomas Lamont managed to have most of the objectionable (to him) provisions taken out of the bill, but failed to defeat separation. This was not so much reform, then, as revenge. The move in the present Congress and present administration to repeal the Glass-Steagall Act of 1933 and permit banks to underwrite securities may be justified by the growing freedom for security houses to associate themselves with money funds and check-writing facilities. It is objected to by Minsky (1984) on the ground that it, and the associated merger movement along state lines, will build up large banks in which the interests of small business may fall further into neglect.

In Italy, the state took over the finance of industry through IMI and IRI, and reformed the banking system *de jure* in 1936. The number of banks fell. The Credito Italiano and Comit sold off their industrial securities and long-term loans to holding companies *de facto* controlled by the state at prices based on their need for liquidity rather than the market value of the assets. The Bank of Italy was given monopoly of note issue, and powers to regulate credit, but left with a large bundle of illiquid assets. Industry, with limited profits and forbidden to borrow from the banks, was forced to turn to IMI and IRI, which raised funds by issuing bonds with state guarantee. Conventions between the three major banks on the one hand and the government and the Bank of Italy on the other in the early 1930s were solidified into the Bank Law of 1936. Credit became a function of public interest, not private, to prevent the domination of banks by industry, and presumably vice versa. Banks of ordinary credit, i.e. making short-term loans, were cut off from long-term investment on which decisions were no longer made by banks but by business and government. Private investors had never overcome the handicap of the colonialized capital market, and banks went in for such repeated 'overtrading' (to use Adam Smith's phrase) that they had to be restrained. This left the provision of long-term finance to government.

Bank concentration

The papers under review bespeak a process of bank concentration in practically every country but the United States, where, if deregulation takes place, a similar path is likely to be followed. In Britain, the merger movement just before and just after the war led to the formation of a big five, now down to three. In France, four major deposit banks remained to be nationalized in 1946. In Germany, mergers of the 1920s led to the four D banks, which the failure of the Danat in 1931 brought down to three. In Italy, we end up with three, in Austria basically one. The concentration of banking in Spain was equally evident as the big six shrank to five and the three major financial centers from three to two.

The position in some countries is even more centralized as decision-making inside a given bank may be undertaken locally or mainly by the head office. W. A. Thomas notes that in Britain in the 1920s the Midland, National Provincial and Westminster all operated in a centralized fashion, with Barclays decentralized, and Lloyds functioning in a compromised fashion (1978, p. 57). Computers now, if not then, may bring detailed local credit information into a central location, but it is hard to believe that small localized business can receive a sympathetic hearing in the metropolis hundreds of miles away. Large firms, as Hardach (1984) emphasizes, have access to the international market when they do not have monopoly profits available for reinvestment. Small business is at a disadvantage as Minsky (1984) mentions for money funds without loan officers, as the Macmillan gap in Britain testifies, as the Small Business Administration in the United States implies, and as the establishment of Mefo-wechsel in the interwar period in Germany indicates.

Here is where a question comes to mind over the IMI/IRI development in Italy. We know that a dual business economy has sprung up, with the development of a large sector of business, especially in the South, that pays no social security charges, or minimum wages, deducted income taxes, and the like. What does it do for finance? Is it served by IMI and IRI, by the large banks in violation of the Bank Law of 1936 insofar as long-term capital is concerned, or has there developed a free private risk-taking capital market of the Pareto-optimal type in contrast to the risk-averse colonized capital market that is open in the North? Is there a possibility that the non-reporting private economy of the South may one day develop into a resilient and robust economy where risky investment is embraced as a private function rather than one left as a residual for government?

Conclusion

The disparate development in the relations between banking and industry in the countries under review leads me to the eclectic or wishy-washy position between the upholders of the Coase theorem – that institutions adapt to underlying demand and supply conditions – and the polar view of institutionalists – that the historical development of institutions determines outcomes.

In Britain, banks clung for the most part to short-term finance, the capital market to long-term, after flirtatious interruptions in the 1860s and in 1919–20, afterwards regretted, and a Macmillan gap only partly filled by the creation of two private and one semi-private finance houses in the 1930s (Thomas, 1978, p. 119). There was no reform. In Germany, the system was subject to cataclysmic shock, but rebounded virtually intact. The same outcome was recorded in Austria, except for the continued concentration of banks and continued government owner-ship of the major bank. France prepared reforms, but hesitancy in putting them through left them virtually meaningless. Spain kept itself outside the main trends, but in 1941 adopted an INI, in imitation of Italy's IRI, but as a positive rather than a reactive policy choice.

The sharpest contrast is between the United States and Italy. Alike in adopting a number of reforms – notably the separation of deposit from investment banking – they differed in that their principal rescue institutions – IRI in Italy and the RFC in the United States – were given very different life expectancies. IRI is now immortal. The RFC has long ago gone to its reward. The Banca di Roma celebrates its centennial in congratulating the country at the happy outcome of the Bank Reform of 1936. In the United States, a Republican administration gets ready to rip out the reforms of the 1930s and return banking to the freedom of its pre-Andrew Jackson days, minus unit banking.

I conclude it would be difficult for any economist to have predicted these outcomes, however effectively we can explain them afterwards. If this strikes the positive economist as heresy, so much the worse.

References

Barber, Clarence (1978), 'On the Origins of the Great Depression', *Southern Economic Journal*, vol. 44, no. 3 (January), pp. 432–56.

Bonelli, Franco (1971), *La crisi del 1907: una tappa dello sviluppo industriale in Italia* (Turin: Fondazione Einaudi).

Borchardt, Knut (1961), 'Zur Frage des Kapitalmangels in der erste Hälfte des 19. Jahrhunderts in Deutschland', *Jahrbucher für Nationalökonomie und Statistik*, vol. 173, pp. 401–21.

Borchardt, Knut (1980), 'Zur Frage der währungspolitischen Optionen Deutschlands in der Weltwirtschaftskrise', in K. Borchardt and Franz Holzheu (eds), *Theorie und Politik in der internationalen Wirtschaftsbeziehungen* (Stuttgart: Gustav Fischer Verlag), pp. 165–81.

Born, Karl Erich (1967), *Die deutsche Bankenkrise: Finanzen und Politik* (Munich: R. Piper).

Bouvier, Jean (1955), *Le Crédit Lyonnais de 1863 à 1882. Les Années de formation d'une banque de dépôts* (Paris: SEVPEN, 2 vols).

Bouvier, Jean (1965/1970), 'The Banking Mechanism in France in the Late Nineteenth Century', translated and reprinted in Rondo Cameron (ed.), *Essays in French Economic History* (Homewood, Ill.: Irwin), pp. 341–69.

Bouvier, Jean (1984), 'The French Banks, Inflation and the Economic Crisis, 1919–1939', *Journal of European Economic History*, vol. 13, no. 2 (Fall, special issue), pp. 29–80.

Cameron, Rondo (1961), *France and the Economic Development of Europe* (Princeton, NJ: Princeton University Press).

Charpenay, Georges (1939), *Les Banques régionalistes* (Paris: Nouvelle Revue Critique).

Clapham, J. H. (1910/1961), 'The Last Years of the Navigation Acts', *English Historical Review*, vol. 25 (two parts, July and October); reprinted in E. M. Carus-Wilson (ed.), *Essays in Economic History* (London: E. Arnold), vol. 3, pp. 144–78.

Cohen, Jon S. (1966), 'Finance and Industrialization in Italy, 1894–1914', dissertation; subsequently published (New York: Arno Press, 1977).

Committee on Finance and Industry (1931), *Report* (Macmillan Report), Cmd 3897 (London: HMSO).

Confalonieri, Antonio (1976), *Banca e industria in Italia* (Milan: Banca Commerciale Italiana, 3 vols).

EEC Commission (1966), *The Development of a European Capital Market* (Segré Report) (Brussels: European Economic Community).

Ferguson, Thomas (1981), 'Critical Realignments: the Fall of the House of Morgan and the Origins of the New Deal', doctoral dissertation in political science, Princeton University, to be published.

Fischer, Wolfram (1962), *Der Staat und die Anfänge der Industrialisierung in Baden, 1800–1850* (Berlin: Duncker und Humblot).

Friedman, Milton and Schwartz, Anna Jacobson (1966), *A Monetary History of the United States, 1867–1960* (Princeton, NJ: Princeton University Press).

Gerschenkron, Alexander (1962), *Economic Backwardness in Historical Perspective* (Cambridge, Mass.: Harvard University Press).

Gordon, Aaron (1952), *Business Fluctuations*, 2nd edn (New York: Harper & Row).

Gordon, Robert J. and Wilcox, James A. (1981), 'Monetarist Interpretations of the Great Depression: An Evaluation and Critique', in K. Brunner (ed.), *The Great Depression Revisited* (The Hague: Martinus Nijhoff), pp. 49–107.

Hansmeyer, Karl Heinrich and Caesar, Rolf (1976), 'Kriegswirtschaft und Inflation (1936–1948)', in Deutsche Bundesbank (ed.), *Währung und Wirtschaft in Deutschland, 1876–1975* (Frankfurt-am-Main: Knapp), pp. 367–429.

Hardach, G. (1984), 'Banking and Industry in Germany in the Interwar Period, 1919–1939', *Journal of European Economic History*, vol. 13, no. 2 (Fall, special issue), pp. 203–34.

Holland, Stuart (ed.) (1972), *The State as Entrepreneur: New Dimensions for Public Enterprise: the IRI State Shareholding Formula* (London: Weidenfeld & Nicolson).

Hoover, Herbert (1952), *The Memoirs of Herbert Hoover*. Vol. III: *The Great Depression, 1929–1941* (New York: Macmillan).

Hoselitz, Bert F. (1956), 'Entrepreneurship and Capital Formation in France and Britain since 1700', in *Capital Formation and Economic Growth* (Princeton, NJ: Princeton University Press).

Irmler, Heinrich (1976), 'Bankenkrise und Vollbeschäftigungspolitik (1931–1936)', in Deutsche Bundesbank (ed.), *Währung und Wirtschaft in Deutschland, 1876–1975* (Frankfurt-am-Main: Knapp), pp. 283–329.

Jeffrys, J. B. (1938), 'Trends in Business Organization in Great Britain since 1856', thesis, London School of Economics; reproduced (New York: Arno Press, 1977).

Kuisel, Richard F. (1981), *Capitalism and the State in Modern France: Renovation and Economic Management in the Twentieth Century* (Cambridge: Cambridge University Press).

Matthews, R. C. O. (1954), *A Study of Trade-Cycle History: Economic Fluctuations in Great Britain, 1832–1842* (Cambridge: Cambridge University Press).

Meltzer, Allan H. (1981), 'Comments on "Monetarist Interpretations of the Great Depression"' (by Robert J. Gordon and James A. Wilcox), in K. Brunner (ed.), *The Great Depression Revisited* (Boston, Mass.: Martinus Nijhoff).

Minsky, H. P. (1984), 'Banking and Industry between the Two Wars: the United States', *Journal of European Economic History*, vol. 13, no. 2 (Fall, special issue), pp. 235–72.

Mishkin, Frederic S. (1976), 'Illiquidity, Consumer Durables Expenditure and Monetary Policy', *American Economic Review*, vol. 66, no. 4, pp. 642–54.

Organization for Economic Co-operation and Development, Committee on Invisible Transactions (1967), *Capital Markets Study* (Paris: OECD, 7 vols).

Pechman, Joseph A. (1983), *Federal Tax Policy*, 4th edn (Washington, DC: Brookings Institution).

Riesser, Jacob (1911), *The Great German Banks and their Concentration* (Washington, DC: US Government Printing Office for the National Monetary Commission).

Rostow, W. W. (1978), *The World Economy: History and Prospect* (Austin, Tex.: University of Texas Press).

Schliemann, Jürgen (1980), *Die deutsche Währung in der Weltwirtschaftskrise, 1929–1933: Währungspolitik und Abwertungskrontoverse unter den Bedingungen der Reparationen* (Berne: Verlag Paul Haupt).

Schwartz, Anna J. (1981), 'Understanding 1929–1933', in Karl Brunner (ed.), *The Great Depression Revisited* (Boston, Mass.: Martinus Nijhoff).

Temin, Peter (1976), *Did Monetary Forces Cause the Great Depression?* (New York: W. W. Norton).

Thomas, W. A. (1978), *The Finance of British Industry, 1918–1976* (London: Methuen).

Toniolo, Gianni (1980), *L'economia dell'Italia fascista* (Rome: Laterza).
Toniolo, Gianni (1981), 'Sintesi dei lavori delle sezioni', in Banca di Roma, *Banca e industria fra le due guerre* (Bologna: Società editrice Il Mulino).
Wanniski, Jude (1977), *The Way the World Works* (New York: Basic Books).
Wicker, Elmus (1980), 'A Reconsideration of the Causes of the Banking Panic of 1930', *Journal of Economic History*, vol. 40, pp. 571–83.

21

1929: Ten Lessons for Today

Lesson 1: Plus ça change, plus c'est la même chose (sometimes)

George Santayana's famous saying that those who cannot remember the past are condemned to repeat it should be taken seriously – but it is important that the right lessons be learned. The building of the Maginot Line is a case in point.

What can we learn about financial crisis? Adam Smith defined it as 'overtrading, followed by revulsion and discredit'. The objects of over-trading may change from crisis to crisis, but the process remains the same. In 1928 the objects were bonds, in 1929 stocks. At various times they were commodities, real estate, shopping centers, oil ventures, and country loans. Even when the growth of 'money' was limited to 'modest' rates, financiers escaped the constraints with innovative financing methods – bills of exchange and banknotes in the nineteenth century, later checking deposits, and then today's CDs, 'repos', credit cards, and even – in Kuwait – postdated checks. When the central bank gets a fix on one M_i, once the market gets the bit in its teeth, it creates new financial instruments, a new money M_j. Or if we stick to the old definition, we see the results in a whipped-up velocity. The rush from money into real and illiquid financial assets proceeds for a time, and then it slows down as the realization dawns that 'chain-letters' don't expand infinitely. A crisis or panic may or may not be the result, with the speculators rushing from real and less liquid financial assets back into money.

Lesson 2: Keynesianism-vs.-monetarism is too narrow an analytical framework

The causes of the 1929 depression are debated between Friedman–Schwartz, who blame monetary policy, and Temin, who ascribes the decline in money to an antecedent decline in spending. In the new *Great Depression Revisited*, edited by Karl Brunner, a few writers admit one international cause to the analysis – the Hawley–Smoot tariff of June 1930 (Wanniski even has it causing the stock market crash of 1929!). But the framework remains too narrow: it omits prices and exchange rates, and numerous factors stemming from World War I – reparations, war debts, overvaluation of sterling, undervaluation of the French franc,

Reprinted with permission from Challenge *(March–April 1983), pp. 58–61.*

excessive long-term lending to Germany and the 'periphery', from the Dawes loan in 1924 to the middle of 1928 when the stock market rise started. It also omits the shift to short-term lending and the piling up of balances in Central Europe.

The Keynesianism–monetarism framework is equally irrelevant today. It still assumes a neat continuity with a small number of variables, and leaves out political factors, shocks, and discontinuities.

Lesson 3: Prices count (though they didn't in 1921)

Modern macroeconomic analysis dismisses price changes, by and large. When a price falls, we would, theoretically, expect the producer's loss to be matched by the consumer's gain. To think otherwise would make us guilty of money illusion. But this is purely *a priori* reasoning at a simple level. It ignores lags. In the 1930s, when prices fell, losers knew immediately, but winners took time to realize that they had gained.

Modern macroeconomics also ignores dynamic effects. The banks of the losers may fail, but the winners are unlikely to start new banks. The fall of prices in the last quarter of 1929 was critical: it led to the aborting of recovery in the spring of 1930, when financial markets perked up briefly. Investment fell away and, with it, income and consumption, leading to bank failures and declines in the money supply.

Why did this kind of financial crisis occur in 1930, but not (except for Britain) in 1921? The fall in prices and the shakeout in commodity speculation in 1921 – as opposed to 1930 – were not serious because the world was still in a seller's market. Goods remained fundamentally in short supply until after 1925. Then European recovery, on top of the uncorrected wartime expansion outside Europe, left supplies heavy in a buyer's market.

Britain was an exception in 1921. There the heavy weight of bank borrowing in 1919–20, and later the appreciation of the pound, meant that low prices gave the country ten years of depression.

Today there are heavy stocks in agriculture, and excess supply in metals such as aluminium, steel, and perhaps in the non-metallic mineral – oil. Despite the recent record of inflation, deflation in primary products cannot be excluded.

Lesson 4: Flexible exchange rates are not a cure-all; on occasion they are poison

In the 1950s and 1960s there was a misplaced enthusiasm for flexible exchange rates. While the experience of the 1970s diminished this somewhat, the enthusiasts continued to ignore an important lesson of the 1930s – a lesson that is applicable today, but with a twist. Even if we leave aside undervaluation and overvaluation, and mercifully forget the economic theories that exchange rates cannot deviate from purchasing-power parity, we must take into account that every depreciation here is matched by an appreciation there. In the 1930s, with commodity stocks heavy and prices drooping, depreciation left prices at home unchanged, but the connected appreciation drove them down abroad. The early depreciations of Argentina, Uruguay, Australia, and New Zealand drove down world prices of wheat, meat, and wool. Much more pervasive was the appreciation of the dollar against the pound in 1931. The pound went from $4.86 in early September 1931 to $3.25 in December of that year. This failed to raise prices in the United Kingdom and the sterling bloc, but drove them down in the United States and the gold bloc. The result was 50-cent wheat and 5-cent cotton.

In the 1970s, the mechanism worked in just the opposite way from the early depression years. Depreciation raised prices in the depreciating country and appreciation left them unchanged: this is because the underlying world tendency was toward inflation. With flexible exchange rates leading to overshooting – now up, now down – an inflationary ratchet developed. It was especially observable in oil, where dollar depreciation produced increases in oil prices and dollar appreciation left them where they were.

It is possible, however, that the ratchet will turn again. As commodity stocks accumulate and prices turn soft, a deflationary trend may be activated. Perhaps it might be wise to move away from flexible exchange rates if we want to bring greater stability to commodity prices and national price levels.

Lesson 5: Beware of sudden halts in foreign lending

The world depression can be said to have begun gradually in Germany and the periphery of developing countries in mid-1928, when the flow of long-term capital to those areas was abruptly stopped, as the investor in New York turned to the stock market and the call-money market that financed it.

The actual precipitant of the October 1929 crash is hard to pin down, Wanniski to the contrary notwithstanding. My candidate is the Hatry crisis in London, in which an entrepreneur tried to parlay his holdings in investment trusts and operating companies into a large purchase of big steel. He was caught using fraudulent collateral for this, and the resultant crisis halted the flow of capital from London to the New York market, and reversed it when interest rates tightened. This led to still higher call-money rates in New York and started a process of liquidation. Once the market fell, 'others' started to withdraw their money from call loans, for fear the stock market would close, and to convert their one-day loans into something much longer.

The lesson that one should not suddenly reverse a lending process is one that leading world banks seem thoroughly to understand today. Following the cheap-money moves of 1970–1 (undertaken to re-elect Nixon), and the oil shock of late 1973, there was serious overtrading in country loans. But the banks kept lending, rescheduling, renewing, providing new monies to developing and socialist countries, and to farm-machinery and oil-producing companies alike.

Today there are newspaper hints that the regional banks are growing jittery over the need to maintain or increase positions where sovereign risk is high, but that the major money-center banks try to whip the regional banks back into line.

Lesson 6: Robbing Peter to pay Paul is dangerous

Money-market banks behaved responsibly in 1929, pulling back slightly after June of that year, the better to position themselves to come to the rescue of the call-money market when and if out-out-town banks and 'others' got the wind up and headed for the exits. When the market actually fell, the banks tried to halt the decline. In so doing, however, they cut off credit to commodity dealers, and apparently to automobile installment companies too. In those years many commodities were shipped to New York on consignment and sold on arrival, rather than bought by an importer prior to shipment. If New York commodity dealers were unable to get credit, they could not buy in normal amounts and at normal prices. In consequence, the collapse of security prices communicated itself to commodity prices, especially of coffee, rubber, hides, silk, and tin, that depended on New York finance. Prices dropped throughout the world, prices that, as Lesson 3 underlines, were important in the particular circumstances to world prosperity and depression.

Banks also behaved responsibly in 1981–2 (though not in the 1970s). In today's context, the banks should take care lest their newfound caution in lending to hard-pressed developing countries and cash-starved corporations lead to harshly restricted credit to less afflicted borrowers, such as small business.

Lesson 7: A lender of last resort is needed in crisis, but there should be some ambiguity as to who it will be and who will be helped, when and how

Walter Bagehot rationalized the lender-of-last resort function in *Lombard Street* in 1873, but the practice and even a competent under-standing of the process (by Henry Thornton, a well-known economist and banker of 1800) go much further back. Financial crisis occurs when there is a rush into money from other assets. The way to stop it is to make clear that there is plenty of money for all (solvent) demanders.

Ambiguities abound. If institutions know they will be saved from any slip into carelessness, they take even less care. This is the moral hazard principle in insurance. The line between the illiquid and the insolvent wavers and shifts when prices fall further. Unlimited help seems unavailable, but limited aid increases the panic to get to the head of the queue.

It used to be an issue who took on the role. In domestic crises it could be the central bank, the treasury or a consortium of leading banks that guaranteed the liabilities of the illiquid units. There was sometimes danger that the process of choosing who would play lifeguard let the failing swimmer drown. Even more ambiguous was choosing an international lender of last resort, since sovereign countries in principle are equal. In 1931 financial collapse spread from Austria to Germany to Britain to Japan to the United States to the gold bloc without a decisive halt, because first Britain was unable longer to play the role, and France and the United States were unwilling to, except on a scale that proved too little and too late.

Accept that a lender of last resort in crisis is necessary. Is it sufficient? D. E. Moggridge, the Canadian economic historian, believes that what was called for in 1929 was not merely halting financial collapse but structural adjustment, perhaps along the lines of the Marshall Plan after World War II. The issue is a profound one, and the respective importance of real and financial factors has been the subject of continuous debate associated with the Great Depression of 1873–1896, and the real Great Depression of 1929–39. The subject will doubtless be revived when the Great Recession of 1974–8? or '9?, if that is what it comes to be called, takes its historical shape.

When financial crises were limited to the developed countries, as in Britain in March 1961, the lender of last resort was the swap network. There was no conditionality; if everything had not been reversed in six months, the International Monetary Fund moved in and took over. When crisis affected the less developed countries, the swap network could not be used, as its members were limited to financially developed countries. The first approach was made to the Paris Club for rescheduling, the second to the International Monetary Fund. Both are slow at decision-making and negotiating. In the summer of 1982, the Bank for International Settlements came into the picture, as it had briefly over the Austrian credits of 1931, with bridging loans to give time for the IMF.

It is now clear, however, that the IMF needs enlarged resources.

Lesson 8: Formalism, politics, and ideology impede crisis-solution

In his history of the Bank of England, Clapham notes that, when it was necessary to pitch in to solve a crisis, the Bank could not afford to be 'overnice'. The point is underlined by the French objection to the Hoover moratorium of 19 June 1931 that halted war debt payments and reparations for a year on the ground that it violated the clauses of the Young Plan (which had just reordered the reparations). It took three weeks to settle the issue and by that time German finances had collapsed. The French were also prone at the time to raise political *quids* to be exchanged for economic *quos*. Austria should not have a second loan until it gave up Zollunion (tariff union) with Germany, and

Germany got no credits until it gave up building the pocket battleship.

In today's world the fear is that debt settlements with Eastern Europe, which are needed for our own financial safety, might become involved in bargaining with the socialist bloc on foreign policy questions. The record shows such a course to be dysfunctional.

Lesson 9: Transitions are dangerous

The formulation of good policy in the 1929 depression was handicapped by three transitions: from the financial pre-eminence of the New York Fed to that of the Board of Governors in Washington; from Hoover to Roosevelt; and from Pax Britannica to Pax Americana. Each change left a transitional gap in policy formation that added to the difficulties. If, as Tobin said, he got the Nobel prize for stating that one should not put all one's eggs in one basket, and if Tinbergen's theory of economic policy, which won him the prize, can be reduced to 'you can't kill two birds with one stone' (one needs as many instrument variables as target variables), my application for the prize offers, 'Don't change horses in midstream', or perhaps better, 'Be very careful if you have to change horses'.

American world economic leadership is slipping, and there is no evident successor to take over. An election in the United States comes in two years, and runs the risk of paralyzing attention to world problems. There is nothing to do about these circumstances except to be wary, very wary.

Lesson 10: Keep the key

Milton Friedman believes in government by rules, not by men. His defense of this position is cogent and admirable. But locking the door and throwing the key away is not advisable in a world of financial crises. Thomas Joplin, a Newcastle timber merchant after the Napoleonic Wars and an astute bank critic, said: 'There are times when rules and precedents cannot be broken; others when they cannot be adhered to with safety'. Bagehot has a similar statement in *Lombard Street*, adding wistfully, 'I confess that this is most inconvenient'. Sir Robert Peel, writing on the Bank bill in June 1844, stated: 'My confidence is unshaken that we have taken all the Precautions which legislation can prudently take against the Recurrence of a pecuniary Crisis. It may occur in spite of our Precautions; and if it be necessary to assume a grave Responsibility, I dare say Men will be found willing to assume such a Responsibility.'

Men are no less needed in the world of finance almost 140 years later. Keep the key.

Index

Abraham, David 254, 263
Abreu, M. de Paiva 278, 288
Acworth, A. W. 106, 107, 110, 112, 134, 175, 176, 179, 182, 183, 185
Adam Smith Lecture 1, 11n.
agriculture 46, 66, 76, 90, 97, 101, 110–11, 113, 114–15, 134, 183, 271
Albion, Robert G. 39
Aldrich, Winthrop 308
Alejandro, Diaz 277, 281, 283
als ob hypothesis 136
Amsterdam 57, 67–8, 69, 70, 93, 157, 159, 193
angel 216
Angell, James W. 13, 181, 185
Antwerp 157, 159, 165 n. 2
Argentina: bank failures 195, 197; Baring crisis 13, 196, 197, 200, 227, 231; bond market collapse (1890) 146; boom in grazing land 195, 229; capital flow 300; central bank 14; deprecia-tion of peso 230, 231; depression (1929) 276; exchange rate 277; farm prices 288; finance (1890–3) 277; foreign lending 201, 237, 275; German selling of securities 200; Italian immigration 196; mortgage bonds 228, 230; overissue of banknotes 200; railroads 191, 195, 200, 230; Roca–Runciman treaty 278, 282; trade with Britain 284; wheat 280
armaments 171, 291, 305
Artaud, Denise 181, 185
assignats 43, 81, 111, 130, 131, 132, 169, 242, 277
astronomers 214
Attwood, Matthias 115
Attwood, Thomas 107–8, 110, 112
Aujac, Henri 263
Australia: bank failures 195, 197, 227, 232; cessation of US investment 300; commodity prices 288; depreciation in exchange rates 275; financial centre 158; land boom 195, 232; railroads 191; silver-lead mines 191; wheat 280
Austria: banking 293, 304–5; British

subsidy 249; building boom 195; Creditanstalt 163, 271, 293, 304, 305; French investments 161; hyperinfla-tion 257; League Loans 256; loans from Britain 122, 181; tariffs on British goods 182; Universal Exhibition 198; war against Prussia 171; Zoll-union with Germany 122, 163
automobile industry 120, 267, 268, 307
avoirdupois 216

Bagehot, Walter 5, 39; anticipated by Thornton 109; on currency 19, 223–5; on English banking 47, 98; on French financial domination 159–60; on interest rates 192; on lender of last resort 34, 72, 160; on panic 22, 205; on payment for war 170; on population movements 150; on savings 76, 98; on universal money 223–4
balance of payments 17, 127 n.8, 145, 172, 248–9, 252, 253, 279, 287
Ballot, Charles 66, 82
bananas 276, 282
Banca Generale 234
Banca di Roma 234, 293, 304
banking and banks: check payments 98; Cobbett's views 20 n.2; crises 135, 295; deregulation 18, 195, 309; English and French compared 86–102; and Euro-pean industry 6, 300–1, 307; failures 195, 197, 270–1; international 163, 272; investment 308; Italian 234, 293, 300–1, 306–7; Japanese 99; Mexican 284; reforms 307–9; Scottish 17–18, 33, 242; Smith's metaphors 18; Swedish 240–2
Banking School 3, 16, 19, 41–3, 109, 114, 172, 231, 249, 262
banknotes: convertibility 43, 95, 161; issue and circulation 45, 46, 48, 71–3, 90, 91, 94–5, 249; land as collateral 59; as legal tender 57; Mexican peso 284; monopoly of issue 55; small-denomination 51; wildcat issuance 277; Wolowski's simile of food 43